Imperial China
1350–1900

Jonathan Porter

ROWMAN & LITTLEFIELD
Lanham • Boulder • New York • London

Published by Rowman & Littlefield
A wholly owned subsidary of The Rowman & Littlefield Publishing Group, Inc.
4501 Forbes Boulevard, Suite 200, Lanham, Maryland 20706
www.rowman.com

Unit A, Whitacre Mews, 26-34 Stannary Street, London SE11 4AB,
United Kingdom

British Library Cataloguing in Publication Information Available

Library of Congress Cataloging-in-Publication Data

Names: Porter, Jonathan, author.
Title: Imperial China, 1350–1900 / Jonathan Porter.
Description: Lanham : Rowman & Littlefield, 2016. | Includes bibliographical
    references and index.
Identifiers: LCCN 2015036923 | ISBN 9781442222915 (cloth : alk. paper) | ISBN
    9781442222922 (pbk. : alk. paper) | ISBN 9781442222939 (electronic)
Subjects: LCSH: China—History—Qing dynasty, 1644–1912. | China—
    History—960–1644.
Classification: LCC DS754 .P67 2016 | DDC 951/.03—dc23 LC record available
    at http://lccn.loc.gov/2015036923

Printed in the United States of America

Imperial China
1350–1900

For Yezi

WITHDRAWN

Contents

Part IV: Ming and Qing Foundations, 1368–1900

Part V: When Worlds Collide, 1500–1870

Part VI: Continuity in Change, 1870–1890

Figures

Preface

This book is a product of more than forty years of teaching mainly undergraduates at the University of New Mexico, as well as study and research on Chinese culture, society, and history. My students, year after year, consciously or not, caused me to think about and question the history of China, and my approach to the subject evolved accordingly. In the meantime, I was busy writing professional papers, articles, books, and all the paraphernalia of academic life, which leaves little space for broader reflection on history. But I often thought that I might turn to such a project as this, perhaps in retirement. Thus, and only then, this book became a reality.

Though I taught courses on Traditional China and Revolutionary China alongside my course on Imperial China, the latter always represented the core of my scholarly interest. It was where I began my study of Chinese history. At Harvard as an undergraduate I was introduced to Asian history in "Rice Paddies," the introductory course taught by John Fairbank and Edwin Reischauer, and followed this with Chinese intellectual history with Benjamin Schwartz. As I began to think about what region of Asia I might eventually focus on, while Japanese history had many attractions, I was especially drawn by Professor Fairbank's narration on China in the nineteenth century, the fascinating juxtaposition of a complex civilization and its decay. At the University of Colorado, where I began my graduate studies, I worked under Earl Swisher, who reinforced my interest, and was introduced to Chinese language by Colonel David Barrett, whose deep appreciation and knowledge of Chinese culture was infectious. I was now a committed student of China. Moving on to advanced graduate work at the University of California at Berkeley, I was privileged to have as my mentors Joseph Levenson, Frederic Wakeman, and Cyril Birch. The influence of all of these in shaping my understanding and appreciation of Chinese history is incalculable, and to them I am deeply grateful. On a more intimate level, two years' study and research in Taiwan at the Stanford Inter-University Program for Chinese Language Studies and the Academia Sinica were invaluable, and in Taiwan I was exposed directly to Chinese society and popular culture.

In a way that I still cannot properly acknowledge, the encouragement and support of my parents in my academic endeavors, particularly when I abandoned the promise of astronomy for history just after Sputnik seemed to open new doors, was something I will always remember. The comments of the anonymous reviewer of my original proposal were extremely helpful initially in enabling me to better define the focus of the book. In particular, the incisive suggestions and sympathetic guidance of the three anonymous reviewers of the completed draft were invaluable in helping me to bring coherence to the manuscript. I am grateful for their diligent attention and clarifications, while the errors that remain are entirely my own responsibility. No book would ever reach fruition without the skilled direction of an able editor. Susan McEachern, editorial director at Rowman & Littlefield, gave me the courage and incentive to continue. Her enthusiasm for the project from early on, her astute advice, and her patience for my slow writing habit helped carry me through to the finish. The careful and professional assistance of Rowman & Littlefield's editorial staff, including Audra Figgins, Jehanne Schweitzer, and Jocquan Mooney helped make this book a reality. Finally, the constant enthusiasm, encouragement, and inspiration of my companion and soul-mate Paige, have been an essential but invisible part of this book.

Introduction

In the mid-fourteenth century a son of a poor peasant family in north China led a rebellion against the Mongols, who had conquered China a century earlier. The Ming dynasty, which he founded in 1368, inaugurated a period of more than 500 years, the last epoch of traditional Chinese history, remarkable for its continuity and stability. In its nationalistic reaction to "barbarian" domination, the Ming returned to pre-Mongol roots in the classical Song dynasty (960–1279) for cultural and institutional models. While the Ming was overthrown after 250 years by Manchu conquerors from the northeast frontier, the Qing dynasty (1644–1912) which they founded effectively perpetuated the institutional and cultural patterns that the Ming had inherited, and continued to elaborate them until the Manchus themselves were overwhelmed by the forces of the modern world in the twentieth century.

The Ming-Qing period was remarkable for its stability, continuity, and the duration of unified rule over the largest contiguous area of East Asia. From its beginnings, Chinese history was punctuated by periods of disunity and political and social fragmentation, often of long duration. Classical China was born in the protracted feudal era of contending states of the Zhou dynasty from the twelfth to the third centuries BCE. The unification of China under the Qin and Han (221 BCE–220 CE) was broken by the medieval era of disintegration lasting more than three centuries. Reunification under the Sui and Tang dynasties (589–906) was again disrupted by a period of division lasting a half-century, before the Song reestablished the empire in 960. The Song lost the northern half of China to the Jurchen invaders in 1126 before it finally fell to the Mongol invasion in

1

1279, but while China was nominally unified under the hegemony of the vast Mongol world empire for another century, the Mongol Yuan dynasty (1279–1368) in many respects had more in common with periods of division than with consolidation.

But successive periods of division were becoming shorter; a very long-range trend toward unification of the Chinese cultural and geographical world was increasingly evident. With the rise of the Ming and Qing dynasties, periodic division came to an end and unification lasted an astounding 500 years until modern times, when the global context of China had fundamentally changed, and had begun to affect the course of Chinese history. Thus it is appropriate to see the Ming-Qing era as standing apart in the long ages of Chinese history, both connected to and arising from China's historical evolution, but representing a distinct climactic stage. How was this?

In one sense the Ming-Qing era stands as a bridge between three thousand years of traditional Chinese civilization and the emergence of modern China from the Nationalist and Communist revolutions of the twentieth century. But the era was more than a transition from one stage of history to another. So in another sense, the Ming-Qing represents the fulfillment of embryonic formations developing since earliest times: The nature of imperial autocracy founded on the moral conception of rulership; the role of the educated elite as custodians of cultural authority; the importance of ritual as the grounding of political and social order; the discourse between monarchy and bureaucracy in the definition of the polity; the evolution of Chinese cultural identity; and Chinese views of the world. These and many other subjects are among the unifying themes of the story of Imperial China told here.

This book views the Ming-Qing period as a largely coherent and unified era in late traditional Chinese history, the consummation of the imperial epoch. Why "imperial"? The word has two meanings which define these times and characterize the history from the fourteenth through the nineteenth centuries. First, "imperial" describes a form of government, and more broadly, a style of rule directed or headed by the dominating power and influence of an emperor and his court. The Ming and Qing were each dynasties of ruling families which, even in their worst moments, exerted a pervasive effect on the entire polity, society, and culture. The dynastic families and their emperors were not mere embellishments on top of the political structure, or largely symbolic but powerless figureheads, as is the case with many modern nominal constitutional monarchies. Some emperors possessed truly awesome powers, more than perhaps any in previous dynastic periods. But even those who were weak or incompetent, and even corrupt and misguided, commanded authority that could not be ignored by their officials and subjects. Imperial power was not to be dismissed, however arbitrary. The basis for this extraordinary authority is one of the problems this book explores. Moreover, before the conception of modern phenomena of nationhood and nationalism arose, the emperor was the expression of cultural identity from high officials down to the lowliest commoners and peasants. Except for his attachment to his home county, and perhaps his province, to which he paid taxes, a poor farmer would know only that he was the subject of the emperor, inconceivably distant, not of a vague notion of China as a nation. While officials were aware of the existence of a larger political entity, *Zhongguo* ("China"), more important was the consciousness of the dynasty, and thus the emperor, whose interests they directly served. Unlike modern symbols of the state such as the national flag, personal loyalty to the emperor was everything, regardless of the worthiness of its object.

Second, "imperial" connotes empire, the rule by a centralized authority over an extensive geographic area (or areas), often embracing diverse ethnic and cultural components. Obvious examples are the British empire of the nineteenth century, geographically dispersed and ethnically varied; the Spanish empire of the eighteenth century; or the Mongol empire of the thirteenth to fourteenth centuries. An empire in this sense need not be ruled by a monarch or emperor. Whether or not an empire is dominated by a homogenous political and military elite and defined by a unitary ideology, it reflects a coherent structure imparted by organizing institutions such as law, language, and political identity. The Ming was barely an empire according to these definitions, since its territorial sway was severely limited, but it continually sought to project influence across its frontiers over diverse territories and ethnic groups. The Qing, however, by these definitions was one of the largest empires in the world. Combined, the Ming-Qing is not just another stage, one following the other, in the long history of Chinese civilization, but a distinct culmination in Chinese historical development.

Some scholars have characterized the Ming-Qing era as the "late-traditional" or even the "neo-traditional" period, and others the "early modern" period. Both names are inherently ambiguous and suggest a subordination to the times that came before or those that followed, which in a chronological sense they were. History is not discontinuous. As this study shows, the Ming and Qing sprang from the soil of earlier ages and fertilized later developments. Yet Imperial China here is understood on its own terms, for the many issues it illuminates in the history of China, but also for world history generally.

Arguably, China's imperial history began with the unification under the Qin dynasty by the First Emperor, Qin Shihuangdi, in 221 BCE. The Qin, though it lasted only to 206 BCE, established a pattern of imperial rule that was repeated in various versions by the major dynasties of the

Han, Sui, Tang, Song, Yuan, Ming, and Qing, as well as by several minor
dynasties ruling parts of China during the interregnums between the great
dynasties, down to the end of imperial rule in the Nationalist Revolution
of 1911. Indeed, after the first comprehensive history of China written
during the Han about 100 BCE, the official historiography of China came
to comprise twenty-five dynastic histories. This record of more than two
thousand years might be enough to establish a definition of what is meant
by "Imperial China." But with a definition so broad, much of the fine
grain, the particular interest of imperial history is lost. Those two millennia were not simply a monotonous repetition of the same old patterns as
some early European observers of China liked to believe. Great changes
occurred during this period as China was repeatedly transformed.

Mark Elvin argues that a fundamental change in the "internal logic"
of Chinese civilization had emerged in the mid-fourteenth century to
characterize Chinese history for the next several centuries. This turning
point was reflected in the "filling up" of the southern and southwestern
frontiers, the increasingly inward-looking society, and the development
of philosophical and intellectual introspection and intuition.[1] A point of
equilibrium between geographic size, institutional structure, and technical competence and skill was reached in subsequent times that became
evident in a general condition of quantitative growth but qualitative
standstill—what Elvin calls a "high-level equilibrium trap."[2]

Robert Hartwell similarly describes a political-demographic transition extending from early to late Song (tenth to thirteenth centuries) that
witnessed the decline and disappearance of the Tang dynasty aristocratic
professional elite and the emergence of local gentry lineages that became
typical of Chinese society thereafter.[3] Why not date the beginning of
"Imperial China" here? While much of the contours of imperial Chinese
society were then taking shape, it was not until the Ming that imperial
absolutism of the Yuan was absorbed, the remnants of aristocratism were
destroyed, and China became increasingly introverted.

While Imperial China can be defined most simply in terms of emperor
and empire—ruling imperial institutions and a geographically and demographically ramified empire—it must be understood more broadly
as exhibiting a complex dynamic of interrelated factors. Imperial China
properly conceived involves the gathering and intensification of patterns
previously arising. Remarkable about this era that distinguishes it from
what preceded it was the formal complexity of Ming-Qing social, political, and economic institutions and their supporting intellectual thought
and ideology.

A word is appropriate here about the organization of the book. Chapters proceed in a roughly chronological progression from the legacy of the
late Song dynasty and the Mongol conquest, to the founding of the Ming

in the fourteenth century and the full flourishing of the imperial style in the late Ming and early Qing, to the decline of the Qing in the nineteenth century. We begin the narrative at roughly 1350 when Zhu Yuanzhang, founder of the Ming dynasty in 1368 and the quintessential autocrat, began his rise to power. We end at approximately 1900 when, although the Qing endured for another decade until the revolution of 1911, the moribund state of the dynasty was giving rise to movements from which a new modern China was to emerge. Chapters individually address thematic issues appropriate to the period discussed or consider aspects of Chinese society, economy, and culture. Part I, The Classical Legacy, establishes the groundwork for the periodization that follows and explores some central defining themes. Part II, The Imperial Way, describes the rise of the Ming, the scope of imperial autocracy, the Ming relationship with the surrounding world, and the disintegration of order. Part III, The High Qing, discusses the Manchu revolution, imperial culture, and absolutism under the Qing. Here we pause the chronological narrative in part IV to explore variations on the theme of Imperial China, including the agricultural foundation; commercial activity and economic trends; the life of the ruling official elite and the literati; the spiritual world of popular religious devotion; science and technology; and the evolving Confucian discourse on thought and learning. Unlike the diachronic approach of the first three parts these themes are treated synchronically, mindful of their overlapping influences in the eighteenth and nineteenth centuries. With part V we resume the chronological narrative, introducing the global context of Imperial China in the nineteenth century; the conflict over opium leading to the Opium Wars; and the Great Taiping Rebellion, inspired by the Christian impact on China. Finally, part VI, Continuity in Change, raises the problem of the possibility of reform, and an epilogue closes with the end of the imperial age and movements that ultimately transformed the imperial order.

Unlike America, which was founded and built by immigrants from old worlds, always looking forward to a new world of limitless possibilities, not backward to the roots they had left behind, China, with an incomparably longer history, has always looked back to shared, common origins that have continuously shaped experiences of the present and expectations of the future. For the Chinese, inheritors of the greatest cumulative human historical record, history is not a dead past but enlivens the present. Historical exemplars of virtue and villainy, morality and depravity, loyalty and betrayal are alive in memory. Not only did traditional officials, scholars, and writers routinely cite such exemplars but even modern radical revolutionaries have done so. One of Mao Zedong's signature movements, the Hundred Flowers Campaign of the 1950s ("Let a hundred flowers bloom, let a hundred schools of thought contend") evoked the Hundred Schools of Thought that flourished in the late Zhou dynasty from the sixth to the third centuries BCE. Always mindful of the relevance of historical precedents in later periods of Chinese history, I have opened each chapter with a brief vignette of an historical event that exemplifies the theme of the chapter that it introduces.

SUGGESTED READINGS

The following sources offer various perspectives on the larger dynamics and periodization of Chinese history and society.

Balazs, Etienne. H. M. Wright, trans., *Chinese Civilization and Bureaucracy: Variations on a Theme* (New Haven: Yale University Press, 1964). A collection of separate provocative essays on political and economic institutions, including bureaucracy, feudalism, and capitalism.

Elvin, Mark. *The Pattern of the Chinese Past* (Stanford: Stanford University Press, 1973). Emphasis on political economy and technology, from the formation of the early empire in the sixth century BCE through the medieval economic revolution to qualitative standstill by the nineteenth century.

Hartwell, Robert M. "Demographic, Political, and Social Transformations of China, 750–1550," in *Harvard Journal of Asiatic Studies* 42.2 (December 1982), 365–442.

Ho Ping-ti. "In Defense of Sinicization: A Rebuttal of Evelyn Rawski's 'Reenvisioning the Qing,'" *Journal of Asian Studies* 57.1 (February 1998), 123–155.

Ho Ping-ti. "The Significance of the Ch'ing Period in Chinese History," *Journal of Asian Studies* 26.2 (February 1967), 189–195. This early article and the following two later articles offer a dialogue on understanding and defining major aspects of the Qing period.

Jenner, W. J. F. *The Tyranny of History. The Roots of China's Crisis* (London: Penguin Books). 1992. An extended interpretive essay on Chinese history and culture.

Liu, James T. C. "The Neo-Traditional Period (ca. 800–1900) in Chinese History. A Note in Memory of the Late Professor Lei Hai-tsung," *Journal of Asian Studies* 24.1 (November 1964): 105–107. An early contribution to the periodization of Chinese history.

Rawski, Evelyn S. "Presidential Address: Reenvisioning The Qing: The Significance of the Qing Period in Chinese History," *Journal of Asian Studies* 55.4 (November 1996), 829–850.

Skinner, G. William. *Marketing and Social Structure in Rural China*. Association for Asian Studies, reprinted from *Journal of Asian Studies* 24.1 (November 1964), 24.2 (February 1965), 24.3 (May 1965). A seminal series of articles by a leading anthropologist of China on the commercial structure of rural society.

Stover, Leon E. *The Cultural Ecology of Chinese Civilization: Peasants and Elites in the Last of the Agrarian States* (New York: New American Library, 1974). An anthropological approach to Chinese popular and elite culture.

NOTES

1. Mark Elvin, *The Pattern of the Chinese Past* (Stanford: Stanford University Press, 1973).
2. Elvin, 298–315.
3. Robert Hartwell, "Demographic, Political, and Social Transformation of China, 750–1550," *Harvard Journal of Asiatic Studies* 42.2 (December 1982), 365–442.

I

THE CLASSICAL LEGACY, 1000–1350

1

Song

The Great Divide

Emperor Xuanzong ("Mysterious Ancestor") of the Tang dynasty was a great patron of culture, of poets and painters, of Buddhism and theatre. His long reign from 712 to 756 marked the efflorescence of the "Golden Age" of the Tang, a time of cosmopolitan brilliance and excitement. Some of the greatest Chinese poets— men like Li Bo and Du Fu—frequented his court. His imperial temple name, Xuanzong, alludes to the mysteries of Buddhism and Daoism still associated with the high culture of the Tang. But Xuanzong's reign was destroyed by rebellion and foreign invasion and he was forced to abdicate his throne and abandon his capital. Order was eventually restored and the capital was reestablished by Xuanzong's successors, who reclaimed control of the north, and the Tang endured for another century and a half.

Emperor Huizong ("Excellent Ancestor") ascended the throne of the Northern Song dynasty in the year 1100. The dynasty, known simply as the Song, was later called the Northern Song because its capital was at Kaifeng on the Yellow River in north China, before the Song was forced to retreat south by invasions from the north. Huizong was to be the last of the Northern Song emperors. His reign was continually disturbed by the advancing Jurchen people from the northeast, the region later known as Manchuria. The Jurchen adopted the dynastic title Jin ("Gold") in 1115, thus asserting equality if not superiority to the Song. The challenge to the Song was unmistakable, and the Song was forced to pay humiliating tribute to the Jurchen rulers in the ultimately futile expectation of buying them off.

11

Foolishly, Huizong sought an alliance with the Jurchen against the Khitan, a nomadic Mongol tribe that conquered the fringes of north China in the mid-tenth century, who were perceived as the more serious challenge. However, with the Khitan in retreat, the Jin became an implacable threat, absorbing ever more territory of north China. Huizong was forced to abdicate under the inexorable Jurchen pressure in 1125. Kaifeng fell the next year, in 1126. Huizong and his court, including the heir apparent, were captured and carried off to the Jurchen capital in Manchuria, where they lived the rest of their lives in exile. The Song succeeded in reestablishing the dynasty under the reign of the Emperor Gaozong ("Eminent Ancestor"), the younger son of Huizong who had fortuitously avoided capture and exile by the Jurchen in 1126. Retreating before the Jurchen invasion, Gaozong eventually established his new capital at Hangzhou, near the coast south of the Yangzi River, and became the first emperor of the Southern Song.

Huizong left an ambivalent legacy. On one hand his reign was marked by the ultimately disastrous foreign invasion of the Jurchen that eventually brought him down, and by costly popular rebellions in the south, provoked largely by his own oppressive rule and the corruption and incompetence of the high officials of his court. Curiously, the popular rebellion of Huizong's reign left its own legacy in popular culture. The leader of the rebellion in Shandong province was Song Jiang, a Robin Hood–like hero who hid out from the authorities with his loyal band of followers in the Liangshanbo marshes. He was eventually betrayed and surrendered. But his adventures entered folklore and became the subject of a later novel, *Shuihuzhuan* (translated variously as "Men of the Marshes" and "Water Margin"), which became a favorite of popular insurgent leaders down to Mao Zedong.

On the other hand, Huizong presided over a lavish court, squandering vast treasure on elaborate buildings, fabulous gardens with strange rocks and rare plants brought from the south at the cost of great human suffering, and the acquisition of extravagant art. The emperor was a patron of Buddhism and Daoism and of artists, and was himself an accomplished painter of birds and flowers.

If Huizong was a pivotal figure in his own dynasty, the Song, losing his throne and his capital and precipitating the retreat and reestablishment of the Song in the south, in a sense he echoed another pivotal emperor Xuanzong of the Tang who reigned four centuries before him; Xuanzong's reign marked a watershed not only for the Tang but also between classical and later traditional China. It is appropriate to think of this era from the reigns of Xuanzong to Huizong as the "Great Divide" in Chinese history, separating social, cultural, and political patterns that had emerged since classical antiquity and a new paradigm that became fully manifested to reach maturity in the time of Emperor Huizong. Thus he was a pivotal figure in a larger sense as well, his reign marking the full emergence of new patterns in Chinese history. Some historians have characterized this turning point as the emergence of "Early Modern China," recognizing the seeming modernity of many subsequent developments. Others have seen it as the beginning of a "Chinese Renaissance." Though both views are appropriate, neither is necessary to appreciate that by the era of the Southern Song, Chinese society and culture had reached a climax of development that prevailed for the next millennium through the Ming and Qing dynasties to the end of the imperial era at the beginning of the twentieth century.

THE CONFUCIAN HERITAGE

The Confucian heritage from ancient times had evolved into a new paradigm, coherent in its salient features, that was to dominate Chinese society for the next thousand years. Its principal elements were:

1. The rise of the civil bureaucracy and the decline of the aristocracy. The establishment of the civil service examination system since its inception in the Han and its reestablishment in the Tang created the dominant route to civil office in government for scholars who had mastered the literary and cultural tradition of Confucian learning. The old aristocracy of birth from the late Han and the medieval period that followed it failed to survive in this new social environment of the late Tang and Song. As products of the examination system, the scholar-literati progressively took responsibility for policy of the Chinese state.

2. The ascendancy of the imperial institution including the emperor and the court. The Confucian-Legalist tension of the late Zhou era of philosophical disputation, the brief and violent first empire of the Qin, and the early Han became internalized in the institutions of central government from the late Tang and Song times.

3. The centralization of military power institutionally in the imperial court and geographically in the imperial capital. By the Song the emperor had managed to bring under central control the previously centrifugal military forces that had weakened the Han and Tang dynasties.

4. Establishment of Confucianism as the dominant ideology of the state and the waning of Buddhism. Under the influence of the great persecution of Buddhism and its institutions in the late Tang and the establishment of the Confucian-oriented civil service examination

system, Buddhism, though still patronized by some emperors partial to devotional religion, ceased to occupy a high cultural and political position, and was relegated to a peripheral role in popular culture secondary to Confucian secular civil culture.

5. The prevalent pattern of rural agrarian society of farmers and agricultural taxpayers. The feudal characteristics of the earlier era gradually gave way since the mid-Tang to an agrarian tax revenue system that reinforced the class of independent farmers, modified in part by tenancy under rural landlords in some regions.

6. Urbanization, growth of commerce, and a money economy. While China remained an overwhelmingly agrarian society, large cities and market towns appeared in ever larger numbers. Interregional trade grew in scope and specialization of commodities, and the economy became increasingly monetized.

7. The end of the cosmopolitan spirit of the early Tang and the increasing inward orientation of Chinese culture and society. The rebellions of the mid-Tang reign of Emperor Xuanzong and the collapse of the Tang empire in central Asia closed off the Silk Road that had sustained cosmopolitan interests of the Tang elite and supported the role of non-Chinese people and religions in Tang society. Late Tang persecution and suppression of Buddhism permanently removed the enlightening influence of alternative religious traditions on the higher levels of Chinese culture.

The new order that emerged in the three centuries or so from the "Great Divide" comprised two principal components that defined the institutional, social, and cultural world of China. First was the imperial institution including the emperor and the apparatus that supported him. Broadly conceived, this was the "court," the high officials and ministers and dynastic clan members who surrounded the emperor. From it emanated edicts, mandates, and policy decisions, and sometimes relatively trivial decisions that shaped the course of the dynasty from the top. Second was the official bureaucracy and the scholar-literati class from which it was drawn. This class is sometimes referred to as the *shi*, a very old term dating back to the early feudal era of the first millennium BCE originally signifying the lowest feudal rank and connoting a warrior or martial role. As the feudal system evolved, *shi* came to be understood as a class of civil elite that governed society. (Confucius was a member of the *shi* class.)

By the eleventh- and twelfth-century Song a self-conception of the ideal scholar official as an omnicompetent custodian of the social order and culture had become firmly established. In his full reach, the literati-official was a poet, essayist, historian, political commentator, painter, administrator, and moralist. James T. C. Liu describes the ideal member of this class:

> For a Confucianist to be regarded as outstanding among his contemporaries, he would have had to be not only gifted but upright, not only worthy but influential. Even in his childhood, he would be noted for remarkable conduct. In his youth he would achieve literary fame at least in prose, if not also in poetry. As time went on he would win further respect for his scholarship in the classics and their philosophical principles, in historical studies, and often in the theory of statecraft as well. He would achieve prominence in government service, where he would demonstrate his moral leadership and wise statesmanship. This would be enough to make him outstanding in his own time.[1]

This description echoes the spirit of Confucius' characterization of his own moral growth from youth to old age:

> The Master said: At fifteen my purpose was set on learning. At thirty I was established. At forty I was without doubts. At fifty I knew the will of heaven. At sixty I was ready to listen to it. At seventy I could follow my heart's desires without exceeding right action.[2]

But the *shi* class was neither monolithic nor homogeneous; a great range of styles and variations was found within its ranks. In many respects this was in fact its great strength, a creative tension that continually invigorated Chinese culture over centuries of change. Two eleventh-century paragons of this newly rising class were Ouyang Xiu (1007–1072) and Su Shi (1036–1101).

Ouyang Xiu was the perfect example of the multicultured and omnicompetent literati-official. Ouyang came from an obscure family in Jiangxi province that only recently had achieved modest success in the civil service examinations. He was born in Sichuan province where his father was posted as an official. After his father died when he was only three, his mother taught him to read and write. By the age of fifteen he had acquired a reputation as a talented scholar and enjoyed history, politics, and poetry. In 1030, at the age of twenty-three, he placed first in the metropolitan *jinshi* ("presented scholar") examination, the highest level in the examination system. He was particularly adept in the ancient prose style and after a period serving in regional offices was appointed to compile the *New History of the Tang*. In 1043 he assumed a key position in the Minor Reform program of Fan Zhongyan (989–1052). As set forth in Fan's "Ten-Point Memorial," the reform's objectives were changes in the selection and evaluation of officials, in examination standards, in promotion of agricultural productivity, and in creation of local militia. The reform program was undermined by bureaucratic factionalism and the measures rescinded in 1045. In the following years Ouyang was again serving in regional posts, but returned to power in the 1060s. Ouyang's ability and prominence enabled him to advance in a career in the central government, rising through the Board of Rites, one of the six functional divisions of the central government, to chancellor of the Hanlin Academy, the highest academic institution, the State Council, and president of the Board of War, where he reformed the military administration. Frequently controversial and criticized for his defense of political factions and his indulgence in wine and women, he resigned from the government in 1069 on the eve of the Major Reform of Wang Anshi and retired in 1071.

There are intriguing parallels between the lives and careers of the two great statesmen and literary figures of the Southern Song, Su Shi and Ouyang Xiu. Su Shi—more commonly known by his familiar name Su Dongpo—was also born in Sichuan where his family had recently emerged into prominence. His mother supervised his education. At age twenty-one he placed second in the *jinshi* examination, positioning him for a distinguished public career. But he was an ambivalent figure, as much a free-spirited literatus and poet as a dedicated bureaucrat. Su entered public service in 1060, serving in regional posts. But he had the temerity to oppose the Major Reform of Wang Anshi in 1069, was relegated to minor positions, and finally dismissed in 1072. He made numerous enemies by his satirical poems ridiculing incompetent and corrupt officials. After a lengthy retirement, Su was recalled in 1086 and rose to high rank by 1091 as president of the Board of Rites. As governor of Zhejiang province in 1089 he was located at Hangzhou. After consulting experts and studying the water supply system, he reconstructed and built new canals, constructed an efficient fresh water supply for the city, and rebuilt West Lake which remains the center of the city's enduring beauty. Always outspoken and controversial, he was banished again in 1094, first to Guangdong province in the south and then to Hainan island. At the time Hainan was considered virtually the most remote destination one could be banished to. Only in 1101 was he recalled by Emperor Huizong, who evidently appreciated a fellow spirit, but died within the year. Su Shi expressed the range of possibilities exhibited even in a single representative of the literati-official class. Su was equally comfortable as an aesthete in the tradition of the great Tang poet Li Bo, with whom he was often compared, and as an engineer building practical water control works to improve the public welfare.

THE BUREAUCRATIC STATE

Both Ouyang Xiu and Su Shi were either directly or peripherally involved in the discourse on the state and reform central to the newly emergent bureaucratic state that was to remain the prevailing pattern for the next millennium through the height of Imperial China. The scholar-official class that had finally achieved hegemony as the political-social elite dominated and continually shaped this discourse. The Minor Reform in which Ouyang participated in the early eleventh century was only a prelude to the more extensive and ambitious Major Reform initiated by Wang Anshi (1021–1086) in 1069. Wang's New Policies rested on his "Ten Thousand Word Memorial" of 1058 which attracted much attention. But it was not until the ambitious young Emperor Shenzong ("Divine Ancestor") came to the throne in 1067 that Wang was summoned to court and received the complete support of the emperor to enact his reforms. The New Policies were radical in their direction and purpose. They sought to make fundamental changes to state finance, taxation, monetary policy, and commerce; military defense and local security; local government administration and personnel; and the civil service examinations and the educational system. The reforms provoked a storm of protest, both from officials and the elite whose vested interests were attacked (the examination and education reforms aroused the most resistance since they challenged the basis of scholar-literati power), but they were challenged for philosophical and political reasons of principle as well. Ouyang Xiu, who was generally disposed to reform, criticized Wang's measures as too radical and unorthodox. Su Shi, true to his character, was more intemperate in his attacks. The most implacable opposition to Wang Anshi came from Sima Guang (1018–1086), the most eminent statesman and prominent historian of the age.

Sima Guang and Wang Anshi are often posed as the great combatants on the polar ends of the debate on reform within the literati-official world. Without the support of the emperor, even if he was only a puppet in the hands of powerful ministers at court, such major policy shifts as Wang's could never be implemented. But it was rarely the emperor who contributed significant substantive ideas to policy discussions. Political debate occurred across a broad range of factions, ideological positions, and narrow personal interests, often conducted in memorials by censors, appointed officials who were charged with remonstrance and impeachment of officials for malfeasance, corruption, and moral failings, as well as criticism of policy. The resistance to Wang's New Policies reached such intensity that he was finally obliged to resign in 1076 in spite of the emperor's support through the end of Shenzong's reign in 1085. Immediately upon the emperor's death, the empress dowager, acting as regent for the new child emperor, recalled Wang's nemesis, Sima Guang, to power as chief councilor. The New Policies were entirely rescinded, but Sima Guang died less than a year later.

Wang Anshi and Sima Guang were exponents of diametrically different political visions. In the most simplistic sense, within the arena of

Confucian discourse, Wang was a progressive and Sima Guang was a conservative. Wang envisioned a radical transformation of society, while Sima opposed fundamental change in the existing order and defended tradition. Yet it is important to understand that both were accomplished scholars and literary figures in the best Confucian tradition. It is not as if Wang derived his prescriptions from an alternative political vision of the world, such as a Marxist in the early twentieth century might have done. Though each derived their visions from different sources in tradition—Wang from authoritative classical models of ideal society such as the *Rites of Zhou*,[3] Sima, as a premier historian, from empirical principles adduced from historical models—both essentially worked within the same classical tradition. Even the political school that Wang's critics sometimes accused him of following, the Legalists of the Zhou and Qin, nevertheless existed within what became the broad Confucian embrace, and made him at most a "Confucian activist."

Prior to the end of the eleventh and early twelfth century the Chinese bureaucratic elite was a cohesive professional status group that consistently sought government service more than any other activity. Access to bureaucratic preferment was based not only on examination success but also on family tradition or service, privilege, and political connections at court. But the expansion of the examination system after the eleventh century created a growing excess of examination candidates and successful graduates exceeding the number of bureaucratic positions actually available. Thus denied the opportunity for government service, for this regional elite whose status was attested by their examination degrees, office holding became only one of a number of alternative careers. An autonomous status-elite based on literary and scholarly qualifications defined by the examinations alone replaced the professional elite of earlier times who specialized exclusively in government service.

The point here is that the understanding of the state and society, and the responsibility for their proper administration and welfare, was entirely encompassed by the hegemony of the new elite that prevailed from the late Northern Song and Southern Song onward. Except for the century-long interregnum of the Mongol Yuan dynasty from the mid-thirteenth to the mid-fourteenth century, this perception endured largely unchanged for the next eight centuries. Imperial China of the Ming and Qing dynasties was shaped in great part by this understanding. Thus it was only in the nineteenth century when China was confronted by a significantly different Western alternative vision of the world that adjustment to that new world order was all the more arduous and traumatic.

SUGGESTED READINGS

Bol, Peter K. "Government, Society, and State: On the Political Visions of Ssu-ma Kuang and Wang An-shih," in Robert P. Hymes and Conrad Schirokauer, eds., *Ordering the World: Approaches to State and Society in Sung Dynasty China* (Berkeley: University of California Press, 1993), 128–192.

Giles, Herbert A. *A Chinese Biographical Dictionary*, 2 vols. (Shanghai: Kelly & Walsh, 1898). A standard English language biographical reference, especially for pre-Ming Chinese history, though somewhat outdated.

Hartwell, Robert. "Demographic, Political, and Social Transformations of China, 750–1550," *Harvard Journal of Asiatic Studies* 42:2 (1982): 355–442.

Hymes, Robert P., and Conrad Schirokauer, eds. *Ordering the World: Approaches to State and Society in Sung Dynasty China* (Berkeley: University of California Press, 1993). Chapters address the Confucian discourse on political reform during the Song. See especially the article by Peter Bol, above.

Kuhn, Dieter. *The Age of Confucian Rule: The Song Transformation of China* (Cambridge: Harvard University Press, 2009). A comprehensive treatment of the Song as a transitional period in Chinese history.

Lin, Yutang. *The Gay Genius: The Life and Times of Su Tungpo* (New York: J. Day Co., 1947). The classic biography of the famous Northern Song scholar-official and poet.

Liu, James T. C. *China Turning Inward: Intellectual-Political Changes in the Early Twelfth Century* (Cambridge: Council on East Asian Studies, Harvard University, 1988). Discusses the important turning point in traditional Chinese history during the Southern Song dynasty.

Liu, James T. C. *Ou-yang Hsiu: An Eleventh-Century Neo-Confucianist* (Stanford: Stanford University Press, 1967). An important biography of a major Northern Song scholar-official involved in the Confucian political discourse of the time.

Smith, Paul J. *Taxing Heaven's Storehouse: Horses, Bureaucrats, and the Destruction of the Sichuan Tea Industry, 1074–1224* (Cambridge: Harvard University Press, 1991).

NOTES

1. James T. C. Liu, *Ou-yang Hsiu: An Eleventh-Century Neo-Confucianist* (Stanford: Stanford University Press, 1967), 2.

2. Translation by the author. See Confucius, Arthur Waley, trans., *The Analects of Confucius (Lun Yu)* (New York: Vintage Books, originally published 1938), II, 4.

3. The *Rites of Zhou (Zhou Li)*, an ancient pre-Confucian classic of dubious authenticity, associated with the founding of the Zhou at the beginning of the first

millennium BCE, depicts the ideal society that supposedly existed then. As such it has been a recurrent resource for radical political thinkers, including the founders of the pseudo-Christian Taiping Heavenly Kingdom of the mid-nineteenth century. See Jonathan D. Spence, *God's Chinese Son: The Taiping Heavenly Kingdom of Hong Xiuquan* (New York: W. W. Norton, 1996), 127–128.

2

The Barbarian Ascendancy

In the late twelfth century an obscure Mongol tribal leader gradually consolidated his control over the steppes in a customary process of defeat and incorporation of neighboring tribal leaders. The legend of Temujin's distant forebears describes the union of a blue-grey wolf and a fallow doe who after traveling together to the headwaters of the Onan River gave birth to the first ancestor of the Borjigin clan, some twenty-two generations before Temujin. The source for this account is the epic narrative, The Secret History of the Mongols[1], *probably a product of oral transmission of unknown provenance, until, much later, the Mongols created a written script in 1204 based on the Uighur-Turkish script.* The Secret History *was written after Temujin's death in 1227. Origin myths of a people are, of course, usually those of the founders who have imposed them under duress on the rest of their society and have become generalized thereafter.[2] Animal fables contained in legends are sometimes oblique references to human events and circumstances.*

In 1206 Temujin gathered the subordinate Mongol tribal chieftains that he had laboriously brought under his sway in the preceding years in a great *khuriltai*. In doing so he created a new nation, what was henceforth to be called Mongolia. Temujin (1162–1227) was acclaimed by the Mongol leaders as Chinggis Khan ("Universal Ruler"). Far off to the south in Hangzhou, the Song could hardly have been aware, much less imagined, what that distant gathering on the Kerulen River in the steppes of Mongolia portended for their future survival.

Although the title of Great Khan was passed down through Temujin's lineage, it was never completely uncontested. On the death of each Great Khan, a *khuriltai* had to be assembled to select his successor. Given the far-flung extent of Mongol tribes, this sometimes took many months or years. Challengers and factions among the Mongols existed by the very nature of their loosely knit tribal society, and when Chinggis' grandson Khubilai claimed the title of Great Khan in 1260 any semblance of unity had evaporated. Divisiveness was to plague the Mongols throughout the building of their empire and their conquest of China to the very end of their rule.

There is a world of difference between this legend of Chinggis' origins and that of any Chinese dynastic founder. A successful first emperor of a Chinese dynasty claimed as a matter of course a Mandate from Heaven to rule. The proof was in the pudding: An unsuccessful aspirant to rule over China could not, by definition, assert Heaven's Mandate because none had obviously been forthcoming to support his claim. Misrule could lead to Heaven's withdrawal of the Mandate. Even the legendary mythology of China describes ancient culture heroes, exemplars of civic virtues whose tireless efforts on behalf of their subjects earned them their place in history. There are no animal fables or stories of migration here. The mythology is prosaic, not epic.

The Mongols could not have come from a tradition and culture more alien to the Han Chinese world of the Song. The legends of Mongol origins arose from a tribal and shamanistic society. The emergence of the Chinese people was a secular and humanistic chronicle. The Mongols' nomadic pastoral economy rested entirely on animal husbandry of sheep, horses, and camels from which all their livelihood derived. China was a sedentary agrarian economy the products of which were grains—millet, wheat, sorghum. In such an intensive agricultural environment large animals had only a peripheral place where, like pigs, or cattle used as work animals, they could be raised efficiently on the margins of settlements. The Chinese consequently had no experience with the products of a pastoral economy such as milk and cheese. Only in modern times when they became part of the Chinese diet did dairy products overcome a deep revulsion associated with barbarian culture. The Mongol's fluid, tribal-based social organization was manifested in their extreme mobility and expansive potential, while Chinese society was hierarchical and strongly family-centered, in which fixed rituals and rigid social relationships predominated. Until well into their era of expansion when they created a written script, the Mongols were a preliterate people preserving only oral traditions of their history. The Chinese had one of the oldest written languages in the world, the longest in continuous use, which by the Song had already created an immense corpus of literature of every kind.

THE MONGOL CONQUEST

Already by the death of Chinggis Khan in 1227, the Mongols had created the largest contiguous territorial empire in the history of the world. It extended from Afghanistan in the west, and the Crimea in southern Russia, across Central Asia, northwest China, to northeast China, including the former Jurchen Jin capital at Beijing, and Manchuria. It was yet to incorporate large parts of the Middle East, Russia, and all of Song China. Chinggis' attack on the Jurchen forced the Jin emperor to abandon his capital at Beijing in 1215 and retreat southward to Kaifeng, the former Song capital on the Yellow River that the Jurchen had taken in 1127, and which now became the Jin capital. At that point China was as yet hardly touched directly by the Mongols, although north China remained under Jurchen occupation until the Mongol conquest of the Jin was completed in 1234. The initial expansion of the Mongols under Chinggis had been comparatively rapid, lasting hardly more than two decades. It was to be more than another half-century before the conquest of China was completed. The Song was the Mongol's most difficult conquest. In China the Mongols for the first time encountered a population of tens of millions living in fortified cities, and in the south many large rivers and lakes and flooded rice fields presented an obstacle to Mongol cavalry.

Khubilai Khan (1215–1294), grandson of Chinggis, was proclaimed Great Khan in a disputed succession in 1260, following the relatively brief reigns of Ögödei (r. 1229–1241), son of Chinggis, and Möngke (r. 1251–1259), Khubilai's elder brother. The problems of succession to Mongol leadership, including those associated with the interludes between the reigns of Chinggis, Ögödei, and Möngke, presaged the internal factionalism and divisiveness among Mongol princes later following Khubilai's long reign. In 1272 Khubilai proclaimed the Yuan ("Prime") dynasty. If their goal was not already clear, it was now. This was an unmistakable declaration of implacable Mongol expansion anticipating the conquest of all China. The adoption of the dynastic title Yuan positioned the Mongols in the line of historical Chinese dynastic successions going back to the very origins of Chinese history, as the Khitan with the Liao dynasty and the Jurchen with the Jin had done before them. It also was to confirm a precedent that became fixed henceforward. Dynastic names had always been proper names of places or peoples, until the Jurchen adopted the name Jin ("Golden"). Henceforth dynastic titles became rhetorical flourishes: Ming ("Radiant"), Qing ("Pure"). The proclamation of the Yuan, however, clearly oriented the Mongols, at least those who acknowledged Khubilai's leadership, toward China. The term had no independent significance for the larger Mongol world, which indeed had by now become partitioned into the four autonomous "khanates" of Persia, Russia ("The Golden Horde"), Central Asia, and China (including the Mongol heartland in Mongolia), all of which theoretically acknowledged the Great Khan. The Southern Song was finally conquered under Khubilai in 1279, completing the Mongol empire at its height.

Khubilai first occupied the Chinese imperial throne as emperor in 1280, ruling from his capital at Beijing. Following Chinese ritual dynastic precedent, Chinggis Khan was posthumously vested with the temple name Taizu ("Supreme Progenitor") of the Yuan. Khubilai was posthumously given the temple name Shizu ("Progenitor of the World") (departing from the normal practice of using *zong* ("ancestor") for emperors succeeding the founder). Khubilai reigned in China very much as a traditional Chinese emperor, at least in form if not always in substance. Even before he became Great Khan, when he administered a large appanage in north China, there were those Mongols who suspected that Khubilai identified too much with his Chinese subjects and that he relied excessively on his Chinese advisors, who sought to convert him to humanistic Confucian values of government. Mongol conservatives and traditionalists generally based in the steppe homeland and anxious to preserve Mongol tribal identity feared that Khubilai was being seduced by Chinese culture, and they opposed his policy of accommodation to Chinese administrative practice. Their fear was not unfounded. Ruling China was not like ruling Mongolia and Central Asia where no entrenched traditions of hierarchical government over sedentary peoples existed. To rule well over the vast population of Song China, especially the south that unlike the north had not experienced centuries of alien rule, Khubilai had to attract the support of the Chinese. That goal required at least the appearance of assimilation of elements of Chinese civilization. The Mongol rulers tended to dress like Chinese of the Song and used titles adapted from Chinese.

Interestingly, Khubilai was significantly aided in his efforts at acculturation by his politically astute wife and empress Chabi. Her personality transcended Mongol traditions of pastoral nomadism. An educated woman, she urged Khubilai to identify with the illustrious Emperor Taizong of the Tang, whose conquests evoked comparisons with Khubilai. But an endemic tension between Mongol tribal pastoralism and Chinese civilization persisted, a fear of identifying with their subjects, engendering a divisiveness that took its toll and that ultimately weakened Mongol rule.

MONGOL RULE

Yuan civil government of China represented a simplification of traditional Song administrative structure. The functions of the Central Secretariat were expanded while the older chancellery and department of state were abolished. The Six Ministries (Personnel, Revenue, War, Rites, Justice, and Public Works) that had become a standard and indispensable part of the Chinese bureaucracy were retained. The Censorate was also retained and its powers were greatly enhanced to provide greater surveillance over a largely alien bureaucracy. The Mongols employed the civil service ranking system of nine levels for officials, each rank comprising a higher and lower echelon, making a total of eighteen ranks. But the civil service examination system was not implemented by the Mongols, marginalizing the Han Chinese. Military administration was vested in the bureau of military affairs, a separate, highly secret organization in which only Mongols were allowed to serve.

As aliens, the Mongols were confronted with the challenge of ruling a population both within China proper and throughout the empire. Khubilai divided the population into four categories: Mongols, *semu*, north Chinese, and south Chinese. Mongols were the elite, the only people permitted to serve in the military administration. But they were few in number, only a few hundred thousand at most available for service. Second in order of status were *semu* (people of varied categories, meaning foreigners) who included various ethnic groups that had come under Mongol sway early on: Uighurs, various other Turkic peoples of Central Asia, Persians, Arabs, and Europeans. Like Mongols, already habituated to Mongol rule, these were considered most reliable. Third in rank were north Chinese, sinicized Khitans, Jurchens, and Koreans. Classified as *hanren* (Han Chinese), as foreigners they were considered more reliable by virtue of their long exposure to foreign rule. Finally, fourth in rank were *nanren* (south Chinese), conquered subjects of the southern Song who were regarded as most resistant to Yuan rule and consequently least reliable. All important positions in government were reserved for the first two categories. Chinese were excluded from the military administration and from the Censorate, and any functions involving security.

The Chinese literati-scholar elite had migrated in large numbers to the regions south of the Yangzi River during the Southern Song as successive waves of barbarian invaders carved off sections of north China that had once been the political heartland of classical Chinese civilization. First the Khitan Liao dynasty incorporated the area around Beijing. Hard on their heels came the Jurchen Jin who were in turn forced southward by the Mongols. The Song lost their capital at Kaifeng on the Yellow River in 1127 and soon the rest of China north of the Yangzi. The Chinese elite displaced from those areas were forced to make new lives for themselves in the south, fitting into the existing social order. Refugees from the conquest, they harbored an abiding antipathy to the invaders. Most were unused to alien rule. Not only were they deeply resentful of the Mongols who had defeated the last refuge of the Song in the south but the conquerors in turn naturally distrusted the southerners.

The exclusion of the Chinese from government office and the suspension of the civil service examinations by the Mongols meant that the Chinese scholar elite confronted diminished opportunities for government service under the Yuan. Even so, aside from involuntary withdrawal from public service, many scholars, from antipathy to the conquerors, unwillingness to collaborate, and loyalty to the Song, refused to serve under the Yuan and voluntarily withdrew from public life. Some simply became recluses; many others in compensation took up alternative occupations such as painting or medicine, or turned to private scholarship, poetry, literary interests, and religion. The Yuan was notable for some of the greatest Chinese landscape paintings. A consequence of these unusual circumstances was that private expressions of culture flourished during the Yuan to an unprecedented degree.

Following the death of Khubilai in 1294, no strong Mongol ruler rose to the fore. Factional struggles for the mantle of the Great Khan continued, fragmenting and weakening the Mongol empire, continuing what had already become irreversible detachment of Yuan China from the steppe heartland of the Mongol people. In the next half-century or more a succession of eight ineffective and weak emperors held the throne. Even before the end of his long reign, Khubilai himself had lost much of the imperial grandeur and competence that had marked his early years. His wife and advisor Chabi died in 1281, removing a strong positive influence in his life. He embarked on disastrous overseas invasions of Japan and Java, failures that cast doubt on his reputation. And he became obese, suffering from alcoholism and deteriorating health.

A principal legacy of Khubilai's policies was the Confucianization of Mongol rule in China—the establishment of the Yuan itself was the most prominent manifestation of this tendency. In contrast, sinicization of the Mongols would have meant the loss of their linguistic identity and distinct ancestry, and did not signify the assumption of rule by the Chinese; they remained excluded from government positions, and few of them were in positions to advise the emperor, as they had Khubilai. Rather, Mongols and *semu* themselves became "Chinese" in the sense of Confucianists espousing Confucian policies and Confucian orientations to the world. In some ways this is just what the Chinese had always anticipated for alien conquerors, the ineluctable assimilation of barbarians to Chinese culture and tradition. It had happened before, as history showed. The recent fate of the Khitan and Jurchen were prime examples. Confucianists had always asserted themselves as the arbiters of the harmonious social and political order—harmony was the premier Confucian virtue and an ordered society was the ultimate Confucian goal. *Jiaohua*, transformative civilizing influence, was the most powerful instrument in the Confucianists' possession. They need only abide and ultimately the barbarians would succumb. Harmony and order were the foundation of dynastic stability and longevity. In civilizing transformation the barbarians would ultimately benefit, although on Chinese terms.

As the Mongol steppes became progressively more dependent administratively on the Yuan central government, the moral strength of the Mongols in pastoral nomadic virtues correspondingly attenuated. Fear of losing their cultural heritage and identity drove rulers such as Khubilai, as it did the early Manchu emperors later on, to follow the hunt and to preserve their barbarian customs. The Confucianization of Mongol administration of China attested to the influence of Chinese civilizing transformation—the Mongols were unable to rule China on their own terms. Ruling successfully a huge sedentary population could only be accomplished on Chinese terms. Considerations of the larger Mongol empire and the Mongolian steppe were irrelevant to domestic Chinese problems. One wonders whether, if the Mongols had seen this problem, they might have simply withdrawn to save themselves. There was not, after all, a large resident population of Mongols and *semu*. But they had already become too deeply committed to China, which long before Khubilai, going back even to Chinggis, was the "jewel in the crown" of the empire. The irony is that sinification was the source of Mongol failure, their ultimate undoing, not of preservation of their rule.

THE MONGOL LEGACY

By 1340 the Mongols had become inextricably implicated in the traditional Confucian discourse on state policy. Confucian political ideology that essentially had no relevance to the wellsprings of the Mongol conquest and its raison d'être shaped the fate of the Yuan. A sharp rift between Reform and Conservative Confucian programs, long latent, now became entrenched in Yuan government. The reappearance of this discourse, so salient in the Northern Song between such leading statesmen as Wang Anshi and Sima Guang, in the efforts of Mongol and *semu* chancellors to strengthen dynastic rule reflects the degree to which, as an historian of the late Yuan has concluded, "The conquerors in China fell captive to the forces of Chinese history, inasmuch as the leading problems of the realm were now entirely Chinese domestic problems."[3]

Following the fall of Wang Anshi in 1085 and the repeal of his New Policies, the Conservatives briefly returned to power during the Yuanyu reign period (1086–1093) following Emperor Shenzong's death. Emperor Huizong, however, reinstalled Wang's reforms, though in an ineffective and half-hearted manner. Gratuitously, the Yuanyu conservative faction was vindictively purged and banished, and its members and their families persecuted, their names engraved on stone tablets as miscreants. Following the fall of Kaifeng in 1126 and the retreat of the Song to the south, Wang's reforms were held responsible for the Northern Song disaster. The Emperor Gaozong (r. 1127–1161) restored the Conservatives to dominance and rehabilitated the Yuanyu faction. Henceforth the reforms of Wang Anshi and his followers were anathema and reform of any kind was held in disrepute. Thus it is all the more remarkable that this bitter legacy should resurface to torment the Yuan almost two centuries later.

From 1340 government swung violently between the extremes of Reform and Conservative state policy. The principal reformer was the Mongol chancellor Toghto, who assumed leadership of the government from 1340. In 1344 Toghto was dismissed after intense criticism and the Conservatives reigned. Toghto was recalled in 1349 and remained in power until the end of 1354. Perhaps the most able Mongol official, he assumed personal command of the armies besieging the last major rebel challenger to the Yuan. But on the eve of success, he was dismissed again as a result of jealous opposition from the opposing faction. The only role of the now ineffectual emperor was to endorse the violent charges and countercharges of the contending factions. The removal of Toghto was a major turning point in the Yuan. It marked the last hope of salvaging Mongol rule. From 1355 the Yuan was essentially doomed.

In an environment of growing regionalism and pervasive rebellion of diverse contenders to succeed the Yuan mandate, Mongol rule rapidly disintegrated. The era from 1355 to 1368 is the story of the ascendancy of the ultimate victor in this struggle, Zhu Yuanzhang, the founder of the Ming dynasty.

Was the Yuan a temporary aberration in the historical logic of Chinese history, an interregnum after which the course of history returned to normal? If the Mongols were merely an interlude, they nevertheless perpetuated and reinforced historical trends that had become manifest in the Song and formed the foundation of Imperial China. However much they may not have foreseen the consequences of their conquest of China, Mongol rule strengthened long-range historical tendencies such as the enhanced autocracy of the imperial government, the rising dominance of civil bureaucracy (quite apart from the fact that the Mongols' civil bureaucracy was largely non-Chinese in composition), the concentration of military power in the imperial court that was already underway in the Song, and the Confucianization of political discourse that was reflected in the factional policy struggles between Reformers under Toghto and his Conservative opponents. If the Mongols in China had remained firmly grounded in inner Asia and ruled the Yuan only as an appanage of the greater empire, somewhat as Khubilai had before his succession in 1260, then they would have remained far more extraneous to the course of Chinese history. But the Yuan became precisely what it aspired to be, a successor dynasty in the traditional Chinese dynastic order.

The Mongols no doubt disrupted many Chinese political and social processes. They rejected merit selection of officials by the examination system, they enforced ranked categories on higher levels of the subject population, and they imposed complicated, rigid hereditary occupational registration on commoner households. But the fundamental structure of Chinese society as it existed prior to the conquest was not permanently altered. Of course, many Chinese regarded the Yuan as anathema and by their determination not to serve the conquerors relegated themselves to a peripheral role that must be endured for the time being. And the Mongols themselves consciously excluded the Chinese from their normal participation in the rule of their own country, their reliance on foreigners underscoring their Otherness. Marco Polo, who belonged to the *semu*, served in the Yuan administration under Khubilai for fifteen years. In his famous *Travels*, he clearly differentiates north China, Cathay, from south China, which he calls Manzi. In his perception and no doubt in that of his Mongol employers, China was not a single integrated entity. Moreover, for all his extraordinarily detailed observations of Chinese society and economy—cities, commerce, technology—he never mentions the Chinese language, certainly the most remarkable cultural attribute of the Chinese. That agents of Mongol rule did not need to know Chinese is a powerful commentary on the persistent alienness of the Mongols in China. Of course, Marco Polo was a Venetian merchant whose outlook was dominated by a commercial world view. But in the end the Mongols became detached from their roots and their fate linked inextricably with China.

Most Chinese elite held ambivalent feelings about the Yuan. In spite of deeply resenting the dominance of people they had always viewed as culturally inferior barbarians and their exclusion from opportunity for service, the Yuan was generally accepted as a legitimate claimant to the Mandate of Heaven, attesting to the degree of Confucianization of the Mongols. Chinese Confucian scholars possessed an abiding faith in the transformative power of Chinese civilization on surrounding peoples. There was never, for the Chinese, an uncrossable racial barrier that prohibited a foreigner from potentially becoming Chinese if he adopted all of the accoutrements of what it meant to be Chinese. Unfortunately, the Mongols, having become entrapped in the Confucian nexus at the higher levels, never permitted themselves to become assimilated at the lower levels of culture, speaking Chinese, adopting Chinese customs, and integrating with the Chinese population through intermarriage, for instance. The Manchus, later heirs of the Jurchen, confronted a very similar situation. Although they attempted to hold on to their Manchu identity (their imposed hairstyle resented so much by the Chinese lasted to the end of the dynasty), they lost their language to all intents and purposes and became "more Chinese than the Chinese."

SUGGESTED READINGS

Cleaves, Francis Woodman, trans. and ed. *The Secret History of the Mongols (Yuan chao bishi)*, 2 vols. (Cambridge: Harvard University Press, 1952). A standard translation of the account of the legendary origin of the Mongols and the rise of Chinggis Kahn. See also the translation by Urgunge Onon below.

Dardess, John W. *Conquerors and Confucians: Aspects of Political Change in Late Yuan China* (New York: Columbia University Press, 1973). A study of the political and economic dynamics during the decline of the Mongol Yuan dynasty.

Elvin, Mark. *The Pattern of the Chinese Past* (Stanford: Stanford University Press, 1973). Emphasis on political economy and technology, from the formation of the early empire in the sixth century BCE through the medieval economic revolution to qualitative standstill by the nineteenth century.

Mote, F. W. *Imperial China, 900–1800* (Cambridge: Harvard University Press, 1999). The most comprehensive treatment of Chinese history from the end of the Tang through the early Qing dynasties. An extremely useful reference, with the caveat that the index has many lacunae.

Polo, Marco. Milton Rugoff, trans. with introduction, *The Travels of Marco Polo* (New York: New American Library, 1961). A good, accessible translation of Marco Polo's famous narration of his travels throughout the Mongol empire.

Rossabi, Morris. *Khubilai Khan: His Life and Times* (Berkeley: University of California Press, 1988). The best biography of Khubilai Khan, who reigned over the Mongol empire at its height.

Urgunge Onon, trans. *The Secret History of the Mongols: The Life and Times of Chinggis Khan. Yuan ch'ao pi shih* (Richmond, Surrey: Curzon, 2001).

NOTES

1. Francis Woodman Cleaves, trans. and ed., *The Secret History of the Mongols* (*Yuan chao bishi*) (Cambridge: Harvard University Press, 1952), 2 vols.

2. An example is the foundation myth of Japan, which according to legend was created by the Sun Goddess Amaterasu, who was the proprietary divinity of the victorious Yamato clan.

3. John W. Dardess, *Conquerors and Confucians: Aspects of Political Change in Late Yuan China* (New York: Columbia University Press, 1973), 157.

3

The Imperial Myth
The Mandate of Heaven

In 1122 BCE (the date is very uncertain) Wu Wang ("The Martial King") of the Zhou, whose personal name was Ji Fa, addressed a gathering of hereditary rulers at Menjin on the Yellow River, east of the Zhou capital on the Wei River. He had inherited the legacy of his father Wen Wang ("The Cultured King") who had died two years earlier and who had borne a deep grievance against the reigning Shang dynasty:

> Now Shou, the King of Shang, does not reverence heaven above, and inflicts calamities on the people below. Abandoned to drunkenness and reckless in lust, he has dared to exercise cruel oppression. He has extended the punishment of offenders to all their relatives. He has put men into offices on the hereditary principle. He has made it his pursuit to have palaces, towers, pavilions, embankments, ponds, and all other extravagances, to the most painful injury of you, the myriads of the people. He has burned and roasted the loyal and the good. He has ripped up pregnant women. Great Heaven was moved with indignation and charged my deceased father Wen to display its terrors, but he died before the work was completed.
>
> On this account I, Fa, the little child, have. . . . contemplated the government of Shang; but Shou has no repentant heart. He sits squatting on his heels, not serving God nor the spirits of heaven and earth, neglecting also the temple of his ancestors, and not sacrificing in it. . . . The iniquity of Shang is full, Heaven gives command to destroy it. If I did not obey Heaven, my iniquity would be as great.
>
> I, the little child, early and late am filled with apprehension. I have received the command of my deceased father Wen . . . and I lead the multitude of you [hereditary vassals] to execute the punishment appointed by Heaven.[1]

Ji Fa's "Great Declaration" came to be included as one of the principal documents in the Shu Jing (The Book of History), *one of the great Classics of the*

Confucian tradition dating back to the early Zhou era. Not only is it a powerful indictment of Shang rule as manifested in the dynasty's last king, but it is also the locus classicus of the doctrine of the Mandate of Heaven.

The Zhou had long been vassals of the Shang, but had rankled under the misrule of the later Shang kings. Wen Wang especially had suffered humiliation. But he had remained restrained, mindful of the obligation of loyalty he bore his sovereign. He died, biding his time, deterred by an abundance of caution from taking action. But there finally came a time when the outrages of Shou, the king of Shang, could no longer be ignored. Wu Wang felt a filial obligation to avenge the wrongs done to his father. But he also claimed more than a merely personal family vendetta. Heaven commanded Wu Wang to end the rule of Shang. By this he justified his act of lèse-majesté. He was clearly anxious to find justification for overthrowing his erstwhile rulers. The doctrine of the Mandate of Heaven which the Zhou created rationalized their action. Was this just a cynical posture to cover what was their ambition for expansion and dominance, like any other rising conquest state in history? Perhaps. But the abundance of caution and anxiety that the Zhou leaders expressed suggests that there was much more to it than that. They were unleashing an instrument that in time could just as well be used against them. Cheng Wang ("The Complete King") succeeded Wu Wang in 1115 BCE when he was still very young. Wu Wang's brother, the Duke of Zhou and a kinsman, the Duke of Shao, served as regents and advisors to the minor king. The Duke of Shao's "Announcement," also included in the Shu Jing, *has been passed down as the principal exposition of the new doctrine of the Mandate:*

> Our king has received [that] decree [of Heaven]. Unbounded is the happiness connected with it, and unbounded is the anxiety. Oh, how can we be other than reverent?
>
> When Heaven rejected and made an end to the decree in favour of the great dynasty of Yin [Shang], there were many of its former wise kings in heaven. The king, however, who had succeeded to them, the last of his race, from the time of his entering into their appointment, proceeded in such a way as at last to keep the wise in obscurity and the vicious in office. The poor people in such a case, carrying their children and leading their wives, made their moan to Heaven. . . . Heaven had compassion on the people. . . . Its favouring decree lighted on our earnest [founders]. Let the king sedulously cultivate the virtue of reverence. . . . [King Shou] acquainted himself with Heaven, and was obedient to it. But now the decree in favour of him has fallen to the ground. Our king has now come to the throne in his youth; let him not slight the aged and experienced.
>
> We should by all means survey the dynasties of Xia and Yin. I do not presume to know and say, the dynasty of Xia was to enjoy the favouring decree of Heaven just for so many years, nor do I presume to know and say it could not continue longer. The fact simply was, that, for want of the virtue of reverence, the decree in its favour prematurely fell to the ground. I do not presume to know and say, the dynasty of Yin was to enjoy the favouring decree of Heaven for just so many years, nor do I presume to know and say, it could not continue longer. The fact simply was that, for want of the virtue of reverence, the decree in its favour fell prematurely to the ground. The

king has now inherited the decree—the same decree, I consider, which belonged to those two dynasties.[2]

Notable here is the almost impersonal operation of Heaven's will; the loss of the decree of Heaven for both the Xia and Shang happened "prematurely," not from the force of military conquest, but from the loss of reverence by their kings. The Zhou have inherited the decree but are not the agents of its loss; they did not seize it by force, it "fell to the ground." And just as truly this may come to pass for the Zhou: Note the words of caution to the king; let him not fail to be reverent. The Zhou leaders acknowledge the inherent danger of the doctrine that they have articulated. Heaven is sovereign. All rulers and their dynasties are subject to its will and must continually demonstrate their worthiness to claim its decree.

THE FORCE OF THE MANDATE

Considering the importance of this foundational doctrine throughout Chinese history, the lack of explicit discussion of the meaning of the Mandate of Heaven or an explanation of its origins and evolution in most if not all secondary sources and none in primary sources is surprising. Charles O. Hucker calls it the "cornerstone of all Chinese political theory."[3] It is merely mentioned as if its significance were to be taken for granted in most works. One highly reputable source, discussing the Ming dynasty, alludes to the Mandate of Heaven without any critical evaluation:

The Ming case demonstrates the enduring validity of the doctrine of the Mandate of Heaven. It was not that the Chinese populace by nature had more tolerance for misgovernment. But the peasantry, maneuverable only en masse, was at the command of an evenly deployed bureaucracy. Unless the scholar-official class agreed to or was compelled to change its allegiance, a dynastic turnover would not occur.[4]

This explains nothing more than that a great inertia inhibited the process of political change. The Mandate was irrelevant: the will of the scholar-official class had taken its place. Yet it is clearly a powerful political and cultural thread running through the fabric of Chinese history, with many nuances and meanings. The Mandate was a preoccupation of emperors and their ministers as well as the Confucian elite from the beginning to the end of every Chinese dynasty. The Jurchen Jin court conducted serious discussions on the issue of their inheritance of the Mandate. Emperor Gaozong of the Song was preoccupied with the legitimacy of his succession considering that his father the ex-Emperor Huizong and elder brother, the designated heir, were held hostage by the Jurchen. The

Kangxi emperor dwelled on the question of the Qing dynasty's claim to the Mandate. Only Khubilai Khan was indifferent, confident in the purely military power that assured Mongol control of China and having come from an alien tradition in which the Mandate was irrelevant.

Let us consider the meanings of the doctrine of the Mandate of Heaven (*tianming*) as it was first propounded by the Zhou rulers and as it subsequently evolved. The word *tian* in a material sense denotes "sky" and associations with sky including "day" and "weather." The original pictographic character (天) may have depicted an anthropomorphic deity (a stick figure with a horizontal line on top that originally depicted a large head), particularly in Zhou culture where it was distinct from the Shang's primordial ancestral deity, Shangdi. If it indeed originally possessed a personal, anthropomorphic aspect, it gradually assumed a more abstract and impersonal sense of the ultimate ethical ground of existence. *Tian* in this sense, however, was very different from the Judeo-Christian concept of Heaven, the home of God and a place where the virtuous aspired to go after death. The material sense of *tian* always coexisted with the moral sense, so that *tianxia*, "under heaven" or "below heaven," signified the entire earthly realm of human habitation—"all under heaven."

Thus Heaven possessed both active and passive modes. On one hand it was a component of the material cosmos; on the other hand it possessed agency, generally understood as benign, or benevolent in ultimate intent, though in action it could inflict violent warnings of moral failures in the form of natural disasters such as earthquakes, or signs in the material heavens. In its active mode, *tianming*, Heaven's decree or the Mandate of Heaven, was bestowed by Heaven upon or withdrawn from human rulers according to their virtuous conduct and demeanor, "reverence" in the language of the Zhou proclamations. To withdraw the Mandate or lose the Mandate of Heaven was called *geming*. The word *ge*, meaning to lose or change, originally meant "to molt," as an animal loses its skin. This, interestingly, suggests a rather passive process of transformation.

Curiously, this ancient word for political change, *geming*, in modern times comes to denote revolution, the modern form of radical political change. Thus the decree of Heaven is divested from Heaven entirely and comes to be vested in the popular will. But the ambiguity was always there. It is sometimes claimed that Mencius, the great successor to Confucius in the late Zhou period, proclaimed a "right to revolt" based on the obligation of the ruler to promote the welfare of the people. In fact, Mencius was not so revolutionary. Agency still resided ultimately with Heaven:

> Mencius said: The people are of supreme importance; the altars of the gods of earth and grain come next; last comes the ruler. That is why he who gains

the confidence of the multitudinous people will be Emperor . . . When a feudal lord endangers the altars of the gods of earth and grain, he should be replaced. When the sacrificial animals are sleek, the offerings are clean and the sacrifices are observed at due times, and yet floods and droughts come [by the agency of heaven], then the altars should be replaced.[5]

Only in predynastic times, in the legendary mists of Chinese history when sages reigned as culture heroes, was there no Mandate because none was required. The Model Emperors Yao and Shun, who according to Chinese mythology reigned in the third millennium BCE, were exemplars of virtue who each passed over their own son to bestow their throne to the most qualified subject in the realm. Yao bestowed the throne on Shun, Shun on Yu. Yu the Great, Shun's successor, who conquered the floods that were ravaging China throughout the Yellow River plain, broke the pattern and passed his rule to his son, thus establishing the hereditary Xia dynasty. The first dynasties, Xia, Shang, and Zhou, brought fallibilities, hereditary succession, and the end of sagely rule. Then Heaven's Mandate came to operate.

In its purest form, as articulated by Wu Wang and the Duke of Shao, the Mandate of Heaven doctrine could potentially countenance any challenge to legitimate rule. It was in this respect a "wild card." How would one distinguish a change of rulers achieved by force of arms from one sanctioned by Heaven as the result of loss of virtue—lack of reverence? Wu Wang and the Duke of Shao were uneasily aware of this dilemma. They had conquered the Shang by military force but claimed to be merely the instrument of Heaven's will. This predicament was to remain an issue throughout Chinese history. A challenger to a dynasty was either rebel or emperor, one or the other; there was no middle ground. However virtuous an aspirant to the Mandate might appear, failure to achieve the throne relegated him to the status of outlaw, rejected by Heaven for lacking sufficient virtue. Nothing succeeds like success—the claim to have received the Mandate was always an ex post facto legitimation. Yet it remained always a powerful influence. Even in the twentieth-century Civil War between the Nationalists and the Communists culminating in the Nationalists' retreat to Taiwan, each side branded the other as rebel (*fei*), with connotations of brigand, robber, bandit, denying any shred of political legitimacy.

If the doctrine of the Mandate had continued to operate in its pristine form, it would have entailed constant political instability and uncertainty. Any challenge to established political authority, regardless of its merit to claim legitimacy, would be encouraged and the established authority would be constantly pressed to mount a defense based on anything more than formal possession. Thus, over the centuries, various safeguards were conceived and introduced, devices that made frivolous or specious challenges by usurpers more difficult to establish.[6] Early on the emperor came to be conceived as the Son of Heaven (*tianzi*), creating a filial relationship between Heaven and the ruler that went beyond the more contractual association that the basic doctrine describes. If the ruler is Heaven's son it became much more difficult to displace that relationship. *Tianzi* remained throughout imperial history the standard usage for the emperor.

Dynasties and their servants, the Confucian ministers of the ruler, were careful, moreover, to emphasize and articulate the rules of legitimate familial succession. Each dynasty had its rules, Ancestral Injunctions, of filial succession by generational descent or priority of birth. The Mandate came to repose in a dynastic rule, as long as that succession was properly observed. This sometimes became a double-edged sword when emperors sought to violate dynastic law for their own ends and Confucian officials defended hereditary rules for their own interests. So serious an issue was this that officials sometimes committed suicide in protest against violations of hereditary principle, as when in the late Qing the Empress Dowager Cixi violated the law of filial succession by appointing her nephew, cousin of the deceased emperor, as the new emperor. Increasingly, absolute loyalty (*zhong*) by the scholar-official class to the throne was demanded and inculcated. Officials were expected to remain loyal unto death upon the defeat of a dynasty, regardless of misrule and corruption that were the leading cause of its loss of the Mandate. For many officials who had served a dynasty at the end, loyalty to their sovereign took precedence over transfer of allegiance to a new dynasty decreed by Heaven. Some went so far as to commit suicide rather than be forced to submit to a new dynasty.

Finally, the correct and proper performance of ritual, established in precedent and dictated by the Confucian Classics, became necessary to continually substantiate the ruler's claim to the throne. Heaven's beneficence was influenced by ritual in the sense that its reverential and assiduous performance reflected the virtue of the performer. Lapse in ritual observance would reveal inattention to the contingency of the Mandate and invite its withdrawal. With the full development of the imperial-bureaucratic state in the early Han dynasty (202 BCE–220 CE) an elaborate cosmological apparatus had been constructed to rationalize the authority of the emperor and the role of the official class in the new order. Under the reign of Han Wudi ("The Martial Emperor of the Han") (140–87 BCE), the Confucian theologian Dong Zhongshu, the chief exponent of the new imperial Confucianism, conceived a moral triad embracing the distinct realms of Heaven, Earth, and Man. Each realm interacted with the other. If their relationship were not in harmony, disorder in all three would result, manifested in unpredictable astronomical events in the realm of

Heaven, natural catastrophes in the Earthly realm, and disruption and rebellion in the Human realm. Dong Zhongshu placed the emperor at the center of this cosmic triad as its balance wheel. By his virtue and the power of his exemplary action, harmony between the three realms would be maintained. If, however, he was inattentive to virtue and his conduct lapsed, signs of disharmony would appear: Unpredicted events in the heavens, such as comets and eclipses; natural catastrophes on earth, such as earthquakes and floods; and social disorder and uprisings among men. Dong used the analogy of the character for king, *wang* (王). The character comprises three horizontal lines joined through their centers by a vertical line. The three horizontal lines stand for Heaven, Earth, and Man. The line that joins them represents the ruler.

Here was the role of the scholar-official: To call to the attention of the emperor and interpret the signs, omens, and portents that indicated moral lapses. The emperor should examine his heart and correct his behavior, thereby restoring harmony in the cosmic triad. An awesome moral burden for the well-being of the universe rested on the ruler, and his Confucian officials functioned like a priesthood guiding him in correct ceremony and ritual performance, to restrain him from the temptation to abuse his power. The memory of the tyrannical First Emperor Qin Shihuangdi, who burned the Classics and buried scholars alive, was still fresh a century later in Dong Zhongshu's time. This was the Confucianists' goal: Dong Zhongshu's creation functioned as a figurative harness, containing the Qin Shihuangdi who struggled to emerge from within every subsequent emperor.

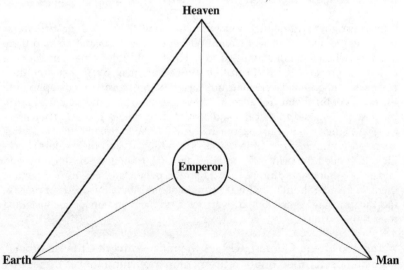

Figure 3.1.　Dong Zhongshu's Cosmic Diagram. Jonathan Porter.

While the elaborate cosmological apparatus of Han imperial Confucianism did not survive the end of the Han, the basic moral assumptions that underlay it and the hypothetical duty of Confucian officials to remonstrate with the ruler did survive. Emperors in later dynasties, when confronted with omens and portents and natural disasters, were often known to publicly castigate themselves for their moral unworthiness and search within their behavior for causes of Heaven's displeasure. But if the Confucians' moral check on unbridled imperial autocracy sometimes worked, there were many instances when official remonstrance unleashed the wrath of the emperor to the ultimate cost to the remonstrator of his life.

A central dichotomy at the core of the doctrine of the Mandate of Heaven had become increasingly evident by the era of the Song if not before, a tension between the deterministic inevitability of the dynastic cycle—that all dynasties come to their full term in the natural course of their evolution—and voluntarism inherent in the dynamic relationship between ruler and Heaven, that continued display of virtue could potentially prolong the life of a dynasty indefinitely. Fatalism mitigated by voluntarism in a sense enlivened the doctrine of the Mandate, sustaining its relevance throughout imperial Chinese history.

WITHDRAWAL OF THE MANDATE

As Zhu Yuanzhang began his final push to expel the Mongols from China, he issued a decree on the Mandate he was about to claim:

> When the right to rule shifted away from the Song, the Yuan dynasty [barbarians] entered and ruled over China. Within the four seas and beyond there are none who have not submitted to it. How could this be the consequence of human powers? It was in truth bestowed by heaven. At that time their ruler was enlightened and their officials good, quite capable of upholding the norms of the realm. Yet even so, knowledgeable men and scholars of firm purpose still sighed that "caps and sandals had traded places." Thereafter, the Yuan officials failed to observe their rulers' "Ancestral Instructions"; they abandoned and destroyed the norms of conduct . . . and their rulers shockingly despoiled the principles of father and son, ruler and servitor, husband and wife, senior and junior . . . And so the people's hearts turned against them. . . . And although that was brought about by the misdeeds of men, in fact the time had come when heaven despised them and no longer sustained their right to rule.[7]

In about 1863 Zeng Guofan, who as the most eminent Chinese official of his age had been called out of retirement in mourning for his father by the Manchu Qing dynasty to defend the dynasty against the revolutionary challenge of the Christian-inspired Taiping Rebellion (1851–1864), issued a stirring proclamation to the scholar-official class:

> From the time of Emperors Yao and Shun and the Three Dynasties until now, through successive generations the sages have sustained our sacred teachings *(mingjiao)* and esteemed the social relationships. The positions of lord and subject, father and son, high and low, honored and common, are as orderly and inconvertible as cap and shoe. But the bandits of Yue, taking their cue from the outer barbarians, venerate the religion of God. From their bogus lords and ministers down to their soldiers and mean people, all are called brother. They say only Heaven is called father. Besides this, all the people's fathers are all brothers and all the people's mothers are all sisters. Farmers are unable to freely cultivate in order to pay taxes, as they call all the fields the fields of the Heavenly King. Merchants are unable to freely trade in order to seek profit as they call all the merchandise the merchandise of the Heavenly King. Scholars are unable to recite the Confucian classics as they have other theories of a so-called Jesus and the New Testament. All of China's several thousand years of propriety, morality, and social relationships, of literature and law, are suddenly dragged in the dust and utterly destroyed. How can this be only a change in our Qing dynasty? It is the most extraordinary transformation in our sacred teachings since its creation, for which our Confucius and Mencius weep in their graves.[8]

Although the contexts of the two declarations, separated by five hundred years, were vastly different, Zeng's rhetoric is strikingly similar to Zhu Yuanzhang's. The sense of outrage over the violation of Confucian hierarchical, filial relationships—the immutable orderliness of social roles, like "cap and shoe"—is the same. Though the barbarian Qing was beginning to show signs that it was losing the mandate, and Zeng might have been forgiven for choosing differently, the Taiping offered a far more radical challenge to Confucian norms. Zeng invokes a powerful idea, *mingjiao*, the traditional moral order contained in the sacred teachings and obligations of the sages, often equated in general with Confucianism. But for Zeng, in a sense, the issue was more than any ruler's or any dynasty's right to rule. It was the universal claim of Heaven to the continuation of a traditional moral order, beyond any particular ruler's virtue. Here we see the generalization of the doctrine of the Mandate of Heaven. Part of this involves reinvestment of the Mandate in all the people, as it had existed in ancient utopian times of the Great Unity *(Datong)* proclaimed by Confucius: *Tianxia wei gong* (All Under Heaven is the public realm). But also, in the passing of the Mandate in the twentieth-century 1911 and 1949 revolutions, the decree of Heaven is no longer received by any one person whose preeminent virtue (reverence) has claimed it. In the process, the Mandate has lost its real meaning as well as its significance to the point that it becomes bandied about in fatuous ways, claimed supposedly for entrepreneurs and the new commercial elite in the twenty-first century People's Republic.

SUGGESTED READINGS

de Bary, William Theodore, Wing-tsit Chan, and Burton Watson, compilers. *Sources of Chinese Tradition* (New York: Columbia University Press, 1960). A comprehensive anthology of translations of selections from Chinese classical works, histories, essays, and literature.

Hucker, Charles O. *China's Imperial Past: An Introduction to Chinese History and Culture* (Stanford: Stanford University Press, 1975).

Legge, James, trans. *The Chinese Classics*, 5 vols. (Hong Kong: Hong Kong University Press, 1970 [1960]). The most complete and authoritative translations of the Classics, still a standard source though betraying the nineteenth-century style of its author.

Mote, F. W. *Imperial China, 900–1800* (Cambridge: Harvard University Press, 1999). The most comprehensive treatment of Chinese history from the end of the Tang through the early Qing dynasties. An extremely useful reference, with the caveat that the index has many lacunae.

Schwartz, Benjamin. *The World of Thought in Ancient China* (Cambridge: Harvard University Press, 1985). An exploration of Chinese thought of the Zhou era by a foremost student of Chinese intellectual history.

Wakeman, Frederic, Jr. *The Fall of Imperial China* (New York: The Free Press, 1975). A standard textbook on the late imperial period from the end of the Ming to the end of the Qing.

NOTES

1. "The Great Declaration," *The Book of History* (*Shu Jing*), James Legge, trans.

2. "The Announcement of the Duke of Shao," *The Book of History* (*Shu Jing*), James Legge, trans.

3. Charles O. Hucker, *China's Imperial Past: An Introduction to Chinese History and Culture* (Stanford: Stanford University Press, 1975), 55.

4. Frederick W. Mote and Denis Twitchett, eds., *The Cambridge History of China*, vol. 7, *The Ming Dynasty, 1368–1644, Part I* (Cambridge: Cambridge University Press, 1988), 556–557.

5. Mengzi (Mencius), trans. with an introduction by D. C. Lau, *Mencius* (Harmondsworth, England and New York: Penguin Books, 1970), VII, B, 14.

6. Frederic Wakeman, Jr., *The Fall of Imperial China* (New York: The Free Press, 1975), 56–57, offers a good discussion of the limitations of the Mandate.

7. Quoted in F. W. Mote, *Imperial China, 900–1800* (Cambridge: Harvard University Press, 1999), 559–560.

8. Zeng Guofan, *Zeng Wenzhenggong quanji* (The Collected Works of Zeng Guofan), 5 vols.; Taipei reprint, 1965, v. 5, *Wenji* (Collected essays), 147–148.

II

THE IMPERIAL WAY, 1350–1650

4

The Rise of the Ming

The auspicious birth of Zhu Yuanzhang, who would become the Ming Emperor Taizu ("Supreme Progenitor"), the first emperor of the Ming dynasty, was recorded in the dynasty's official Veritable Records (shilu), *using the ceremonial titles that would retroactively be conferred on his mother and father.*

His Majesty's father Renzu moved . . . to Anhui during the Yuan Dynasty. Diligent, frugal, honest, and upright, people revered him as an elder. His mother, the Empress Dowager Chen, gave birth to four sons. His Majesty was the third. During her pregnancy, she once dreamed of a Daoist coming from the northeast, to the wheat field south of her house, who put a white powdered pill in her palm. It was a radiant object and it grew steadily. "This is delicious and edible," said the Daoist. The empress dowager then swallowed it. Waking up, she confided the dream to Renzu. She still scented fragrance in her mouth. . . . On the following day Taizu was born; the room was saturated with a crimson aura . . . It was October 24, 1328. Following that, lights flashed several times at night. Sighting it from a distance the neighbors were terrified, thought it was a fire and all rushed to help. When they arrived they found nothing and were quite astonished.[1]

Such fanciful, magical language was used to describe all dynastic founders in Chinese history. It attested that the Mandate had already been passed by Heaven to the one who would become its successful claimant and served to squash by priority any competing claims that might arise later. Portents and signs revealed the will of Heaven. The appearance of religious and secular saviors or leaders in other times and places, of course, were announced in similar fashion, from Jesus to Mao Zedong.

As Zhu Yuanzhang rose in prominence in the contest with his rivals for the Mandate, supernatural deeds and powers continued to be attributed to him; the initial claim of his auspicious birth could not be taken for granted.

Chu was stricken by severe drought. His Majesty was worried. Yang Yuanhao, a native of Chu, said, "There is a dragon shrine in the Pozi Pool in the northern valley of Mount Feng southwest of Chu. Whenever there was a flood or drought people who went there to pray always found their wishes fulfilled. After praying, if fish leap or tortoises emerge, it is the omen of rain." Hearing this His Majesty held a fast, purified himself in a bath, and went there to make a prayer. After praying he stood on the cliff west of the pool; for a long while he saw no sign of fish or tortoise. He then bent his bow and fixing an arrow, invoked a prayer: "The drought is so severe that I prayed on behalf of the people. The spiritual beings have thrived on this land, so how could they ignore the people? I am making an agreement with the deities: If it does not rain within three days, they may not be housed in this shrine." Having thus vowed, he shot three arrows in to the sky and departed. Three days later, heavy rains fell.[2]

Now, in 1354, the future emperor is no longer a passive instrument of Heaven's will. Though still unequal, the relationship between them is now reciprocal. This story is reminiscent of Mencius' statement that "when sacrificial animals are sleek, the offerings are clean and the sacrifices are observed at due times, and yet floods and droughts come, then the altars should be replaced."[3]

THE MAKING OF AN EMPEROR

Zhu Yuanzhang grew up in extreme poverty in the Huai River region of north central China, between the Yellow and Yangzi River watersheds. He was the youngest boy in a family of four sons and two daughters. The Huai region, like most of north China, was afflicted by conditions of chaos and civil war attendant on the decline of the Yuan dynasty in the 1340s, aggravated by endemic drought, floods, famine, and epidemic plague. In rapid succession his father, mother, and eldest brother were carried away by plague. The survivors, like many others in the region, lived on grass and tree bark. Only by the kindness of a local minor landlord were they able to find a plot to bury their parents and brother.

Setting aside the mythological explanations for the rise of the dynastic progenitor of the Ming, in these waning years of the Yuan the conditions favored the incubation of rebellion and struggle between diverse contestants for the Mandate. These conditions became increasingly entangled and mutually reinforcing from the mid-fourteenth century. Hardly a

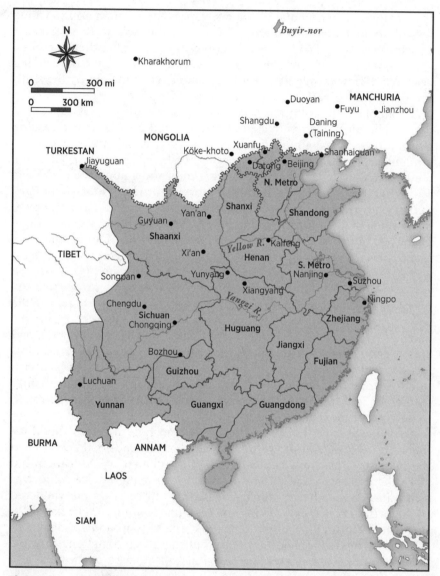

Figure 4.1. Ming China provinces.

generation after the death of the Great Khan Khubilai in 1294, a rapid succession of eight weak emperors occupied the Yuan throne, while government gradually unraveled below them. Weakness at the center invited growing dissentions among Mongol generals and princes, many of whom acted as virtually autonomous warlords. Political collapse was accompanied by economic problems, especially inflation. Aggravating these human crises were natural disasters. The Yellow River flooded catastrophically in 1344. Its course periodically shifted hundreds of miles, entering the sea north or south of the Shandong peninsula, devastating vast areas of low farmland. From 1333 famine was endemic. By the 1340s rebellions were breaking out everywhere.

The ambiance of political, social, and economic disintegration, magnified by the alien Mongol conquest, engendered a sense that a turning point in history was imminent. Religious movements in the chaotic environment of power struggles, peasant rebellions, and natural disasters bred eschatological doctrines predicting impending apocalyptic change. The White Lotus society, a Buddhist movement whose roots went back to the Song, invoked the expectations of the descent to earth of Maitreya, the Buddha of the future, from the Pure Land, when he would inaugurate a new age of peace and salvation. Conflated with the Maitreya doctrine, Manichaeism, espousing the universal struggle between forces of light and darkness, portrayed Maitreya as the "Radiant King" (*Ming Wang*). Followers of the White Lotus believed that a descendent of the Song Emperor Huizong, captured by the Jurchen, would appear to restore the Song. They wore red cloth head bands to identify themselves, giving the name Red Turbans to their rebellion. Thus a prevalent chiliastic mood spread across the affected regions of north central China. Floods, famine, locusts, and plague provoked massive movements of refugees. When hundreds of thousands of these refugees were impressed into labor gangs by the Mongol chancellor Toghto for the Yellow River restoration project, these popular movements became further energized.

Zhu Yuanzhang's father had once pledged him to a local Buddhist monastery. Now, with no resources, nowhere to find food, Zhu joined the monastery as a novice. He received a rudimentary education, but since the monastery lacked the means to feed many novices, Zhu was sent out as a mendicant monk. For perhaps three years he wandered through the Huai region, living by begging. Nothing might have distinguished him in this environment, just one of thousands of displaced refugees living from hand to mouth. But there was something unusual about Zhu Yuanzhang. First, his physical appearance was formidable if not frightening. He was tall and strongly built. His complexion was dark. A high ridge commanded his forehead; he had a large nose, large eyes, big ears, and a prominent jutting chin. His startling physiognomy must have made an impression on everyone he met. Moreover, he possessed innate ability and intelligence and his experiences added to his rudimentary education.

Much later, when Zhu became emperor his remarkable appearance became a source of ridicule among those around him, or so he imagined, and a cause of his extreme paranoia. In official portraits made of him after he became emperor, his features were progressively softened. In the first portrait from 1368, the year he ascended the throne, his swarthy features are clearly evident. In the second, made in 1377, he appears as a handsome middle-aged emperor. In the last from 1397, one year before his death, he looks like a rather benign grandfather—all of his remarkable features have vanished.[4]

The Red Turban rebellion broke out in earnest in 1351. Zhu, wandering as a monk, evidently joined their secret organization in 1352 when he was twenty-four. Not long thereafter he placed himself under the patronage of one of the Red Turban leaders, Guo Zixing, who soon came to appreciate Zhu's abilities. Guo gave his foster daughter, née Ma, to Zhu in marriage, a bond that was to become a significant influence in Zhu's career. Zhu proved himself an able leader. He formed a military unit around twenty-four village friends who became constant supporters. Zhu was a rising star, and his force soon grew to twenty to thirty thousand troops. In the disintegration of Yuan authority and the fragmentation of social order, society had become thoroughly militarized, creating opportunities for upward mobility for those with extraordinary talent. Patron-client relationships between warlord leaders and their followers were the strongest bonds, replicating in many ways the conditions surrounding the rise of the Mongols under Chinggis Khan.

As Zhu's fortunes rose, he increasingly became an autonomous figure contending with other such secular and religious warlords. He began to attract scholar advisers who recognized his talent and aspiration to become emperor. Although at first he was considered a leader of the Red Turbans, as other leaders were defeated and the movement waned Zhu gradually disassociated himself from it. Later he would deny his Red Turban and White Lotus associations and move instead toward Daoism, more acceptable to the Confucian scholar-literati elite whose support he cultivated and would need. In 1356 Zhu occupied the great Yangzi River city of Nanjing, which became his base. From there he campaigned east and west along the Yangzi valley. The turning point in the civil war came in 1363 when in great naval battles on Boyang Lake, west of Nanjing, he decisively defeated his principal rival Chen Youliang. Zhu emerged as the strongest power and could now clearly be perceived as a future emperor. In 1364 he reorganized his army based on preexisting Yuan dynasty models into a system of guards units (*wei*) of 5,000 soldiers and battalions (*qianhu suo*) of 1,000 soldiers, the so-called *Weisuo* system. In 1368 Zhu launched a northern expedition under his most trusted general Xu Da, who took the Mongol capital at Dadu (later renamed Beiping, "The North Pacified"). The Mongol emperor fled north to the steppes, extinguishing the Yuan dynasty.

Now victorious, Zhu Yuanzhang proclaimed his new dynasty the Ming ("Radiant"), a name that resonated with his movement's Red Turban and Manichean origins. Although playing down his early rebel associations as unseemly for an emperor of a stable political order, Ming nevertheless co-opted lingering nostalgic adherents to the Maitreya doctrine.

China did not employ a continuous calendar, such as the Gregorian or Julian calendar in the West. Years were numbered sequentially by political periods such as reigns of rulers or by repeating mathematical cycles. Prior to the Ming, emperors adopted reign names which were political slogans that reflected the rhetorical style that the ruler and his ministers wished to project. As conditions or circumstances changed, reign names were often changed to achieve auspicious results, so that one emperor's reign might be designated by several reign titles. Calendar enumeration of years began over again with each new reign name, however short its duration might be. (For example, Song Huizong had seven reign names: Jianzhong ["Establish the Center"] 1101, Jingguo ["Restoration of Order"] 1101–1102, Chongning ["Venerate Peace"] 1102–1107, Daguan ["Great to Behold"] 1107–1111, Zhanghe ["Government of Harmony"] 1111–1118, Chonghe ["Abundant Peace"] 1118–1119, and Xuanhe ["Comprehensive Peace"] 1119–1120.) Zhu Yuanzhang in 1368 adopted the reign name Hongwu ("Vast Military Power"), rather appropriate to the means of his great accomplishment. The first year of the Ming and of his reign is therefore designated the first year of Hongwu. But beginning with the Ming and continuously thereafter through the Qing, reign names became coterminous with actual imperial reigns, one reign name for each emperor. Henceforth we may refer to an emperor unambiguously by his reign name, such as Hongwu 1368–1398.

An emperor might be identified by any one of three designations: His family and personal given name (e.g., Zhu Yuanzhang), his posthumous temple name (e.g., Taizu), or his reign name (e.g., Hongwu). His personal name, however, was taboo during his lifetime and for the duration of his dynasty. His temple name, of course, was only declared after his death and consequently was unknown during his reign. It was thus by his reign name that he was known. In official writings and memorials to the throne he was addressed as *Tianzi* ("Son of Heaven"), but of course this title did not uniquely identify any one emperor. Heretofore we have used the posthumous temple name to refer to an emperor (e.g., Song Huizong) in order to avoid the confusion of using many reign names for one emperor. Henceforth we will use the reign name if not the personal name. But it is important to note the correct style. It is incorrect to say Emperor Hongwu—the correct form that will be used here is the Hongwu emperor. (For instance, if one likens Franklin Roosevelt's "New

Deal" to a reign name, one would not say "President New Deal" but rather "The New Deal president.")

SHAPING THE MING

When Zhu Yuanzhang ascended the throne at age forty, he left behind one era of his life and entered a very different one that was to last another thirty years until his death in 1398. But the manner of his struggle for the Mandate no doubt deeply influenced his personality and behavior as emperor. His education outside the Confucian tradition, though he came to master the traditional official documentary style, made him suspicious and contemptuous of Confucians who now populated his government. He suspected, not without reason, that they ridiculed him behind his back for his vulgar manners and odd appearance. Though he showed great solicitude for the common people from whom he came, his proclivity for violence and uncontrollable rages against those he suspected of incompetence and disloyalty grew. As he became ever more paranoid his tyrannical behavior had a lasting effect on his successors throughout the Ming and continued into the Qing. (The nature of the Hongwu emperor's tyrannical behavior will be explored further in the following chapter.)

Much of the formal central government structure created by the Hongwu emperor was a legacy of the Yuan, although like the Yuan it was based on earlier Chinese models. In 1368 a Central Secretariat was created, comprising chief counselors of the left (senior) and the right (junior). Beneath the Secretariat and reporting to it were the Six Ministries, including ministries of Personnel, Revenue, Rites, War, Justice, and Public Works. The Chief Military Commission, a powerful body that supervised the military system, was created earlier in 1362. The Censorate, charged with impeachment of officials for malfeasance and corruption, powerful under the Yuan, was a weak organization in the early Ming. The last components of central government structure in the area of scholarship and ideology were the National University occupying the top of the pyramid of local Confucian schools, and the Hanlin ("Forest of Brushes") Academy to which the most eminent Confucian scholars were assigned to draft important documents of state and serve as advisors to the court. Finally, the Great Ming Code (*Da Ming Lu*), closely based on the Tang dynasty law code, went through repeated revisions through the Hongwu reign and was published in its final version in 1397. However, all this changed in 1380 as a result of the Hu Weiyong conspiracy.

The process of founding the Ming continued through the reigns of the first five emperors from 1368 to 1435. Two of these, short reigns, were relatively inconsequential. In the first, the Hongwu reign; the third, the Yongle reign; and the fifth, the Xuande reign, the contours of the Ming, and indeed of imperial China until the twentieth century, were largely drawn.

Zhu Yuanzhang fathered twenty-six sons and sixteen daughters. Even before 1368 he became concerned with the management of his large progeny of children and heirs and the issue of succession. One problem was to obviate potential struggles that might arise between them, yet as he grew to distrust the regular civil and military bureaucracies, he saw his heirs as more dependable supporters. In 1369 the emperor promulgated the Ancestral Injunctions (*zuxun*). Its primary purpose was to specify the selection of the heir apparent. But in its broad purposes, it had far-reaching consequences. As Ming imperial house law, its significance in creating a kind of constitutional structure of the Ming was parallel to that of the Great Ming Code, and like the Code, Zhu revised and added to the Injunctions throughout his reign to 1395, when it was finalized. The Ancestral Injunctions prohibited his descendants from any involvement in civil society. He invested his male heirs as princes ruling over regional fiefdoms. One unforeseen consequence of the exclusion of Zhu's descendants from employment and education was that by the late Ming they numbered in the hundred thousands and incurred a tremendous fiscal burden on the dynasty. Later additions to the Injunctions imposed binding imperatives on his descendants that went far beyond issues of inheritance.

The Injunctions stipulated that only children of Empress Ma could succeed to the throne; sons of secondary wives and concubines were disqualified. Zhu Yuanzhang's fourth son Zhu Di was generally recognized to be the most able, most like his father in many respects. He was invested as Prince of Yan, the northeastern region including Beiping. But Zhu Di was believed to be the child of one of Zhu Yuanzhang's concubines, perhaps a Korean woman. In any case, Zhu chose his eldest son, Zhu Biao as the heir apparent. As fate would have it, Zhu Biao died in 1392 and the other two older sons also died before their father. That left Zhu Di as the eldest surviving son. But following strict laws of primogeniture Zhu Yuanzhang designated Zhu Biao's eldest son Zhu Yunwen, born 1377, as the new heir.

Upon the death of Zhu Yuanzhang in 1398, Zhu Yunwen ascended the throne as the Jianwen ("Establishment of Civic Virtue") emperor, the name reflecting a traditional polarity of *wu* (martial) and *wen* (civil) in the symbolic rhetorical figures of founding emperors. The new emperor proceeded vigorously to establish his own style as ruler. But he was clearly mindful of the powerful threat from his uncle, who in spite of the explicit directions of the Ancestral Injunctions brooded over what he saw as the injustice of the selection of his nephew and his perceived right as his father's eldest surviving son to succeed to the throne. In 1399 the Prince of Yan, claiming violations of the Injunctions by the Jianwen emperor and the legitimacy of his own cause, raised the banner of revolt. The Prince of Yan's strength lay in his military resources based in the north, including Mongol cavalry units. The civil war was bitterly fought but ended with Zhu Di's capture of the capital at Nanjing in 1402. The Jianwen emperor and his family perished in the burning of the palace. Since their bodies were unrecognizable rumors abounded that the emperor had actually escaped and would return to reclaim his throne—as such apocryphal stories so often accompany the assassination of a monarch. Zhu Di assumed the throne as the Yongle ("Perpetual Peace") (1402–1424) emperor. Though he was nominally the third emperor of the dynasty, his reign marked the second founding of the Ming. Throughout his reign Zhu Di was haunted by his act of usurpation and sought to expunge the record of his predecessor, attempting to turn the clock back to the end of his father's reign. He claimed that he was actually a legitimate son of Empress Ma, though ironically a legend arose that the empress was infertile or had borne no sons to Zhu Yuanzhang.

The Yongle emperor assiduously cultivated the imperial ideal of the Chinese monarch. He was a supremely active emperor, a tireless ruler, as confident on horseback leading his armies in the field as he was at home in the court directing his government officials. (The growth of imperial autocracy will be examined in the following chapter.) Suffice it to note here that in 1380 the Hongwu emperor in a fit of violent paranoia had abolished the organs of central government including the Central Secretariat. He commanded that his actions were binding on his successors and could never be reversed. Zhu Di was bound by the Ancestral Injunctions. To facilitate central government operation, the Yongle emperor began to rely increasingly on grand secretaries, Confucian officials serving in lower central government positions who had been individually elevated by the Hongwu emperor to aid in routine central government administration. Gradually grand secretaries assumed the functions of the former chancellors, although they never possessed the semiautonomous power that chancellors enjoyed. Collectively they came to be designated the Grand Secretariat (*neige*). Grand secretaries always come from the ranks of the Hanlin Academy, and Hanlin scholars were in turn all graduates of the highest metropolitan level (*jinshi*) of the civil service examinations. Thus the Grand Secretariat represented the influence of the Confucian scholar-official class, whose role in policy-making in the Chinese state had gradually expanded since the Northern Song, in the Yongle reign. However, the emperor greatly expanded the use of eunuchs as his personal agents in government. Eunuchs, having no independent social base or autonomy outside the court, were creatures of the emperor, completely subordinate to his will. Increasingly they assumed secretarial functions as their education improved and became a virtual bureaucracy in their own right. The Yongle emperor delegated substantial executive authority to his most competent eunuchs.

The Yongle emperor's most ambitious project was his decision to relocate the capital from Nanjing ("Southern Capital") to Beiping ("The North Pacified") in the north, the former Mongol capital of Dadu, where as Prince of Yan he had established his base of power. Early in his reign he made plans for the new capital, and construction of the imperial city proceeded slowly from about 1407. Government functions were gradually moved to the north. The new capital, renamed Beijing ("Northern Capital"), was completed after some setbacks in 1421. The emperor selected the location for the imperial tombs north of the city at a site exhibiting appropriate auspicious features as determined by *fengshui*, the Chinese science of geomancy. His tomb, the construction of which he supervised and which was completed in 1418, was the largest and most central of the thirteen tombs of the Ming emperors to be buried there. Of all of his endeavors the one dearest to his heart, the building of Beijing was the most extraordinarily costly of his ambitious projects, absorbing the energies and resources of a large number of provinces and regions of China. It had permanent fiscal consequences since the Beijing area was relatively poor, unable to sustain a city of that size. To supply the new capital and the armies that would be dispatched from there, the Grand Canal linking the Yangzi valley with the north had to be reconstructed. The permanent cost of supplying Beijing became a huge drain on the state treasury. The immense construction project elicited much official opposition. Soon after the city was formally dedicated a lightning storm started a fire that engulfed a large portion of the recently finished Forbidden City including three great throne halls. Such an adverse event could only be interpreted as a sign of Heaven's displeasure, a warning that the Mandate was in jeopardy. The emperor was appropriately contrite though unknowing of what moral flaws might have caused the disaster.

The term "Ming empire" is a misnomer. The Ming was never an empire in the way that the Qin, Han, and Tang dynasties were empires, extending their political control by means of military conquests, trade and economic expansion, and cultural influence far beyond the boundaries of China Proper. Although the Ming had defeated and pushed the barbarians back into their traditional homelands, it never succeeded in establishing durable and lasting control beyond the limits of Han ancestral regions that defined China Proper. The "Ming empire" was not significantly larger than the Song, which had never broken out of its barbarian confinement. Nevertheless, the Yongle emperor possessed grandiose imperialist ambitions. Toward southeast Asia and beyond, the maritime world known to the Chinese as Nanyang ("The Southern Ocean"), the emperor adopted an active posture more assertive than any emperor before or since. In 1407 he sought to annex the Vietnamese state of Annam, initiating a costly and ultimately disastrous war lasting twenty years. Over the course of his reign, he dispatched almost fifty ambassadorial missions to the numerous states and rulers of Nanyang as far west as the Middle East and Africa. Among these missions are counted the seven spectacular maritime expeditions launched under the command of the eunuch admiral Zheng He from 1405 to 1433 (the last sent out under the Yongle emperor's successor).

To the north, across the continental frontier of inner Asia, the emperor sought to defeat and destroy the lingering threat of the Mongols, now divided into competing tribal confederations. Between 1410 and 1424 the emperor personally led five immense military expeditions into the steppe seeking to overawe alternately the Oirats (western Mongols) and the Tartars (eastern Mongols). While registering some signal successes, the Ming offensives were in the end pyrrhic victories. The Yongle emperor died while returning at the head of the fifth expedition in 1424, and the Mongol threat remained elusive. All of the Yongle emperor's projects, the Annam war, the maritime expeditions, the Mongolian campaigns, the construction of Beijing, and the restoration of the Grand Canal were enormously costly and extravagant, taking a tremendous toll on the fiscal and political viability of the state. The exactions on Vietnam for timber for the construction of ships and palaces alone was a significant cause of the Annamese resistance.

The Yongle reign was marked by ambivalent orientations, rooted in part in Zhu Di's background as an experienced military leader and as patron of civil government. On one hand, his expansive military efforts and his construction of the northern capital drew on his Mongol influences, and even his maritime initiatives, largely anathema to Confucian officials, were based on Mongol precedents. On the other hand, the Yongle emperor's reconstruction of civil government and bureaucracy, even to the extent that it was infused with growing eunuch influence, represented the Confucian imperial ideal, if nevertheless sometimes weakened by tyrannical actions. Zhu Di was originally canonized as Taizong ("Supreme Ancestor") but later in the Ming his temple name was elevated to Chengzu ("Accomplished Progenitor") recognizing that he had completed the work of consolidating Ming rule.

THE GOLDEN AGE

The Yongle emperor was succeeded by his eldest son Zhu Gaozhi, with the reign title Hongxi ("Vast Prosperity") (1425–1426). He could hardly have been a greater contrast with his father. Generally uninterested in military affairs and not physically robust, he showed a proclivity for learning and administration, much to the delight of his Confucian teachers. It soon became evident that the Hongxi emperor was the hope of the Confucian bureaucracy. He had not been associated with his father's policies, and he soon began to reverse many of the Yongle emperor's programs, canceling the scheduled maritime voyage of Zheng He, issuing a general pardon, and beginning a process of returning the capital to Nanjing. Devoted to reforming the central government in the direction of Confucian moderation, he endeavored to rule as an exemplary Confucian monarch. Unfortunately, the Hongxi emperor died less than a year after assuming the throne. He was succeeded by his eldest son, Zhu Zhanji who became the Xuande ("Comprehensive Virtue") emperor (1426–1435).

The Xuande emperor in many respects shared the best attributes of his predecessors. He followed his father's model of a Confucian monarch but he possessed military talent, having accompanied his grandfather, the Yongle emperor who favored him, on military campaigns and hunting expeditions. At the same time, he was an accomplished painter, calligrapher, poet, and writer, and a patron of the arts, much in the tradition of Song Huizong. He built on and continued the central government reforms his father had started and regularized the civil administration of the provinces through the institution of the provincial governor (*xunfu*). The emperor exhibited a sincere concern for the popular welfare. Once while traveling he saw a farmer plowing his field. He stopped to try his hand at the plow. Afterward, he observed to his attendants, "After taking only three turns at the plow, we are already unequal to the labor. What if one does this constantly? Men always say there is no toil like farming, and they are right!"[5]

Perhaps in a gesture toward his grandfather he dispatched the much-delayed seventh and last maritime expedition under Zheng He in 1431. But he also ended the disastrous twenty-year Annam war when Chinese military commanders were decisively defeated by the insurgency in 1427, and recognized the existing government of Annam. His mother, the Empress Dowager Zhang, was an important influence on the character of his reign who continued her beneficent influence as regent for her grandson, the Xuande emperor's son. (We shall return to her influence in the following chapter.)

The Xuande reign is considered the Ming dynasty's "Golden Age," a time of stability and harmony in civil and military affairs. During the Xuande period we witness the ascendancy of civil over military influences, although on another note this tendency was accompanied by the decline of the *weisuo* military system created by the Hongwu emperor. With the end of the Xuande reign in 1435 the various competing forces contingent on the rise of the Ming out of the era of late Yuan turbulence were largely resolved. New issues and sources of weakness leading to the ultimate decline and fall of the Ming now came to the fore.

As constructed by Zhu Yuanzhang over the course of his reign from the early 1360s, the Ming owed its institutional form almost entirely to the Yuan. Though Zhu rejected, like all Chinese, alien Mongol rule and its degrading attitude toward its Chinese subjects, the influences of the Yuan military system and its elite authoritarian style bore most heavily on his experience as he rose to power in the waning years of the Yuan. Chinese Confucian officials and scholars, for all their indispensable service to making the state function, were regarded as instruments of the emperor, not as autonomous agents in a partnership between bureaucrats and autocrats. Zhu harbored a deep suspicion bordering on pathological hatred of the Confucian literati class that pervaded his entire reign and echoed the Mongol suspicion of their Chinese subjects.

Yet by the end of the Xuande reign in 1435, the Confucian official elite had emerged from the wilderness to claim the dominance it enjoyed in pre-Yuan, Song times. A traditional Confucian education became the foundation for success in the civil service examinations, which in turn was the principal path to a civil service career in the Confucian bureaucracy. Parallel to this development, the influence of the military elite waned, particularly under the onslaught of Zhu Yuanzhang's purges, and civil officials assumed a large measure of control over the military establishment. But, finally, in a sense permanently compensating for the seeming victory of the Confucian civil service, the power of eunuchs grew exponentially stronger through the Yongle and Xuande reigns to the point that a succession of eunuch dictators dominated the later Ming and even challenged the authority of the emperor.

SUGGESTED READINGS

Chan, Hok-lam. "The Rise of Ming T'ai-tsu (1368–1398): Facts and Fictions in Early Ming Official Historiography," *Journal of the American Oriental Society* 95.4 (1975): 679–715. An excellent study of the background and rise of Zhu Yuanzhang, the founder of the Ming dynasty.

Dardess, John W. *Conquerors and Confucians: Aspects of Political Change in Late Yuan China* (New York: Columbia University Press, 1973). A study of the political and economic dynamics during the decline of the Mongol Yuan dynasty.

Dardess, John W. *Ming China, 1368–1644. A Concise History of a Resilient Empire* (Lanham, Maryland: Rowman & Littlefield, 2012). A brief study of the Ming organized by thematic subjects, including frontiers, emperors, governance, literati, and outlaws.

Dreyer, Edward L. *Early Ming China: A Political History, 1355–1435* (Stanford: Stanford University Press, 1982). A careful analysis of early Ming political developments by a leading Ming scholar.

Goodrich, L. Carrington, and Chaoying Fang, eds. *Dictionary of Ming Biography, 1368–1644,* 2 vols. (New York: Columbia University Press, 1976). An essential and reliable reference for the study of the Ming.

Hucker, Charles O. *China's Imperial Past: An Introduction to Chinese History and Culture* (Stanford: Stanford University Press, 1975).

Hucker, Charles O., ed. *Chinese Government in Ming Times: Seven Studies* (New York: Columbia University Press, 1969). Studies by major students of the Ming on local and fiscal administration, education, politics, bureaucracy, and the military system.

Mote, F. W. *Imperial China, 900–1800* (Cambridge: Harvard University Press, 1999). The most comprehensive treatment of Chinese history from the end of the Tang through the early Qing dynasties. An extremely useful reference, with the caveat that the index has many lacunae.

Mote, Frederick W., and Denis Twitchett, eds. *The Cambridge History of China,* vol. 7, *The Ming Dynasty, 1368–1644,* Part 1 (Cambridge: Cambridge University Press, 1988).

Taylor, Romeyn. "Yuan Origins of the Wei-so System," in Charles O. Hucker, ed., *Chinese Government in Ming Times* (New York: Columbia University Press, 1969), 23–40. See Charles O. Hucker, *Chinese Government in Ming Times,* above.

Twitchett, Denis, and Frederick W. Mote, eds. *The Cambridge History of China,* vol. 8. *The Ming Dynasty, 1368–1644,* Part 2 (Cambridge: Cambridge University Press, 1998). The volumes of the *Cambridge History of China* on the Ming dynasty, with chapters contributed by authorities in their respective fields, constitute the most complete and essential reference for this period.

NOTES

1. Quotation adopted from Hok-lam Cham, "The Rise of Ming T'ai-tsu (1368–1398): Facts and Fictions in Early Ming Official Historiography," *Journal of the American Oriental Society* 95.4 (1975): 691, from *Taizu shilu (Veritable Records of Ming Taizu).*

2. Quotation adopted from Hok-lam Chan, 696, from *Taizu shilu (Veritable Records of Ming Taizu).*

3. Mengzi (Mencius), trans. with an introduction by D. C. Lau, *Mencius* (Harmondsworth, England and New York: Penguin Books, 1970), VII, B, 14.

4. See L. Carrington Goodrich and Chaoying Fang, eds., *Dictionary of Ming Biography, 1368–1644* (New York: Columbia University Press, 1976) (hereafter *DMB*), plates 1 and 2 following 278.

5. *DMB,* 283.

5

Autocrat, Bureaucrat, Empress, Eunuch

In 221 BCE King Zheng of the state of Qin, aided by Legalist advisors and ministers, conquered and annexed the last surviving states of the Zhou. The decentralized feudal order of Zhou founded by Wen Wang and Wu Wang eight centuries earlier had come to its end and the Mandate passed, it seemed, to the Qin. The conquest of the Zhou elevated the Chinese world from a collection of contentious autonomous states to a unified empire on an unprecedented scale. Wang (king), a once exalted title in the days of the Shang and early Zhou, had been cheapened and diminished through the Warring States era of the late Zhou and was no longer appropriate to describe the ruler of this new world order. A new title for ruler had to be invented suitable to the new political reality. Thus King Zheng adopted the title First Emperor of the Qin (Qin Shihuangdi). Huangdi ("emperor") was a quasi-divine term that designated a universal ruler; Shi (First), because the Qin proclaimed a dynasty that would last ten thousand years, each successive emperor to be numbered in sequence. Qin Shihuangdi, then, was the first emperor of China, inaugurating an entirely new era. Forever after he was the prototypical autocrat. A perennial tension throughout Chinese history was thus born between the theoretically unbridled authority of the supreme monarch and the mitigating influence of his civil officials without whom he would be unable to rule.

The emperor was guided by adherents of the Legalist school, the principal antagonists of the Confucianists at the end of the Zhou. The Legalists were deeply contemptuous and suspicious of the educated shi class to which Confucians belonged—the Ru ("weaklings") they called them. Han Feizi, the great synthesizer of Legalist theory, writing on the authority of the ruler, advocated the ruthless suppression of the nattering educated class of the Zhou:

In listening to a learned man, if the ruler approves his words, he should officially adopt them in his administration and appoint the man to office; and if he disapproves his words, he should get rid of the person and put an end to his heretical doctrine. Actually, however, what is regarded as right is not officially adopted in administration and what is regarded as wrong is not stamped out as heretical doctrine. Thus, what is right is not employed and what is wrong is not eliminated—this is the way to chaos and ruin. . . .

Therefore, those who practice humanity and righteousness should not be upheld, for if upheld, they would hinder concrete accomplishment. Again, those who specialize in refinement and learning should not be employed, for if employed, they would distrust the laws.[1]

Li Si, the ruthless grand councilor of the Qin, carried this advice to its logical conclusion:

Of old, the empire was scattered and in confusion, and there was none able to unite it into one. This was because the feudal lords all became active together, and in their discussion they harped on the past so as to injure the present, and made a display of empty words so as to confuse the truth. Men valued what they themselves privately studied, thus casting into disrepute what their superiors had established.

At present Your Majesty possesses a unified empire, has laid down the distinctions of right and wrong, and had consolidated for himself a single (position of) eminence. Yet there are those who with their teachings mutually abet each other, and who teach others what is not according to the laws. When they hear orders promulgated, they criticize them in the light of their own teachings. Within (the court) they mentally discredit them, and outside they criticize them upon the streets. To cast disrepute on their ruler they regard as a thing worthy of fame, to accept different views they regard as high (conduct); and they lead the people to create slander. If such conditions are not prohibited, the imperial power will decline above, and partisanships will form below. It is expedient that these be prohibited.

Your servant suggests that all books in the bureau of history, save the records of the Qin, be burned; that all persons in the empire, save those who hold a function under the control of the bureau of scholars of wide learning, daring to store the Shi *[Classic of Poetry], the* Shu *[Classic of History], and the discussion of the various philosophers, should go to the administrative and military governors so that these books may be indiscriminately burned. Those who dare to discuss the* Shi *and* Shu *among themselves should be executed and their bodies exposed in the market place. Those who use the past to criticize the present should be put to death together with their relatives. Officials who see or know (violators of these regulations) without reporting them, should be considered equally guilty.*[2]

Accordingly, one of the most the most heinous crimes ever perpetrated in Chinese history, the burning of the books and the killing of scholars as a program of ideological control, was committed, permanently consigning the Qin to the condemnation of later scholars until Mao Zedong took Qin Shihuangdi as his model during the Great Chinese Cultural Revolution in the 1960s during the Cultural Revolution.

THE CONFUCIAN-LEGALIST ACCOMMODATION

The Qin created a stark tension between the Legalist theory of the absolute monarch and the Confucian tradition of conscientious public service. The Qin's tyranny assured its speedy demise; it fell to rebellion in 206 BCE after the succession of only the second emperor. Out of the chaos of civil war, the Han emerged in 202 BCE. The Han's reaction to the Qin's radical authoritarianism was to return to the former ways. But there was no desire to restore the discredited feudalism of the Zhou. Thus the Han gradually began to recruit an educated bureaucracy of appointed officials. Those best qualified, of course, were Confucians who followed a tradition of education and public service. The early Han emperors began the process of creating the rudiments of a civil service examination system based on merit. But at the same time it was never assumed that a bureaucracy could rule itself; it required the firm hand of an authoritarian monarch ruling a centralized state that would guarantee the perpetuation of a system of selection of officials by merit. The triumph of this accommodation occurred under the reign of Han Wudi ("The Martial Emperor") (140–87 BCE), supported by the new Confucian imperial ideology of Dong Zhongshu. "The Legalist victory [of the Qin], while seeming to destroy Confucianism, in reality created the stable society in which it could triumph. The Confucian victory [of the Han], far from destroying Legalism, made the Legalist empire all but indestructible."[3]

Thus an enduring modus vivendi was reached between Confucianism and Legalism, between the imperial ruler and the bureaucracy of officials. The dynamic tension between them tilted to one side or the other, but remained a powerful creative force throughout imperial Chinese history. The enduring dream of the Confucian was a humane ruler who exemplified Confucian virtues and who esteemed and respected his Confucian advisors. The highest Confucian political virtue was the function of remonstrance to the ruler, with the expectation that the ruler should listen with humility. But as Li Si, articulating a very different view, had said, "To cast disrepute on their ruler they regard as a thing worthy of fame; to accept different views they regard as high conduct."[4] The official frequently laid his life on the line to uphold the Confucian ideal before his emperor.

IMPERIAL AUTOCRACY IN ACTION

Zhu Yuanzhang was the incarnation of Qin Shihuangdi. The Ming rose out of the Yuan absolutist state, and in such an environment, the Qin example, whether consciously emulated or not, possessed a powerful attraction, including the perspectives of Han Feizi on the scholar class, and the actions of Li Si, justified as with both of them in the name of creating a stable order. Although necessarily relying on their services, from the beginning the Hongwu emperor sought to methodically control and intimidate the officials. One means was to fix the content of the civil service examinations so as to limit the scope of their knowledge. Another was laws that prohibited interference in government matters by officials, a goal that seems paradoxical since government matters were their business. Yet another, far more fearful and brutal, was public flogging of offending officials before the court, a procedure so violent that it often led to the crippling or death of the subject. Last was the use of eunuchs as a rival source of power to officials. The basis of the rising influence of eunuchs lay in their function as checks on the civil bureaucracy and instruments of autocracy.

The Hongwu emperor's pathological suspicion and fear of officials, with whom he yet could not do without, was exhibited in a series of astonishingly brutal, expansive purges of bureaucrats and military officers. Early in his reign he had shown a proclivity for capricious execution of opponents or those he imagined were his opponents. He was extremely intolerant of even the hint of official malfeasance. In 1376 it came to his attention that documents used by local officials to report grain tax shipments were being pre-stamped prior to completion, when transit losses could be calculated and deducted. This was an innocent practice of the responsible officials intended to expedite reporting by obviating the invalidation of documents that would otherwise contain inaccurate figures because losses were unaccounted for. Enraged by what he believed was corruption, the emperor ordered the summary execution of all officials connected with the practice. Thousands were killed in what came to be known as the Case of the Pre-stamped Documents.

Hu Weiyong had been an early follower of Zhu Yuanzhang since the 1350s when he had earned Zhu's respect. In 1373 Hu was appointed to the Central Secretariat, and in 1377 rose to chief councilor. Hu consolidated his position of influence by advancing his allies and removing his opponents. He was increasingly apprehensive over the emperor's irrational violence exhibited in the Pre-stamped Documents Case. His ambitious behavior attracted growing opposition from the censors, who charged that Hu was plotting a coup d'état and the assassination of the emperor. When Hu's alleged plot was revealed to the emperor, he ordered the immediate execution of Hu, his conspirators, and their entire families. The purge, which went on for more than a decade, extended to thousands of others who were only tenuously connected with Hu Weiyong or guilty merely by association. The purge was revived with increased ferocity in 1390, leading to a reign of terror from 1390 to 1395 involving everyone who might be imagined to have had a connection with Hu. Lan Yu, one of the most successful Ming generals, who had led armies in the southern Yunnan region and against the Mongols, was executed on trumped-up charges of treason in 1393. The purge expanded to decimate the class of military officers. By Hongwu's death in 1398 most of the upper ruling elite had been devastated. It is estimated that up to thirty thousand people were killed in the Hongwu emperor's attempts to intimidate the civil and military bureaucracies.

When Hu Weiyong's alleged conspiracy was revealed in 1380 the Hongwu emperor concluded that the Central Secretariat (*zhongshusheng*), with its quasi-autonomous role as the highest organ of central government, was a permanent threat to his own power. He therefore abolished the Secretariat, the Censorate, and the Chief Military Commission, effectively decapitating the formal structure of the central government. The emperor became his own councilor. The Six Ministries, no longer responsible to the Secretariat, were raised in rank and now reported directly to the emperor individually. The Military Commission was replaced by five regional military commissions reporting individually to the emperor. The Censorate was soon restored but with reduced powers. To handle the huge influx of paperwork no longer mediated by the secretariat, the emperor appointed secretaries from among officials concurrently serving in lower ranks to assist and advise him. Later institutionalized in the following Yongle reign as the Grand Secretariat, they were purely servants who possessed no autonomous authority such as the former chief councilors had enjoyed.

Enhancing the emperor's personal control over the government, twelve guard units (*wei*) at the capital were placed directly under the emperor's command as the Imperial Guards. The chief of these was the Embroidered Uniform Guard (*jinyi wei*) which was responsible for police work and surveillance, becoming the most important instrument of repression.

The year 1380 was a watershed in Ming and later imperial history. The Hongwu emperor decreed in the Ancestral Injunctions that his successors were henceforth forever prohibited from restoring the Secretariat and its functions. His will was obeyed. This was the entering wedge for eunuch influence which grew over the following reigns to become a vast institutional apparatus serving the emperor's exclusive interests. The absolute power of the monarch was now unmitigated by formal institutions of government, much as the Legalists of the Qin had advocated.

THE IMPERIAL-BUREAUCRATIC ORDER

How could such unrestrained tyranny be tolerated? Why were the emperor's commands, however awful and terrifying, obeyed? Why did his subjects fail to exercise any restraining influence? The easy answer, of course, is that the emperor possessed obedient instruments of terror in his loyal police and military units, his personal servants such as the eunuchs, and among subservient officials who hoped that by currying his favor they would escape his wrath (though they rarely did) that overwhelmed the vastly larger number of his victims. Yet this somewhat metaphysical question points to the fundamental basis of imperial autocracy in China—the ritual, institutional, and customary sources of the emperor's role. Zhu Yuanzhang, like Qin Shihuangdi, may have been the mightiest of monarchs, but even the most incompetent and weak emperors held in their hands the capacity to demand absolute obedience to their will. So essential was the imperial institution to the imperial-bureaucratic polity of China since the Qin and Han invented it that to threaten the manifestation of its existence in any single emperor would have endangered the entire structure, including its other half, the scholar-official class who were the custodians and representatives of the higher cultural ethos of Chinese civilization. Understanding this all too well, the scholar-officials were unwilling to bring down the entire edifice to save some individuals. One who possessed the moderating influence of the Classics such as the Xuande emperor (1426–1435) would eventually come along. Scholar-officials had to believe that Li Si was an aberration.

No understanding of the Chinese imperial-bureaucratic system can be gained without an appreciation for its complex processes. Government was as much a matter of procedure and ritual as it was of policy and action. It was not just a cohort of men serving in differentiated offices debating and implementing decisions. Bureaucratic officials were embedded in a vast infrastructure of detailed rules, minute procedures specified in written regulations and unwritten conventions and customs that the Qin could not even have dreamed of. Actions and precedents taken within this matrix were methodically recorded. China produced as a result the world's largest body of bureaucratic records. The inertia of the system was in the long run the greatest source of strength of the bureaucracy against the unrestrained imperial will of the monarch.

At a fundamental level the central government was divided between the Outer Court and the Inner Court. The Outer Court comprised the formal government institutions, headed until 1380 by the Secretariat, and including the Six Ministries, the Censorate, and the Hanlin Academy. The Inner Court, so called because it was located within the palace and close to the emperor, was originally made up of informal agencies including the Grand Secretariat and the diverse offices staffed by eunuchs.

Bureaucracy is all about communication. The functions of government were carried out through an infrastructure of strictly controlled communication. Virtually all decisions were taken in response to memorials received from officials, answered by orders in the form of imperial edicts and rescripts. Memorials were received by the Transmission Office (*tongzhengsi*) established in 1377 in the Outer Court. From there they were passed to the Palace Secretariat (*wenshufang*), since 1432 staffed by eunuchs in the Inner Court, which in turn passed them to the Directorate of Ceremonial (*silijian*), the center of eunuch authority in the Inner Court. After the staff of the Directorate of Ceremonial presented the memorials to the emperor for preliminary review they were transmitted to the proper ministry for recommendation of appropriate action and to the Grand Secretariat for deliberation. From there they passed back up the line to the emperor for decision and implementation in the form of edicts. By the mid-fifteenth century this process was dominated and effectively controlled by eunuchs, who were able to modify and even veto recommendations of the Grand Secretariat.

The actions and words of the emperor and his court were systematically recorded daily in the Diaries of Action and Repose (*qijuzhu*). This "imperial diary" was condensed daily into the Daily Records (*rili*). This body of records was in turn compiled into the Veritable Records (*shilu*) for each reign. The Veritable Records were used by the following dynasty to write the official dynastic history of its predecessor, in the case of the Ming, the *Ming Shi*. The Veritable Records, all of which survive for the Ming and Qing, are the most important historical source for the last five hundred years of Imperial China. Unequalled by any other country, they comprise 7,000 chapters for the Ming. They were not tamperproof, however. The Veritable Records for the Hongwu reign were extensively edited and revised by the Yongle emperor to hide the record of his usurpation of the Jianwen emperor, who was largely made to disappear from the historical record.

At the core of the imperial-bureaucratic order was the civil service examination system. The Hongwu emperor had implemented the examinations early in his reign after they had remained dormant in the Yuan. Then, dissatisfied with the results, he had temporarily abandoned them. The system was revived permanently in 1384. The Confucian curriculum of the examinations ensured the Confucianization of the civil service and the domination of Chinese society by the scholar-gentry class through the Ming-Qing era. The civil bureaucracy in the Ming numbered approximately fifteen thousand officials, five thousand instructors in government schools, and perhaps another four thousand petty district officers. Graduates of the first qualifying level of the examinations, assigned to local schools at the district, department, and prefectural levels, received a stipend and were exempt from labor service. At this level their status was somewhat nebulous, still essentially commoners. As they worked their way up the examination ladder, those who were successful and graduated at the highest level, the triennial metropolitan examination, received the distinguished degree of "presented scholar" (*jinshi*) and would likely be appointed to a provincial or central government position.

For all his brutality, the Yongle emperor lived up to expectations of a great emperor, if not the Confucian expectations for one. The ambiguous relationship of monarch and minister in this era is exemplified by the Yongle emperor (1402–1424) and Minister of Revenue Xia Yuanji (1366–1430). Xia earned his second level examination degree in 1390 and entered the National University where he attracted the attention of the Hongwu emperor. He was assigned to the Ministry of Revenue by the Yongle emperor and rose to be minister of revenue from 1405 to 1421. As an expert on financial affairs he organized support for Yongle's ambitious projects including the annexation of Annam, the northern Mongolian campaigns, the maritime expeditions under Zheng He, and the construction of the new capital at Beijing. He possessed detailed knowledge of country-wide funds and grain supplies, carrying with him demographic figures on population, households, tax supplies, and shortages. Unlike Wang Anshi, the great Northern Song statesman, he was not an innovative reformer but followed orthodox methods, combining fiscal expertise and Confucian virtues. Although completely honest and blameless, he was impeached by his enemies in 1421 and imprisoned by the Embroidered Uniform Guard. Surviving prison, he was recalled by the Yongle emperor's successor in 1424 and continued his career until his death in 1430. He was close to both the Hongxi and Xuande emperors, in the period of financial restraint after the extravagances of the Yongle reign. Following conservative policies, Xia advised against further maritime expeditions and the continuation of the Annam war. Xia Yuanji enjoyed the reputation of a true Confucian official commanding the esteem of the civil bureaucracy. On his death bed in 1424, the Yongle emperor was reported to have said, "Yuanji loved me."[5] As a sign of remorse, this was a rare tribute from one of the most powerful and vindictive Ming emperors to an exemplary Confucian official. It illustrates one dimension of the tension that existed between the Legalist autocrat and the Confucian official. At its best, this tension was ultimately a source of strength in the imperial-bureaucratic system that had evolved from the stark conflict between the Legalist monarch of the Qin and the Confucian officials of the Han.

THE PALACE

In addition to the imperial institution and the civil bureaucracy, the palace constituted a third but highly unpredictable component of government. Family intruded into the conduct of government through the influence of the wives and consorts of the emperor. Empresses and dowager empresses stood outside the formal institutional structure but at times exerted great political influence. Their authority, while entirely customary, was based on the direct influence of a favored consort on the emperor, the filial status accorded to motherhood if the consort were the mother of the heir apparent, and the more nebulous status of an able consort among court officials. Empresses and empress dowagers could and often did act as arbiters between emperors, especially if they were minors or were weak, and eunuchs and officials. The best empresses were educated and were in no way inferior to scholar-officials, yet they were not allowed to sit for the examinations. While they often exercised a moderating influence, however, they could also be a corrupting influence when they pursued personal goals of aggrandizement driven by ambition and jealousy.

The Empress Ma (1332–1382), who exercised a strong beneficial restraint on her husband Zhu Yuanzhang, exemplified the best tradition of palace influence. She was entrusted as a small child by her impoverished parents to her father's close friend Guo Zixing, one of the contenders for power in the late Yuan civil war. She worked in the fields as a child and consequently her feet were left unbound. While she was largely self-taught, she became literate and well-read. After Zhu Yuanzhang entered Guo's bodyguard, Guo gave her to Zhu in marriage in 1352. She served as Zhu's secretary in charge of documents and records. She showed great compassion for Zhu's officers, once rescuing some of them from a Mongol attack, and distributed clothes to his troops. As empress after Zhu ascended the throne, she intervened in some of his harsh decisions to mitigate his anger. As empress she emulated Khubilai Khan's wife Chabi, wearing clothes made of patched and mended coarse silk, while she continued to study literary texts. Zhu remained devoted to her until her death. She possessed an innate good sense, and after her death the absence of her restraining influence on the Hongwu emperor was evident in his growing irrational conduct.

THE RISE OF EUNUCH POWER

Autocracy and brutality toward the official class became progressively routine and institutionalized in the Yongle reign (1402–1424). The Yongle emperor's distrust of the officials who had served the deposed Jianwen emperor (1399–1402) led him to inflict a bloody purge on all those in the civil service bureaucracy and military who had been associated with the previous reign. No doubt his sense of guilt for his usurpation magnified the ferocity of his purge. Rivaling the extent of his father's purges, the Yongle emperor's victims may have numbered in the tens of thousands.

While regularizing the organization of the Outer Court and the Grand Secretariat in the Inner Court, at the same time the Yongle emperor depended increasingly on eunuchs as advisors and agents. Eunuch power grew accordingly until during later reigns, when they came to control the throne and the administration of the state. Eunuchs in the Hongwu reign were organized under the Directorate of Palace Servants (_neishijian_). In 1384 the Hongwu emperor had prohibited eunuchs from corresponding with officials, becoming literate, wearing official uniforms, or holding civil and military ranks. In the Yongle reign eunuchs were organized into twenty-four offices with various responsibilities related to palace functions. The center of eunuch power rested in the Directorate of Ceremonial. With increasing formality, eunuchs ceased to be merely personal tools of the emperor and became an institutionalized bureaucracy in their own right. The Embroidered Uniform Guard, revived in the Yongle reign, operated the northern and southern prisons in the capital, where arrested officials were tortured and flogged. Cooperating with the guard but largely displacing its function, the Eastern Depot (_dong chang_), a spy organization with wide authority staffed by eunuchs, was established in 1420. Later still, the Western Depot (_xi chang_) was set up in 1477 to spy on other secret service branches. But eunuchs themselves were not immune from being purged.

The Xuande reign (1426–1435) was the pivotal point in the growth of eunuch power. Although the Xuande emperor aspired to rule as a humane monarch and strengthened the civil bureaucracy, he introduced changes that were to vastly expand eunuch authority. In 1426 he established the Palace School (_neishutang_) for the education of eunuchs that opened the door to unlimited eunuch influence. Eunuchs henceforth mastered the language and techniques of bureaucratic organization, allowing them to become an autonomous bureaucracy rivaling the official civil bureaucracy with much the same organizational rationale. The Directorate of Ceremonial drew its members from the Palace Secretariat which became the training ground for appointments to the Directorate. The heads of the Directorate of Ceremonial grew more powerful than the former councilors, abolished by the Hongwu emperor, embracing executive, legislative, and judicial powers. Thus the Directorate developed into a quasi-imperial authority, with power to approve or disapprove recommendations of the Grand Secretariat, control appointment and dismissal of ministers, and influence the formulation of policy. By the end of the fifteenth century there were ten thousand eunuchs in the palace. By the end of the dynasty in the mid-seventeenth century eunuchs numbered seventy thousand in the palace alone, perhaps one hundred thousand in the entire country, vastly exceeding the size of the regular civil bureaucracy.

Wang Zhen was one of the first students in the Palace School for eunuchs to receive a Confucian education. He later gained complete influence over the heir apparent Zhu Qizhen. When the Xuande emperor died in 1435, Zhu Qizhen was only eight years old. There was no provision in the Ancestral Injunctions for succession of a minor emperor or a regency to rule on his behalf. The Empress Dowager Zhang, mother of the Xuande emperor, first proposed a more mature successor, but decided to uphold the rights of the heir apparent. Placing Zhu Qizhen on the throne, she summoned the leading grand secretaries, pointed to her grandson, and told them this was the new emperor. Although the Ancestral Injunctions prohibited anyone from acting as a formal regent, Grand Empress Dowager Zhang assumed the position of the leading member of a de facto regency for the new Zhengtong ("Orthodox Succession") reign (1436–1449), with three grand secretaries and Wang Zhen, who was appointed to the Directorate of Ceremonial in 1435. Throughout the reigns of her husband, son, and now grandson, Zhang exercised a powerful stabilizing influence in the best tradition of the palace, until her death in 1442. Suspicious of the ambition of Wang Zhen and his power over the youthful emperor, she worked to restrain his influence. At one point she ordered Wang to commit suicide but relented under pressure from the grand secretaries and Wang's pleading.

Wang restrained himself for the remainder of Zhang's regency, but with the death of Grand Empress Dowager Zhang, all fetters were removed from Wang Zhen, who now became the first of the infamous "eunuch dictators." At this time the Mongol Oirat leader Esen, who aspired to become Great Khan, was threatening the Ming military frontier. The young Zhengtong emperor delighted in participating in military maneuvers. Pandering to his master, Wang proposed, against vigorous remonstrance from officials, that the emperor personally lead his armies in a campaign to defeat the Mongols in 1449 with Wang acting as field marshal. Hastily assembled, the army, though huge, was ill-prepared, poorly supplied, and badly led. After marching into the steppe, when the army encountered evidence of Esen's strength and the perilous situation it was entering it began to withdraw. Attacking the retreating army, the Mongols annihilated the Ming rear guard. When the army encamped at the undefended town of Tumu for the night the Mongols attacked and destroyed the entire army, capturing the emperor himself. Wang Zhen perished at the hands of his own officers. Thus ended the sorriest episode of imperial ineptness of the Ming.

Esen rejoiced that he had in his hands the perfect hostage to extort concessions from the Ming court. But the government ignored the fate of the unfortunate emperor and installed his brother as the Jingtai ("Bright Prosperity") emperor (1450–1456) in 1450. Realizing that his hostage was valueless, Esen returned Zhu Qizhen to the court, but the new emperor, enjoying his unexpected elevation, sought to marginalize him. Although the Jingtai reign brought stability and restoration of order, officials of the former Zhengtong emperor conspired to restore their patron to the throne. Their opportunity came in 1457 when they forced their way into the palace with a unit of the Imperial Guard and in a coup d'état placed Zhu Qizhen back in the throne as the Tianshun ("Obedient to Heaven") emperor (1457–1464).

When the Tianshun emperor died in 1464, his son, still in his teens, was enthroned as the Chenghua ("Accomplished Transformation") emperor (1465–1487). While he was still a young child, the Xuande emperor's former consort, Empress Dowager Sun, had given him a palace nursemaid, Lady Wan. Although twice his age, Wan Guifei ("Honored Consort") became his favorite consort, ranking second only to the empress. The Chenghua emperor's complete devotion to her permitted her to exercise great influence on the court, involving pervasive corruption and the appointment of large numbers of unqualified personnel. She introduced an ambitious eunuch from her staff, Wang Zhi, who rose to be the second notorious eunuch dictator. In 1477 he established with the emperor's authorization the Western Depot (*xi chang*) which became the instrument of his reign of terror, more feared even than the Eastern Depot. Wang was finally removed by the emperor in 1483 after vigorous opposition from other eunuchs.

Wan Guifei died in early 1487, predeceasing the Chenghua emperor by only a few months. The emperor left only one son, by Lady Ji, a Yao aborigine (as, incidentally, was Wang Zhi) who had been brought into the palace as a concubine after one of the southern campaigns. Zhu Youtang, then, who was half-minority, rather small and dark complexioned, ascended the throne in 1488 as the Hongzhi ("Expansive Rule") emperor (1488–1505). Here, at last, was the model emperor whose advent Confucian officials so earnestly hoped for, comparable to the Xuande emperor in his sincere commitment to ruling in partnership with his ministers and to Confucian teachings and ethical values. He dismissed thousands of corrupt officials appointed by Wan Guifei, members of her family, eunuch collaborators, and disreputable Buddhist and Daoist hangers-on. To his credit, very few were executed. The Ming History (*ming shi*) assessed his reign in glowing terms, reflecting the Confucianists' favorable views

The Ming held the realm throughout a succession of sixteen rulers. . . . Xiaozong [the Hongzhi emperor] was alone in having the ability to maintain his governing in humility and modesty, to be diligent in governing and to have deep concern for the people, ever vigilant to uphold the Great Way of guarding the realm's riches and not abusing his powers, maintaining the purity and uprightness of his court, and assuring that the people would enjoy abundance.[6]

Unfortunately, it wasn't to last. Yet even under the Hongzhi reign the eunuch bureaucracy expanded to surpass the civil bureaucracy in size.

DISSIPATION OF IMPERIAL RULE

The Hongzhi emperor was the last of the Ming emperors who were seriously and conscientiously engaged in government. He was succeeded by emperors who could hardly have been more different in their indifference to rule well and responsibly. Willful, self-indulgent, and incompetent, they abandoned government to an uneasy partnership of ministers and powerful eunuchs. Zhu Houzhao, the Zhengde ("Rectification of Virtue") emperor, reigned from 1506 to 1521. Flagrantly disregarding his duties, he roamed the streets of the capital in disguise, encouraged by his eunuch companions. He was frequently drunk. He squandered vast resources from the state treasury on such personal whims as a separate residential palace with its own military exercise field and a hunting zoo, lavish expenditures on lanterns for the lantern festival, and a Mongol yurt encampment within the Forbidden City.

In 1506, taking advantage of the emperor's self-indulgence in musical entertainments, the eunuch Liu Jin rose to a position of commanding power as the third of the eunuch dictators. He carried out another reign of terror against his opponents and critics until he finally lost favor with the subservient emperor and was arrested and executed in 1510. For the rest of his reign the emperor engaged in foolish military adventures with favorite officers. After an accident in which he almost drowned when his small boat capsized and he fell ill, he died in 1521 without an heir.

After considerable negotiation and deliberation over ritual proprieties and dynastic precedents, the younger cousin of the Zhengde emperor, Zhu Houcong was enthroned as the Jiajing ("Auspicious Tranquility") emperor, reigning from 1522 to 1566. At first his actions and behavior boded well for his reign. Under the influence of his chief grand secretary, he promoted austerity in contrast to the lavish expenditures of his predecessor, dismissed unqualified officials and eunuchs, and curbed the eunuch bureaucracy. But this early positive momentum dissipated as he became absorbed in a long-running controversy over ritual related to the status of his relatives, and his chronic poor health caused him to become obsessed with Daoist practices of immortality and sexual potency. He became increasingly erratic, disregarding the responsibilities of government entirely. After a failed assassination attempt by a group of palace ladies driven to extremity by the emperor's constant harassment and perverse behavior, he withdrew to a separate palace in the imperial city and for the rest of his reign had no further contact with the court. The emperor's health progressively worsened until he died in 1566, probably from the effects of arsenic and lead poisoning associated with the Daoist elixirs he had indulged in.

The Jiajing emperor's withdrawal from government opened the way for the resurgence of eunuch power. By the late 1540s the head of the Directorate of Ceremonial held absolute power over the eunuch bureaucracy, displacing the Grand Secretariat. Yet another powerful instrument of eunuch autocracy was created in 1552 in the Palace Army (*neiwufu*) comprising eunuchs.

With the reigns of Zhengde and Jiajing spanning six decades of the sixteenth century, the imperial institution had declined significantly since the reigns of Hongwu and Yongle two centuries earlier. Whatever their faults, and there were many, the latter emperors were constantly engaged in the establishment and ruling of the empire, never out of touch with their officials and ministers. The former emperors, however, ruled largely by default, their often misguided attempts to interfere in the conduct of government leading to mismanagement, conflict, and corruption. The administration of the state fell to a tense accommodation between the civil bureaucracy of Confucian officials and the autonomous eunuch bureaucracy.

The relationship between monarch and minister in this changed environment was exemplified by the failed reigns of Zhengde and Jiajing, and Grand Secretary Yang Tinghe (1459–1529). Yang earned the highest civil service examination degree (*jinshi*) in 1478 at the age of nineteen and entered the Hanlin Academy. He was promoted to minister of revenue and grand secretary in 1507 and in 1513 he became head of the Grand Secretariat. After an obligatory two-year period of mourning for his father he was recalled to service as minister of personnel and grand secretary. He frequently remonstrated with the Zhengde emperor over his irresponsible behavior, but escaped punishment. During the emperor's military adventure in the south in 1521, Yang took full charge of the government in Beijing, enhancing his reputation in the process. The emperor's death without an heir presented a serious issue of succession. Yang forcefully interpreted the Ancestral Injunctions to permit the designation of the emperor's younger cousin as his successor as if he were his younger brother. During the interregnum between the death of the emperor and the arrival at the capital of the new emperor and his enthronement, Yang was in absolute power for thirty-seven days. He issued a lengthy edict in the name of the new emperor-to-be proclaiming new policies and reforms as well as correction of previous abuses. More than 148 thousand superfluous officials were dismissed, taxes were reduced, Daoist priests were discharged, large numbers of women brought into the palace to serve the emperor's sexual regimen were released, and useless military units were disbanded.

Even before the Jiajing emperor ascended the throne a major crisis developed that eventually led to the undoing not only of Yang but seriously impaired the entire reign. The new emperor insisted that his own collateral family be elevated to a status equal to the primary dynastic line. For Confucian officials, this was a fundamental violation of state ritual. It provoked a controversy that pitted many officials, including Yang, against the emperor supported by sycophantic officials on the other side. Assuming an authority not unlike the former councilors, from his powerful position as grand secretary Yang at first rejected the emperor's edicts, but he was eventually forced into retirement in 1524. He was later stripped of all honors by the vengeful emperor for his opposition in the rites issue, reduced to commoner status, and died in 1529. Years later the emperor questioned Grand Secretary Li Shi about the accumulated grain reserve in the imperial treasury. Li responded:

> "The grain now stored up is enough to meet several years' demand. It results from the government's having weeded out many superfluous officials and having practiced strict economy in the early years of Your Majesty's reign." At this the emperor sighed and said: "This was due to Yang Tinghe's meritorious service which we should not forget."[7]

Once again, here was a reflective, perhaps remorseful expression of appreciation by an emperor for his loyal official. And Yang Tinghe was loyal, but not loyal in the sense that he would do the monarch's bidding regardless of his conscience, as any eunuch would. Yang, like most "good" Confucian officials, was loyal to the higher moral order that embraced both bureaucrat and emperor, even if they had to pay the ultimate penalty for opposing the imperial will, something the Qin Grand Councilor Li Si would not tolerate. The highest goal to which a Confucian official could aspire was the enduring esteem of his colleagues and the judgment of history, which would outlast his death and cast luster on his family for generations afterward.

It is a strange irony, perhaps, in the evolution of Ming autocracy, that the early emperors, employing the newfound power of eunuchs as an instrument to expand their power, were the most autocratic and tyrannical, whereas the later emperors, acceding to the expansion of eunuch power, were less tyrannical, becoming themselves instruments of eunuch power. Moreover, the most competent emperors, all reigning in the early Ming—Hongwu, Yongle, Xuande, and Hongzhi—gave way to incompetent emperors in the later Ming—Zhengde, Jiajing, and Wanli. In a reversal of roles tyrannical emperors were succeeded by tyrannical eunuchs; eunuch dictators replaced dictatorial emperors. In between were "good emperors" such as Xuande and Hongzhi set against "evil eunuchs" such as Wang Zhen, Wang Zhi, and Liu Jin.

But against this evolutionary pattern the Confucian scholar-official class, its independent survival seemingly gravely imperiled by the brutal purges of the Hongwu and Yongle emperors, endured to become permanently entrenched as the dominant political force by the mid-Ming. From the Xuande reign, decision-making power was centered in the consultative relationship between the emperor and his ministers. However weak and vulnerable they might be individually—they were after all classically regarded as *Ru* ("weaklings")—collectively they were the ultimate arbiters of political change in Chinese civilization. The political insignificance of the *Ru* against the towering power of the Qin monarch had undergone a fundamental transformation.

SUGGESTED READINGS

Crawford, Robert B. "Eunuch Power in the Ming Dynasty," *T'oung Pao*, second series, 49.3 (1961): 115–148. A detailed description of the organization and apparatus of eunuch authority.

Dardess, John W. *Ming China, 1368–1644: A Concise History of a Resilient Empire* (Lanham, Maryland: Rowman & Littlefield, 2012). A brief study of the Ming organized by thematic subjects, including frontiers, emperors, governance, literati, and outlaws.

Dreyer, Edward L. *Early Ming China: A Political History, 1355–1435* (Stanford: Stanford University Press, 1982). A careful analysis of early Ming political developments by a leading Ming scholar.

Goodrich, L. Carrington, and Chaoying Fang, eds. *Dictionary of Ming Biography, 1368–1644*, 2 vols. (New York: Columbia University Press, 1976). An essential and reliable reference for the study of the Ming.

Huang, Ray. *1587. A Year of No Significance: The Ming Dynasty in Decline* (New Haven: Yale University Press, 1981). An engaging and provocative study of the decline of the Ming based on biographical portraits of major figures of the Wanli reign.

Hucker, Charles O., ed. *Chinese Government in Ming Times: Seven Studies* (New York: Columbia University Press, 1969). Studies by major students of the Ming on local and fiscal administration, education, politics, bureaucracy, and the military system.

Mote, F. W. *Imperial China, 900–1800* (Cambridge: Harvard University Press, 1999). The most comprehensive treatment of Chinese history from the end of the Tang through the early Qing dynasties. An extremely useful reference, with the caveat that the index has many lacunae.

Mote, Frederick W., and Denis Twitchett, eds. *The Cambridge History of China*, vol. 7, *The Ming Dynasty, 1368–1644*, Part 1 (Cambridge: Cambridge University Press, 1988).

Tsai, Shih-shan Henry. *Perpetual Happiness: The Ming Emperor Yongle* (Seattle: University of Washington Press, 2001). A competent examination of the crucial reign of the Yongle emperor of the Ming.

Twitchett, Denis, and Frederick W. Mote, eds. *The Cambridge History of China*, vol. 8. *The Ming Dynasty, 1368–1644*, Part 2 (Cambridge: Cambridge University Press, 1998). The volumes of the *Cambridge History of China* on the Ming dynasty, with chapters contributed by authorities in their respective fields, constitute the most complete and essential reference for this period.

Wu, Silas H. L. *Communication and Imperial Control in China: Evolution of the Palace Memorial System, 1693–1735* (Cambridge: Harvard University Press, 1970). This seminal study on the crucial role of the memorial system as an instrument of imperial power in the Qing dynasty is useful also for understanding official communication in the Ming and in general.

NOTES

1. William Theodore deBary, et al., compilers, *Sources of Chinese Tradition* (New York: Columbia University Press, 1960), 141, 147.

2. Derk Bodde, *China's First Unifier: A Study of the Ch'in Dynasty as Seen in the Life of Li Ssu (280?–208 B.C.)* (Leiden: E. J. Brill, 1938), 82–83.

3. Edwin O. Reischauer and John K. Fairbank, *East Asia: The Great Tradition* (Boston: Houghton Mifflin, 1958), 108.

4. Bodde, 82.

5. L. Carrington Goodrich and Chaoying Fang, eds., *Dictionary of Ming Biography, 1368–1644*, 2 vols. (New York: Columbia University Press, 1976) (hereafter cited as *DMB*), 534.

6. Quoted in F. W. Mote, *Imperial China, 900–1800* (Cambridge: Harvard University Press, 1999), 635.

7. *DMB*, 1545.

6

The Ming and the World

The Yellow River, rising in the high Tibetan plateau, flows eastward, descending into northwestern China. There it turns abruptly northward, then east, and then south, describing a great "horseshoe bend," cutting deeply into the loess highlands, an overburden of fine, wind-blown soil that remains in suspension in the turbulent water of the river. Finally, where the shorter Wei River closes off the opening of the horseshoe, the river turns east through deep gorges. Past the gorges, pouring out onto the lowlands, the current slows, releasing its burden of silt and building the great north China plain all the way to the sea. The plain is thus a secondary alluvium of loess deposited by water.

The Yellow River received its name from the astonishing volume of fertile yellow silt that it carries throughout its course through north China. The upper Yellow River highlands around the Wei River and the lower Yellow River plain were the birthplace of the Chinese people, who, relying on the fertile soil and the abundance of water for irrigated agriculture, built their civilization. Neolithic peoples, the ancestors of the Chinese, in the highlands and plains, joined to create settlements, control water for irrigation and to protect against floods, and to cultivate millet and other grains. Later, as the complexity of their society increased, they cooperated to build walls around their villages to maintain order and defend from marauders. Ultimately, they developed writing and the higher attributes of organized human society, walled towns became cities, and civilization—people living in cities—emerged. These were the foundations of the Shang and Zhou societies of the second millennium BCE.

As they moved outward from the settled valleys toward the north, northeast, and northwest, settlers, perhaps driven by pressures of growing population and the search for new opportunities, encountered land that while still fertile was less able to sustain permanent settled agriculture. Farther from the Yellow River and its tributaries, water to supply irrigation was less abundant. Pushing even farther out they would reach the steppe grasslands or the forbidding desert that was incapable of supporting agriculture of any kind. In these different environments, ecological adaptations emerged, from marginal agriculture mixed with animal husbandry to full nomadic pastoralism. The changes were gradual, both in terms of the physical gradient of geographical environments and in terms of the evolution in time of adaptive cultures to those environments. But the result was a process of differentiation between polar cultural and economic modes: agriculture versus pastoralism, sown versus steppe, sedentary settlement versus nomadism, static versus fluid society. Thus a margin was created, a threshold between contrasting cultural patterns, the closed, self-contained core and the open, limitless but dependent periphery.

To the south of the Yellow River watershed the situation was different and far more complicated. There the transition was from dry land irrigation of open plains dominated by a continental climate to wet, lush, mountainous regions dominated by a maritime climate. Wet rice cultivation took over from broadcast cultivation of millet and wheat. The process of expansion into the south went on for many centuries of settlement and adaptation and was not fully completed until the Song period.

As the locus of a great civilization on the Eurasian continent, China was remarkably isolated from other civilizations such as India, Mesopotamia, and the Mediterranean. China Proper, bounded by seas on the east and south, mountainous jungles on the southeast, the Tibetan escarpment to the west, and deserts and steppe to the north, is a large but compact area comprising the principal watersheds of the Yellow and Yangzi Rivers. Communication with the outside world was difficult or impossible in almost any direction. To the east was the vast Pacific Ocean, to the south impassible jungles, to the west the immense Tibetan plateau, to the north the Gobi Desert and the steppe and taiga of Siberia. To attempt to travel in any of these directions led nowhere. Only to the northwest, up the Gansu Corridor, between the desert and the mountains of Tibet, and across Central Asia between the forbidding deserts and mountains, along the arduous route that came to be known as the Silk Road, was it possible to reach other settled civilizations. The only other route was from the south China coast, through the islands of Southeast Asia, to the Indian Ocean.

Depending on political dynamics of the core and the periphery, the Chinese expanded and contracted within these imposing physical limits. The regions surrounding China Proper, including the northeast basin and forests that later were known as Manchuria, the steppe and forests

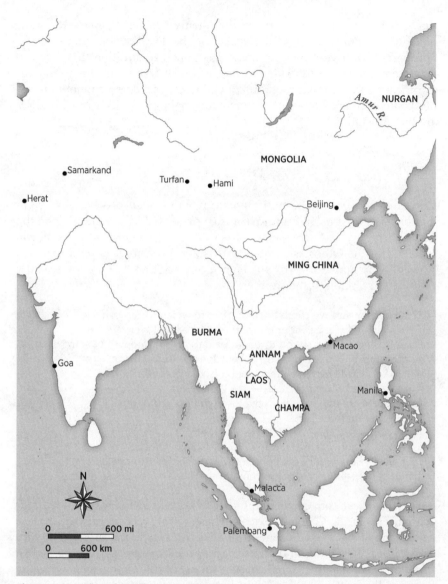

Figure 6.1. Ming China in Asian context.

of Mongolia, the deserts and mountains of Central Asia known as Chinese Turkestan, and Tibet, and including China Proper itself, can all be conceived together as belonging to Greater China. The boundaries of this area were always ambiguous because modern concepts of geopolitical boundaries meant little in ancient times. Excluding Mongolia proper, the area is roughly equivalent to the territory of the People's Republic of China. China Proper is the realm of the Han people, the Chinese "proper." The government of China recognizes in addition fifty-five minority nationalities within Greater China. In modern times this presents a significant issue of what constitutes "Chineseness." Are the many minorities Chinese in any sense other than being political subjects of China? Or are they the Other?

THE OTHER

Han Chinese identity, the cultural pattern of the inner core, was formed in the consciousness of the cultural contrast presented by the margin and the outer periphery, the sense of We associated with sedentary agricultural society and the Other associated with shifting pastoral nomadism. "An Ancient Marching Song" by the eighth century poet Li Qi expresses the Chinese perception of the frontier:

> In the blazing sun we climb the mountain to watch for beacon fires;
> in the yellow dusk we water our horses by the Jiao River.
> The marchers' alarms sound through the dark gritty gloom of blowing sand,
> more melancholy than the song of the Chinese princess' lute.
> We make a crude camp ten thousand li from city walls,
> where rain and snow swirl across the vast desert.
> Tartar geese cry mournfully flying through the night,
> as tears stream from Tartar children's eyes.
> News comes that the Jade Gate is still cut off,
> so we must soon sacrifice our lives to follow the war chariots.
> Year after year we bury the bones of war in the desert wasteland,
> that in vain may we see grapes brought in tribute to the house of Han.[1]

The historical concept of the Other is conveyed by many words for "barbarian" in the Chinese lexicon. These terms, rooted in Han Chinese culture, have evolved in usage from ancient times to the present. In very early times the Shang and Zhou had specific names for the barbarian tribes across the inner Asian margin to the north. In the west were the *Rong*, in the east were the *Yi*, in between were the *Hu*, applied especially to Mongol and Tartar tribes and Turks later. During the Han, the Xiongnu, known in the West as the Huns, and other northern barbarians were called *Di*. Aborigines and savages to the south were called *Fan*. In the Song the most pejorative word for barbarians was *Lu*, meaning a prisoner or slave. The Mongols of the Yuan dynasty referred to those foreigners ranked second only to Mongols in their administration as *Semu*, "people of assorted categories," applied to Khitans, Turkish peoples, other Central Asians, and Europeans. A more generic term for barbarian was *Huawai*, "beyond the pale of civilization." In subsequent conventional usage *Yi* became the general term for all barbarians or foreigners, including those who arrived on the scene much later, such as Westerners who came by sea. Although for the most part seemingly neutral, all terms applied to foreigners were inherently pejorative in their cultural context.

As foreign presence in China increased significantly in the late eighteenth century, other names for Westerners appeared, based on physical appearance and behavior and clearly pejorative, such as *yangguizi*, "foreign devil," *dabizi*, "big nose," and *hongmao fan*, "red-haired barbarians." The most neutral term, currently in general use in official contexts, is *waiguoren*, literally "foreigner," or more colloquially, *laowai*, "respected foreigner."

The Chinese always allowed that barbarians could be assimilated to Chinese civilization and would be accepted as Chinese to the degree that assimilation was successful. A foreigner may adopt a Chinese name, dress as a Chinese dresses, become as proficient in the language as a Chinese and to all intents and purposes be Chinese. In contrast, the Japanese view is quite different. No matter how completely a foreigner assimilates Japanese culture he may never become Japanese and by law may not adopt a name that would identify him as Japanese. Chinese culture tends toward inclusion, not exclusion. The Chinese view was validated by abundant experience of frontier interaction, where barbarian peoples became drawn into the Chinese cultural orbit and lost the elements of their alien culture. A graphic example of this attitude is the term *shu*, "cooked," also "experienced," and thus "tamed," applied to barbarians both on the northern frontier and in the southern minority regions who became at least partially assimilated. The opposite of *shu* was *sheng*, "raw," "uncooked," "unacquainted with civilization," thus "wild." For instance, the Jurchen people of eastern Manchuria that were considered least assimilated to Chinese ways during the Ming were called the "wild Jurchen."

Inherent in the Han perception of the inner Asian barbarians was the menace they posed to civilization of the core. But paradoxically, their threat often came not simply from their "unsoftened native vigor. . . . They became really dangerous to the extent that they became civilized, and versed in the arts of organization, production, and war."[2] The Han Chinese view of the barbarians was nevertheless highly ambivalent. The Jesuit priest Matteo Ricci adopted Chinese culture of the elite so completely that he was accepted among them and admired for his learning, though he never abandoned his Christian calling. The Jesuit Johann Adam Schall von Bell became president of the Imperial Astronomical Bureau under the Qing, an official civil bureaucratic position. The Manchus before their conquest of China in 1644 assimilated Confucian culture and practice so thoroughly that they came to be considered by some "more Chinese than the Chinese," which facilitated the Chinese acceptance of Qing rule. And yet, in the end, as Qing rule deteriorated in the nineteenth century, the barbarian origins of the Manchus came back to haunt them, they lost the Mandate, and Chinese rebels and revolutionaries condemned them as alien usurpers. In a sense the People's Republic of China's vigorous official recognition of minority nationalities tends to preserve the concept of foreignness rather than their assimilation and incorporation into the national unity.

THE TRIBUTE SYSTEM

Foreign relations throughout the Ming and most of the Qing were largely encompassed by the tribute system. First established in the Han dynasty (202 BCE–220 CE), resumed in the Song and reestablished at the beginning of the Ming in 1368 by Zhu Yuanzhang, the tribute system was a highly ritualized and formalized institution that governed interaction between China as the suzerain power and surrounding states as (theoretically at least) tributary vassals. In form it was very much a reflection of the Chinese proclivity for bureaucratic control and record keeping. Recognized tributary rulers were vested or confirmed in their positions by the emperor, the Chinese calendar was conferred on the tribute state as the symbol of the universal Chinese order, and the tributary rulers were expected to send tribute missions at regular intervals to the Chinese court. Elaborate regulations governed the reception and conduct of tribute missions. Tallies were issued to each tribute state specifying in precise detail the size and frequency of its mission, the manner of its reception at the capital, and its duration. The mission submitted tribute gifts to the court reflecting the local products and arts of the country. The emissaries were received in audience by the emperor, lavished with gifts in return, always more valuable than what they had brought, entertained at a great banquet, housed in official hostels, and finally permitted separate trade on the side. The court's treatment of tribute missions was carefully calibrated according to the status and importance to the Chinese of the respective tribute state. It was very important therefore to ensure that a mission was not bogus, since the benefits from trade were extremely lucrative, and precautions were taken through the tally system to eliminate fraudulent missions.

One byproduct of the tribute system was the collection of intelligence on foreign countries and peoples in order to ensure the integrity of the system. The Chinese penchant for taxonomy and record keeping dictated the compilation of compendia of descriptions of tributary states and dis-

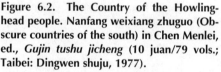

Figure 6.2. The Country of the Howling-head people. Nanfang weixiang zhuguo (Obscure countries of the south) in Chen Menlei, ed., *Gujin tushu jicheng* (10 juan/79 vols.; Taibei: Dingwen shuju, 1977).

Figure 6.3. The Country of the Forked-tongued people. Nanfang weixiang zhuguo (Obscure countries of the south) in Chen Menlei, ed., *Gujin tushu jicheng* (10 juan/79 vols.; Taibei: Dingwen shuju, 1977).

tant foreign lands that might some day have to be dealt with. One such compendium was *Investigation of the Eastern and Western Oceans* (*Dongxi yang kao*), published about 1617, mainly relating to Japan and Southeast Asia.[3] The *Comprehensive Illustrated Encyclopedia* (*Gujin tushu jicheng*) published in 1728 includes a subsection of "frontier barbarians" in the main section on geography. Entries on tribute states based on Ming and early Qing sources describe their history of relations with China and their behavior. Entries on Western countries include the Portuguese and Dutch. Following these textual entries is a long series of illustrations of typical inhabitants of diverse countries of the south and west accompanied by very brief captions, titled "Obscure Countries of the South" (*Nanfang weixiang zhuguo*). While some of these illustrations are identifiable as actual people, most are entirely fanciful and imaginary. We find here humans with the heads of birds, fire-breathing devils, mermen with bodies like fish, men

Figure 6.4. An English woman and an English man. Fu Heng, et al., eds., Huang Qing zhigongtu (Illustrations of tributary peoples of the Great Qing), in *Yinying wenyuange Siku quanshu* (Taibei: Shangwu yinshuguan, 1986), v. 594, 425.

without stomachs, and men with three-fold bodies.[4] A third compendium, *Illustrations of Tributary Missions of the Qing Dynasty (Huang Qing zhigong tu)* published in the Qianlong reign (1736–1796) is an identification manual of natives of foreign countries having nominal tribute relations with China in the mid-eighteenth century. Examples of both men and women are included. The texts that follow the very realistic drawings give the location of the country, chronology of relations with China, some typical character traits, and dress and physical appearance. While the illustrations are remarkably detailed, differentiating accurately between various foreigners, the accompanying texts preserve many of the pejorative stereotypes toward barbarians of earlier times.[5]

From the Chinese perspective, the tribute system had neither fiscal nor commercial objectives. It was managed by the Ministry of Rites and was designed to affirm Chinese centrality as the one civilization and the role of the emperor as son of heaven (*tianzi*). Secondarily, the tribute system's purpose was to manage foreign trade by bringing it under the umbrella of a centrally controlled institution and drastically reduce its volume. A rig-

Figure 6.5. A Polish woman and a Polish man. Fu Heng, et al., eds., Huang Qing zhigongtu (Illustrations of tributary peoples of the Great Qing), in *Yinying wenyuange Siku quanshu* (Taibei: Shangwu yinshuguan, 1986), v. 594, 421.

orous ban on all maritime trade outside the tribute system was issued in 1372 and was not repealed until 1567, when it had ceased to be effective. The tribute system's ritual function is evident in the missions dispatched by the court in 1368 to Korea, Vietnam, Champa, and Japan announcing the founding of the Ming by Zhu Yuanzhang. Tribute missions were received in return from Korea, Annam, and Champa in 1369, from Java in 1370, Japan, Siam, Cambodia, and Samudra in 1371, and the Ryukyu Islands in 1372. The tribute system clearly expressed China's hierarchical view of the world. No other country in this sinocentric world view was the equal of China, the "Middle Kingdom." Civilization was singular, not plural, and the emperor as son of heaven was its universal ruler who recognized no equal. During the Southern Song, it is true, the emperor was forced to recognize the Jurchen Jin emperor as an equal, and by virtue of the large tribute paid to the Jin to secure a military armistice, even superior. The official rhetorical relationship between the two courts was a delicate one. But this was a practical expedient dictated by survival. The

Song emperor swallowed his pride, even against the objections of some courtiers, but always preserved the mental reservation that the Jurchen, though very powerful, were inherently inferior.

MING FOREIGN AFFAIRS

China's active engagement in "foreign affairs," as distinct from the more passive "foreign relations" involved in the routine tribute system, focused principally on Japan, Southeast Asia, and the Mongols. Relations with Japan depended very much on political conditions within Japan at any one time. While the Ming sought to establish regular tribute relations with Japan, it was the most recalcitrant of peripheral states, not willingly acknowledging Chinese suzerainty. The Ashikaga shogun Yoshimitsu was eager to expand trade with China and welcomed Chinese envoys, who were dispatched in 1399 and 1403. Trade continued to 1410, but Yoshimitsu's successor Yoshimochi disliked the Chinese and reversed the receptive policy. Japanese trade missions under the tribute system resumed a century later, but became embroiled in endemic piracy along the China coast, which was at first instigated by Japanese. The Ming court became obsessed with efforts to suppress piracy and repeatedly appealed to Japan to interdict it. But by the mid-sixteenth century piracy was almost entirely in Chinese hands, over which Japan, which was by then gripped in nation-wide civil war, had no control.

The *Ancestral Injunctions* of Zhu Yuanzhang in 1395 listed countries, all in Southeast Asia, that were never to be invaded. The Yongle emperor ignored this prohibition when as part of his hegemonic program of foreign aggrandizement he invaded Annam early in his reign in 1407, with the intention of annexing it as a permanent dependency. During his reign (1402–1424) sixty-two missions were dispatched to Southeast Asia, eliciting ninety-five missions in return, far more numerous than the tribute system called for and reflecting the emperor's active diplomatic efforts toward Nanyang ("The Southern Ocean"). Zheng He's maritime expeditions (to be considered later) were part of this offensive. In the meantime the Annam enterprise ground on in an inconclusive war. When the Xuande emperor (1426–1435) came to the throne he ended the protracted war in 1427 and withdrew Chinese presence from Nanyang. His reign marked the end of engagement with Southeast Asia and the beginning of the Ming's isolation in international affairs.

The northern frontier of inner Asia, however, was a different matter. Having thrown off the Mongol yoke in 1368, the Ming remained obsessed with the problem of the restless Mongols until almost the end of the dynasty. The Ming's worst nightmare was the prospect of the rise of another Chinggis Khan who would unify once again the Mongol tribes and hurl them against China. This fear almost came to pass when Timur (1336–1405), a descendant of Chinggis Khan, ruler of a vast Middle Eastern empire, launched a large military expedition intending to conquer China in 1405. But Timur died and the expedition was canceled before it had hardly begun and before the Yongle emperor had even learned of it. The rise of Esen of the Oirat Mongols, who aspired to become another Chinggis, caused great consternation in the Ming court. But after he defeated the Ming forces and captured the emperor in the Tumu fiasco, Esen failed to take Beijing and his threat subsequently fizzled. Finally, the rise of Altan Khan in the 1540s and 1550s presented the last great Mongol threat to the Ming. Altan made frequent raids on the border, alternating demands for favorable tribute concessions with military offensives. In 1550 he unsuccessfully besieged Beijing. Raids continued sporadically along the northern border into the 1560s.

In between these major crises, Mongol pressure along the border from west to east rarely abated. The efforts of the Ming to counter this pressure involved a range of responses, from active military intervention across the frontier line of defense to passive withdrawal and a defensive posture. The Ming approach sought to treat different Mongol groups separately, employing the tactic of divide and rule. On the eastern frontier in southeastern Mongolia the Uriangkhad Mongols were relatively "tame," having continuous close contact with the Ming. In the center were the Tartars, the Mongols "proper," the most restive, who posed a persistent threat. In the west on the northeast fringes of Mongolia the Oirat Mongols were less threatening because they were more remote; the Ming sought to play the Oirats and the Tartars against each other.

The Yongle emperor, whose power as Prince of Yan before his accession was based near the frontier and who included Mongol cavalry in his army, assumed an aggressive approach to the Mongol problem. Between 1410 and 1424 he led five massive military expeditions into the steppe, counterparts of his maritime expeditions to the south. In 1410 the first campaign inflicted a major defeat on the Tartars but failed to crush them. The 1414 campaign was directed against the Oirats who were moving east against the Tartars, and the army drove them back to the west. After a respite, by 1421 the Tartars were again threatening the border. The emperor led a third expedition in 1422 which ended inconclusively. The fourth campaign in 1423 was smaller and withdrew when it was learned that the Tartars had been defeated by the Oirats. In 1424 the emperor led his last campaign north to engage the Tartars but withdrew when he failed to encounter them, and died in the field in 1424. The expeditions had failed to make significant gains or stabilize the frontier in spite of battlefield victories. No further expeditions were launched until the disastrous campaign of 1449 when the emperor was taken prisoner by Esen.

After the Yongle reign the Ming lost control over the outlying areas, and aggressive defense was replaced by passive defense. In 1472 a proposal to build a line of walls along the frontier was advanced, essentially rebuilding and expanding the Qin Great Wall of the third century BCE. Construction began in 1474 and the project progressed rapidly, increasing in intensity in the mid-sixteenth century and into the first part of the seventeenth century, producing the Great Wall as it is seen today. Although the walls changed the character of defensive warfare, they never solved the endemic problem of the Mongol threat. As the Ming withdrew behind the Great Wall line, the ultimate effect was as much psychological as it was instrumental in securing China's security. It became a symbol of China's isolation, defining a sharp separation between the Han people of the sedentary core and the shifting Others of the frontier, where before a disturbingly ambiguous transition zone had existed.

In the Ming view of the world a persistent tension existed between divergent orientations, south and north, the sea and the steppe, the maritime world and the continental frontier. The two capitals, Nanjing and Beijing (identical parallel government structures were maintained in each even after Beijing became the official capital) reflected this tension. Nanjing was the economic center of the lower Yangzi basin, the breadbasket of China. It was the launching site for the great maritime expeditions of the Yongle reign and represented the Ming's maritime orientation. Beijing was the strategic frontier military center, close to the defensive Great Wall line. It was the launching site for the Yongle emperor's Mongolian campaigns and represented the Ming's continental orientation. In a sense the resolution of this tension was foreordained. It was actually determined early in the Ming with the Yongle emperor's construction of Beijing. It was after all from the north that China felt constantly threatened, where issues of security were immediate and strongly felt. Although piracy along the coasts arose for a time in the mid-sixteenth century, it never posed a serious threat to China's existence. No challenges came from the direction of the south, from Nanyang.

Inner Asia remained the preoccupation of the Ming. Yet in the long run this Inner Asian orientation was portentous because in their consciousness of the world around them it never prepared the Chinese for the more serious challenge that would ultimately come from the sea, whereas after the Manchu conquest the north ceased to have any relevance. And yet, more ominous still, even China's limited experience of the south and west through Nanyang failed to prepare them for the onslaught that was to come.

CHINA'S APPROACH TO THE WEST

Beyond "foreign relations" as conducted under the routine tribute system, beyond "foreign affairs" of the crises issues of Japan, Annam, and the Mongols around the East Asian periphery of China were larger issues of the world beyond. When the Yongle emperor launched his seven great maritime expeditions under the command of the eunuch admiral Zheng He, his objective was to assert Chinese hegemony over a world largely known, if only dimly, to the Chinese through the experience of the tribute system. Exploration and discovery of new worlds were never his motive. Yet in their scope and extent the voyages of Zheng He raise provocative questions.

The first voyage launched in 1405 and returning to Nanjing in 1407 set the model for all the subsequent voyages. The fleet comprised more than sixty-three large ships, as many as two hundred smaller support ships, and embarked more than twenty-seven thousand personnel. The largest ships, called "treasure ships," were approximately four hundred feet in length, one hundred sixty feet in beam, drawing twenty-five feet with a displacement of twenty-five to thirty thousand tons, and carried nine masts with huge sails. The fleet sailed through Southeast Asia and across the Indian Ocean to Calicut, the commercial entrepôt on the southwest coast of India, stopping along the way at Champa, Java, Palembang, Samudra, Achin, and Ceylon. At Palembang, on the island of Sumatra, Zheng He engaged in battle the fleet of a notorious Chinese pirate, killing five thousand of his men, and took him back in chains to the capital at Nanjing, where he was executed. The second and third voyages from 1407 to 1409 and 1409 to 1411, respectively, were each launched almost immediately following the return of the previous voyage and followed the itinerary of the first voyage with little variation. On the third voyage Zheng He abducted the king of Ceylon from his palace and brought him back to China to chastise him for the disrespect he showed to the first expedition. The fleets returned with tributary ambassadors from the places they visited and brought lavish gifts in return.

With the fourth expedition, which sailed in 1413 and returned in 1415, the emphasis of the remaining voyages changed. The fleets reached farther, beyond the familiar ocean pathways traveled by Chinese merchants for centuries. The fourth fleet reached Aden and Hormuz on the Persian Gulf. The fifth and sixth voyages, sailing in 1417 to 1419 and 1421 to 1422 respectively, reached Hormuz and traveled on to ports on the east African coast. The fleets brought back spectacular tribute, including lions, leopards, dromedaries, ostriches, zebras, rhinoceroses, antelopes, and giraffes. The last evoked great excitement and awe in the court, as they were believed to be unicorns (*qilin*), an auspicious beast in Chinese cosmology. The expeditions were temporarily suspended following the return of the sixth voyage while the Yongle emperor was engaged in establishing his new capital at Beijng and were not resumed during his lifetime. But after a hiatus of ten years, the Xuande emperor dispatched the seventh and last voyage in 1431, returning in 1433, which reached Hormuz and east Africa, while a contingent of Chinese traveled overland to Mecca. Zheng He died in 1433 after the return of this voyage and they were never resumed.

Might Zheng He's fleets have reached farther, perhaps continued their course down the east African coast, rounded the Cape of Good Hope, sailed up the west African coast, entered the Mediterranean, and crossed the Atlantic to "discover" America seventy years before Columbus? However awesome the size and power of Zheng He's great treasure ships, however vast his armada, however skilled his navigators, however great the resources that propelled him, it was not to be. In *1421: The Year China Discovered America* (later reissued as *1421: The Year China Discovered the World*) Gavin Menzies, a retired British Royal Navy submarine commander, claims just this, that Zheng He's fleets circumnavigated the globe from 1421 to 1422, when they reached and explored the Atlantic coasts of Africa, North and South America, the Caribbean, and Greenland, and the Pacific coasts of South and North America, New Zealand, and Australia. According to Menzies they planted colonies in New England and in the California San Francisco Bay area.[6] Menzies' hypothesis relies on the poor documentation kept of the sixth voyage, which sailed from 1421 to 1422, opening the door to wild speculation about its destination. The Chinese allegedly accomplished this stupendous feat of flawless navigation and discovery in a mere two-and-a-half years. By contrast the Europeans required at least a century to accomplish similar feats in their "discovery" of Asia.

Unfortunately, there is absolutely no plausible evidence for any of Menzies' claims. They are based only on speculation, inference, flimsy coincidences, and a wishful imagination. Yet his hypothesis forces us to consider what the failure of this alternative meant. Above all, it was a matter of motive and commitment. The Europeans drove outward upon the seas in an implacable quest for wealth and religious conversion. The Portuguese navigator Vasco Da Gama rounded the Cape of Good Hope with only three small ships carrying a few hundred men that would have been dwarfed by Zheng He's immense treasure ships, and landed at Calicut almost one hundred years after Zheng He first came there. Asked by the Zamorin, the local ruler, why he had come, Da Gama famously replied, "We have come for Christians and spices."

China had different priorities. The construction of Beijing, as expensive as the treasure fleets, became the Yongle emperor's obsession, and in his later years preempted his attention to Nanyang. The transfer of the capital to Beijing in 1421 while the sixth voyage was abroad contributed to his declining interest in maritime expeditions. The goal of overawing the countries of Nanyang with China's wealth and power, a significant motivation of the voyages, ceased to exert a hold on the imperial imagination. Certainly, no other exponents of such ambitious enterprise existed. The voyages were eunuch operations, commanded by eunuchs, extensions of imperial power. Confucian officials such as Xia Yuanji deplored them for their immense cost and meager results and saw them for what they were, manifestations of imperial ego.

If the Chinese possessed the capacity, they had not the will for global conquest. The voyages had no commercial motive, no driving mission to convert others to their way of life. Nothing better illuminates this difference in motives between China and the Portuguese than what each brought back. The Chinese returned with "face," that is, prestige, and trophies to prove it—a giraffe! The Portuguese returned with rich cargoes of valuable spices and an unquenchable drive for more.

THE WEST'S APPROACH TO CHINA

One hundred years after the end of the Ming maritime expeditions to the West, the Portuguese had established themselves on the south China coast and were trading in circumvention of Ming commercial prohibitions. By 1557 they acquired a permanent base on the tiny peninsula of Macau, renting the land from local authorities. Arriving with the Portuguese were Jesuit missionaries who more than the merchants initiated the first intensive contact with the early modern West. The pioneer of the Jesuit evangelical mission in Asia was Francis Xavier, who after proselytizing in India landed in Japan in 1549. In India Xavier had adopted the traditional Christian approach to the meek and humble who were the objects of his evangelical efforts. It was said that he could "speak in tongues" through the power of faith, overcoming the language barrier. In Japan, where he encountered considerable interest in Christianity, the Japanese often asked him, what do the Chinese believe? If the Chinese, who they looked up to as the progenitors of their civilization, were inclined to Christianity they would be persuaded in favor of the new faith.

Thus Xavier turned to China as the goal. He arrived at Shangquan island off the south China coast in 1552 seeking entry to the country. But the door was closed to him, and staying on past the trading season late in the year as the merchants departed with the monsoon he died in disappointment there. More priests followed Xavier but while residing in Macau they had no better success. Finally, the Jesuit father-visitor Alessandro Valignano, after visiting Japan and contemplating the forbidding problem, in 1577 adopted a new strategy focused on China. The priests would abandon Xavier's approach to the humble and instead would accommodate to Chinese customs and study Chinese language and learning with a view to better understanding their goal. Valignano sent for the learned and talented Italian Jesuit Matteo Ricci, who arrived at Macau in 1582. Ricci pioneered the new strategy, studying in Macau and becoming fluent in Chinese. He managed by dint of great persistence to enter China, residing near the great trading city of Canton just inland from Macau. To gain access to the literate class, he first dressed as a Buddhist priest, which he imagined would be his counterpart. But he soon discovered that the literati looked down on Buddhists, and instead he adopted the dress of a Confucian scholar-official and diligently studied the Confucian classics. This, and his wide learning, quickly brought him access to the official class. Gradually working northward he eventually arrived in Beijing in 1601, where he built a church, and died there in 1610.

What particularly interested Ricci's interlocutors was not his religious message but his knowledge of mathematics and astronomy, the basis of the calendar, which was his entrée. The calendar was the foundation of the Chinese cosmic order, but because of the retarded development of mathematics in China, it had many inaccuracies. Just then Europe was experiencing new scientific developments in algebra, trigonometry, and the astronomical discoveries of Copernicus and Galileo. Interestingly, the Jesuits though aware of the new developments were prohibited by the Church from teaching them as they were considered heresy. Ricci was no scientist; he called for other Jesuits trained as scientists to follow him. They brought clocks, scientific instruments, and translations of scientific works. Jesuits following Ricci were appointed to the Imperial Astronomical Bureau (*qintian jian*) where they worked on reforming the calendar and on astronomical predictions.

Johann Adam Schall von Bell (1591–1666), a German Jesuit who was trained as a scientist, was sent to China and arrived at Macau in 1619. After studying Chinese there he arrived in Beijing in 1623. He was appointed to the Imperial Astronomical Bureau in 1630. His appointment survived the fall of the Ming and the Manchu conquest, and he was appointed by the Qing to head the Astronomical Bureau, a significant achievement for a foreigner. In his capacity as a scientist he helped reform the calendar, translate works on astronomy and mathematics, supervise the construction of astronomical instruments, and even taught the Manchus to cast cannons.

It was not long before new arrivals to the evangelical field in China, the Dominicans and Franciscans, challenged the Jesuit strategy of accommodation. The central issue was whether the Jesuit acceptance of Confucian learning and particularly Confucian rites was an acceptable route to conversion. Potential Chinese converts would resist conversion if ancestor worship, the foundation of the Confucian family system, were prohibited as inconsistent with Christian faith. The Jesuits argued that ancestor worship was merely a secular observance, not a religious rite, but the other orders regarded it as heresy. This controversy, which went on for many years and embroiled the Church, was as much about Church politics as about faith. The Rites Controversy was finally resolved in 1742 when the Church banned the acceptance of Chinese rites by the Jesuits. In response the Chinese emperor ordered the expulsion of the missionaries, the evangelical mission collapsed, and the Jesuits were officially condemned. The great goal of converting China to Christianity had failed.

The problem revealed so clearly here is the weight and balance of early Western influence on China. The Jesuit fathers made very few converts to Christianity among the Chinese literati whom they hoped would lead the way to the conversion of the country, although they were somewhat more successful among members of the palace and the ruling house. For a time their intimate relations with the Chinese emperor—the first Manchu emperor, the Shunzhi emperor (1644–1661) called Adam Schall "grandpa" (*mafa*)—and the Jesuit fathers had lively debates on religion and science with the Shunzhi emperor's successor, the Qing Kangxi emperor (1662–1722). But in the end the Jesuit hopes came to nothing. Instead the Chinese incorporated their scientific expertise as a subordinate practical technology. The Jesuits on the other hand had tended to succumb to Chinese influence, as barbarians always had, in accepting Chinese rites, unable to preserve their cultural autonomy. The question really was, who was converting whom?

China's experience of the West and the world beyond the Asian periphery in the sixteenth and seventeenth centuries was very different from what it would become later. The maritime expeditions toward the West during the Yongle reign looked not forward to a new world but backward to the tribute system established in the Hongwu reign, and before it to the Song, that validated China's traditional view of its place in the world. The Jesuit approach to China during the Wanli reign and later looked forward, a harbinger of things to come. But contact with the West through the Jesuits was so limited in scope and so constrained by traditional assumptions about foreigners that it offered little appreciation of what lay behind them. Neither the maritime voyages nor the Jesuit experience prepared China for the great forces that were even then changing the world and were soon to be thrust upon them.

SUGGESTED READINGS

Attwater, Rachel. *Adam Schall: A Jesuit at the Court of China, 1592–1666.* Adapted from the French of Joseph Duhr, SJ (London: Geoffrey Chapman, 1963). An English-language biography of the pioneering Jesuit scientist in China through the Ming-Qing transition.

Dardess, John W. *Ming China, 1368–1644: A Concise History of a Resilient Empire* (Lanham, Maryland: Rowman & Littlefield, 2012). A brief study of the Ming organized by thematic subjects, including frontiers, emperors, governance, literati, and outlaws.

Dreyer, Edward L. *Early Ming China: A Political History, 1355–1435* (Stanford: Stanford University Press, 1982). A careful analysis of early Ming political developments by a leading Ming scholar.

Dunne, George H., SJ. *Generation of Giants: The Story of the Jesuits in China in the Last Decades of the Ming Dynasty* (Notre Dame, Indiana: University of Notre Dame Press, 1962). A popular account of the Jesuit religious and scientific enterprise in Ming China.

Elvin, Mark. *The Pattern of the Chinese Past* (Stanford: Stanford University Press, 1973). Emphasis on political economy and technology, from the formation of the early empire in the sixth century BCE through the medieval economic revolution to qualitative standstill by the nineteenth century.

Gernet, Jacques. Janet Lloyd, trans., *China and the Christian Impact: A Conflict of Cultures* (Cambridge: Cambridge University Press, 1985). The study of Christianity in China since the Ming by a leading authority.

Goodrich, L. Carrington, and Chaoying Fang, eds. *Dictionary of Ming Biography, 1368–1644,* 2 vols. (New York: Columbia University Press, 1976). An essential and reliable reference for the study of the Ming.

Hucker, Charles O., ed. *Chinese Government in Ming Times: Seven Studies* (New York: Columbia University Press, 1969). Studies by major students of the Ming on local and fiscal administration, education, politics, bureaucracy, and the military system.

Levathes, Louise. *When China Ruled the Seas. The Treasure Fleet of the Dragon Throne, 1405–1433* (New York: Oxford University Press, 1994). A popular account of eunuch admiral Zheng He's maritime expeditions.

Ma Huan. J. V. G. Mills, trans. and ed., *Ying-yai Sheng-lan: The Overall Survey of the Ocean's Shores* (Cambridge: Cambridge University Press, 1970). An account of Zheng He's maritime expeditions by a Chinese participant in the voyages.

Menzies, Gavin. *1421: The Year China Discovered America* (New York: William Morrow, 2003). The dramatic but completely unreliable and controversial account of the imaginary achievements of Zheng He's sixth voyage.

Mote, F. W. *Imperial China, 900–1800* (Cambridge: Harvard University Press, 1999). The most comprehensive treatment of Chinese history from the end of the Tang through the early Qing dynasties. An extremely useful reference, with the caveat that the index has many lacunae.

Mote, Frederick W., and Denis Twitchett, eds. *The Cambridge History of China,* vol. 7, *The Ming Dynasty, 1368–1644,* Part 1 (Cambridge: Cambridge University Press, 1988).

Mungello, D. E. *Curious Land: Jesuit Accommodation and the Origins of Sinology* (Honolulu: University of Hawaii Press, 1985).

Rowbotham, Arnold H. *Missionary and Mandarin: The Jesuits at the Court of China* (Berkeley: University of California Press, 1942). Another popular but reliable account of the Jesuit missionary enterprise in China.

Schütte, Josef Franz, SJ. John J. Coyne, SJ, trans., *Valignano's Mission Principles for Japan,* vol. I, parts I & II (St. Louis: The Institute of Jesuit Sources, 1980). A scholarly study and translation of the Jesuit father-visitor Alessandro Valignano's investigation of the Christian prospects in Japan and China.

Spence, Jonathan D. *The Memory Palace of Matteo Ricci* (New York: Viking, 1984). The fascinating story of Matteo Ricci's use of memory skills to recommend himself to Chinese scholar-officials.

Trigault, Nicola. *China in the Sixteenth Century: The Journals of Matthew Ricci: 1583–1610.* Trans. by Louis J. Gallagher (New York: Random House, 1953). The journals translated from Latin of Matteo Ricci, the pioneer of the Jesuit evangelical mission in China, containing detailed and astute observations of Chinese culture and society.

Tsai, Shih-shan Henry. *Perpetual Happiness: The Ming Emperor Yongle* (Seattle: University of Washington Press, 2001).

Twitchett, Denis, and Frederick W. Mote, eds. *The Cambridge History of China,* vol. 8. *The Ming Dynasty, 1368–1644,* Part 2 (Cambridge: Cambridge University Press, 1998).

Wong, George H. C. "China's Opposition to Western Science during Late Ming and Early Ch'ing," *Isis* 54 (1963): 29–49. The Chinese reaction to Western science introduced by the Jesuits. To be treated cautiously; see Nathan Sivin in the *Selected Bibliography.*

Young, John D. "An Early Confucian Attack on Christianity: Yang Kuang-hsien and his *Pu-te-i,*" *Journal of the Chinese University of Hong Kong* 3.1 (1975): 159–186. A thorough account of Yang Guangxian's attack on Christianity.

NOTES

1. Translation by the author.

2. Mark Elvin, *The Pattern of the Chinese Past* (Stanford: Stanford University Press, 1973), 41.

3. Zhang Xie, ed., *Dongxi yang kao* (12 *juan*) in *Yinying wenyuange siku quanshu* (Taibei: Shangwu yinshuguan, 1986), 594: 137–277.

4. Chen Menglei, ed., *Gujin tushu jicheng,* 10,000 *juan* / 79 volumes (Taibei: Dingwen shuju, 1977).

5. Fu Heng, et al., eds., *Huang Qing zhigong tu*, 9 *juan*, in *Yinying wenyuange siku quanshu* (Taibei: Shangyu yinshuguan, 1986), 594: 395–441.

6. Gavin Menzies, *1421: The Year China Discovered America* (New York: William Morrow, 2003).

7

Luan

Disintegration of Order

Three centuries after the Zhou dynasty was founded by King Wu and the Duke of Zhou, the Spring and Autumn Annals *recorded in brief, cryptic entries the historical events from 722 to 481 BCE. The annals documented the disintegration of the Zhou feudal order that had by then become increasingly apparent. The end of the* Spring and Autumn *period was the age of Confucius (551–479 BCE), to whom the editing of the* Annals *was traditionally attributed. Even before Confucius' time the once firm foundation of the hierarchical social and political system on which family cohesion and civil order depended had begun to erode under the pressures of political competition among the feudal states, economic development, and the challenge of emerging new social classes. In editing the* Spring and Autumn Annals, *Confucius had allegedly employed a subtle method of obliquely praising and blaming events recorded in the* Annals. *Confucius was the first in a succession of commentators who, confronted with the slow disintegration of the old order, sought to diagnose the ills of the time and offer remedies that they hoped would be adopted by a powerful prince. While they took different approaches—the Legalists offering authoritarian solutions, the Daoists advocating withdrawal from the insidious effects of society—order was the preeminent concern of all schools of thought. Their goal was to recreate or restore the lost order of the past—now an ideal—or to create an entirely new order to replace it. Disorder and turmoil (*luan*) which threatened their times was the condition they feared and deplored.*

Order is meant here in the wider sense: "The condition in which everything is in its proper place, and performs its proper functions."[1] *Order arose from respect for human relationships in the family, in society at large, and in politics, particularly preserved in ritual observances (*li*), which were the external* *manifestation of eternal principles (*li zhe, tianli zhi jiewen*). Confucius stated the fundamental role of* li *as the foundation of the social order in his doctrine of the "rectification of names" (*zhengming*), that a name (*ming*) designating a role (such as son) and the normative behavior associated with it must correspond, that is be rectified (*zheng*), for order to prevail in society. Behavior must be correct and appropriate to the meaning of any role in society. A son who behaves in an unfilial way toward his father is no son. In the* Analects Confucius *spoke of this:*

> Duke Jing of Qi asked Master Kong about government. Master Kong replied, saying, Let the prince be a prince, the minister a minister, the father a father, and the son a son. The Duke said, How true! For indeed when the prince is not a prince, the minister not a minister, the father not a father, the son not a son, one may have a dish of millet in front of one and yet not know if one will live to eat it.[2]

For the Chinese, from ancient times, order was an imminent moral condition, not transcendental, not conferred or reserved by a transcendent god. No supramundane sanctions preserved the social order, only human responsibility, the innate moral instinct and cultivation of man. Whether man was innately good or innately evil (the Confucianists and Legalists differed sharply on this issue), he was capable of perfecting the ideal social order. The perfectible ideal was expressed in the *Great Learning* (*Da Xue*), one of the Four Books of Confucianism that was exalted by the Neo-Confucian school of Zhu Xi since the Song:

> The ancients who wished to illustrate illustrious virtue throughout the kingdom, first ordered well their own states. Wishing to order well their own states, they first regulated their families. Wishing to regulate their families, they first cultivated their persons. Wishing to regulate their persons, they first rectified their hearts. Wishing to regulate their hearts, they first sought to be sincere in their thoughts. Wishing to be sincere in their thoughts, they first extended to the utmost their knowledge. Such extension of knowledge lay in the investigation of things.
>
> Things being investigated, knowledge became complete. Their knowledge being complete, their thoughts were sincere. Their thoughts being sincere, their hearts were then rectified. Their hearts being rectified, their persons were cultivated. Their persons being cultivated, their families were regulated. Their families being regulated, their states were rightly governed. Their states being rightly governed, the whole kingdom was made tranquil and happy.
>
> *From the Son of Heaven down to the masses of the people, all must consider the cultivation of the person the root of everything besides.*[3]

If the immanent human social order depended on the preservation of social status, hierarchy, proper place in society, and moral cultivation, disorder arose from dysfunctional behavior and the failure to maintain ritual relationships. Symptoms of disorder were manifested in instability in family relationships; economic conditions causing dislocation of people from settled lives, driving them into new occupations and new areas; and movement and infiltration of outsiders and rootless people with no settled place in society. Official malfeasance and corruption, dereliction of official responsibilities, and declining morale among the civil bureaucracy were further symptoms of disorder. *Luan,* the perception of chaos and disorder in the political sphere, infected social and intellectual life as well; the Chinese idiomatic phrase *luan qiba zao* ("all at sevens and eights") expresses this attitude. The spreading influence of the intuitionist philosophical movement of Wang Yangming in the sixteenth century, seeming to undermine the more orthodox tradition of Neo-Confucianism that emphasized established social order, was popular among the new commercial classes, another source of the sense of social disorder in the mid-Ming. At the highest level of the court and the emperor, disorder appeared in capricious brutality and oppressive treatment of officials. Of course, execution of malefactors was always justified to maintain social order, but vindictive treatment of the innocent violated the moral order. Pervasive execution and physical torture of enemies became a dysfunctional influence through much of the later Ming. Proper, diligent, and respectful observance of ritual (*li*), from the family up to the Son of Heaven, was the surest reflection of the enduring order; *luan* was its absence.

THE EROSION OF ORDER

Long before signs of disorder and decline converged in the late Ming, as they had in the *Spring and Autumn* era of the late Zhou, the symptoms they reflected were incubating in the early reigns. By the end of the unsuccessful reign of the Jiajing emperor in 1566, the fabric of order was beginning to unravel. It was not that the dynasty did not stumble on for another eighty years, but one has to ask at what point its inner light had been extinguished. The dynasty endured not because it possessed a great inner resilience and creative energy but because of the sheer momentum of its vast institutions and the absence of a viable alternative. But the alternatives were soon to emerge.

The Longqing ("Surpassing Blessing") emperor, succeeding the Jiajing emperor in 1567, began his reign by reversing or correcting many of the abuses of his father's reign, declaring remission of oppressive taxes, granting amnesties to his enemies, and returning confiscated estates to their owners. But it soon became apparent that the new emperor had no aptitude for state affairs. He suffered from a speech impediment that prevented him from speaking at court and evidently had diminished mental capacity. The official reforms at the inception of his reign were actually the work of the new junior Grand Secretary Zhang Juzheng. His short undistinguished reign ended in 1572 with the accession of the Wanli ("Universal Order") emperor who enjoyed for forty-six years the longest reign (1573–1619) of the Ming. In contrast to his father, the Wanli emperor was exceptionally intelligent and precocious, and held out great promise of restored vitality for the imperial institution. As a child he was brought up under the strict tutelage of Zhang Juzheng and chief eunuch Feng Bao, as well as by his mother and the empress dowager. Positive expectations seemed to be born out during the first decade of his reign while Zhang Juzheng dominated the government as senior grand secretary, but they were not fulfilled. The half-century of the Longqing and Wanli reigns became a tale of decline of imperial competence and pervasive misrule. The Wanli emperor was determined to name his third son heir apparent over the strict claim of his eldest son, violating the dynastic rules set out in the *Ancestral Injunctions* and evoking bitter opposition of officials. The succession dispute lasted from 1586 to the end of his reign, setting ministers and officials against each other. When he failed to get his way, the emperor became disillusioned with government, withdrew completely from court, and refused to conduct official business for years at a time. His petulant behavior had a corrosive effect on the morale of the civil bureaucracy, which was forced to struggle on without central direction.

For a time at the beginning of the Wanli reign it seemed that dynastic decline might be halted and the early vigor of the imperial government restored. The career of Zhang Juzheng (1525–1582), perhaps the most capable official of the entire dynasty, seemed to belie the general sense of malaise. He had entered the grand secretariat at the beginning of the Longqing reign in 1567. He was responsible for drafting the last will of the Jiajing emperor (1522–1566) and the accession edict of the Longqing emperor, eliminating abuses of the previous reign and announcing reforms. He became the influential chief tutor of the heir apparent, the future Wanli emperor, a stern taskmaster who constantly urged frugality. The heir apparent came to idolize him. With the accession of his pupil in 1572, Zhang became senior grand secretary, a very powerful position from which he effectively ruled over the Inner and Outer Courts and enjoyed virtually unchallenged dominance over government for a decade until his death in 1582.

Zhang was no ideologue, nor was he a prominent Confucian scholar in his own right. He was essentially a political activist and a realist who sought to restore the institutional vigor of the early Ming reigns. He promoted austerity in government and responsible fiscal administration. In 1581 he introduced the "single whip" taxation system, the first overhaul of tax administration since the eighth century Tang eight hundred years earlier. The new system commuted diverse and confusing taxes in kind into a single payment in a single registry (*yitiaobian*). The name was a homophone for "single whip" and the familiar name stuck. Revenue collections and fiscal austerity replenished the treasury, which in 1582 held enough funds for nine years' expenditures. In 1578 he inaugurated an ambitious cadastral survey. He appointed Qi Jiguang, the most talented and innovative military leader of the Ming, who had earlier suppressed piracy on the south coast, to the command of the crucial military region east of the capital. Under Zhang's regime, the imperial bureaucracy reached an unprecedented level of efficiency.

However, already in 1577 a major personal crisis undermined Zhang's administration. All officials were expected and required to observe twenty-seven months of mourning on the death of a parent, an observation of filial piety which generally meant returning to one's ancestral home and adopting a frugal lifestyle. It was a requirement that was waived only in extraordinary circumstances. For some officials it could be a welcome "sabbatical" of sorts. But for a minister like Zhang it would have interrupted and perhaps ended his entire program. When in 1577 Zhang's father died, the emperor dutifully urged Zhang to remain in office, granting him a waiver from the mourning requirement. In this case the error was not the emperor's good intentions but Zhang's seemingly political self-serving motive in accepting the waiver. The incident provoked a storm of criticism from officials from all quarters, demands for Zhang's resignation or impeachment for violating this fundamental stricture of Confucian filial piety. Retaliating against his critics, Zhang in 1579 ordered the abolition of Confucian private academies from which much of the criticism emanated. But from this time until his death his effectiveness was undermined. And the beginnings of pervasive and destructive bureaucratic factionalism that dominated the remaining years of the Ming were becoming clear.

A fundamental issue connected Zhang Juzheng's waiver of the mourning obligation and the Wanli emperor's attempt to name his third son his heir in violation of the *Ancestral Injunctions*. The importance of observing correct ritual was critical in governing. Ritual was the manifestation of the cosmic moral order, whether for the emperor or for the Confucian official. Ritualistic exercises involving the emperor must be performed regularly and faithfully. On these exercises rested the whole confidence in the authority of the Son of Heaven. Filial piety was a foundational principle of the Chinese moral order. In a society founded on the fabric of ritual one could no more pick and choose what rituals to observe than one could choose what laws to follow in a society founded on law. To do so would challenge the organizational foundation of the state and society. Both cases revealed the incipient erosion of order in the later Ming.

Zhang Juzheng had projected an image of the frugal, virtuous Confucian minister. When he died in 1582, it came to light that he had accumulated vast wealth and that in private he had lived in lavish style. The emperor, who had been so much under the thrall of his tutor, was shocked and disillusioned by the discrepancy between Zhang's image and the reality. Zhang's influence was quickly rooted out. But more important in its lasting effects, the emperor henceforth assumed a negative and suspicious attitude toward his officials and his duties. To the despair of the court he became perverse, venal, avaricious and dissolute, squandered immense sums from the state treasury on extravagant but useless projects (refusing to draw on his own ample personal treasury), and promoted oppressive taxation schemes. In 1596 he dispatched eunuchs to the provinces as tax collectors and mining intendants who extorted money from the common people with threats of confiscation and baseless claims to land. In 1582 the Ming had turned a corner. Zhang Juzheng's programs could not be institutionalized. They never amounted to true reform in the meaningful sense but rather idiosyncratic efforts at restoration of older models, which without his continued guidance soon evaporated after his death. The hopeful promise of Zhang Juzheng was an illusion.

BUREAUCRATIC FACTIONALISM

The emperor gradually became more isolated within the palace walls as his power became more dysfunctional. With an almost palpable sigh of relief, the Taichang ("Exalted Prosperity") emperor, the heir that Wanli had fought so bitterly but unsuccessfully to replace, succeeded the long, painful reign of his father in 1620. The tremendously extravagant ceremonial projects of the Wanli emperor were halted, and oppressive taxes rescinded, millions of *taels* were released from the palace treasury, eunuch tax collectors were recalled, and oppressive taxes abolished. But the new emperor died after only one month on the throne.

The private academies that Zhang Juzheng had closed in 1579 because of their intense criticism of his activist administration and his exemption from mourning leave were the seedbeds of a rising wave of bureaucratic factionalism that ultimately came to cripple the ability of the civil bureaucracy to respond constructively to crises. In the late Ming the academies became the locus of groups of like-minded officials and scholars who identified as parties. Since the Song, political parties among officials (*dang*), had been banned or strongly discouraged as anti-Confucian. Yet they tended to embrace Confucian orthodoxy and what they saw as strict ethical behavior. In general, they represented the antithesis of administrative rationalization and reform along the lines or Zhang Juzheng's policies, although Zhang was in no sense a true reformer either. They opposed the Grand Secretariat because grand secretaries tended to be the source of centralizing institutional and fiscal organization. They supported the Censorate as a platform to attack the policies and their advocates that they opposed, and were intent on maintaining a loose organization in the civil bureaucracy. So what measures did the parties support? Their approach tended to be voluntaristic. They believed that the public spirit of moralistic Confucians could accomplish great feats without the need for a technical administrative apparatus. Administrative talent was defined not by objective bureaucratic expertise but by personal virtue.[4]

Parties were not coherent, integrated organizations in the modern sense. They were rather loose associations of similarly inclined officials who were oriented by ideology, not by programs, and defined more by who they opposed than by what they supported. Their doctrinaire attitudes made them quarrelsome and destructive. The Donglin Academy, located in the lower Yangzi delta in Donglin prefecture of Jiangsu province, China's intellectual center of gravity, was founded in 1604 and quickly became the principal focus of factional politics. From 1605 political struggle became endemic, paralyzing the government.

The eldest son of the Taichang emperor was enthroned as the Tianqi ("Announced by Heaven") emperor in 1621. While still a child in the palace of his grandfather, the Wanli emperor, he had fallen under the influence of his nurse Madame Ke and an ambitious eunuch in the service of his mother. Wei Zhongxian became the future emperor's close confidant. The child was evidently mentally deficient, physically weak, and poorly educated. He exhibited little interest in the affairs of government. Upon his accession, his mentor Wei Zhongxian rose rapidly in power. Though Wei was illiterate, he assumed the all-powerful position of head of the Directorate of Ceremonial in the eunuch bureaucracy and inaugurated a reign of terror against his critics and opposing officials, mainly the Donglin partisans. Of the four famous "eunuch dictators" of the Ming, Wei was the most vicious. Violent partisan struggle ensued through the 1620s, involving Wei Zhongxian and his allies, Donglin partisans, and officials and eunuchs outside the partisan alignments.

In 1624 Wei became head of the Eastern Depot, the powerful eunuch agency of police investigation and intimidation. In the same year the battle came to a climax when Yang Lian, a censor and Donglin leader, submitted a devastating memorial charging Wei with twenty-four high crimes and misdemeanors. Yang Lian's accusations, as explicit as they were, rocked the court and led to a flood of supporting memorials attacking Wei and his allies. Wei struck back in a furious campaign of retaliation lasting to 1626 that purged the government of Donglin partisans and eliminated most of his enemies including Yang Lian. Academies were targeted for destruction, especially those associated with the Donglin movement, including the Donglin Academy itself. At the same time a movement was instigated by Wei's sycophantic official supporters to erect "living shrines" in Wei's honor throughout the provinces, and in 1627 a proposal was made to honor Wei with ritual observances similar to those accorded to Confucius himself. Clearly the Ming official establishment had become mired in dysfunctional behavior.

SPREADING MALAISE

Powerful eunuch dictators, having no means to institutionalize their power, never outlasted the emperor on whom their influence depended. The emerging personality cult surrounding Wei Zhongxian thus quickly collapsed when his patron, the Tianqi emperor, died in 1627. As the emperor had no surviving sons (he was twenty-one at the time of his death), he was succeeded by his younger brother, who assumed the reign title of Chongzhen ("Lofty Good Fortune") in 1628 at the age of seventeen. Wei was dismissed and shortly thereafter committed suicide when orders for his arrest and interrogation were issued. The accession of the Chongzhen emperor offered some cause for hope; he was reasonably conscientious and intelligent, but he was inhibited by indecision and an inability to lead at a time when imperial leadership was most critical.

The Ming was so extensive geographically and demographically complex that challenges to its stability both from within and without could either be effectively ignored until they hopefully went away—if they did not soon escalate beyond a critical point—or could be dealt with by routine, ponderous bureaucratic responses. If they did rise to a higher level of crisis, challenges were rarely addressed with dynamic, long-range strategies. Chinese government, including both the imperial administration and the civil bureaucracy, to say nothing of the eunuch bureaucracy during the Ming, operated according to largely repetitive and unarticulated functions, both driven by and inhibited by ritualistic and moralistic assumptions. It was not that creative responses were impossible but that it was extremely rare that such responses could be sustained over a sufficient period of time. A case in point is the far-reaching reforms of Wang Anshi during the Northern Song. In normal times crises could usually be solved, however ineptly, given these structural and ideological weaknesses. But commitment to traditionalistic and ritualistic models militated against innovation in response to major challenges to order. Solutions to crises depended on a modicum of effective operation of the civil bureaucracy, however inefficient, and a sufficient energy of imperial leadership from the court (which is not to say that the kind of vigorous direction exercised by, for instance, the Yongle emperor was in any sense the norm). When these elements were absent or ineffective, then crises became intractable.

Thus the instability that inflicted the south China maritime periphery since the early Ming ban on maritime trade and the restrictive operation of the tribute system became a festering issue throughout the mid-sixteenth century. The tribute system was designed as a kind of safety valve to funnel trade through an institutional structure of tightly regulated tribute missions. This broke down around 1510 when competing missions arrived from regional Japanese feudal domains. Armed clashes occurred between competing, already highly militarized Japanese tribute missions, and by the 1520s illicit trade developed as the tribute system broke down. Large scale pirate raiding along the south China coast increased in the 1520s and 1530s, at first led by Japanese but eventually almost entirely involving Chinese of the maritime provinces. Successive Ming commanders dispatched to suppress the illicit trade were unable to capture pirate leaders, who enjoyed support among the general coastal population, or to destroy their trading enclaves. Ming efforts to suppress the illicit trade were ineffective because local elites were deeply implicated in the trade and local authorities who were complicit in the trade simply resisted orders to cooperate in suppression efforts. Again, bureaucratic inertia, willful or not, blunted effective action. A renewed ban on all trade in the 1550s had the effect of increasing the intensity of pirate raids, which escalated to large-scale invasions inland and the seizure of walled towns by pirate armies. Solving the piracy crisis eventually depended on a complex of interrelated circumstances. The marginal character of the south China maritime world did not draw in other regions. But, for the same reason, the government was able to ignore the problem until policies aggravated the situation. And only in part did bureaucratic competence and persistence, reflected in the appointment and consistent support for the brilliant tactician Qi Jiguang, finally address the problem directly. When the ban on maritime trade was lifted in 1567 the crisis evaporated.

Conditions in the upper Yellow River watershed of Shaanxi and Gansu provinces within the Great Wall a century later were very different from the southeast maritime periphery. The northwest *loess* highlands west of the Yellow River had experienced decades of endemic poverty due to environmental degradation and attendant economic depression. From the early seventeenth century the already marginal agriculture of the region was eroded by adverse weather conditions, drought, and plagues of locusts, aggravated by administrative misrule, corruption, and ruinous taxation resulting from the Wanli emperor's incessant tax increases to pay for his extravagant projects. By the late 1620s famine had become endemic in Shaanxi province, leading to mass starvation, infanticide, cannibalism, and outbreaks of epidemic disease. Local peasant uprisings broke out frequently from 1628. Conditions were not unlike those prevailing in the Huai River region of north China in the 1340s during the late Yuan, which spawned the rebellion of Zhu Yuanzhang.

The northwest encapsulated the general social and political malaise of the late Ming. Peasants driven from their lands in desperation joined bands of unpaid transport workers and soldiers who had deserted their units as a result of prolonged pay arrears. These diverse constituents formed the rank and file of groups of "roving bandits" that supported themselves by constant marauding, preying on the very population from which they themselves had arisen. Pacification efforts by the Ming were generally ineffective, hampered by competing regional jurisdictions and the debased condition of the Ming military forces. Small bands of a few thousand, simply armed, grew as they coalesced into larger groups, formed around charismatic leaders who arose out of the conditions of poverty and disorder. Such leaders adopted colorful titles that appealed to the romantic traditions of popular resistance and rebellion: "The Unmuddied," "Heaven-disturbing Monkey," "Lone Wolf," "Friend of the Red Army," and "The Dashing King." Government counteraction often involved inducing rebel leaders to surrender by offering them leniency, absorption into the regular army, and resettlement. But recidivism was common because the root conditions of the region that promoted rebellion were never addressed.

CONTENDERS FOR THE MANDATE

Two principal leaders emerged from the impoverished peasant families of northern Shaanxi. Zhang Xianzhong was registered in the *weiso* military system, but was dismissed from the army for misconduct. He was physically large and powerful with an unpredictable personality. In 1630 he led a small raiding party, roaming and plundering. Although several times induced to surrender, he showed a proclivity for recidivism. By 1637 his army grew to three hundred thousand as he moved east into central China between the Yellow and Yangzi Rivers. Zhang suffered a series of defeats at the hands of government forces—in 1638 he was allowed to retain his army and temporary base—but by 1641 he had recovered from near total defeat after losing his entire army in 1640. Given the chaotic social and economic conditions, a population of new followers was readily available. In 1644 he moved southwest into Sichuan province where he established his new base.

Li Zicheng, also from a peasant family in northern Shaanxi, led an unsettled early life and like Zhang Xianzhong showed a proclivity for violence. After enlisting in the army, he joined a mutiny in 1630. His growing band of followers expanded south and east, increasing to thirty to forty thousand by 1634. His army was almost completely destroyed by a Ming counteroffensive in 1638, but by 1640 his forces were resurgent. By the end of 1641 his army had expanded to one hundred thousand and had grown to four hundred thousand a year later. While both bands were in constant movement, their mobility gave them a significant advantage over pursuing government forces.

Although frequently approaching annihilation, rebel forces were constantly swelled by endemic conditions of famine and ruinous taxation in the northwest. The problems that had bred rebellion had become essentially intractable. The point of no return for the Ming was passed in 1641. By that year the last major efforts to deal with both domestic rebels and the Manchu threat across the frontier were exhausted.

Now resurgent, Li Zicheng consolidated his movement from 1641 as he began to make a conscious transition from random plundering to a more stable regime. In 1641 he captured the Yellow River city of Loyang. He began a deliberate effort to cultivate an image of Confucian orthodoxy, restraint, benevolence, and social reform, seeking to attract local scholar-gentry to his cause. He took Xi'an, the capital of Shaanxi province, in 1643, where he proclaimed his new dynasty, the Shun ("Obedient to Heaven"), and created the skeleton of formal administrative structures.

From the north, the simultaneous pressure of Manchu raids across the Great Wall made a coordinated and focused campaign by the Ming against the rebels virtually impossible, even if such a possibility was actually still feasible at the time, which is questionable. The Manchus raided across the Great Wall in the Beijing area for the first time in 1629. Raids resumed in 1636 and again in the Beijing region and the Shandong peninsula from 1638 to 1640. The court was forced to withdraw forces deployed against the rebels in the northwest to deal with the Manchu invasion, dividing resources and energy between two threats while defeating neither.

The Manchus were descended from the eastern Jurchen, borrowing institutions and organizational models from both Mongols and Chinese. They were a seminomadic people living in the forest margins of Manchuria along the border with Korea. The founder of the embryonic Manchu state was Nurhaci (1559–1626), for the Manchu people rather like what Temujin was for the Mongols. But unlike the early Mongols, the Manchus had a long history of interaction with the Ming through the framework of the tribute system and their frontier administration. Nurhaci was a minor tribal chieftain of the Aisin Gioro clan in the confederation of Jianzhou Jurchen. The Jianzhou guard was a projection of the *weiso* military system into frontier society as a means to stabilize shifting ethnic frontier tribes. Originally without a written language, the Manchus adopted a new language in 1599 based on the Uighur-Mongol script. As they expanded into the central plain of Manchuria, they absorbed Chinese craftsmen, traders, and farmers who provided the basis for settled organization. From the 1580s Nurhaci created an entirely new military-social system that enrolled all Manchu families in a series of eight banners, subdivided into smaller units called *niru* (arrow). By 1615 there were three hundred *niru*. As Mongols and Chinese of the northeast frontier were brought under Manchu organization, parallel Mongol and Han banners were created. At first there were four, later an additional four were created for each group, Manchu, Mongol, Han, for a total of twenty-four banners. Banners were identified by flags of four colors (yellow, white, red, blue), either plain or bordered.

The Manchu horizon was constantly expanding. In 1616 Nurhaci proclaimed himself emperor of the Later Jin ("Golden") dynasty, consciously adopting the dynastic name of the Jurchen dynasty of the twelfth and thirteenth centuries. As Nurhaci used his own reign period names, this act unmistakably marked a challenge to Ming sovereignty over the eastern frontier. The Manchus had become in a sense external rebels against their Ming suzerain in the Ming tribute system. Nurhaci announced "Seven Great Grievances" against the Ming in 1618 to justify his attack on Ming forces in southern Manchuria, and in 1619 for the first time defeated the Ming army there. A new capital was established at Shenyang in 1625. When Nurhaci died in 1626 he was succeeded by his eighth son Hong Taiji, under whom the Manchus expanded east into Korea and west into Mongolia. In 1636 Hong Taiji proclaimed the Qing ("Pure") dynasty, breaking the connection with the former Jurchen Jin dynasty and symbolically in no uncertain terms declaring the Manchu intention to replace the Ming. The die was cast. Qing ("Pure") clearly suggested an indictment of the Ming ("Radiant"), now sullied by corruption and incompetence.

Manchu propaganda was successful in attracting increasing numbers of Chinese to the new dynasty. Effective Ming defense was often vitiated by constant factional struggles in the court, involving baseless charges and impeachments of sometimes successful officials and generals. In the northeast, Yuan Chonghuan conducted an energetic offensive against the Manchus that was marked by victory over Manchu forces in 1626. But he was dismissed by eunuch Wei Zhongxian. In 1628 he was recalled by the Chongzhen emperor, but again when the Manchus breached the Great Wall in 1629, Yuan was unjustly charged with treason in 1630 and executed. Yuan's removal resulted in the complete collapse of Ming defense. In the northwest, Hong Chengchou was governor-general of Shaanxi province in 1631 where he repeatedly defeated Li Zicheng. Because of his success in the northwest he was brought east to coordinate defense against the Manchus in 1639. Impatient for immediate results, the emperor urged Hong into precipitous action. Hong was defeated and taken prisoner in 1641 and held in secret by Hong Taiji. Persuaded to join the Manchus, from 1644 he served the Qing until his death in 1665, heading the Office of Pacification at Nanjing, coordinating the entire Qing campaign of conquest of the south. Mistreatment of officials, corruption, and inconsistent policies paralyzed the Ming responses to the crises.

In early 1644, Li Zicheng launched his army from Xi'an for his final offensive, heading northeast to Beijing. So demoralized had the dynasty become that he met no resistance and entered the city on April 25. Faced with complete collapse, the Chongzhen emperor climbed an artificial hill in the Forbidden City and hanged himself. Thus ended ignominiously the Ming dynasty after two hundred seventy-six years and sixteen reigns.

At first Li's army observed discipline. But soon order gave way to widespread confiscation of wealth from officials and residents of the city, looting, and killing. Li proved himself unable or unwilling to restore order and was wracked by indecision. In the east, blocking the Manchus from moving south of the wall, the Ming general Wu Sangui held the eastern end of the Great Wall at Shanhaiguan where the wall meets the sea northeast of Beijing. Wu's intentions were unclear. Li Zicheng, acting prematurely, led his army east to engage Wu. He was soundly defeated and fell back to Beijing. On June 3 Li declared himself emperor of the Shun ("Obedient to Heaven") dynasty which he had previously proclaimed a year earlier at Xi'an, and having melted down vast amounts of looted treasure, he evacuated the city in the direction of Xi'an. Shortly thereafter the Manchus, in alliance with Wu Sangui, entered Beijing.

THE SOUTHERN MING

When news of the Chongzhen emperor's death and the rebel capture of the capital reached the south, general panic erupted. In the secondary capital at Nanjing consternation prevailed among loyalist Ming officials. Various contenders to succeed the Chongzhen emperor were sought out or emerged from among Ming imperial princes who had escaped the rebellion and invasion of the north. Although one, the Prince of Fu, was considered less able than another, the Prince of Lu, he enjoyed significant official backing perhaps because he was perceived as more compliant. When Shi Kefa, the most influential official of the south, shifted his initial support from the Prince of Lu, the Prince of Fu assumed the title of Protector of the State (*jianguo*) in June and shortly thereafter was enthroned at Nanjing as the Hongguang ("Vast Brilliance") emperor.

Shi Kefa assumed command of the Ming military forces in the Yangzi region. But the regime lacked sufficient revenues to support its forces, which were given freedom to raise their own supplies in the areas where they operated and appoint their own personnel. The enervating factionalism that had plagued the court continued at Nanjing, and the Hongguang court was divided by its inability to decide whether to focus on the rebels or the Manchus as the principal enemy threat. By early 1645 the Manchu armies reached the Yangzi. Failing to persuade Shi Kefa to surrender, in May they perpetrated a ten-day massacre of the city of Yangzhou where Shi Kefa was based, captured and executed him as a warning against further resistance. The Ming lost their most able commander. Nanjing fell in June and the Prince of Fu was captured and executed.

The conquest of the south might have proceeded more rapidly from that point had not the Manchus issued an order in July that all subjects on pain of death must adopt the Manchu hairstyle, which required shaving the front of the head and braiding the hair at the back in a queue. This decree, which was severely enforced, evoked furious opposition and inflamed the resistance, galvanizing opposition to the Manchus.

Another Ming contender, the Prince of Tang was chosen as Protector of the State at Fuzhou, the capital of Fujian province on the south China coast, in July 1645. He was enthroned as the Longwu ("Eminent Martial Virtue") emperor in August. This regime lasted until the next year, when it was overtaken by the Manchu advance. The last of the Ming claimants to the throne, the Prince of Gui, became Protector of the State at Zhaoqing, west of Canton in Guangdong province in the far south, and ascended the throne as the Yongli ("Perpetual Succession") emperor in December 1646. This last peripatetic court, constantly on the move and shifting bases to escape the inexorable Manchu conquest, persisted for many years in increasingly abject conditions until it was driven across the border into Burma, where it was finally extinguished ignominiously in 1662.

The "Southern Ming," as the sorry succession of pretenders to the Ming throne after the fall of Beijing in mid-1644 came to be called, was never more than a lost cause supported by die-hard loyalists and self-serving opportunists. After the death of Shi Kefa in 1645, the Southern Ming forces were little more than a motley collection of local militia, pirates, adventurers, and ex-rebels over which the successive courts exerted little direction and offered virtually no central support. It would be an error to see a vestige of an imperial state in the hopeless resistance to the Qing conquest. Against all logic, the leaders of the refugee courts of the "Southern Ming" harbored completely imaginary hopes that their cause would somehow succeed and the Qing conquest would be reversed.

Who lost the Ming? observers have asked. The question presupposes that blame must be assigned, that we can point a finger of accusation, most probably at the Chongzhen emperor.[5] But why should the Ming be different from any previous dynasty? Why should we expect that failure would have somehow eluded it? Why vest such an onus on Chongzhen? In late Ming times, as in many other times, many actors worked in often divergent directions: Emperors, reformers, partisans, eunuchs, rebels, and loyalists. Over the course of the dynasty more than one Ming emperor had failed to meet his responsibilities and the expectations of his officials, and address the challenges that faced his regime, but the dynasty had survived. Why should the Chongzhen emperor be the exception? The dynasty could survive this time also. In the right circumstances, the Manchus could have been held back. The peasant rebels were almost defeated on several occasions. Officials could have risen above petty factional struggle. Eunuchs could have been curbed. In some crucial way the convergence of influences, weaknesses, and failures, coupled with a pervasive sense of weariness at the core, were fatal.

The causes of the Ming failure lie deep in the early years of the dynasty, rooted in the formation of the Ming itself: Elevated autocratic power unmitigated by a balance of constituent influences; punitive and capricious discipline of the civil bureaucracy; untrammeled exercise of gratuitous violence by emperors and eunuchs; expansion and reliance on eunuchs for extralegal activities; and dereliction of responsibility by emperors. Above all, the steady erosion of ritual (*li*), the network of interacting roles, status, positions, and observances that bind together the normative social and political structure as the foundation of ordered human society had failed the Ming.

SUGGESTED READINGS

Atwell, William S. "From Education to Politics: The Fu She," in William T. de Bary, ed., *The Unfolding of Neo-Confucianism* (New York: Columbia University Press, 1975), 333–367. A useful account of the principal political faction at the end of the Ming.

Dardess, John W. *Ming China, 1368–1644: A Concise History of a Resilient Empire* (Lanham, Maryland: Rowman & Littlefield, 2012). A brief study of the Ming organized by thematic subjects, including frontiers, emperors, governance, literati, and outlaws.

Fairbank, John K., ed. *Chinese Thought and Institutions* (Chicago: The University of Chicago Press, 1957). A formative anthology of articles on institutional, intellectual, and social history by leading scholars. Particularly relevant here is Charles Hucker's article on "The Tung-lin Movement of the Late Ming Period."

Goodrich, L. Carrington, and Chaoying Fang, eds. *Dictionary of Ming Biography, 1368–1644*, 2 vols. (New York: Columbia University Press, 1976). An essential and reliable reference for the study of the Ming.

Huang, Ray. *1587. A Year of No Significance: The Ming Dynasty in Decline* (New Haven: Yale University Press, 1981). An engaging and provocative study of the decline of the Ming based on biographical portraits of major figures of the Wanli reign.

Hucker, Charles O., ed. *Chinese Government in Ming Times: Seven Studies* (New York: Columbia University Press, 1969). Studies by major students of the Ming on local and fiscal administration, education, politics, bureaucracy, and the military system.

Michael, Franz. *The Origin of Manchu Rule in China: Frontier and Bureaucracy as Interacting Forces in the Chinese Empire* (New York: Octagon Books reprint, 1965). A pioneering study of the rise of the Manchus and the formation of the Manchu state.

Mote, F. W. *Imperial China, 900–1800* (Cambridge: Harvard University Press, 1999). The most comprehensive treatment of Chinese history from the end of the Tang through the early Qing dynasties. An extremely useful reference, with the caveat that the index has many lacunae.

Mote, Frederick W., and Denis Twitchett, eds. *The Cambridge History of China*, vol. 7, *The Ming Dynasty, 1368–1644*, Part 1 (Cambridge: Cambridge University Press, 1988).

Parsons, James Bunyan. *Peasant Rebellions of the Late Ming Dynasty* (Tucson: University of Arizona Press, 1970). A definitive study of the rebellions of Li Zicheng and Zhang Xianzhong and their political and social milieu at the end of the Ming.

Schwartz, Benjamin. *The World of Thought in Ancient China* (Cambridge: Harvard University Press, 1985).

So, Kwan-wai. *Japanese Piracy in Ming China during the 16th Century* (East Lansing: Michigan State University Press, 1975). Japanese piracy in the sixteenth century evolved to embrace extensive Chinese piracy presenting a significant threat to the Ming maritime world.

Spence, Jonathan D. *The Death of Woman Wang* (New York: Penguin Books, 1979). An engaging local history of a county in Shandong province in the seventeenth century impacted by natural disasters and Manchu raids.

Spence, Jonathan D., and John E. Wills, Jr., eds. *From Ming to Ch'ing: Conquest, Region, and Continuity in Seventeenth-Century China* (New Haven: Yale University Press, 1979). An important collection of nine essays on the Manchu-Chinese conflict and its aftermath in the mid-seventeenth century.

Struve, Lynn A. *The Southern Ming, 1644–1662* (New Haven: Yale University Press, 1984). The comprehensive, definitive study of the struggle of the refugee Ming forces following the Manchu conquest of China.

Twitchett, Denis, and Frederick W. Mote, eds. *The Cambridge History of China,* vol. 8. *The Ming Dynasty, 1368–1644,* Part 2 (Cambridge: Cambridge University Press, 1998).

NOTES

1. *Oxford English Dictionary,* 1933 (reprinted 1961), vol. VII, 182.
2. Confucius, Arthur Waley, trans., *The Analects of Confucius* (*Lun Yu*) (New York: Vintage Books, originally published 1938), XII, 11.
3. James Legge, trans., *The Four Books,* 4–7. Emphasis added.
4. One might be tempted to see here the "Red" mode of action of Mao Zedong versus the technical "Expert" mode of Deng Xiaoping adumbrated in the political discourse of the Ming parties.
5. See F. W. Mote, *Imperial China, 900–1800* (Cambridge: Harvard University Press, 1999), 781–784, 801–804, for an extensive discussion of this issue.

III

THE HIGH QING, 1650–1800

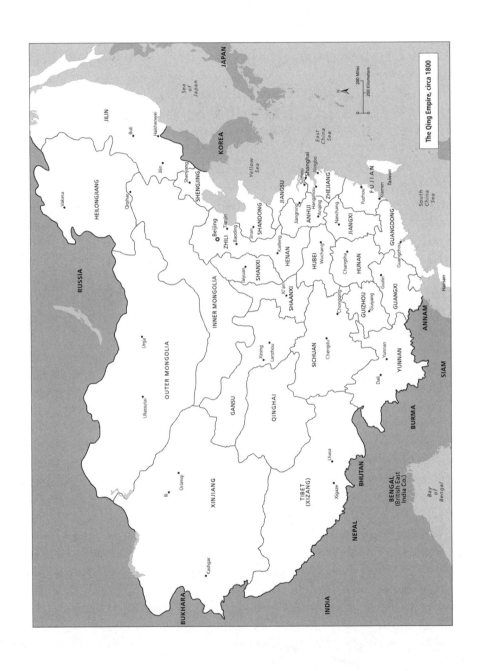

The Qing Empire, circa 1800

8

The Manchu Revolution

Where the Great Wall, built by the Ming in the fifteenth century, crossed the barren hills north of Beijing and descended to the sea, it blocked the narrow littoral that stretched from the broad central China plain on the south to the coastal region known as Liaoning on the northeast. Here, where the wall meets the sea, a massive fortress-gate guarded passage between the two regions. Shanhaiguan ("The Gate between Mountains and Sea") became the pivot of a protracted struggle for possession of the Mandate of Heaven.

The rich central basin of Liaoning, drained by the Liao River and its tributaries, and the surrounding mountains and highlands were known since early times as the Northeast (Dongbei). Later the area was called the Three Eastern Provinces, or Manchuria in foreign terminology. The Liao basin is enclosed by mountain ranges to the east, north, and west. On the east, bordering Korea, are the Long White Mountains; far to the north the Amur River (Heilongjiang) divides the Northeast from Siberia; to the west are the mountains and highlands of eastern Inner Mongolia. In its geographical complexity, the Northeast was a frontier margin of China Proper, encapsulating the greater Sino-inner Asian cultural and political interactions. Chinese farmers and merchants had gradually migrated into the Liao basin, extending their traditional intensive sedentary agricultural society into the Northeast. In the forests and rivers of the mountains of the north and east, descendents of the Jurchen, a Tungusic people, pursued a mixed seminomadic culture of hunting, fishing, animal husbandry, and farming. On the west the Mongols followed a fully nomadic pastoral steppe economy of herding and animal husbandry, including sheep, horses, and camels. The Ming, extending its efforts of control outward beyond the Great Wall, sought to exploit, in the interests of its own security, the constant interactions of the diverse groups and tribes of the frontier. Its objective was to preempt the emergence of any confederation of tribal leaders powerful enough to challenge Ming hegemony over the frontier. On the ethnically and geographically ambiguous margin of empire, the Ming assiduously combatted the prospect of the resurgence of barbarian power. Ironically, in the long run it was the very intervention by the Ming officials in constant tribal rivalries, internecine struggles, and shifting semi-feudal confederations that was the key to the emergence of a leader who would challenge the Ming.

NURHACI

And so it was that a petty Jurchen tribal chieftain, Nurhaci, united his people into a powerful new force and founded a new state. Thus the stage was set for the preliminary rehearsal of a larger drama. Nurhaci was the realization of the Ming's worst nightmare, the emergence of another Chinggis Khan. Nurhaci (1559–1626) rose from small beginnings through rivalry with other tribal leaders. Unlike Chinggis Khan, who rose out of a pure and distant nomadic steppe environment, Nurhaci benefited from constant interaction with various frontier ethnic groups, Chinese, Mongol, Jurchen, and Korean. These shaped the dynamics of his and his successors' development. In incessant wars with other tribal leaders, by age thirty Nurhaci had consolidated control over the Jianzhou region in the east. In the last decades of the sixteenth century he was on his way to creating a new military-social organization based on units, called *niru*, of three hundred men and their families. By 1615, *niru*—by that time there were three hundred—were organized into banners (*gusan*) each headed by a prince (*beile*), originally the sons of Nurhaci. In order to prevent feudal concentration of power under a single *beile* commanding one or more banners, banners were supported by noncontiguous land allotments, and military forces organized for campaigns were drawn from units belonging to several separate banners. Nurhaci thus created a proto-bureaucratic organization in contrast to the traditional tribal feudalism of the Jurchen. In 1599 a written language was created based on the Uighur-Mongol script and thereafter the name Manchu was adopted by Nurhaci's successor in 1636, a reflection of the new emergent Manchu identity. (The problem of Manchu identity will be discussed more fully in the following chapter.)

The expansion of Manchu hegemony first over the Northeast and then over Korea, Mongolia, and finally China was a gradual affair lasting a century or more. At first, Nurhaci probably did not envision the founding of a larger empire beyond creating a unified confederation of Jurchen tribes, including a powerful alliance with the western Mongols. During a Ming military campaign intended to stabilize the disintegrating Jianzhou confederation, Nurhaci's father and grandfather were both killed. This event prompted Nurhaci to launch a vendetta against the Ming forces in the region, with whom he had formerly been on peaceful terms. Nikan Wailan, a local Chinese adviser to the Ming commander who was held responsible for the killings, was killed in 1586. The event was later included in Nurhaci's "Seven Great Grievances" charged against the Ming. Nurhaci launched his first direct attack on the Chinese, taking the city of Fushun in Liaodong ("Eastern Liao") in 1618. The Manchus were now clearly in rebellion against the Ming. By 1621 all of Liaodong was under Nurhaci's control and a new Manchu capital was established at Liaoyang (later Shenyang). The Ming now had a serious problem on their hands that would occupy them continuously until their ultimate defeat in 1644.

In the process of moving down into the central agricultural basin of Manchuria the Manchus absorbed and attracted many Chinese of Liaodong. An important strength of the Manchus was their ability to assimilate outsiders, somewhat as the Mongols who were numerically weak had used *semu* (Uighurs, Khitans, and Europeans) in their administration. But the Manchu practice was much more systematic, as the Chinese provided vital technical, administrative, and economic skills that the Manchus lacked. The Liaodong Chinese in turn often acquired Manchu names and customs, making them a loyal inside force supporting the Manchus. Chinese who were captured by the Manchus before the creation of the Chinese banners in 1601 were incorporated into Manchu society as either slaves or bondservants. Bondservants served their Manchu masters in diverse ways, some ultimately in very high positions of trust.

Nurhaci anticipated that frontier tribal feudalism would continue after his death under a collective leadership of his sons, the *beile* or princes. Yet his creation of the banners already had introduced a measure of rational bureaucratic organization, and the incorporation of Chinese with bureaucratic experience reinforced this tendency. The four senior banner leaders, the *hosoi beile*, formed a deliberative council of princes ambiguously suggesting the perpetuation of collegial rule, but also a sort of council of state under a monarch. Thus was introduced a conflict between aristocratic tribal rule and monarchical rule. When Nurhaci died in 1626 the issue came to the fore in the question of succession to Nurhaci's rule. Acting collectively, the *hosoi beile* gathered to debate the selection of a successor. The *hosoi beile* had grown to eight in 1622 with the addition of the remaining banner chiefs. After the senior *beile* ruled themselves out of consideration, the council chose Nurhaci's eighth son, Hong Taiji.[1]

From his accession, Hong Taiji was determined to reduce the power of the feudal princes and enhance the authority of the monarch. To do so he relied on Chinese collaborators from Liaodong. His Chinese advisers advocated the adoption of traditional Chinese bureaucratic institutions.

In 1631 the Ming model of central government divided into Six Ministries (Civil Service, Revenue, War, Rites, Justice, and Public Works) was adopted and by 1636 a Literary Office (*wen guan*) for secretarial assistance and the Censorate were added, now all reorganized into the Three Inner Courts (*nei san yuan*). Thus Hong Taiji had created a bureaucratic state on the Chinese model. In the same year he declared the inception of the Qing dynasty and adopted a new name, Manchu. By posing a new dynastic name Qing ("pure") against the Ming ("radiant"), the Manchus indicated their intention to contest the Mandate of Heaven.

Hong Taiji clearly admired the Chinese and relied on Chinese collaborators to build his administrative organization as well as for military planning. This process of sinification was deeply resented by traditional Manchu tribal leaders and many of the *beile*, who feared the erosion of Manchu culture and tradition and of their own power. This abiding issue was to emerge openly later on following the death of Prince Regent Dorgon who perpetuated Hong Taiji's policies. When the southern Manchurian city of Songshan fell to the Manchus in 1642 they captured the Ming commander there, Hong Chengchou. Hong had earned a reputation as the most successful Ming general leading the campaign against the rebels in the northwest. As a consequence of his successes there he was transferred by the court in 1641 to the northeast in hopes of stemming the Manchu advance. Aware of his reputation and ability, Hong Taiji persuaded Hong to join the Manchu cause. Hong served the Qing loyally, drafting proclamations and state documents as only a Chinese scholar could, advising Hong Taiji on policy, and later eventually heading the office for pacification of Jiangnan at Nanjing from 1645 to 1648. There he enacted policies of administrative pacification of the south. Hong Chengchou was typical of many lesser Chinese turncoats who were essential to Manchu success.

In the course of Hong Taiji's reign, as he came to rely increasingly on Chinese advisers and Chinese bannermen, the complexion of the Manchu-Qing regime changed accordingly. Elected by his equals, *hosoi beile*, Hong Taiji began as primus inter pares, a prince among princes; he ended as an imperial autocrat, the *beile* reduced in power and subjected to his will. Nurhaci had not envisioned the ultimate conquest of China; such a future would not have seemed possible then. He had declared himself emperor of the Later Jin in 1616, emulating the ancestral frontier dynasty of the Jurchen. With Hong Taiji the prospect of creating a greater entity, a new dynasty that would contest the Mandate of Heaven with the Ming, only gradually formed on his expanding horizon. The die was finally cast with his proclamation of the Qing in 1636.

The Manchus created a shadow Chinese state on the frontier margin of China before their direct conquest in 1644. Chinese scholars were attracted and recruited and employed in high positions. Confucianism was adopted as the state ideology and Confucian classics and history were translated into Manchu. The full Chinese central government structure was adopted by 1631. The Manchus projected a favorable image of stability and order in contrast to the growing disorder of the last years of the Ming. Thus the Manchus grew into China; the last act was the military conquest of China Proper. Though accompanied by many violent episodes, it was less violent by comparison, for instance, to the Mongol conquest of the Southern Song because of this. In the course of this transformation the Manchus had to abandon their habitual practices of pillage and enslavement of populations and the massacre of foreigners. Although the Manchus were still raiding across the Great Wall and gathering booty in 1642–1643, when the *beile* Amin slaughtered Chinese in two cities in 1630, he was arrested by Hong Taiji and eventually died in prison in 1640.

DORGON

When Hong Taiji died in 1643, the Manchu armies were poised outside the Great Wall in Liaodong, awaiting the opportunity that would open the door to China to them. Hong Taiji was succeeded by his six-year-old son Fulin, who ascended the throne as the Shunzhi ("Prosperous Rule") emperor. He would be the first Manchu emperor of China. Because Fulin was a minor, Hong Taiji's younger brother Dorgon (1612–1650), the fourteenth son of Nurhaci, assumed direction of the government as prince regent. Dorgon was a powerful exponent of the new bureaucracy and the principal architect of the new order forged under the reign of his older brother. He was to become a virtual dictator until his death in 1650.

Blocking the Manchu armies from entering China was the Ming general Wu Sangui, stationed at Shanhaiguan where the Great Wall meets the sea. Wu was one of the most able Ming generals, from a military tradition whose family were Chinese natives from Liaodong. In that sense, Wu looked both ways across the cultural divide that separated Manchus from Chinese. In the meantime the "roving bandit" Li Zicheng, the "Dashing Prince," had launched his final thrust from Xi'an northeast through Shaanxi toward Beijing, intent on toppling the Ming. Li had adopted the traditional accoutrements of imperial rule: scholar-officials to lend his regime Confucian legitimacy, Confucian rites and institutions, and a dynastic title, Shun ("Obedient to Heaven"). He reached the capital in April 1644 and entered the city on April 25 encountering virtually no resistance. The last Ming emperor hanged himself on Coal Hill the day before, thus ending the Ming dynasty.

This triad of personalities, Dorgon, Wu Sangui, and Li Zicheng perfectly encapsulated the issues attendant on winning the Mandate of

Heaven. Li Zicheng, a native son, though beginning with all the liabilities of a marauding rebel, had consolidated the other roving bandits under his authority and evolved to become an imperial contender. It was Li who led his armies into the capital to overthrow the Ming. At that point Li might have risen to sit on the throne as the first emperor of a new dynasty, as other domestic rebels such as Zhu Yuanzhang had in the past. Zhu had overcome the other challengers in a long civil war and had destroyed the Yuan to found the Ming. But Li Zicheng was no Zhu Yuanzhang. He possessed neither the military genius nor the administrative adeptness of his predecessor. Somehow, either through failure of will or incompetence and inability to control his followers, Li lost the Mandate as soon as he was in a position to claim it. In the first days following the rebels' entry into the capital, their occupation degenerated into chaos, rebel leaders executing Ming officials and relatives, rebel followers engaged in plunder of the wealth of the city. Li was unwilling or unable to discipline his followers, and perhaps simply lacked the vision of a successful founder. Stripped of the façade of imperial contender, the inherent character of the rebels as plundering bandits stood revealed.

The Manchus under Dorgon, on the other hand (though rebels themselves from beyond the Great Wall), projected an image of stability and order. Their own assumption of the accoutrements of Confucian imperial rule was not a façade. Though barbarians from beyond the pale, the Manchus had consciously adopted the posture of being "more Chinese than the Chinese." The contrast with the rapacious and disloyal domestic rebels could not be lost on the Chinese subjects of the Ming. Moreover, after 1631 the Manchu armies were no longer purely Manchu/Jurchen. They comprised, in addition to the Manchu banners, Chinese and Mongol banner troops and artillery manned by Chinese trained by the Portuguese. Though the Manchu cavalry was a formidable striking force capable of crushing its enemies in the field, they depended on regular troops and artillery to besiege walled cities. Unlike the Mongols, for instance, the Manchus alone did not possess overwhelming military superiority.

So what was Wu Sangui to do? Wu was torn between conflicting influences. On one hand he was a Han Chinese, a loyal subject of the Ming emperor. But the emperor was dead and the rebels grasped the throne. Should he submit to Li Zicheng as the prospective new emperor, a fellow Han, defending China against the alien Manchus? But it was increasingly clear that the rebels would never be more than rebels. Another, personal motive allegedly affected Wu's actions. His father was being held hostage by Li in Beijing and appealed to his son to surrender to Li. Moreover Wu's concubine, the legendary beauty Chen Yuanyuan had also been taken by Li. When Wu rejected his father's appeal, Li executed his father. This, and his jealousy over the fate of his beloved Chen Yuanyuan, drove Wu to seek revenge, so the probably apocryphal account goes. On a higher plane were considerations of state and political loyalty. Wu alone did not possess the military strength to restore the Ming, and the fate of other Ming loyalist forces and Ming royal contenders in the south was unknown.

Wu Sangui, between the domestic rebel Li Zicheng and the foreign rebel Dorgon, stood at the critical moment in the decision of the Mandate of Heaven. In early May Wu defeated two rebel forces sent out against him, perhaps intended by Li to test his strength. A subsequent offer by Wu to negotiate was preempted when Wu learned that Li was leading his entire army toward Shanhaiguan. At that point Wu turned to Dorgon, urging him to join his army in crushing the rebels. On May 27, backed by Manchu banners which came through the Great Wall, Wu routed Li's army which fell back on Beijing. It seems obvious that Wu and Dorgon envisioned different outcomes from this expedient alliance. Ironically, while Wu offered the Manchus the profits of plunder, their traditional source of support, Dorgon had already commanded a change of policy from plunder to occupation. The Manchus, severely strained for revenue, had found that the Northeast could no longer support their vastly expanded organization; they had every intention of moving permanently down into the Central Plains. Li reentered Beijing on June 3 and belatedly ascended the throne as the emperor of the Shun dynasty. The next day, after melting down for transportation all of the gold and silver that could be gleaned from the city, Li abandoned the capital, fleeing westward with his tattered armies.

Wu Sangui and Dorgon reached Beijing on June 6. Dorgon promptly claimed the throne for the Qing, proclaiming that the Manchus had legitimately inherited the Mandate. He could credibly make the point that it was not the Manchus but the roving bandits that had destroyed the Ming; the Manchus were absolved of the charge of disloyalty. Wu was sent west in pursuit of the fleeing rebels with the title "Prince Pacifier of the West." A similar title had already been conferred on him earlier by the Chongzhen emperor to induce him to come to the aid of the capital as the rebels advanced, but it had been too late.

The Shunzhi emperor, Hong Taiji's successor, ascended the throne at Beijing on October 30. But for the next six years, until his premature death in 1650 at the age of thirty-eight, Dorgon was the virtual dictator of China. As Dorgon continued to rely heavily on Chinese bannermen and collaborators, his regime was marked by accommodation with the Chinese and increasing sinification. Yet both Hong Taiji and Dorgon were ambivalent about the dangers of sinification, mindful of the loss of tribal identity experienced by previous conquest dynasties such as their forebears, the Jurchen Jin. Although Dorgon relied on his brothers Ajige and Dodo, neither were serious opponents of his policies and the tension between himself and the other Manchu princes gradually became acute. Thus the conflict between Manchu tribal feudalism and Chinese imperial autocracy remained unresolved.

WINNING THE MANDATE

Ultimately it was the Chinese, the collaborators and turncoats advising Hong Taiji and Dorgon who advocated the permanent conquest of China, and men like Wu Sangui who saw the Manchus as more worthy successors of the Ming, who were the arbiters of dynastic change. Yet while the Manchus securely held the imperial throne in the summer of 1644, the issue was far from decided. The entire south, the Yangzi valley, the rich Jiangnan region, beyond that the far south, and Sichuan in the west were yet to be conquered. Ming loyalism and anti-Manchu resistance festered there. This division might have become the status quo, with the Qing ruling north China and the Central Plain, the northern, predominantly wheat culture of the Yellow River watershed separated roughly from the southern, predominantly rice culture of the Yangzi River watershed, just as the barbarian Khitan Liao and the Jurchen Jin dynasties coexisted with the Southern Song. But the various southern Ming regimes were inherently unstable and had inherited many of the same problems that proved fatal to the Ming. A modus vivendi was actually considered by the Nanjing regime and a peace mission dispatched to the north in August 1644. But the mission was barely acknowledged and treated with contempt by the Manchus. And Dorgon, encouraged by his Chinese advisers, was determined that the Qing should unify all China. In any case, officials and literati at Nanjing were afflicted by unrelenting factional bickering, polarization, and an air of unreality, oblivious to the threat that confronted them. The principal task of the Manchus was to win over the loyalty of the official elite and educated Confucian literati. The most powerful obstacle to winning the elite was enduring Ming loyalism. Loyalty to the Ming arose not so much from any sense of regret for the loss of the dynasty— the Ming's failures, after all, were all too obvious to many—but from a fundamental Confucian moral imperative of filial piety that required unconditional loyalty to one's sovereign regardless of a calculation of merit. Of course there were just as many who had no such scruples, seeing in the Qing an opportunity to serve. But this dilemma between resistance, including suicide, and surrender and service nevertheless remained.

In their approach toward the Chinese of the south the Manchus exhibited considerable ambivalence. They were confident in their rightful succession to the Mandate and their determination to rule all of China. Resistance therefore was intolerable. But unlike the ferocious Mongol conquest, they wished to achieve their objective with the acknowledgement by the Chinese of their legitimacy. On one hand they were willing to show leniency, but where leniency was unavailing they showed great severity. While offering a welcoming hand they also could display an iron fist. Their certainty in the justice of their cause and their concern that the Chinese truly submit led to policies that seriously alienated Chinese and made conquest more difficult. In June 1644 Dorgon decreed that all Chinese must adopt the Manchu style of dress and wearing the hair. The latter required shaving the front of the head and braiding the long hair at the back into a queue. For the Manchus this would demonstrate submission by the Chinese to a uniform practice and also make identification of loyal subjects from resistors fairly easy. The penalty for failure to obey was severe: "lose your hair or lose your head." Unquestionably this command stiffened resistance of many Chinese, elite and commoners alike. The issue was not merely some idle matter of vanity. It touched on a deep moral issue. In the Confucian moral tradition of filial piety, one was obligated to retain one's body intact as one had received it from one's parents. (That is why decapitation was a far more shameful form of execution than strangulation.) The Chinese viewed haircutting as a mutilation and a dishonor as well as a barbaric act.

The Manchus had no intention of ruling China remotely from Manchuria, and in any case the region's capacity to sustain the Manchu-Chinese population was strained. As the Manchu banners with their attendant population moved into north China they had to be settled on new lands. They expropriated large areas of the best farmlands in the Beijing region, resettling the former Chinese residents on poorer lands, enslaving much of the population. This policy caused great hardship to the Chinese and resentment against the Manchus.

Large numbers of Ming officials and gentry in north China had changed allegiance to the Qing before the fall of Nanjing in June 1645. But the south remained the center of resistance. Particularly the Jiangnan region south of the Yangzi between Nanjing and the coast, the rich center of traditional literati culture and Confucian scholarship, confronted the Manchus with the strongest determination to defend the Ming. As the Qing armies moved south the Ming general Shi Kefa, renowned for his ability, honesty, and loyalty, moved his forces to defend Yangzhou on the north bank of the Yangzi. The city was famous for its affluence and flourishing literati culture. As Dorgon approached the city in May 1645 he appealed to Shi Kefa to surrender, praising his character and promising to honor him. Unavailing against the general's determination, the Manchus launched a bitter siege that ended May 20. What followed was a ruthless ten-day massacre of the city's population in which an estimated eight-hundred thousand died. Shi Kefa, captured and brought before Dorgon, was unyielding and was promptly executed. His sacrifice made him an emblem of resistance and an enduring national hero. The brutal contrast between the pitiless massacre of Yangzhou, which evoked the Mongol destruction of cities that refused to surrender as a warning to others, and the genuine efforts of persuasion and assimilation of the Chinese under-scores the ambivalence of Manchu behavior. Following the surrender of Nanjing and the ignominious flight of the refugee Southern Ming court in 1645, Dorgon issued an edict, severe in tone, to the people of Jiangnan. He charged three crimes against the Ming: Ming ministers made no effort to strike against the rebels following the fall of Beijing; they enthroned a Ming successor, the Prince of Fu, in Nanjing who had no imperial man-date; and their generals failed to attack the roving bandits but themselves ravaged the population. The edict promised amnesty and employment to those who surrendered but severe punishment to those who continued to resist.

> I have solemnly accepted the Mandate of Heaven, and so arrayed the six armies to subdue and punish the guilty. All civil and military officials in each locale who take the lead in surrendering their towns and territories will be meritoriously advanced one degree in rank. Those who obstinately [deny] the Mandate and do not submit will be massacred and their wives and chil-dren taken prisoner.[2]

The edict confidently claimed the Mandate for the Qing. Following the fall of Nanjing most officials accepted the Qing. But still there were many, including whole families, who expressed their loyalty to the fallen Ming by suicide, acknowledging the dynasty which had granted their degrees and employed them.

The firm resolve of the Manchus convinced most of the futility of active resistance. Yet nevertheless profoundly suspicious of the scholar-gentry elite, especially of the Jiangnan region who were perceived as insuffi-ciently submissive to higher authority, the Manchus lost no opportunity to intimidate this crucial class. When widespread cheating and bribery in the provincial examinations came to light in 1657, the government reacted ferociously. Hundreds of malefactors were executed and thousands of family members banished into slavery. The campaign of intimidation ex-tended into the next reign following the death of the Shunzhi emperor in 1661. In several of the wealthiest prefectures of Jiangnan it was revealed that up to 13,500 gentry were delinquent in paying their land taxes. Tax delinquency was nothing new but to the Manchus it reflected a cavalier attitude and laxness among the gentry. A series of decrees demanded immediate payment on penalty of severe punishment. A protest of hun-dreds of students occurred in 1661. The subsequent crackdown and arrest of offenders led to the degrading and dismissal of thousands of officials and gentry before the case was brought to an end in 1662.

The Manchus were extremely sensitive to any expression of the perception of the alienness of the conquerors among the educated elite, which could be interpreted as subversive challenge to Manchu rule. This concern did not diminish with time but persisted throughout the dynasty, rising at times to almost paranoid heights. Zhuang Tinglong, a wealthy Jiangnan merchant, sponsored an ambitious history of the Ming based on a work written in the last years of the Ming. The work appeared in 1660. Carelessly or thoughtlessly edited, the book used the personal names of early Manchu rulers, taboo under the reigning dynasty, Ming reign titles for Southern Ming reigns after 1644, and obsolete late Ming titles. These errors, though unintentional, were considered at least slanderous to the reigning dynasty and at worst treasonable. Once again the government reaction was swift and violent. Everyone associated with the work was arrested and punished, including even the printers, seventy were executed, and families were enslaved to Manchu households before the case ended in 1663.

These cases are reminiscent of the persecutions of officials during the early reigns of the Ming, when sometimes the mere suggestion of treason led to the killing of thousands of victims. The difference is that although the Hongwu emperor was pathologically afraid of conspiracies against his rule, his paranoia did not originate from his ethnic origins, as it did for the Manchus. If anything, his insecurity arose from his obscure and common background. The Manchu leaders, on the other hand, were confident in their Confucian learning. Also, the Manchu persecutions had as their objective the intimidation of a specific class and they ended fairly quickly; they did not ripple through the literati and official elite for years, as was the case in the fourteenth century. And while the Manchu action could be ferocious, it did not entail the unrestrained violence exhibited by the early Ming rulers.

Upon the death of Dorgon, who had become a virtual emperor himself, in 1650 Fulin, the Shunzhi emperor, assumed direct rule at the tender age of twelve. Almost immediately a process of denunciation of Dorgon for his arrogation of imperial power and self-exaltation began. Many of his supporters were purged. The new emperor was determined to act as a reforming emperor in the Confucian mode to restore official support for the new government that Dorgon's high-handed behavior was in danger of jeopardizing. Dorgon had severely curtailed eunuch power. But the Shunzhi emperor revived the thirteen palace directorates, the organization of eunuch activities of the Ming, but with numerous additional restrictions, in 1655. Yet to a significant extent the emperor continued much of Dorgon's policies of sinification and accommodation. In addition to his mother the Empress Dowager Xiaozhuang (1613–1688), the empress dowager of Hong Taiji, the emperor relied heavily on his leading Chinese grand secretary Chen Mingxia. Chen had placed third with honors in the last metropolitan examination under the Ming in 1643, and was appointed to the Hanlin Academy. Because he had submitted briefly to Li Zicheng in 1644 he was persona non grata to the Southern Ming court and in 1645 submitted to the Manchus, who appointed him to his former rank. The emperor admired Chen for his vast scholarship and erudition but was suspicious of his loyalty. Eventually in 1654 Chen audaciously proposed to another official the restoration of Ming hairstyle and court dress. Oddly, he seems to have been deaf to the sensitivity of his masters to the hint of persistence of Chinese loyalist sentiments. Chen was impeached for numerous crimes of corruption and was executed. Nothing perhaps better exemplified the Manchu fear of sinification gone too far. Later, in a manner we have observed as typical of other emperors' ambivalent feelings toward their favorite ministers who betrayed them, the Shunzhi emperor, responding to an unkind comment by one of his ministers about Chen, replied "Chen Mingxia, after all, was good."[3]

KANGXI

The Shunzhi emperor died of smallpox in 1661 at the age of twenty-three. He designated his son Xuanye as his heir, in part because Xuanye had contracted smallpox and survived and was thus already immune from the disease that particularly ravaged the Manchus. Xuanye, who was only seven years old, ascended the throne as the Kangxi ("Vigorous Prosperity") emperor. As demanded by his youth, a council of four regents, all Manchu princes—Oboi, Soni, Suksaha, and Ebilun—assumed actual power. Three of them were relatively inconsequential and were soon set aside by the strongest and youngest, Oboi. All of the regents resented Dorgon's policy of accommodation and were determined to revive traditional Manchu tribal institutions and customs and strengthen Manchu dominance which they saw as having been eroded under Dorgon and the Shunzhi reign. With the collusion of the Grand Empress Dowager Xiaozhuang, they cast aside the Shunzhi emperor's will and fabricated a false will that confessed to numerous offenses favoring accommodation. This fabrication provided the justification for reversal of the policies of the Shunzhi emperor.

The scope of eunuch power was again reduced. The Manchus were able to dispense with the use of eunuchs except within the palace because they had an alternative the Ming did not. Bondservants, Chinese captured by the Manchus in Liaodong before the creation of the Chinese banners in 1601, were utterly loyal, as were eunuchs, having no social or political prospects outside of their service. They were slaves of their master, yet they themselves could own slaves, accumulate wealth, and hold office. The bondservants of the upper three banners personally served the emperor and were constituted as the Imperial Household (*neiwu fu*) by 1628.

The regency revived the institution which became the Imperial Household bureaucracy serving the direct and personal needs of the emperor. Though most bondservants, like eunuchs, served in anonymous positions under the Imperial Household, some rose to great heights of power, though never like eunuch dictators during the Ming. The famous example is Cao Yin, who administered the Nanjing imperial textile factory, which supplied the Imperial Household with silk fabrics, for the Kangxi emperor. Cao became a trusted confidential informant for the emperor, while his family rose to great wealth and influence. His grandson, Cao Xueqin, was the author of China's most famous novel, *Honglou meng* ("Dream of the Red Chamber"), which is a loose autobiographical depiction of the life of a wealthy extended family during its heyday and its decline.[4]

Oboi, having successively eliminated the weakest regents, behaved like one of the infamous eunuch dictators of the Ming, intimidating and executing officials who opposed him. The young Kangxi emperor, resentful of Oboi's tyranny, bided his time. Finally in 1669 he plotted with loyal Manchu allies to arrest the regent, who died in prison the same year. The Kangxi emperor assumed direct power at the age of fifteen. He was a precocious child, read widely in Chinese classics and history, and though he retained the frontier skills of the hunt and the military encampment he was equally at home in the Confucian world of the literati-official class. Abandoning the atavistic tribalism of the Oboi regency, he made conscientious efforts to finally win over the Chinese Confucian elite. He sponsored vast literary works of scholarship such as the definitive Kangxi dictionary of Chinese (*Kangxi zidian*) containing over forty thousand words, and a huge dictionary of literary phrases and allusions, the *Peiwen yunfu*. Seeking to lure into Qing service the last illustrious holdouts among Chinese scholars of the south, in 1678 he appointed a commission to hold the *boxue hongci* ("broad learning and vast erudition") examination of 1679. Of the 188 candidates who were summoned (not all were persuaded to sit for the examination), 50 passed and were awarded degrees. These constituted a commission to write the history of the Ming (*Mingshi*), a prestigious project that each dynasty undertook for its predecessor.

As sinification expanded the range of Chinese who were increasingly comfortable with the Manchus, and Han gradually accepted the legitimacy of the dynasty (the Manchus, after all, had always insisted that it was not they but the roving bandits who had destroyed the Ming),

Manchu identity and vigor was correspondingly eroded. As assimilation to Chinese bureaucratic culture increased, the military virtue and effectiveness of the banner elite declined. As time passed fewer and fewer Manchus possessed skills bred in the tribal frontier. Moreover, Manchu banner soldiers settled forcibly on lands originally expropriated from Chinese became increasingly impoverished as they lost their original work ethic. Progressive indebtedness of Manchu commoners, who were expected not to work for their livelihood, was the result. Ineluctably, what Hong Taiji feared and the conservative Manchu elite of the Shunzhi and Oboi eras warned of came to pass. By the end of the dynasty few Manchus, thoroughly sinicized, even knew their own language.

But at least Qing rule was secure—or almost so. The last challenge came in 1674 with the Revolt of the Three Feudatories (*sanfan zhi luan*). The three great Chinese military allies of the Manchus who had pursued the rebels and the Southern Ming pretenders into the south became ensconced there as powerful, virtually autonomous princedoms: Wu Sangui in Yunnan, Shang Kexi in Guangdong, and Geng Jinghong in Fujian. Nominally loyal to the Qing but practically beyond the reach of Qing control, their existence was certainly a thorn in the side of the dynasty. When the aged Shang Kexi in 1673 requested permission to retire and return to his homeland in the north, an opportunity was presented to the government to eliminate this anomaly. The court suggested to the others that they also should retire. While at first nominally agreeing to do so, they had been forced into an awkward position. The emperor had grasped this risky course knowing that it would precipitate a rebellion. Faced by an emperor who would not yield to their proposals for a compromise, the three rebelled. Together, possessed of large armies and considerable resources, they could well have toppled the dynasty. The Qing mobilized Manchu, Mongol, and Chinese banners and a large number of regular Chinese troops. But they were poorly served by timid and incompetent commanders, and at first war went badly for the Qing as the rebels thrust northward taking several provinces south of the Yangzi. It was a mark of Manchu success in winning the Mandate that Chinese for the most part remained loyal to the Qing. The dynasty also commanded superior resources of the Jiangnan region. By 1676 the rebels were faltering and the Qing forces began to win consistent victories under new leadership. The rebellion was finally defeated in 1682.

The protracted transition from Ming to Qing rule of China had taken a century, from Nurhaci's revolt against the Ming northeast frontier command in revenge for the killing of his father and grandfather in 1583

to the final conquest of the last Chinese holdouts in the south in 1682. Revolutions are not won in a day and winning the Mandate of Heaven by the Manchus was one of the most complex revolutions in Chinese history.[5] The modern successor to this protracted event, the transition from Qing to the People's Republic of China, was almost equally prolonged, lasting from the rise of the Nationalist revolutionary movement under Sun Yatsen in the 1890s to the Communist victory in 1949. Winning the Mandate of Heaven—*geming*—in a literal sense defines the process of revolution in traditional China. But revealingly—and not by accident—the term *geming* also denotes the process of revolution in modern China. And yet, what kind of "revolution" was it that the Manchus won? Revolution implies vast political, social, and economic change, the world turned over. When all was said and done, the Qing was really in most respects the Ming. No drastic reforms were ever introduced by the Manchu founders, not by Hong Taiji, not by Dorgon, not by the Shunzhi emperor. In the end the Qing retained original Ming institutions mostly unchanged. What changed was perhaps the degree of efficiency with which they were implemented and the level of autocratic authority by which the Qing ruled China. In a sense at this great midpoint of Imperial China the Manchu achievement was paradoxically a revolution without revolution. What the Manchus achieved was not the redefinition of Imperial China (and not a mere hiatus in the historical logic of traditional China as the Mongols had been) but for all their fire and thunder the full acceptance of themselves as legitimate and worthy inheritors of Chinese civilization.

SUGGESTED READINGS

Chang, Michael G. *A Court on Horseback: Imperial Touring and the Construction of Qing Rule, 1680–1785* (Cambridge: Harvard University Press, 2007). Impressive imperial tours of southern China by the Kangxi and Qianlong emperors were an essential means to gauge popular acceptance of Manchu rule and assert imperial power.

Crossley, Pamela Kyle. *The Manchus* (Oxford: Blackwell Publishers, 2002). A general history of the Manchus by a leading student of the Qing dynasty.

Elliott, Mark C. *The Manchu Way: The Eight Banners and Ethnic Identity in Late Imperial China* (Stanford: Stanford University Press, 2001). A definitive study of the Manchu banner system and the issue of Manchu identity.

Guy, R. Kent. *Qing Governors and Their Provinces: The Evolution of Territorial Administration in China, 1644–1796* (Seattle: University of Washington Press, 2010). A study of the development of Manchu-Chinese provincial administration in the early Qing.

Hucker, Charles O. *China's Imperial Past: An Introduction to Chinese History and Culture* (Stanford: Stanford University Press, 1975).

Hummel, Arthur W., ed. *Eminent Chinese of the Ch'ing Period (1644–1912)*. 2 vols. (Washington, D.C.: Library of Congress, 1943–1944). In spite of its age this remains the essential comprehensive biographical reference for the Qing.

Kessler, Lawrence D. *K'ang-hsi and the Consolidation of Ch'ing Rule 1661–1684* (Chicago: University of Chicago Press, 1976). An authoritative study of the Kangxi emperor and the early Qing.

Michael, Franz. *The Origin of Manchu Rule in China: Frontier and Bureaucracy as Interacting Forces in the Chinese Empire* (New York: Octagon Books reprint, 1965). A pioneering study of the rise of the Manchus and the formation of the Manchu state.

Mote, F. W. *Imperial China, 900–1800* (Cambridge: Harvard University Press, 1999). The most comprehensive treatment of Chinese history from the end of the Tang through the early Qing dynasties. An extremely useful reference, with the caveat that the index has many lacunae.

Oxnam, Robert B. *Ruling from Horseback: Manchu Politics in the Oboi Regency, 1661–1669* (Chicago: University of Chicago Press, 1970). An excellent companion to Lawrence Kessler's study above (*K'ang-hsi and the Consolidation of Ch'ing Rule 1661–1684*) on the conflict between tribal and bureaucratic politics in the establishment of Manchu rule. See also Silas Wu's *Passage to Power* and Jonathan Spence's *T'sao Yin and the K'ang-hsi Emperor* below. Together, these studies represent the core of the specialized studies of this brilliant emperor.

Parsons, James Bunyan. *Peasant Rebellions of the Late Ming Dynasty* (Tucson: University of Arizona Press, 1970). A definitive study of the rebellions of Li Zicheng and Zhang Xianzhong and their political and social milieu at the end of the Ming.

Peterson, Willard J., ed. *The Cambridge History of China*, vol. 9, *The Ch'ing Empire to 1800*, Part 1 (Cambridge: Cambridge University Press, 2002). *The Cambridge History of China* volumes 9, 10, and 11 (like the twin volumes on the Ming) are the standard authorities of the Qing dynasty by leading scholars of their respective fields.

Rowe, William T. *China's Last Empire: The Great Qing* (Cambridge: Harvard University Press, 2009). A thoughtful, comprehensive history of China under the Qing empire organized into ten chapters on various thematic subjects, including government, society, commerce, rebellion, restoration, imperialism, and revolution.

Spence, Jonathan D. *The Death of Woman Wang* (New York: Penguin Books, 1979).

Spence, Jonathan D. *Ts'ao Yin and the K'ang-hsi Emperor: Bondservant and Master* (New Haven: Yale University Press, 1966). A masterful examination of the relationship between a powerful Chinese bondservant and his emperor and the secret memorial system created by the emperor to communicate with his trusted advisers.

Spence, Jonathan D., and John E. Wills, Jr., eds. *From Ming to Ch'ing: Conquest, Region, and Continuity in Seventeenth-Century China* (New Haven: Yale University Press, 1979).

Struve, Lynn A. *The Southern Ming, 1644–1662* (New Haven: Yale University Press, 1984). The comprehensive, definitive study of the struggle of the refugee Ming forces following the Manchu conquest of China.

Struve, Lynn A., ed. and trans. *Voices from the Ming-Qing Cataclysm: China in Tigers' Jaws* (New Haven: Yale University Press, 1993). Translations of participants' accounts and memoirs of the Manchu massacre of Yangzhou in 1645.

Wakeman, Frederic, Jr. *The Fall of Imperial China* (New York: The Free Press, 1975). An excellent textbook covering the period from the end of the Ming to the end of the Qing. Early very useful chapters examine peasants, gentry, merchants, and the dynastic cycle.

Wakeman, Frederic, Jr. *The Great Enterprise: The Manchu Reconstruction of Imperial Order in Seventeenth-Century China*, 2 vols. (Berkeley: University of California Press, 1985). The definitive and lengthy study of the Manchu conquest and its aftermath. An essential work on what Wakeman sees as one of the greatest transitions in Chinese history.

Wakeman, Frederic, Jr., and Carolyn Grant, eds. *Conflict and Control in Late Imperial China* (Berkeley: University of California Press, 1975). A diverse collection of nine essays by leading scholars covering the period from the Manchu conquest to the early Republic.

Wu, Silas H. L. *Passage to Power: K'ang-hsi and his Heir Apparent, 1661–1722* (Cambridge: Harvard University Press, 1979). A careful study of the difficult issue of the Kangxi emperor's selection of, or failure to select, an heir and its political consequences.

NOTES

1. Hong Taiji is evidently a title, meaning something like "great prince," not a personal name; its origin is obscure. Hong Taiji's personal name is unknown. An earlier common name for Hong Taiji was Abahai, which the author, against contrary evidence, prefers. But scholarly consensus accepts Hong Taiji. See Arthur W. Hummel, ed., *Eminent Chinese of the Ch'ing Period (1644–1912)* 2 vols. (Washington, D.C.: United States Government Printing Office, 1943–1944), 1–3; and Giovanni Stary, "The Manchu Emperor 'Abahai': Analysis of an Historical Mistake," *Central Asian Journal* 28.3–4 (1984): 296–299.

2. Quoted in Frederic Wakeman, *The Great Enterprise: The Manchu Reconstruction of Imperial Order in Seventeenth-Century China*, 2 vols. (Berkeley: University of California Press, 1985), vol. 1, 582.

3. Wakeman, vol. 2, 987.

4. Arthur W. Hummel, ed., *Eminent Chinese of the Ch'ing Period (1644–1912)*, 2 vols. (Washington, D.C.: United States Government Printing Office, 1943–1944), 737–739, 740–742. See also Jonathan D. Spence, *Ts'ao Yin and the K'ang-hsi Emperor: Bondservant and Master* (New Haven: Yale University Press, 1966).

5. The definitive study of the Manchu revolution is Frederic Wakeman's two volume work, *The Great Enterprise: The Manchu Reconstruction of Imperial Order in Seventeenth-Century China*.

9

Style and Substance
Imperial Culture

The Kangxi emperor in the fifty-sixth year of his reign on December 23, 1717 read to the assembled members of the court and high officials of the central government a Valedictory Edict, part of which reads:

> *I am now close to seventy, and have been over fifty years on the throne—this is all due to the quiet protection of Heaven and earth and the ancestral spirits; it was not my meager virtue that did it. Since I began reading in my childhood, I have managed to get a rough understanding of the constant historical principals. Every emperor and ruler has been subject to the Mandate of Heaven. Those fated to enjoy old age cannot prevent themselves from enjoying that old age; those fated to enjoy a time of Great Peace cannot prevent themselves from enjoying that Great Peace.*
>
> *Over 4,350 years have passed from the first year of the Yellow Emperor to the present, and over 300 emperors are listed as having reigned, though the data from the Three Dynasties—that is, for the period before the Ch'in burning of the book—are not wholly credible. In the 1,960 years from the first year of Ch'in Shih-huang to the present, there have been 211 people who have been named emperor and have taken era names. What man am I, that among all those who have reigned long since the Ch'in and Han dynasties, it should be I who have reigned the longest?[1]*

While expressing a suitable humility before Heaven which had protected his reign for so many years and a modest assessment of his abilities, the Kangxi emperor's edict exudes a quiet sense of self-confident possession of the historical legacy inherited by the Manchus. Here the emperor does not anchor his reign in the prior history of his own people but in the great tradition of Chinese civilization. The Qing dynasty which the Manchus founded on the ruins of the Ming is not viewed here as a violent interruption in the historical progress of Chinese civilization since the most ancient times, but as a logical and rightful succession bestowed by Heaven's Mandate. The Qing, rising from barbarian roots on the northeastern frontier margin of China, established a powerful aura of largely peaceful legitimate sway over the Han Chinese population of China Proper and the frontier regions of Inner Asia beyond. This achievement was more than merely political and military; it also involved a cultural mastery with important implications for both the last era of Imperial China and for modern China that emerged from it. The peace and prosperity that prevailed over the first half of the Qing period following the completion of the Manchu conquest in retrospect has come to be known as the "High Qing." This era spanned the reigns of three magnificent emperors roughly from 1680 to 1800. These were the glory years of the Qing. This not only was qualitatively a time of great stability and prosperity. Two of the three emperors, the Kangxi emperor (r. 1661–1721) and the Qianlong emperor (r. 1736–1796) each reigned for sixty years, the longest reigns in Chinese history. The sheer length of these two reigns together, separated by the shorter but no less brilliant reign of the Yongzheng emperor (r. 1722–1735), contributed quantitatively to the sense of continuity and self-confidence of these times, already adumbrated in the Kangxi emperor's Valedictory Edict.

IMPERIAL GRANDEUR

Chinese emperors ever since Qin Shihuangdi, the first emperor in 221 BCE, tended to be viewed through a stereotypical lens (note that in his Valedictory Edict the Kangxi emperor alluded to 211 emperors with reign names in the previous two millennia). Certain personality attributes indeed did tend to recur regularly, particularly as the dominant Confucian construction of emperorship became entrenched after the Han dynasty and the medieval era of division. However individualistically disposed an emperor might have been when he ascended the throne, he had already been conditioned by the influences of his immediate family and palace attendants, and his behavior was thereafter shaped by the powerful Confucian bureaucracy from whose ever-present influence he could escape only with difficulty. And yet as we have seen in the case of the Ming emperors, from the pathological behavior of Zhu Yuanzhang, the Hongwu emperor, to the astounding expansive ambition of the Yongle emperor, to the pathetic indecision of the last, the Chongzhen emperor, a great variation in competence and self-image existed in practice. Emperors often displayed idiosyncrasies of character that, in spite of the strait-jacket of court and official institutional ideology, had the capacity to exert great influence on their times.

The three grand emperors Kangxi, Yongzheng, and Qianlong were above all no cookie-cutter monarchs. Each of their reigns was distinctive in its own way, especially the two longest, molding the imperial culture of the High Qing. Kangxi, a patron of culture, was broad-minded and inquisitive. Yongzheng, masterful administrator, was diligent, engaged, and obsessive. Qianlong, the universal ruler, was self-possessed and acquisitive. The Kangxi ("Vigorous Prosperity") emperor ascended the throne in 1661 at the age of seven. In designating his heir, his father, the Shunzhi emperor appointed as regents four high Manchu bannermen, eventually dominated by Oboi. In 1669 at the age of fifteen the emperor cast aside the regency and assumed personal rule. The Kangxi emperor was a precocious child who read avidly in the Confucian classics, history, and literature. Barely a generation removed from the frontier tribal environment of the Manchu homeland, the emperor was remarkable for his command of Chinese culture. So confident was he in his possession of Confucian morality that in 1670, reversing the usual roles of Confucian teacher and emperor, he issued the Sacred Edict, sixteen maxims exhorting proper behavior among the public, to be read by officials in every village throughout the empire twice a month. Chinese emperors, especially the powerful ones, often sought to assert their sway over the intellectual and moral climate of their times by sponsoring ambitious literary projects. The expansive Ming Yongle emperor sponsored the huge *Encyclopedia of the Yongle Reign* (*Yongle dadian*), the largest such project up to this time. The Kangxi emperor sponsored several such works of scholarship including the *Ming History* (*Ming shi*), the officially approved history of the previous dynasty; the *Rhyming Thesaurus of Phrases* (*Peiwen yunfu*) completed in 1711; the huge Kangxi dictionary (*Kangxi zidian*), the most comprehensive dictionary of the Chinese language with approximately forty thousand characters, in 1716; and the massive *Comprehensive Illustrated Encyclopedia* (*Gujin tushu jicheng*), finally printed in 1728 after the emperor's death, comprising ten thousand Chinese volumes (*juan*).

While the Kangxi emperor assiduously maintained his Manchu cultural roots, conducting imperial hunts in the imperial parks north of the Great Wall and practicing the Manchu martial skills of horsemanship and the bow, he was at the same time greatly attracted by Chinese elite culture, especially of the south, the Jiangnan region of the lower Yangzi valley that was the center of gravity of the Confucian literati culture. The affluent life of the Yangzi city of Yangzhou, supported by the wealthy salt merchants of the region who lavishly patronized literati painting and scholarship and established private libraries and academies, he particularly admired. Invoking that fascination, he recruited learned scholars to be his secretaries and advisers to work in the Southern Study (*nanshufang*) which he established in the imperial palace. It was these men who worked on the literary projects under the emperor's direction. Projecting his interest in southern culture into the south, he led six southern tours between 1684 and 1707, the ostensible purpose of which was to inspect river conservancy works on the Yellow River. Although the emperor was inquisitive and interviewed officials along his routes, these were hardly intimate affairs. His retinue of Manchu clansmen, court officials, eunuchs, attendants, as well as his military bodyguard numbered in the tens of thousands and imposed a significant burden on the local resources, both private and public, of the regions through which they passed.

Bitter factional rivalry among several of the Kangxi emperor's sixteen surviving sons (he had altogether thirty-five sons) marred the last two decades of his reign. By the Manchu rule of succession any male child of the ruler could be designated heir by consultation among the royal princes, as Hong Taiji was selected upon Nurhaci's death. This rule contrasted with the Chinese custom by which the eldest son of the principal empress succeeded his father, a method which obviated factional alliances around competing contenders for the throne. The emperor's hesitation and his ambivalence regarding his sons contributed to the uncertainty of the succession. Only in the last hours of his life as he lay dying did the emperor name his fourth son his heir, a relative dark horse who had not participated in the factional struggles. The fourth son, who was already forty-four at the time, ascended the throne in 1722 as the Yongzheng ("Harmonious Rectitude") emperor. Understandably, considerable doubt about the legitimacy of the fourth son's claim and suggestions of conspiracy cast a pall over the succession. One such accusation among many was the evidently spurious charge that the child Yinzhen, the Yongzheng emperor, was the illegitimate son of the Kangxi emperor by a low-ranking concubine who had entered the palace only six months before she gave birth. The Yongzheng emperor spent the first years of his reign suppressing the factions and eliminating several of his brothers as possible challengers. In a harbinger of later Communist factional rhetoric, the emperor referred officially to two of his brothers as "That disreputable person" and "Black-hearted monster."

Perhaps because of the Yongzheng emperor's maturity and experience by the time of his accession, he was an unusually hard-working and diligent monarch, in stark contrast to so many of the incompetent and self-indulgent Ming emperors. The new emperor made it his business to be personally involved with the administration of government down to the smallest details. He was constantly engaged, communicating with his trusted officials, almost to the point of obsession. He was thus one of the most authoritarian of monarchs, much more so than the often lax rule of his father, but he was also a benevolent despot, sincerely attentive to the welfare of the people. He had been well-schooled in Confucian learning in his younger years but was also deeply attracted to Chan Buddhism. Virtually all of the Yongzheng emperor's energies were absorbed in political and economic reforms. He wrote lengthy and detailed responses to his officials' memorials reporting on provincial administration. (His comments were written as rescripts interlineally on the original memorials in vermillion ink.) Consequently he devoted little attention to cultural projects such as those of his father and subsequently of his successor. But his fiscal prudence and administrative efficiency left the Qing treasury flush with revenue. If the Yongzheng court was not culturally brilliant but rather businesslike and methodical, his reign laid the material foundation for the imperial grandeur of the last two-thirds of the eighteenth century. Often viewed with suspicion over his disputed succession and dismissed for his colorless authoritarian rule, his brief thirteen year reign (he died prematurely and unexpectedly in 1735) was one of the most successful in Chinese history.

Determined to avoid the bitter factionalism that had marked his own succession, at the beginning of his reign the Yongzheng emperor wrote his choice for heir on a piece of paper, sealed it in a box, and placed the box behind a tablet in the throne hall, to be opened only upon his death; though the palace officials knew the location of the box, only he knew the name within it. The emperor's fourth son, thus designated by his father, ascended the throne in 1736 at the age of twenty-four as the Qianlong ("Heaven's Abundance") emperor. Because he had come to the throne without the suspicions that surrounded his father's accession, the Qianlong emperor reigned with a secure confidence in the legitimacy of his rule. He aspired to be—and to a great extent he brilliantly succeeded to be—the supreme universal ruler. His vision transcended by far that of his forebears as Manchu monarchs who commanded the Chinese world of the conquest. The Kangxi emperor saw himself poised in the legacy of legitimate Chinese emperors extending back two thousand years; the Qianlong emperor claimed much more. Under his reign the Qing expanded the boundaries of the empire in "Ten Great Campaigns" of which the emperor was extremely proud, to include Mongolia, the distant reaches of what became Chinese Turkestan or Xinjiang ("The New Frontier"), Tibet, as well as the various ethnic populations of the southwest. Except for the Muslim population of the northwest, he personally mastered the languages and practiced the religions of all of them—Manchu, Chinese, Mongol, Tibetan. He viewed himself as the embodiment of the Buddhist *chakravartin*, transcendent universal ruler, the "Wheel Turner."

The Qianlong emperor sought not only to command the physical expanse of the empire but also to possess its material, spiritual, and cultural dimensions as well. Thus he became obsessively acquisitive, collecting art and objects and crafts of every variety, including Western examples such as mechanical clocks and music boxes, and curiosities of nature. Knowing his proclivity, when he travelled local merchants and literati were fearful that he might notice some precious object and ask for it, a request that could not be denied. It was said that when he visited the great Confucian temple at Qufu in Shandong province, the local custodians wrapped in red bunting the spectacular stone pillars of the portico carved with coiling dragons lest the emperor attempt to remove them to Beijing. His arrogance in collecting everything led to his unfortunate habit of branding famous paintings with his large vermillion imperial chop or seal, sometimes more than once on the same painting, and writing his own appreciative colophons on the paintings. Although this diminished the value of the paintings—some say destroyed it—it became a mark of the collector's art-historical connoisseurship. In one sense the amassing of this huge collection, amounting to hundreds of thousands of items, which became a sort of museum in its own right, contributed to the preservation of culture that otherwise might have been scattered or lost.[2]

The literary counterpart of this collecting mania was the *Complete Library of the Four Treasuries* (*Siku quanshu*), an immense project to collect and print, and thereby preserve all of the extant written editions in the classics, history, philosophy, and belles lettres. The project, suggested by the eminent scholar Zhu Yun (1729–1781), was begun after a tepid response from the official class to the emperor's proposal, under the editorial direction of Ji Yun (1724–1805) in 1773 and employed a large staff of scholars plus 1,400 copyists and a complex administrative apparatus to conduct a broad search of public and private libraries and personal collections throughout the empire. Works submitted were copied and returned to their owners. More than 11,000 works were examined of which almost 3,500 complete texts were copied and included in the final compendium. The precedents for this huge enterprise of literary mastery were the Ming *Yongle Encyclopedia* and the Kangxi emperor's *Comprehensive Illustrated Encyclopedia*. It seems the Qianlong emperor sought to emulate and perhaps to surpass these when he embarked on his project. As large as they were the *Complete Library* exceeded them in size. Too large to print using the wood block printing process of the day, seven manuscript copies comprising thirty-six thousand volumes each were issued between 1782 and 1787 and stored in various cities. All of the copies were partially or completely lost and destroyed in uprisings and wars through the nineteenth century.

The Qianlong emperor's efforts were not confined to collecting existing work; he himself produced a stupendous body of written work and paintings. He wrote poetry compulsively, but badly. His collected poetry fills 282 volumes, including 43,800 poems, more than any other poet in Chinese history. Examples of his calligraphy, including his inscriptions on valuable paintings, are considered pedestrian. His self-congratulatory record of his *Ten Great Campaigns* (*Shiquan ji*) alone comprises fifty-four volumes of essays and poems. The emperor delighted in being depicted in portraits in various poses or identities, many of these painted by the Jesuit court painter Father Giuseppe Castiglione (1688–1766), who worked in the European style with perspective very different from the traditional Chinese one-dimensional paintings. The emperor was represented as a Confucian literatus, a Daoist monk, a Buddhist bodhisattva, a hunter, a connoisseur, even a knight errant, thus possessing the full spectrum of cultural personalities embraced by the empire.

Like his grandfather, the Kangxi emperor, the Qianlong emperor led a series of southern tours between 1751 and 1784. Although these also may be seen in the light of the assertion of imperial control over the Chinese cultural heartland, their ostensible motive was different. The emperor's mother, the Empress Dowager Xiaosheng, accompanied him on the early tours. As a Confucian filial son, the emperor was extravagantly devoted to his mother, visiting her daily, solicitous of her every need. Attending to the comfort of the aging empress made these tours even more expensive than they might otherwise have been. If the nevertheless arduous journey to the south were too taxing for the empress, the emperor on her seventieth birthday constructed in the palace a replica of a Suzhou street capturing the languid charm of the southern style that she so enjoyed.

The Qianlong emperor abdicated the throne in 1795, the sixtieth year of his reign, as a gesture of filial respect in order not to exceed the reign of his grandfather who had also occupied the throne for sixty years. Sixty years was also a great cycle in the Chinese calendrical system, after which the cyclical year names repeated in the next cycle. Each year in the sixty-year cycle has a unique designation such that there is always an ambiguity between a certain year of one cycle and that of the preceding or following cycle. The emperor, then in his eighty-fifth year, was still in reasonably good health, though his memory was failing. But he did not surrender power and continued to rule, if not reign, under the reign of his son, the Jiaqing emperor (1796–1820), until his death in 1799.

THE MULTICULTURAL EMPIRE

In the age of the High Qing by the middle of the Qianlong reign, China had reached a pinnacle of grandeur unmatched in every measure by any previous dynasty with the possible exception of the golden age of the Tang one thousand years before. The early Qing Manchu emperors ruled over a prosperous, stable, and extensive empire. The military campaigns conducted by the Kangxi and particularly the Qianlong emperors incorporated the vast regions of northern Manchuria, Mongolia, Chinese Turkestan, and Tibet into Greater China, creating the largest consolidated territorial empire in Chinese history. (Only the Mongol empire was larger, but it was not a centralized empire under a single monarch ruling from China. The Qing empire was larger than the present People's Republic of China.)

The traditional political, economic, and social institutions inherited and subsequently refined by the Qing reached an unparalleled level of maturity and integration. The imperial bureaucratic system, which was the envy of the West at this time, in spite of the progressive enhancement of autocratic rule by the court, effectively managed a complex, hierarchical regional administration from the central government down to the lowest county levels. Complex problems of food production, land reclamation, expansion of arable land, interregional transportation, price control, taxation, and irrigation and flood control were all successfully addressed. Civil service recruitment, appointment, and discipline of officials based on objective, rational criteria produced a generally well-educated, technically proficient official class.

Expanding agricultural productivity and the introduction of New World crops such as the sweet potato, maize, and peanuts led to a rising standard of living that supported the enrichment and spread of material culture. The rise in literacy and popular education contributed to a corresponding growth of a flourishing print culture, visual arts, and theatre. Great libraries established by the wealthy lower Yangzi salt merchants and literati connoisseurs paralleled imperial sponsored enterprises of encyclopedic collections of the Kangxi and Qianlong emperors.

Under the Manchus, though themselves a conquest elite, traditional Confucian values and orthodox Confucian learning inherited from the Song and Ming achieved their widest acceptance and deepest penetration. Not only did the Manchu elite become thoroughly sinicized through an extended process of acculturation to Chinese civilization beginning in Manchuria even before the conquest, but minority ethnic regions within China Proper in the south, southwest, and northwest were brought more fully into the dominant Han cultural order through internal conquest and assimilation. The literati-scholar class, guardians of official Confucian ideology, displayed a more thorough adherence to traditional orthodoxy while broadening the scope of classical learning. So secure were the Manchu rulers in their command of Confucianism that, as in the case of the Kangxi emperor's Sacred Edict of 1670, they confidently lectured the populace on Confucian moral behavior.

The general peace and prosperity engendered by the confluence of these conditions led to a large growth in population during the seventeenth and eighteenth centuries. While population statistics for premodern China are notoriously uncertain, the population is estimated to have grown from approximately sixty million at the beginning of the Ming to more than three hundred million by the end of the eighteenth century. While expanding agricultural productivity based on more efficient farming, new crops, and land reclamation kept pace with population growth, the increasingly adverse ratio of population to land would eventually become a negative consequence of the very prosperity of the High Qing. In some senses the sheer quantitative magnitude of these features of the High Qing—territorial extent, political and social integration, expansion of material culture, sinicization and acculturation, population growth—became themselves qualitative attributes of this era.

While the Ming, in a kind of nationalistic reaction to the Mongol conquest, had become increasingly introspective, building walls to defend against the outsiders across the inner Asian frontier and along the coast, the Qing thrust outward. The Manchus were reacting to no foreign conquest, since the Ming military administration lay lightly over the northeast frontier; indeed, in the decades before the invasion of China, Nurhaci had actively built a confederation embracing diverse peoples and cultures, Mongol, Turkic, Tibetan, Korean, Chinese, and Manchu and their languages, traditions, and folk cultures. It was no conceptual leap from the founders' fledgling empire to the much vaster cosmopolitan cultural empire of the Qing. However much the Manchus enthusiastically adopted the Confucian inheritance of the Song and Ming, their legacy was much more than this, arising as well from their inner Asian frontier origins. Thus the Qing extension of Chinese political administration of China Proper to Mongolia, Turkestan (named Xinjiang, "New Frontier," in the eighteenth century), and Tibet, far beyond the traditional cultural realm of classical Chinese civilization, was unprecedented in Chinese history. That the Qing was a multilingual empire is attested to by the name plaques on official buildings and temples which were carved in the four languages of Chinese, Manchu, Mongol, and Tibetan. Moreover, the Qing was not just multicultural in a de facto sense as a consequence of its far-flung conquests; it was multicultural in vision and outlook as well. Multiculturalism, at least for the court if not for the literati class, was an explicit value. The Qing monarchs, and especially the Qianlong emperor, consciously presented themselves as universal, cosmopolitan rulers, in the diverse meanings as defined in Confucian, Buddhist, Mongol, and Turkic cultures. In this sense the vision of a multicultural empire far transcended the classical Chinese notion of the Son of Heaven's (*tianzi*) rule over All Under Heaven (*tianxia*) radiating outward from an explicitly Chinese cultural center over all other peoples in his sway, who were thereby in varying degrees acculturated to the Confucian order.

THE EMPIRE OF THE SCHOLAR

Qing emperors were exceedingly powerful figures, influencing profoundly the shape and development of empire. But imperial culture was not monolithic. On one hand were the emperor, his court (in the sense of high level clansmen, imperial family members, and officials whether Manchu or Chinese who served his will), and the "conquest elite," the Manchu and Han bannermen who were the basis of the Manchu conquest of China and their descendants. This group shared a cultural outlook that owed much to their multicultural frontier origins. On the other hand was the overwhelmingly Han Chinese civil service bureaucracy which pervaded the entire empire from the imperial capital down to every local district. The bureaucracy was almost entirely recruited from the successful graduates of the civil service examinations, which were held at the prefectural, provincial, and metropolitan levels two or three times every three years. Generally speaking, only those men who passed the highest level examination at the capital, which accorded them the coveted and highly exclusive *jinshi* ("presented scholar") degree, were eligible for appointment to office. Even so, there were far more eligible officials-in-waiting than there were actual official positions. The most common initial appointment was to a district magistracy in one of the approximately 1,500 districts in the Qing regional administration. The substance of the examinations was based on the Neo-Confucian orthodoxy, which all aspiring candidates thus were forced to master. The entire regimen of preparation and study which began at an early age imposed a rigorous discipline on the literati-scholar class. Some chose not even to attempt the endeavor, or abandoned their attempt after initial failure, but were thereby relegated to second class status, though they might nevertheless pursue distinguished literary careers. The rest who chose to sit for the examinations faced an arduous course that led as often to disappointment as to success. For those beginning the process of preparation at the district level there was a chance of only one in six thousand that they would pass the highest metropolitan examination. Only approximately three hundred aspiring scholars passed the examination every three years and were presented to the throne (hence "presented scholar") for a supplementary examination before the emperor. The top three were specially singled out for high honors and were appointed to the Hanlin ("forest of brushes") Academy, the highest central government establishment of learning charged with composing important documents and official works; the first-place graduate (*zhuangyuan*) stood at the pinnacle of the empire-wide scholar elite.

Not surprisingly in view of the competition, the examination system exerted a pervasive influence on the scholar-official class. It engendered a powerful, if not homogeneous, self-conception among the ruling bureaucratic elite, the anointed custodians of the teachings of Confucianism (*mingjiao*). As such, whatever their political subordination to the omnipotent monarch, this class stood apart from the emperor, Son of Heaven, who was the preserver of cosmic harmony and order as the beneficiary of the Mandate of Heaven. Moreover, the class was driven by a strong ethic of service from Neo-Confucian teaching to "improve the world" (*jingshi*). For scholar-bureaucrats, intellectual study as a passive activity went hand-in-hand with active public service—each informed the other. This imperative of the "unity of knowledge and action" was deeply imbedded in the moral vision of the scholar-official.

Of course, no single career pattern governed the life of the scholar-official. Some officials served mainly in the central government, some in the provincial administrations; some served all of their lives, some in only one or two posts. Wang Huizu (1731–1807) was one who exemplified the culture of this class. Wang's family was from Zhejiang province in east central China, part of the academically prominent Jiangnan region of the lower Yangzi valley. His father, who was a minor county official, died when he was ten and his family struggled in poverty. Wang nevertheless passed the first examination at the prefectural level in 1747 at sixteen to earn the *shengyuan* ("born official") degree. This lowest level degree did not qualify the recipient for office but did confer a respected status. Instead Wang became a private secretary, first with his father-in-law who was a district magistrate and specialized in judicial affairs. He served in this capacity for thirty-four years under sixteen different officials in Jiangsu and Zhejiang, becoming an expert in local provincial judicial administration. In the meantime he received the second level *juren* ("recommended man") degree at the provincial examination in 1768, and finally the highest *jinshi* ("presented scholar") degree at the metropolitan examination in Beijing in 1775 after failing the examination three times. The *jinshi* degree qualified Wang for appointment as a district magistrate in Hunan province. He served in two further appointments as magistrate in 1788 and 1790 in Hunan before retiring in 1793. After retirement Wang devoted himself to scholarship. He produced two celebrated guides to local administration printed in 1785 and 1793 based on his long experience as a private secretary. Late in life he developed a strong interest in practical history and compiled an index in sixty-four volumes (*juan*) to biographies in the twenty-four official dynastic histories, completed in 1783, and two guides to historical works published in 1790 and 1801.

Wang's interests did not extend to philosophy and literature, including poetry, which was the case with many other scholar-literati. But he was acquainted with a large number of prominent scholars of the day, such as the famous historian Zhang Xuecheng and Zhu Yun, the instigator of the *Complete Library of the Four Treasuries* under the Qianlong emperor. Such scholars and officials belonged to a nation-wide intellectual community among whom ideas and scholarly work were constantly circulated.

A counterpoint to Wang Huizu, who illustrates the spectrum of official careers, was Chen Hongmou (1696–1771). Chen was from the southern province of Guangxi, a relatively poor and academically disadvantaged region compared to the Jiangnan region where Wang Huizu was raised. Guangxi was the home of several ethnic minority populations, but Chen was Chinese Han. He achieved the *shengyuan* degree in 1716 at nineteen and in 1723 passed both the second and third level examinations. He held several central government positions before being appointed prefect (an administrator of a prefecture, a division of a province comprising a number of districts) in Jiangsu province in 1729. Thus began Chen's long career in provincial administration, rising from mid-level positions in which he generally distinguished himself, to provincial governorships in seven different provinces (three separate appointments in Shaanxi province) and governor-general of Guangdong and Guangxi. In 1763 Chen returned to Beijing, rising to Grand Secretary. Upon retirement in 1771 just before he died he was awarded the esteemed honorary title of Grand Tutor to the Heir Apparent. Chen would not have had such a remarkable and distinguished career serving at the highest levels of regional and central government if he had not enjoyed the trust and confidence successively of both the Yongzheng and Qianlong emperors. Though Chen, like Wang Huizu, was not noted for philosophical and literary works (he condemned the writing of poetry and belles lettres as useless), he compiled compendia of abstracts on community life, education of youth, education of women, and morality in official life: He was an administration maven.

CONQUEST AND ACCULTURATION

A central concern of Chen Hongmou was the acculturation and education of non-Han ethnic minority peoples of the northwest and southeast regions of China Proper, where he served extensively as provincial governor. Chen's conviction that Han, Manchu, and ethnic minority peoples all belonged to a common, shared humanity, possessing equal moral and intellectual capacities, comported very well with his patron the Yongzheng emperor's explicit policies. While the Manchu emperors embraced an inclusive cultural world view of shared historical legitimacy with all peoples, as reflected in the Kangxi emperor's Valedictory Edict, they did not thereby surrender their Manchu cultural identity. Nurhaci had required all subjects of his expanding empire to adopt the unique Manchu hairstyle (the head shaved in front, hair braided in a queue in back) as a means of counteracting tendencies toward ethnic-racial separatism. At the same time the rhetoric of his and his successors' state was rooted in Manchu origins and culture, and involved such separatist measures as a ban on Manchu-Chinese intermarriage and prohibition of Chinese Han immigration to Manchuria, reinforced by the construction of the Willow Palisades across southern Liaodong.

Manchu rule and Manchu identity presented a paradox. The problem for the Manchus as a conquest elite, unlike that for the Mongols before them, was that they chose not to rule China remotely from their homeland in Manchuria but to immigrate south of the Great Wall into China Proper. Dorgon made it a policy to move the Manchu banners and supporting population into north China, where they were resettled on lands expropriated from Han population especially in the region surrounding Beijing. Forced to abandon their former mobility and economic reliance on booty, it would be only a matter of time before they inevitably lost their frontier tribal customs and way of life that were so much the source of their formidable military power. Much later, in the mid-nineteenth century, the Western imperialist powers, barbarian invaders in their own way, arrived in China by sea. The contrast with the Manchu conquest is instructive. The Westerners ruled by remote control, from foreign enclaves in treaty port cities. Only sojourners in China, while remaining securely at home in their own countries, they could exert their cultural influence immunized by their physical separation from the traditional force of assimilation exerted by Chinese civilization.

The Manchus made strenuous efforts to resist sinification and preserve their ethnic and cultural identity. During the minority of the Kangxi emperor, the Oboi regency reversed the assimilationist policies of Dorgon and the Shunzhi emperor, but following his assumption of personal rule, the emperor resumed the former policies, encouraging and promoting Han Chinese in the court and establishing the Southern Study (*nanshufang*) in the imperial palace, where he could consult and study with Chinese scholars. The Chinese cultural elite exerted a tremendous seductive attraction for all levels of the Manchu conquest elite (this corps of Manchu officers may have numbered no more than two thousand individuals). For the emperors from Kangxi to Qianlong, on down the Manchu hierarchy, southern culture of the lower Yangzi Jiangnan region was irresistibly fascinating—manifested in the numerous southern tours made by both the Kangxi and Qianlong emperors. Nothing could contrast more with the cold, rugged northern frontier than the sensuality of southern life and the soft natural beauty of the landscape. Manchu bannermen stationed in garrisons south of the Great Wall, with little occasion to exercise their martial skills in a time of peace and stability, and living in enforced idleness while they were prohibited from entering trades and professions, were softened by exposure to the refined culture of the leisured Chinese literati and became immersed in theatre, drama, music, painting, poetry, raising flowers, and keeping pets. Rather quickly the formerly fearsome Manchu warriors lost their social distinctiveness and became progressively impoverished as their limited stipends were absorbed in maintaining a life of ease, striving to emulate the life of the literati. Manchus and Mongols both lost the ability to use and understand their native languages. The Qianlong emperor was outraged when in audiences Manchus were unable to speak coherently in Manchu, for which he severely castigated them.

This erosion of Manchu culture was fatal. By the late eighteenth century the vaunted eight banners had become useless as a mainstay of imperial power. Although the Qianlong emperor became obsessed with preserving "Manchuness" and exhorted his Manchu subjects to practice the old ways of Manchu speech, riding, and archery, in which he was proud of his own competence, by the late eighteenth century the course of sinicization had gone so far that any efforts to restore Manchu nativism were of no avail. Sinicization of the Manchus had proceeded inexorably from the inception of Manchu rule, from the Kangxi emperor's unapologetic admiration for Chinese civilization, through patronage of Chinese literati and Confucian institutions—the Qianlong emperor visited the Confucian shrine at Confucius' birthplace in Shandong nine times—to mastery of Han culture by the Qianlong emperor.

The distinction between Confucianization and sinicization may be raised again here. There is no doubt that the Manchus were Confucianized. They mastered the Confucian Classics, competed successfully in the civil service examination system, wrote and practiced traditional Confucian literature and arts, debated state policy in Confucian terms, and associated eagerly with Chinese Confucian scholar-literati. In many of these respects the Mongols of the Yuan were also Confucianized. But they were not sinicized to the same degree. They preserved their native language, their ethnic identity with their steppe heritage, and their social customs. The Manchus, on the other hand, however much they may have made gestures toward cultural preservation, lost their native language, their traditional customs, and their connection with their frontier roots. They were progressively sinicized. Only because their names were different were they forced to acknowledge that they were Manchu, not Han.

The harbingers of a very different cultural order, challenging both Chinese and Manchu alike, had already appeared in China by the late Ming.

Jesuit missionaries had arrived at Macau, the Portuguese settlement established in the mid-sixteenth century on the south China coast near Canton, and by the end of the century had penetrated the Ming empire and were slowly working their way up to Beijing, their destination. To the extent that Jesuit Christian teachings posed a radical challenge to a still vital Confucian ideology, the challenge was premature, conversions were limited to a few members of the scholar-literati elite, and their impact was small. After the conquest, the Manchu elite at first appeared to be more receptive to the Christian message, perhaps because their more naive indigenous shamanistic religious culture presented less of an obstacle to sophisticated Christian faith. The Shunzhi emperor (r. 1644–1661) fell under the influence of the Jesuit missionary Adam Schall von Bell, so much so that the emperor addressed him affectionately as "grandpa."

For a time it seemed that the Jesuits would achieve their ultimate goal of converting the emperor of China, after which the whole country would presumably incline to their message. But the moment passed. What was really the vector of the Jesuit influence was their mediation of Western mathematics and astronomy, in which they assiduously developed their skills, knowing the value the Chinese placed on calendrical science. Western influence through the Jesuits reached its height in the Kangxi reign when the emperor admitted them to his court and where he carried on extensive conversations over mathematics and astronomy as well as Christian doctrine. But when in 1705 papal legate Bishop Maillard de Tournon arrived in China to condemn the Jesuit policy that accommodated Christian practices to Chinese rites (the Dominicans had vehemently objected that ancestor worship was a religious practice, not a benign secular social observance, that violated Christian doctrine), the emperor would not compromise and the entire evangelical mission came to an end by 1742. Although Western science had a lasting impact on China, Christianity did not touch the bedrock of Confucian culture.

The eighteenth-century Jesuit Catholic enterprise, though a failure, was the prelude to the late nineteenth-century Protestant Christian assault on China, which brought with it much of the rest of Western cultural influence. Unlike the Manchus, whose invasion was unheralded by any cultural influence on China, the Western invasion of China was prefigured by its first impact on the China coast. Early Western experience in China of the Jesuits was similar to the Manchu experience: cultural assimilation could come only on Chinese terms. But later a change took place. The Manchus could conquer (and administer) China but could not dominate it culturally without themselves becoming acculturated—indeed successful conquest was ultimately dependent on cultural assimilation. The West came to dominate China culturally (at least in part) but ultimately could not really conquer it. Conquest in a true sense had to occur on Chinese cultural terms. Thus the West sealed itself off in cultural and political enclaves whereas the Manchu enclave in the northeast was a way station to cultural absorption.

SUGGESTED READINGS

Atwell, William S. "From Education to Politics: The Fu She," in William T. de Bary, ed., *The Unfolding of Neo-Confucianism* (New York: Columbia University Press, 1975), 333–367. A useful account of the principal political faction at the end of the Ming.

Backhouse, E., and J. O. P. Bland. *Annals and Memoirs of the Court of Peking* (Taipei: Ch'eng Wen Publishing Co. (reprint), 1970). A subjective, dated, and not entirely reliable, but entertaining narrative of events and personalities from the end of the Ming to the end of the Qing.

Brown, Claudia. *The Great Qing: Painting in China, 1644–1911* (Seattle: University of Washington Press, 2014). An excellent coverage of painting during the Qing.

Chang, Michael G. *A Court on Horseback: Imperial Touring and the Construction of Qing Rule, 1680–1785* (Cambridge: Harvard University Press, 2007). Impressive imperial tours of southern China by the Kangxi and Qianlong emperors were an essential means to gauge popular acceptance of Manchu rule and assert imperial power.

Crossley, Pamela Kyle. *A Translucent Mirror: History and Identity in Qing Imperial Ideology* (Berkeley: University of California Press, 1999). An excellent exploration of Manchu-Chinese cultural identity focusing on the Qianlong reign.

Crossley, Pamela Kyle. *The Manchus* (Oxford: Blackwell Publishers, 2002). A general history of the Manchus by a leading student of the Qing dynasty.

Crossley, Pamela Kyle. *Orphan Warriors: Three Manchu Generations at the End of the Qing World* (Princeton: Princeton University Press, 1990). In this and the previous book (*The Manchus*), the foremost scholar of the Manchus in the Qing examines the significance of Manchu rule and culture.

de Bary, W. T. *The Trouble with Confucianism* (Cambridge: Harvard University Press, 1991). In six insightful essays one of the most eminent students of Confucian thought discusses the tensions and predicaments within the Confucian tradition.

de Bary, William Theodore, ed. *The Unfolding of Neo-Confucianism* (New York: Columbia University Press, 1975). An anthology of fourteen articles on the thought and practice of Neo-Confucianism.

Elliott, Mark C. *Emperor Qianlong: Son of Heaven, Man of the World*. Library of World Biography, Peter Stearns, ed. (New York: Longman, 2009). A brief popular study of one of the greatest Qing emperors.

Elliott, Mark C. *The Manchu Way: The Eight Banners and Ethnic Identity in Late Imperial China* (Stanford: Stanford University Press, 2001). The characteristic military-social institution that encompassed all Manchus since the early seventeenth century before the Manchu conquest is analyzed here in the context of Manchu cultural identity.

Fairbank, John K. ed. *The Cambridge History of China*, vol. 10, *Late Ch'ing, 1800–1911, Part 1* (Cambridge: Cambridge University Press, 1978).

Fairbank, John K., and Kwang-Ching Liu, eds. *The Cambridge History of China*, vol. 11, *Late Ch'ing, 1800–1911, Part 2* (Cambridge: Cambridge University Press, 1980).

Feuerwerker, Albert. *State and Society in Eighteenth-Century China: The Ch'ing Empire in Its Glory* (Ann Arbor: University of Michigan, Center for Chinese Studies, Michigan Papers in Chinese Studies no. 27, 1976). This short monograph studies social and political dimensions of the "High Qing."

Guy, R. Kent. *Qing Governors and Their Provinces: The Evolution of Territorial Administration in China, 1644–1796* (Seattle: University of Washington Press, 2010).

Hummel, Arthur W., ed. *Eminent Chinese of the Ch'ing Period (1644–1912)*, 2 vols. (Washington, D.C.: Library of Congress, 1943–1944). In spite of its age this remains the essential comprehensive biographical reference for the Qing.

Kahn, Harold L. *Monarchy in the Emperor's Eyes: Image and Reality in the Ch'ien-lung Reign* (Cambridge: Harvard University Press, 1971). A detailed study of the construction of the imperial persona as seen in the Qianlong emperor.

Meyer-Fong, Tobie. *Building Culture in Early Qing Yangzhou* (Stanford: Stanford University Press, 2003). Following its destruction in the Manchu invasion, the reconstruction of Yangzhou cultural monuments is examined in four case studies.

Mote, F. W. *Imperial China, 900–1800* (Cambridge: Harvard University Press, 1999). The most comprehensive treatment of Chinese history from the end of the Tang through the early Qing dynasties. An extremely useful reference, with the caveat that the index has many lacunae.

Naquin, Susan, and Evelyn S. Rawski. *Chinese Society in the Eighteenth Century* (New Haven and London: Yale University Press, 1987). An examination of political, social, and economic themes in Qing China, focusing on the flourishing of related institutions in the eighteenth century.

Peterson, Willard J., ed. *The Cambridge History of China*, vol. 9, *The Ch'ing Empire to 1800*, Part 1 (Cambridge: Cambridge University Press, 2002). *The Cambridge History of China* volumes 9, 10, and 11 (like the twin volumes on the Ming) are the standard authorities of the Qing dynasty by leading scholars of their respective fields.

Rowe, William T. *China's Last Empire: The Great Qing* (Cambridge: Harvard University Press, 2009). A thoughtful, comprehensive history of China under the Qing empire organized into ten chapters on various thematic subjects, including government, society, commerce, rebellion, restoration, imperialism, and revolution.

Rowe, William T. *Saving the World: Chen Hongmou and Elite Consciousness in Eighteenth-Century China* (Stanford: Stanford University Press, 2001). A masterful study of the career of an influential scholar-official reformer in the eighteenth century.

Smith, Richard J. *China's Cultural Heritage: The Ch'ing Dynasty, 1644–1912* (Boulder: Westview Press, 1983). A fascinating and informative description of the many dimensions of elite and popular culture in the Qing period.

Spence, Jonathan D. *Emperor of China: Self-portrait of K'ang-hsi* (New York: Alfred A. Knopf, 1974). An intriguing portrait of the Qing's most remarkable emperor skillfully presented in his own words by one of the most intellectually fertile China scholars.

Spence, Jonathan D. *Ts'ao Yin and the K'ang-hsi Emperor: Bondservant and Master* (New Haven: Yale University Press, 1966). A masterful examination of the relationship between a powerful Chinese bondservant and his emperor and the secret memorial system created by the emperor to communicate with his trusted advisers.

Wakeman, Frederic, Jr. *The Fall of Imperial China* (New York: The Free Press, 1975). An excellent textbook covering the period from the end of the Ming to the end of the Qing. Early very useful chapters examine peasants, gentry, merchants, and the dynastic cycle.

Wakeman, Frederic, Jr. "High Ch'ing: 1683–1839," in James B. Crowley, ed., *Modern East Asia: Essays in Interpretation* (New York: Harcourt, Brace, World, 1970), 1–28. This essay is the origin of the characterization of seventeenth-century Qing as the "High Qing."

NOTES

1. Quoted from Jonathan Spence, *Emperor of China: Self-portrait of K'ang-hsi* (New York: Alfred A. Knopf, 1974), 144–145.

2. The collection is now contained largely in the National Palace Museums of Beijing, China, and Taibei, Taiwan.

10

Imperial Absolutism
Monarch and Minister

Huang Zongxi (1610–1695), one of the most eminent Confucian scholars of the seventeenth century, spanned the Manchu conquest and remained an implacable Ming loyalist, refusing to serve the Qing in spite of earnest efforts to attract him. His essay, "A Record of Perseverance in Adversity in a Time of Darkness" (Mingyi daifang lu), was a devastating indictment of imperial despotism:

> In ancient times All Under Heaven was the master, the sovereign was the guest. The sovereign's whole life was devoted to being the custodian of All Under Heaven. Now the sovereign is the master, All Under Heaven is the guest. Everywhere there is no place under Heaven left in peace and quiet by the sovereign. Hence to get what he doesn't have, he slaughters the flesh and blood of All Under Heaven, casts asunder the sons and daughters of All Under Heaven, in order to extend his own personal possessions, with never the slightest remorse, saying: I must secure my descendants' inheritance. Having attained this, he then crushes the marrow of All Under Heaven, disperses the sons and daughters of All Under Heaven, in order to serve his own personal lust, considering it as natural, saying: This is the benefit of my personal property. Thus the one who brings the greatest harm to All Under Heaven is none other than the sovereign himself.[1]

His indictment applied as much to the Ming as the Qing.

Always hanging over the Ming and Qing rulers was the imputation of illegitimate power, authority not founded on the realization of the perfect moral order that prevailed in antiquity. The Record of Rites (Li Ji), a Classic allegedly dating from the Zhou era before the age of Confucius, famously asserted that when the Great Way (Da dao) prevailed, All Under Heaven belonged to the public realm (tianxia wei gong), that is, the universal order inhered in the communal

151

sphere. Here was a simple but powerful idea that the realm was a community, not the property of one or a few. Only when the Great Unity (Da tong), a utopian concept of a perfect harmonious order, declined, came the rise of dynastic rule, with the implication that dynastic rule was somehow not only imperfect but illegitimate.

Another renowned Ming loyalist Gu Yanwu (1613–1682) also wrote a critique of centralized authoritarian government advocating, however quixotically, a return to the decentralized quasi-feudalism of ancient times. If local provincial officials served permanently and hereditarily in one place, rather than being frequently rotated out and banned from serving near their home districts, they would exhibit a strong attachment to serving the people responsibly.

Remarkably, neither Huang Zongxi nor Gu Yanwu were punished for their antiauthoritarian views. The Kangxi emperor hoped to overcome their refusal to serve the new dynasty by wooing them with honors. But the *Mingyi daifang lu* was proscribed during the Qing, and though it may have tarnished the luster of the emperor, it had little or no effect on imperial power, which grew during the course of the dynasty.

Before we examine further the problem of imperial absolutism in the High Qing, we must clarify the meaning of various terms for this phenomenon. *Absolutism* is the exercise of unconditional power, usually by an individual, thus an *autocrat*. *Autocracy* by extension is supreme government by an individual claiming independent or self-derived power, an autocrat, usually connoting a monarch or other civil or secular ruler. Absolutism and/or autocracy do not in themselves necessarily imply illegitimate or tyrannical power. *Despotism*, the rule of a *despot*, on the other hand, though in certain circumstances may describe the condition of absolutism or autocracy, refers to arbitrary, oppressive, unjust, and illegitimate exercise of power. However, absolutism or absolute rule may involve *personal rule*, the exercise of power unmediated or unrestrained by established institutions. Huang Zongxi's essay, *Mingyi daifang lu*, in its rhetorical thrust is especially an indictment of despotism. Note that unconditional power is not unlimited power; all power is limited in some way, whether by physical, moral, institutional, or other restraints. Finally, we must differentiate power from *authority*. The latter is understood to derive not from coercive force but from concepts of moral or legal right, that may or may not provide legitimacy for the exercise of power.

In practice, the power of the emperor was always mitigated by the civil service bureaucracy as a whole or by individual officials, especially the emperor's ministers serving at the highest levels of government. Moreover, concentration of power in the emperor's hands was sometimes itself a source of weakness that limited his power. But the power of the emperor was enhanced by the weakness of alternative sources of power and authority that were capable of challenging his own.

One check on absolutism in early times was the "prime minister" or chief councilor, who, as the leading regular official of the realm, mitigated the authority of the monarch. But the prime ministerial function had declined since the Northern Song when powerful chief councilors such as Wang Anshi and Ouyang Xiu had dominated their age, though with often radically competing agendas. Even so, no minister was ever able to maintain his preeminence for very long lacking imperial favor. The chief councilor was never free from the suspicion of usurpation of power, if not from the emperor himself then from jealous officials who constantly undermined his position. The death knell for the prime ministership finally came early in the Ming when the vastly powerful Hu Weiyong, chief councilor to the Hongwu emperor, was purged and executed in 1380 when the paranoid monarch believed he was conspiring to over-throw the emperor (though there may have been some truth in the sus-picion). The Hongwu emperor famously decreed that the position never be resurrected by his successors, and his wish was respected even by the Manchus, though no doubt for different reasons. One consequence of this truncated government was that the emperor had to assume the burden of daily attention to administration formerly carried by his chief minister. This did not work very well for many Ming emperors, the most notable being the Wanli emperor (1573–1620), who refused to see his ministers or appear in court for years at a time. The early Qing emperors, however, were exemplars of administrative diligence.

PERSONAL RULE

During the reign of the Shunzhi emperor (1644–1661) the tendency to-ward growing autocracy that had begun under his predecessor Hong Taiji and his uncle Prince Regent Dorgon was temporarily reversed fol-lowing the regent's death in 1650. Dorgon was a powerful exponent of enhanced imperial power and the corresponding reduction of the power of the Manchu princes, pursued especially through the process of sinici-zation. The Shunzhi emperor continued sinicization, employing Chinese as officials and advisers. He revived the Thirteen Offices, the Ming system of eunuch administration, which became a kind of personal bureaucracy under the powerful chief eunuch Wu Liangfu. The traditional conserva-tive Manchu princes, increasingly sidelined by Dorgon, brooded over their reduced influence. Dorgon had aspired to imperial power himself.

When he died prematurely in 1650 at the age of only thirty-eight, the conservatives moved to purge his supporters and rescind his policies. Though the Shunzhi emperor assumed direct rule with the end of Dorgon's regency, the influence of the conservatives, who wished to preserve original Manchu governing institutions and the collegial tribal feudal leadership bequeathed by Nurhaci, was pervasive. The emperor's physical constitution was weak. When he died of smallpox in 1661 at the age of only twenty-two, the conservative leaders conspired to produce a forged will, an imperial mea culpa that confessed to mistaken policies of sinicization and improper reliance on eunuchs. The new emperor, his father's third son, named heir because he had survived smallpox and was thus immune from the disease, ascended the throne as the Kangxi emperor at the age of seven. Necessarily, the conservative faction led by Manchu regent Oboi ruled in his name, confirming traditional Manchu influence and opposition to sinicization.

Rankling under the arrogant domination of Oboi, who one by one eliminated the other regents, the emperor quietly bided his time. In 1669, with the support of Manchu banner guardsmen, he deftly acted to remove Oboi and assumed personal rule at the age of fifteen. The Kangxi emperor's long reign (1662–1722) of sixty years witnessed the irreversible resumption of sinicization and the reliance on Chinese institutions and advisers. His reign laid the foundations of Manchu-Chinese synarchy. Autocratic rule was enhanced with the inauguration of a secret palace memorial system and use of bondservants as personal agents to replace eunuchs in an expanding imperial household bureaucracy. But the Kangxi emperor was no despot. He exhibited unusual leniency toward corruption and official failures. He confessed he did "not like killing," and unlike Zhu Yuanzhang, the Ming Hongwu emperor, there were no mass executions under his reign. Indeed, his failure sometimes to act decisively was seen as weakness that undermined imperial authority.

The most serious manifestation of the emperor's indecision was the succession crisis that preoccupied the last fifteen years of his reign from 1708 to 1722. The Manchus had no established procedure for choosing the ruler's successor, unlike the Chinese system by which the heir was the eldest son by the principal empress. Instead, since the death of Nurhaci when a council of Manchu elders and princes chose Hong Taiji, the heir apparent could be any legitimate son of the emperor. Yinreng, the emperor's second son, was named heir apparent in 1676, but over the next three decades it became clear that he was incompetent, corrupt, and unfilial. He was deposed by the emperor in 1708, brought back later, and finally deposed for good in 1712, without a successor being named. Factions formed around Yinreng and others among the emperor's sons, creating constant turmoil within the court that sullied the last years of the reign. The issue remained unresolved until the emperor's death in 1722.

With the accession in 1722 of the Kangxi emperor's fourth son, Yinzhen, to the throne as the Yongzheng emperor, the tentative and formative nature of the previous period was brought to an end. The Yongzheng emperor's relatively short reign of only thirteen years ending in 1735 was eclipsed by the spectacular reigns of his father and son, each occupying the throne for sixty years. But the Yongzheng reign was a turning point toward greatly enhanced personal rule. The new emperor, then already in middle age, displayed an obsessive attention to minute detail, reviewing memorials and reports from his officials and ministers and responding with lengthy rescripts, often working long into the night. He was a "workaholic" and perhaps that contributed to his unexpected early death. But more than any other emperor he was the quintessential autocrat.

During the first years of his reign the Yongzheng emperor concentrated on the vigorous suppression of cliques persisting from the last years of his father's reign. Only when the festering factionalism that continued to surround his brothers was eliminated could stable imperial rule prevail. This involved sometimes ruthless action against Manchu princes and their official allies alike. Only one of his numerous brothers, Prince Yinxiang, the thirteenth, escaped his wrath to become his trusted confidant. The emperor wrote extensively and at length in an argumentative and admonitory style in edicts and discourses. Addressing the danger of factionalism, he wrote a "Discourse on Factions" (*pengdang lun*) that condemned factions and cliques among officials. His argument used the identical title of the celebrated essay of the Northern Song statesman Ouyang Xiu (1007–1072), but whereas the latter defended responsible alliances among like-minded officials, the Yongzheng emperor drew the opposite conclusion. Categorically rejecting all alliances among officials, the emperor's essay unequivocally asserted the absolute moral and political authority of the monarch and the proper subordination of subject to ruler. The ruler's authority was absolute and unchallengeable:

> Worthy men are the men of whom We approve, and you ought therefore to approve of them; unworthy men are the men We dislike, and you ought therefore to dislike them. . . . A man's greatest duties are his duty to his prince and his duty to his parents. Suppose a man's father has an enemy and the son is friendly with him; or suppose the father is fond of someone and the son takes him as an enemy. Is this the right course for a son? In sum, only if each man takes his prince's likes and dislikes as his own will everyone be able to reform his evil ways and turn to the good. For prince and minister to be of one mind means good fortune for the state.[2]

THE POWER OF SECRECY

The instrument of the Yongzheng emperor's autocratic government and the medium through which he communicated with his officials in writing was the palace memorial, the system inaugurated by his predecessor the Kangxi emperor. Communication through secret palace memorials (*zouzhe*), unlike open, routine official memorials (*tiben*), was conducted in secret. Palace memorials bypassed the cumbersome and slow process of reception, registration, and viewing by regular central government offices; they were sent directly to the emperor by separate personal couriers, often for his eyes only. They were in practice therefore far more personal, informal, and often intimate, enabling the emperor to rely on trusted officials on a personal basis. The development of the palace memorial system went hand-in-hand with another agency of imperial autocracy established in the Yongzheng reign, the Grand Council (*junji chu*) (literally, bureau of military affairs). It was established in 1726 as an ad hoc group of high metropolitan officials advising the emperor on military campaigns in central Asia early in the reign. The Council could act quickly and expeditiously, bypassing the ponderous processes of the central ministries. Communication between the councilors and the emperor was by palace memorials. The Grand Council, however, had no autonomous power or even at first any formal legal existence, and thus in no way diminished the monarch's power. Members of the Council, high Manchu and Chinese officials, served concurrently with their formal official positions and ranks by which they were identified.

The inception of the Grand Council significantly diminished the role of the Outer Court, the formal institutions of central government including principally the Grand Secretariat and the Six Ministries. The process of decision making, formerly visible in open consultation among metropolitan and provincial officials, was now increasingly hidden from public view. Communicating individually with his trusted advisers, only the emperor was fully aware of all aspects of the formation and implementation of policies. Those officials authorized to communicate through palace memorials could report secretly to the emperor on the activities and behavior of other officials. This had a powerful psychological effect on all officials who might be confronted by the emperor. What did the emperor know and how did he know it? The emperor became omniscient. Officials never knew who might be reporting on them. Since all reporting officials could report cases of malfeasance and corruption, or even trivial breaches of etiquette, they all in effect became censors, and the formal and more public censorial function was correspondingly eclipsed.

The content of palace memorials was virtually uninhibited by formal rules and ritual observances and could involve any subject, from important issues of policy and military campaigns, to detailed reports on weather conditions, market prices of commodities, popular moods, minute reports on activities and movements of officials, and intimate references to details of personal life. The language of the Yongzheng emperor's rescripts, written in vermillion ink interlineally or at the end of memorials, later returned to the memorialist, could be flattering, candid, and even sometimes brutally frank and personal:

> When you were serving in the Board [of Punishments] you were an outstanding official. As soon as you are posted to the provinces, however, you take on disgusting habits of indecisiveness and decadence. It is really detestable . . . you take your sweet time about sending in memorials and there isn't a word of truth in them! You have really disappointed my trust in you, you ingrate of a *thing!*[3]

Palace memorials were always person to person, never office to office. They were the vehicle by which the emperor developed extraordinary personal relationships and reliance on his most trusted officials. Reporting officials were forbidden to share the content of palace memorials with others and were required to write them personally, not delegate them to their secretaries (which presented a difficulty for less skilled memorialists).

THE TRUSTED MINISTER

Zhang Tingyu (1672–1755) rose in the metropolitan administration in the late Kangxi reign, when his father served as grand secretary. He received his *jinshi* degree in 1700, served in the emperor's Southern Study and thereafter was promoted to senior ministerial offices. Upon the Yongzheng emperor's accession, he enjoyed the emperor's particular favor, rising to the office of grand secretary in 1725. When the Grand Council was created, Zhang became one of the first grand councilors, serving continuously there until his retirement in 1750. The emperor bestowed many honors and gifts on his trusted minister, including the highest honor that could be conferred on an official, posthumous enrollment in the Imperial Ancestral Hall. After the Yongzheng emperor's death, his successor the Qianlong emperor continued to rely on Zhang. By this time he was getting old, but his repeated requests for permission to retire were not granted until 1750. He had served for fifty years.

It was held that the emperor's trust in his minister should be reciprocated unquestioningly. The Qianlong emperor, more than his father, was vindictive and intolerant of officials' weaknesses. When Zhang Tingyu sought assurance that the promise of posthumous enrollment in the Imperial Ancestral Hall would be honored after his death, the emperor was naturally annoyed. No doubt age clouded Zhang's judgment. Ceremony and the observance of proper ritual were all-important. Zhang committed two serious ceremonial faux pas, sending his son in his place to the palace to thank the emperor for the confirmation of his honor and announcing his retirement departure at the time the emperor's eldest son had died. The emperor, furious, rescinded the posthumous honor. Even so, Zhang had served a long and distinguished career and the emperor restored the honor after Zhang's death in 1755. He was the only Han Chinese official ever to be so honored.[4] Serving under the personal rule of three autocrats in succession, Zhang Tingyu was an exemplar of the loyal and trusted minister.

The parallel career of Nian Gengyao is a lesson in the perils inherent in the life of such a trusted minister. Nian Gengyao (d. 1726) was a member of the Chinese Bordered Yellow Banner, one of the upper three banners under the emperor's control. His father had been a provincial governor and, like Zhang Tingyu, Nian received his *jinshi* degree in 1700 and subsequently served for a time in the central government. His sister became a concubine of Yinzhen, the future Yongzheng emperor. In the meantime Nian was appointed governor and then governor-general of the western province of Sichuan. Unfortunately, he became involved in the factional politics surrounding the succession to the Kangxi emperor and supported Yinzhen's brother Yinti for a time. When Yinzhen ascended the throne in 1722 he was nevertheless reconciled with Nian, and showered him with honors; their communications through palace memorials were exceptionally personal and informal. Commanding the expanding Qing conquests in Tibet and central Asia at this time, Nian now had risen to a position of great influence, regarded as a hero. But his power made him arrogant—it was claimed that he sat in the emperor's presence—and it is said that supporters in Sichuan erected shrines to him, an act of lèse-majesté. He lost the favor of the emperor, who chastised him in memorials. Impeached by other officials, perhaps out of jealousy, he lost his command and was degraded in rank. In 1726 a bill of indictment of his misdemeanors listed ninety-two crimes. He was sentenced to be executed but was permitted to commit suicide. It is probable that the emperor was determined long before to get rid of Nian Gengyao because he knew too much about the disputed succession.[5] One has to wonder, "What was he thinking?" If Nian had only behaved in a manner befitting a humble, loyal minister before a fearsome, all-powerful autocrat, might he have been spared? In somewhat less portentous but likewise critical circumstances, what explains the ethical lapses of Zhang Tingyu, or of the eminent and powerful Ming Grand Secretary Zhang Juzheng under the Wanli emperor, who violated the indispensable Confucian mourning ritual of retirement on the death of a parent? Both should have known they were treading on thin ice.

By the early eighteenth century, Manchu and Chinese high officials were serving the state in comparable roles. Ortai (1680–1745) exemplified the crucial influence that increasingly sinified Manchus could have in the highest levels of government. A member of the Bordered Blue Banner, commanding a knowledge of both Manchu and Chinese, Ortai earned his *juren* degree in 1669 and thereafter served in the Imperial Household. He advanced to become governor-general of Yunnan and Guizhou in 1726 and governor-general of Guangxi in 1728, successfully dealing with ethnic minority issues that were salient in those provinces, including the pacification of the Miao aborigines. In the course of his career he was accorded numerous honors by the Yongzheng emperor. He was promoted to grand secretary in 1732, president of the board of war, and the grand council where he served as a faithful adviser to the emperor. He continued in this capacity under the Qianlong emperor, and was rewarded, like Zhang Tingyu, with enrollment in the Imperil Ancestral Hall. During his illustrious career as a scholar-official Ortai was an influential patron of both Manchu and Chinese officials.

All of these examples illuminate the perennial problem of the delicate relationship between monarch and minister, however trusted he may be.

IMPERIAL PARANOIA

The instruments of autocratic personal rule forged in the Kangxi and Yongzheng reigns, the secret palace memorial system of communication and the Grand Council operating directly under the emperor, were perpetuated under the Qianlong emperor (1736–1796). What began as ad hoc responses to specific exigencies became routinized institutions. The Qianlong emperor did not share the intensity and obsessive attention to administrative detail of his father. He abandoned or reversed some of the more severe and interventionist fiscal and economic policies of the Yongzheng emperor, opting for a more laissez-faire style of government. However, he was if anything less tolerant of small failings, to say nothing of large transgressions, of his officials. His vermillion rescripts were short and to the point, not the long diatribes of his father. The decline of Zhang Tingyu's fortunes from the Yongzheng to the Qianlong reigns reveals not only the weakness of a long-serving loyal minister in old age but the Qianlong emperor's demanding expectations of performance and his hypercritical attitude toward lapses in behavior.

Sensitivity regarding the alien origin of the Manchu dynasty was a preoccupation of every emperor, if not of their own subjects, ironically in spite of the progressive sinicization and acceptance of Manchu rule by the second half of the eighteenth century. The suspicion of sedition

lurked just below the surface of imperial satisfaction with Qing achievements. Some cases of alleged sedition turned out to be trivial or largely
imaginary. One of the strangest cases came to light in 1728. Yue Zhongqi
was the governor-general of Sichuan and Shaanxi provinces, posted at
the Shaanxi capital of Xi'an. Yue Zhongqi was a descendant of the great
Song hero General Yue Fei (1103–1142). After the Jurchen had conquered
north China in 1127, pushing the Song into the south and founding the Jin
dynasty, Yue Fei campaigned back into the territory north of the Yangzi
River, aiming to recover the north from the Jurchen. It was a brave cause,
popular but unlikely to succeed given greater Jurchen power. In the
meantime the Song court was negotiating a treaty with the Jurchen that
would involve buying them off with a large annual indemnity. Yue Fei's
actions jeopardized the treaty. He was lured back to Hangzhou, the Song
capital, where he was imprisoned and died in jail at the hands of the Song
chief councilor Qin Gui. Ever afterward he was perceived as the supreme
exemplar of loyalty and patriotism, betrayed by evil ministers. It is said
that on his back were imprinted the words *Loyal to the Last* (*jin zhong bao
guo*). He remains to this day the hero of the People's Liberation Army as
an exemplar of loyalty to the state.

The Manchus, descendants of the Jurchen, now ruled China. Yue
Zhongqi was believed by some to be plotting his own rebellion to requite
China's loss to the Jurchen and throw off Manchu rule. Because of his dubious historical association, it is somewhat surprising that the Yongzheng
emperor trusted Yue as much as he did. In 1728, Zeng Jing, an obscure
scholar from Hunan who had written a tract excoriating the emperor
and the Manchus and was plotting a revolt, sent a messenger to Xi'an to
persuade Yue to lead a rebellion. Yue Zhongqi naturally had to act with
great circumspection, given his illustrious ancestor. Any lapse in dealing
with the seditious proposal would have cast grave suspicion of treason
on himself. Through deft questioning of the messenger he managed to
trick him into revealing the scope of the plot by Zeng Jing. As the case unfolded, Zeng Jing and other parties to the plot (there were very few) were
identified, arrested, and brought to Beijing for interrogation. It emerged
that Zeng Jing had been deeply influenced by a well-respected late-Ming–
early-Qing scholar Lü Liuliang (1629–1683) who had written influential
essays on Neo-Confucian thought. Reexamining these tracts revealed that
Lü had condemned the barbarian origins of the Manchus. From the beginning the Yongzheng emperor took a very personal interest—it was after
all he who was attacked by Zeng Jing's tract—and carried on an intense
correspondence with Zeng while the latter was in confinement, bringing
him to confess and retract his charges, and to acknowledge the error of
his anti-Manchu sentiments.

Zeng Jing was pardoned in spite of considerable opposition from high officials including Prince Yinxiang, the emperor's brother and trusted advisor. A lengthy record of the case, *Dayi juemi lu* ("A Record of Righteous Principles to Awaken the Deluded"), was printed under the emperor's direction and distributed throughout the empire in 1730. For the Yongzheng emperor the purpose of the Record of Righteous Principles was to burnish the image of the Manchus as legitimate successor to the Mandate of Heaven and refute the significance of race in ruling China.[6]

This entire affair is reminiscent of the process of Thought Reform (*sixiang gaizao*) applied to class enemies and bourgeois restorationists in the Anti-Rightist Campaign and the Cultural Revolution in the 1950s and 1960s. Then, victims were subjected to an intense regimen of criticism, self-criticism, and confession leading to acceptance back into society as reborn "reds," exactly the process Zeng Jing was put through, instead of simple execution or imprisonment as enemies of the state. The Yongzheng emperor's paranoia and excessive concern with thought reform here is remarkable. It would have been so much simpler to execute the conspirators—the case for sedition was certainly proven. Indeed, reflecting their very different dispositions, the Qianlong emperor immediately upon ascending the throne in 1736 and disregarding his father's precedent, rearrested and executed Zeng Jing, banned the *Dayi juemi lu*, and ordered all copies sought out and destroyed.

A few years later in 1751 the specter of sedition reappeared in the case of the bogus memorial, confirming the Qianlong emperor's fears of an undercurrent of sedition running among his Han subjects. A spurious document purporting to be a memorial to the throne by a high official, Sun Jiagan, was discovered in Guizhou and soon appeared widely in other provinces. The false attribution of the memorial to Sun Jiagan was probably owing to his reputation for frankly remonstrating with the Yongzheng emperor, for which he had been alternately rewarded and punished. Although the emperor ordered every copy of the bogus memorial destroyed, it evidently leveled personal attacks on the emperor and challenged Manchu legitimacy. After a ruthless empire-wide investigation lasting two years, the alleged perpetrator, a low-ranking military official, was arrested and executed.

In an empire the size of the Qing with its vast population, one might expect a certain number of anomalous appearances of political dissidence, however perilous such acts might be for their authors. What is remarkable is the ferocity of the emperor's response to any such hints of sedition, suggesting a deep-seated anxiety about the security of Manchu rule, bordering on irrationality. Autocrats, the more autocratic they are, do not rule with great peace of mind.

The most bizarre case of alleged sedition arose in 1768 in the great Sorcery Scare. A popular belief held that if a person possessing occult powers, a sorcerer, clipped some hair from a victim he could possess the soul of that person for nefarious ends. By blowing or scattering a narcotic powder into a person's face the victim would be immobilized long enough for the perpetrator to clip off the end of his queue. The mandatory Manchu hairstyle imposed on all subjects as a mark of submission made obtaining a sample of hair relatively easy, but since cutting one's queue was an expression of political resistance ever since the early Manchu conquest, it also had large political and cultural ramifications. Incidents of queue clipping were first reported in the Jiangnan region in the spring of 1768. The emperor immediately became personally involved, ordering local officials to rigorously investigate and report incidents of queue clipping. Soon many cases were reported from surrounding regions. The emperor hectored regional officials to get to the bottom of what seemed to him to be a pervasive conspiracy and to identify its source. Those who fell under suspicion were generally transients such as beggars, itinerant peddlers, and wandering monks, all of whom had low status in society. When apprehended they were usually tortured to extract information about the conspiracy. Popular fears of sorcery spread accusations against apparently rootless strangers and vagabonds. Under the constant badgering of the emperor, the panic fed on itself. But unlike previous sedition cases, no leader or instigator of this alleged conspiracy could be identified because there was none. No master sorcerer existed. More ominously, although popular panic was real and engendered what is familiar in many social contexts as mob mentality, in the end it was the emperor who was the mob. As the sorcery scare wound down to its conclusion toward the end of the year with no definitive results, it was finally his trusted ministers who were able to muster the temerity to tell him that the entire case was a mistake. Though he never admitted as much, the emperor had been deluded and rushed to judgment on a course that none could halt except at his peril.[7]

LITERARY INQUISITION

Ultimately more serious for the Manchus than random or isolated individual acts of resistance to their rule was the potential opposition to alien rule by the entire class of the literati-scholar elite. This class was the arbiter of dynastic success in the long run; the policy of assimilation from Hong Taiji to the Shunzhi and Kangxi emperors had been directed to winning over the educated Chinese elite. The Manchus harbored a deep suspicion of the loyalty of the literati class, whose demographic center of gravity was the lower Yangzi region of Jiangnan. There the Manchus had encountered the most vigorous resistance to their conquest. The southern tours of the Kangxi and Qianlong emperors were thus specifically aimed at this region. Literati opposition would be revealed in their habitual medium of expression, their writings. Ever vigilant because it was ever fearful of literati sedition, the court acted often brutally against both blatant and insidious manifestations of disloyalty.

In the last decades of the eighteenth century the court launched a massive literary inquisition to discover, expose, punish, and expunge incidents of criticism, disloyalty, slander, and sedition in all forms of literature. The campaign began seemingly innocently enough in 1773 as a byproduct of the compilation of the great *Complete Library of the Four Treasuries* (*Siku quanshu*) project sponsored by the Qianlong emperor. As the process of collecting and copying works for inclusion in the encyclopedia proceeded, works deemed dangerous or unworthy according to various criteria were singled out for destruction and their authors as well as relatives and associates were punished. As the campaign gathered momentum after 1776, there was something reminiscent of the sorcery scare a few years earlier: a tendency to take on an unstoppable life of its own as officials throughout the empire were caught up in the emperor's fervor. Even a democratic society is not immune from such irrational fears of sedition; witness the McCarthy anti-Communist campaign in America in the 1950s, where guilt by association affected many victims.

The literary inquisition of the 1770s was prefigured in less comprehensive literary persecutions during the Shunzhi and Kangxi reigns. A wealthy Zhejiang merchant and aspiring scholar Zhuang Tinglong assembled a group of scholars to compile a history of the Ming dynasty based on an earlier, late-Ming draft history. After the work was published in 1660, it was discovered to contain defamatory remarks on the Manchus and careless errors, such as the use of Ming reign titles instead of Qing titles, and references to the personal names of early Manchu rulers, the use of which was taboo in the reigning dynasty. Whether or not the work, which was considered mediocre, was intentionally treasonous, the Oboi regency inflicted a savage inquisition from 1661 to 1663, during which the compilers, publishers, and even purchasers of the history were arrested and executed, altogether seventy persons, and their families enslaved. A similar case occurred in 1713 in the later Kangxi reign. Dai Mingshi (1653–1713), who earned his *jinshi* in 1709 at the age of fifty-seven, published a collection of essays and an edition of the Confucian *Four Books*. He was interested in collecting oral accounts of the Southern Ming courts after 1644 and writing a history of that period. In one of his essays seeking information, he used Southern Ming reign titles instead of Qing reign titles of the period. Dai and his collaborators were arrested but only Dai was executed in 1713 and all of his literary works were banned. The relatively lenient treatment by the emperor reflects the more relaxed atmosphere of the Kangxi reign.

The literary inquisition unfolding in the 1770s was far greater in scope and severity. It was aimed at the subjugation and intimidation of an entire class, the scholar-literati elite, not merely a few individuals. Authors of proscribed works, sometimes completely innocent of offense, their families, and associates were ferociously punished. More than three thousand titles, 151,725 volumes, were burned, inflicting an irrecoverable loss on Chinese literature that dwarfed the infamous Qin burning of the books in the third century BCE. Like the prosecution of the sorcery scare of 1768, the Qianlong emperor was himself the engine behind the movement.

THE RULE OF LAW

Absolutism reached its height in the extraordinary unbroken continuity of the Kangxi, Yongzheng, and Qianlong reigns. If instruments of coercion were concentrated in one place, institution, or person, such as a prime minister, imperial autocracy could not prevail. But when the instruments of imperial power were dispersed in, for instance, the imperial guard, banner officers, eunuchs, bondservants, and the provincial constabulary, autocracy was unlimited. Moreover there were always persons who saw opportunities for advancement and influence by pandering to imperial favor, taking advantage of others' errors and planting suspicions. This was the ruler's advantage and strength. Information is power. The palace memorial system of secret one-to-one communication between the emperor and reporting officials was the central medium of autocracy. Only the emperor was aware of everything and controlled the flow of information.

Confucius had said, "A man of true nobility (*junzi*) is not a tool."[8] This was the classical statement that an official is not a mere obedient cog in the machinery of state, that officials possess an autonomous responsibility to a moral order higher than the monarch. But under the Yongzheng and Qianlong emperors, officials were closer than ever before to being tools of the autocrat. The Yongzheng emperor's *Discourse on Factions* had unequivocally asserted as much.

When the emperor kept his own counsel, when he possessed the absolute right to make all decisions great and small, a dilemma was created, the problem of imperial competence. What if the emperor were deluded, incompetent, or made erroneous decisions? Serious abuse of power and error uncorrected was possible. Thus it was that Heshen managed to rise to an unchallenged position of power, corruption, and abuse for two decades at the end of the Qianlong reign. Heshen (1750–1799) was a young Manchu bannerman and palace guard when he came to the emperor's attention in 1775. Enjoying the emperor's unreserved favor, he rapidly rose to minister in the Grand Council, commandant of the capital police, minister of revenue, lieutenant-general of the Manchu Bordered Blue Banner, grand secretary, and official in the *Complete Library of the Four Treasuries* office. He was permitted to ride horseback in the Forbidden City, ordinarily reserved for only those high ministers too frail to walk. So completely was he trusted by the emperor that he could be criticized only at the peril of vicious retaliation. Some of his extraordinary power seems to have rested on the Qianlong emperor's psychological dependence in his old age on his young favorite.

Even after the emperor abdicated the throne in 1796 Heshen was untouchable as long as the Qianlong emperor continued to hold power under the reign of his successor. But as soon as he died in 1799, Heshen's power immediately collapsed, he was arrested, and permitted to commit suicide. His accumulated wealth was calculated at eight hundred million *taels*, equivalent to twenty times the annual imperial revenue.

However exalted the monarch's power, there were limits to imperial absolutism. First, the emperor rarely, if ever, actually initiated policies. Rather, proposed courses of action came to him through palace memorials. He selected policies to be executed from options presented to him after referral to the Grand Council, the Grand Secretariat, or one of the Six Ministries. Thus, the official bureaucracy, especially its highest levels, retained the power to propose. Second, China under the Qing was governed by the rule of law. Actions from the lowest to the highest levels were constrained by laws and statutes. Much more so than present day People's Republic of China, law could not be violated or ignored with impunity. There were two kinds of law, *fa*, enshrined in the Statutes of the Great Qing Dynasty (*Da Qing huidian*), and *li*, precedent arising from tradition. *Fa*, statutory law and regulations, always malleable, was established two millennia previously by the Legalists, the School of Law (*fa jia*), as the foundation of the first empire of the Qin, and every dynasty thereafter. *Fa* emanated from the ruler himself, the emperor's word was *fa* in the form of rescripts and edicts that were successively codified in the *Da Qing huidian*. But *li*, ethical law, arose from historical precedent based in the accumulated wisdom of the Classics, guarded by its custodians, the literati-official class. The emperor could rarely ignore *li*, even the precedent of his predecessors' decisions. To an extraordinary degree literati and officials were willing to sacrifice their lives in the defense of ethical law, against the arbitrary power of the autocrat to rule by statutory law alone.

SUGGESTED READINGS

Backhouse, E., and J. O. P. Bland. *Annals and Memoirs of the Court of Peking* (Taipei: Ch'eng Wen Publishing Co. (reprint), 1970). A subjective, dated, and not entirely reliable, but entertaining narrative of events and personalities from the end of the Ming to the end of the Qing.

Bartlett, Beatrice S. *Monarchs and Ministers: The Grand Council in Mid-Ch'ing China, 1723–1820* (Berkeley: University of California Press, 1991). The definitive study on the formation and operation of the Grand Council in the Qing.

Chang, Michael G. *A Court on Horseback: Imperial Touring and the Construction of Qing Rule, 1680–1785* (Cambridge: Harvard University Press, 2007). Impressive imperial tours of southern China by the Kangxi and Qianlong emperors were an essential means to gauge popular acceptance of Manchu rule and assert imperial power.

Ch'ü T'ung-tsu. *Local Government in China under the Ch'ing* (Cambridge: Harvard University Press, 1962). The best general study of the critical level of local government in the Qing period.

Crossley, Pamela Kyle. *A Translucent Mirror: History and Identity in Qing Imperial Ideology* (Berkeley: University of California Press, 1999). An excellent exploration of Manchu-Chinese cultural identity focusing on the Qianlong reign.

Crossley, Pamela Kyle. *The Manchus* (Oxford: Blackwell Publishers, 2002). A general history of the Manchus by a leading student of the Qing dynasty.

de Bary, W. T. "Chinese Despotism and the Confucian Ideal: A Seventeenth-Century View," in John K. Fairbank, ed., *Chinese Thought and Institutions* (Chicago: University of Chicago Press, 1957), 163–203. An important discussion of Huang Zongxi's critique of imperial despotism.

Elliott, Mark C. *Emperor Qianlong: Son of Heaven, Man of the World.* Library of World Biography, Peter Stearns, ed. (New York: Longman, 2009). A brief popular study of one of the greatest Qing emperors.

Fairbank, John K., ed. *Chinese Thought and Institutions* (Chicago: The University of Chicago Press, 1957). A formative anthology of articles on institutional, intellectual, and social history by leading scholars. Particularly relevant here is Charles Hucker's article on "The Tung-lin Movement of the Late Ming Period."

Fairbank, John K., and Kwang-Ching Liu, eds. *The Cambridge History of China,* vol. 11, *Late Ch'ing, 1800–1911, Part 2* (Cambridge: Cambridge University Press, 1980).

Feuerwerker, Albert. *State and Society in Eighteenth-Century China: The Ch'ing Empire in Its Glory* (Ann Arbor: University of Michigan, Center for Chinese Studies, Michigan Papers in Chinese Studies no. 27, 1976). This short monograph studies social and political dimensions of the "High Qing."

Guy, R. Kent. *The Emperor's Four Treasuries: Scholars and the State in the Late Ch'ienlung Era* (Cambridge: Harvard University Press, 1987). The best comprehensive study of the *Siku quanshu* and its significant impact.

Guy, R. Kent. *Qing Governors and Their Provinces: The Evolution of Territorial Administration in China, 1644–1796* (Seattle: University of Washington Press, 2010). A study of the development of Manchu-Chinese provincial administration in the early Qing.

Huang, Pei. *Autocracy at Work: A Study of the Yung-cheng Period, 1723–1735* (Bloomington: University of Indiana University Press, 1975). This monograph documents the enhanced autocracy of the Yongzheng reign.

Hummel, Arthur W., ed. *Eminent Chinese of the Ch'ing Period (1644–1912)*, 2 vols. (Washington, D.C.: Library of Congress, 1943–1944). In spite of its age this remains the essential comprehensive biographical reference for the Qing.

Kahn, Harold L. *Monarchy in the Emperor's Eyes: Image and Reality in the Ch'ien-lung Reign* (Cambridge: Harvard University Press, 1971). A detailed study of the construction of the imperial persona as seen in the Qianlong emperor.

Kuhn, Philip A. *Soulstealers: The Chinese Sorcery Scare of 1768* (Cambridge: Harvard University Press, 1990). Explores the fascinating story of the sorcery scare of the Qianlong reign and its ultimate complete lack of substance as a reflection of imperial paranoia.

Mengzi (Mencius). Trans. with an introduction by D. C. Lau, *Mencius* (Harmondsworth, England and New York: Penguin Books, 1970).

Metzger, Thomas A. *The Internal Organization of the Ch'ing Bureaucracy: Legal, Normative, and Communication Aspects* (Cambridge: Harvard University Press, 1973). A detailed and prodigious analysis of the operation of the Qing bureaucracy.

Mote, F. W. *Imperial China, 900–1800* (Cambridge: Harvard University Press, 1999). The most comprehensive treatment of Chinese history from the end of the Tang through the early Qing dynasties. An extremely useful reference, with the caveat that the index has many lacunae.

Nivison, David S. "Ho-shen and his Accusers: Ideology and Political Behavior in the Eighteenth Century," in David S. Nivison and Arthur W. Wright, eds., *Confucianism in Action* (Stanford: Stanford University Press, 1959, 207–243). The vast case of corruption under the late reign of the Qianlong emperor is explored here.

Oxnam, Robert B. *Ruling from Horseback: Manchu Politics in the Oboi Regency, 1661–1669* (Chicago: University of Chicago Press, 1970). An excellent companion to Lawrence Kessler's study (*K'ang-hsi and the Consolidation of Ch'ing Rule 1661–1684*) on the conflict between tribal and bureaucratic politics in the establishment of Manchu rule. See also Silas Wu's *Passage to Power* and Jonathan Spence's *T'sao Yin and the K'ang-hsi Emperor*. Together, these studies represent the core of the specialized studies of this brilliant emperor.

Peterson, Willard J., ed. *The Cambridge History of China*, vol. 9, *The Ch'ing Empire to 1800*, Part 1 (Cambridge: Cambridge University Press, 2002). *The Cambridge History of China* volumes 9, 10, and 11 (like the twin volumes on the Ming) are the standard authorities of the Qing dynasty by leading scholars of their respective fields.

Rawski, Evelyn S. *The Last Emperors: A Social History of Qing Imperial Institutions* (Berkeley: University of California Press, 1998). A unique exploration of the institutional structure of late imperial rule, including social organization and court rituals.

Rowe, William T. *China's Last Empire: The Great Qing* (Cambridge: Harvard University Press, 2009). A thoughtful, comprehensive history of China under the Qing empire organized into ten chapters on various thematic subjects, including government, society, commerce, rebellion, restoration, imperialism, and revolution.

Rowe, William T. *Saving the World: Chen Hongmou and Elite Consciousness in Eighteenth-Century China* (Stanford: Stanford University Press, 2001). A masterful study of the career of an influential scholar-official reformer in the eighteenth century.

Spence, Jonathan D. *Treason by the Book* (New York: Viking, 2001). An intriguing case of treason thoroughly and obsessively investigated by the Yongzheng emperor is thoroughly explored here.

Wakeman, Frederic, Jr. *The Fall of Imperial China*. New York: The Free Press, 1975. A standard textbook on the late imperial period from the end of the Ming to the end of the Qing.

Wakeman, Frederic, Jr. "High Ch'ing: 1683–1839," in James B. Crowley, ed., *Modern East Asia: Essays in Interpretation* (New York: Harcourt, Brace, World, 1970), 1–28. This essay is the origin of the characterization of seventeenth-century Qing as the "High Qing."

Wakeman, Frederic, Jr., and Carolyn Grant, eds. *Conflict and Control in Late Imperial China* (Berkeley: University of California Press, 1975). A diverse collection of nine essays by leading scholars covering the period from the Manchu conquest to the early Republic.

Watt, John R. *The District Magistrate in Late Imperial China* (New York: Columbia University Press, 1972). A competent study of this critical interface between imperial bureaucratic hierarchy and the local population.

Wu, Silas H. L. *Communication and Imperial Control in China: Evolution of the Palace Memorial System, 1693–1735* (Cambridge: Harvard University Press, 1970). This seminal study on the crucial role of the memorial system as an instrument of imperial power in the Qing dynasty is useful also for understanding official communication in the Ming and in general.

Wu, Silas H. L. *Passage to Power: K'ang-hsi and his Heir Apparent, 1661–1722* (Cambridge: Harvard University Press, 1979). A careful study of the difficult issue of the Kangxi emperor's selection of, or failure to select, an heir and its political consequences.

NOTES

1. Huang Zongxi, *Mingyi daifang lu*, in Yan Yiping, compiler, *Baibu congshu jicheng* (Taibei: Yimen yinshuguan (reprint), Daoguang 19 [1840]), 2b.

2. Quoted in David S. Nivison, "Ho-shen and His Accusers: Ideology and Political Behavior in the Eighteenth Century," in David S. Nivison and Arthur F. Wright, eds., *Confucianism in Action* (Stanford: Stanford University Press, 1959), 228.

3. Quoted in Philip A. Kuhn, *Soulstealers: The Chinese Sorcery Scare of 1768* (Cambridge: Harvard University Press, 1990), 213.

4. Arthur W. Hummel, ed., *Eminent Chinese of the Ch'ing Period (1644–1912)* (Washington, D.C.: Library of Congress, 1943–44), 54–56.

5. Hummel, ed., *Eminent Chinese,* 587–590.

6. An engaging account of the Zeng Jing case is found in Jonathan D. Spence, *Treason by the Book* (New York: Viking, 2001).

7. The sorcery scare of 1768 and its implications are extensively explored in Philip A. Kuhn, *Soulstealers: The Chinese Sorcery Scare of 1768* (Cambridge: Harvard University Press, 1990).

8. Confucius, *Lun yu* book II, paragraph 12.

IV

MING AND QING FOUNDATIONS, 1368–1900

11

The Good Earth

Somewhere in central China a man and a woman, let us call them Wang Lung and O-lan, worked their field.

Moving together in perfect rhythm, without a word, hour after hour, he fell into a union with her which took the pain from his labor. He had no articulate thought of anything; there was only this perfect sympathy of movement, of turning this earth of theirs over and over to the sun, this earth which formed their home and fed their bodies and made their gods. The earth lay rich and dark, and fell apart lightly under the points of their hoes. Sometimes they turned up a bit of brick, a splinter of wood. It was nothing. Sometime, in some age, bodies of men and women had been buried there, houses had stood there, had fallen, and had gone back into the earth. So would also their house, some time, return to the earth. They worked on, moving together— together—producing the fruit of this earth—speechless in their movement together.[1]

The Chinese landscape was shaped by cultivators who grew food for subsistence since Neolithic times. Chinese mythology describes a succession of legendary primordial culture heroes. Fuxi was the prototypical Paleolithic man, a hunter-gatherer; Shennong, the Neolithic farmer, invented domestic agriculture; and Huangdi, the prototypical emperor, invented civilization. This mythological narrative is in a sense a memory of the manner of emergence of Chinese civilization from sedentary roots in what was and still is the core area of settlement in the Yellow River basin and the North China plain. In this narrative is reflected the gradual transition from presocial humans, through the Neolithic revolution, to the higher institutions of civilized society. Shennong, whose name means simply farmer or "sacred agriculturist," was the progenitor of the agrarian order, the First Farmer. The Chinese view of their origins, therefore, is not based on the struggle of mythic gods and men, as in the ancient Greek myths, or the vast migration of primordial ancestors from some ancient homeland, as the Vedic memory preserves, or the supernatural creation of a chosen people, in the Judeo-Christian legend, but on the mundane evolution of human ancestors out of the land itself. Whether or not this narrative is a "true story" of Chinese origins is irrelevant; perception is everything. It shapes the way a people understand themselves—the way Wang Lung and O-lan understood their place—just as much as the Judeo-Christian myth shapes the way the people belonging to that tradition understand their place in the world.

Chinese farmers, mainly individually and at times collectively, labored intensively for their livelihood.[2] What they didn't consume or sell, and

Figure 11.1. Shennong, the First Farmer. Li Ung Bing, *Outlines of Chinese History* **(Shanghai, 1914), public domain.**

sometimes more than they could spare, was taken by the state in taxes and levies. While agriculture experienced changes over millennia—reclamation of land from lakes, rivers, seacoasts, and deserts; extension of cultivation to hillsides and (increasingly) unfavorable soils; and introduction of new, nourishing crops—the agricultural world changed very little before modern times. Only seldom were Chinese farmers pioneers, and when they were it was largely because they were forced by natural and human adversities to migrate to find better opportunities in less-crowded land. Population change, both growth and decline, drove changes in the agrarian world. Agrarian population had shifted westward in a significant migration in the late fifteenth century as a result of population growth. Subsequently, the population of many areas declined precipitously as a result of war, civil upheaval, and epidemics during the Ming-Qing transition in the mid-seventeenth century. Farmers migrated in large numbers into depopulated regions, reclaiming abandoned farmland in the late seventeenth century, contributing to economic recovery by the early eighteenth century. Change at the fundamental agrarian level was slow and gradual, and was overwhelmingly cyclical. Farmers emerged from the soil, worked and lived on the land their entire lives, and returned to the soil to begin the process again.

THE CHINESE LANDSCAPE

China Proper, the area bounded by the East China Sea on the east and the southeast, the mountainous jungles of Southeast Asia on the south, the Tibetan escarpment on the west, and the wastes of the Gobi desert and the Great Wall on the north, comprises six diverse geographical regions defined by the major watersheds and the mountain ranges that divide them. In the upper Yellow River basin of the northwest the river cuts through the *loess* highlands, an alluvium of fine, wind-blown soil lying to a depth of hundreds of feet in some places. *Loess* soil is fertile, but the climate, dominated by the continental weather system of inner Asia, is dry; irrigation is often necessary to supplement scarce natural rainfall. The Yellow River descends from the northwest highlands into the northeast plains, essentially a secondary alluvium of eroded *loess* deposited by the river over many millennia. Here the climate is also dominated by northern monsoons blowing off the deserts and steppes of inner Asia. But the land is rich and flat and easily cultivated. The North China plain is the most extensive agriculturally productive region of China.

South of the North China plain, set off by an imaginary boundary roughly corresponding to the course of the Huai River, the lower Yangzi River basin is composed of rich agricultural lands divided by mountain ranges. Lakes and water courses break up the landscape, and the warmer climate is dominated by the maritime monsoons of the south, flowing up from the South China Sea, so rainfall is normally plentiful. To the west, up the lower Yangzi valley and beyond the deep gorges through which the river plunges, is the great Sichuan basin, so named from the four tributaries that join the Yangzi there. Contrasting to the highlands across the range of mountains to the north, this upper Yangzi basin is China's most prolific region, influenced by the southern maritime climate, but isolated by surrounding mountains.

Further south across the mountains bordering the Sichuan basin on the south, the remote highlands and mountains of southeast China provide rich irrigated soil. Lastly, to the southeast the coastal region and its hinterland, broken by mountainous terrain and numerous rivers, receives abundant rainfall from the maritime monsoons, and the semitropical climate permits two or three crops per year.

From west to east and north to south ecology, physical environment, and climate vary greatly. Approximately 40 percent of China Proper is arable land, cultivated with broadcast grains such as millet and wheat in the north to intensively irrigated crops, mainly rice, in the south. This area supported a population that grew from roughly 80 to 100 million in the early Ming to 450 million in the mid-Qing. China in premodern, imperial times was fundamentally an agrarian society in which at least 80 percent of the population lived and worked on the land. The other two sectors of the economy, commerce and traditional handicraft industry, were relatively small compared to agriculture and subordinate to it.

ECONOMY AND SOCIETY

The various strata of society, including the imperial bureaucracy representing the state, the scholar-gentry elite, and the peasant masses, viewed the economy from very different perspectives. Peasant labor and the farmer class generally were not only respected but valued as the foundation of the social order. The ancient Confucian adage (shared to some extent by other schools as well) that since the ruler labors with his mind while the commoner labors with his muscles, the ruler's function is to rule over the commoner while the commoner's function is to support the ruler. This captures the notion of the shared responsibility of the two primary orders of traditional agrarian society.

From the state's point of view the economy was fundamentally a producer of revenue, largely if not exclusively from agricultural taxes. While this was an essentially exploitative and extractive attitude, Mencius insisted that the ruler must be motivated by a benevolent regard for the people. The Yongzheng emperor, whatever his authoritarian proclivities, espoused a strong egalitarian view of humanity wherein all people, including minority peoples, belong to a single family. Both higher-level policy makers, including the emperor and his ministers, and lower-level officials, were mindful of peasant welfare and agricultural conditions in various parts of the country. While the state generally did not engage in policies of active economic development, it recognized the need both to maintain social stability, through, for instance, tax amnesties for areas hit by natural disasters such as flood and drought, and to promote agricultural expansion and land reclamation to meet the rising population. A well-regulated and productive agrarian society that met the basic needs of the common people ultimately was the basis for political stability.

From the scholar-gentry's point of view, the economy supported their lifestyle and indirectly maintained the high culture of the literati-scholar class. It is true that lower members of the literati were to all intents and purposes effectively commoners, but they were not involved directly in agricultural production themselves. Members of the scholar-gentry class, those who held civil service examination degrees above the first prefectural level, were not always supported exclusively from rents from land owning. Official emoluments and commercial enterprise were often significant, if uncertain and unreliable sources of income. Although wealth alone was not an accurate measure of high social status, investment in land was in the long run the steadiest source of economic security, both for the scholar-gentry and for the peasantry.

From the point of view of the peasants, the economy simply provided their basic subsistence. While the state was farthest removed from direct participation in economic production, and the scholar-gentry elite occupied an intermediate position, as primary producers the peasants were intimately involved with all aspects of the economy. For this reason peasant livelihood was directly affected by economic fluctuations, including especially natural calamities such as drought and floods, and human-caused disturbances such as war and civil uprisings, but also market fluctuations in commodity prices and exactions of taxes and extraordinary levies and fees. The peasantry was embedded in a customary economy that depended less on money exchange than on barter and exchange in kind at the local level. The peasant's life was never far from the margin of existence.

HOME AND HEARTH

The family was the fundamental unit of agrarian society; the individual's life was entirely defined within the context of the family. The family was simultaneously a social entity, an economic construction, and a physical entity. The single Chinese word *jia* signifies family, household, house, and home. A typical household included five to seven persons, although the number varied according to a family's relative wealth. Thus the household might include the male head of the family and his wife, one or two aged parents, one or two children, and the wives of grown sons. A very poor family could consist of only the head of household and his wife, and perhaps one child, or a single male and his relative. A prosperous family could support three or, rarely, four generations under one roof, considered an ideal. But households of this size or larger tended to break up into nuclear families as sons left the household to establish their own separate households.

Peasant houses were generally one to three rooms, larger if the family was prosperous. The stove in the main room was the essential feature. Above the stove, in a niche in the wall, or on a paper image, resides the figure of the kitchen god or god of the stove (*zaojun* or *zaoshen*). He oversees the daily life of the family, which he witnesses from his central location. Every year before the New Year he returns to Heaven to report on the family's affairs. Before sending him on his way it is customary to smear some sugar on his lips so that he will be sure to report only good things to the emperor in Heaven.

Marriage was the most significant social institution that structured the family. A son was not considered an autonomous adult until his marriage, which could occur as early as fifteen, and even more so until he had produced a son of his own. Then, as part of the family hierarchy producing sons (it was hoped), he assumed the responsibilities of adulthood. A woman left her natal family to join that of her husband and usually fell under the authority of her mother-in-law. A daughter-in-law was often a valuable addition to the human resources of the family. Until her sons in turn married, her status remained low. But once she herself became a mother-in-law, she became the de facto matriarch within the household.

LAND TENURE

The farm associated with a household was not an area of contiguous fields such as is typical of a small farm in the West. The Chinese family did not live on its farmland surrounding the farmhouse and outbuildings. Instead, its land was scattered in small plots, usually long strips of varying sizes interspersed with similar plots of other households. The distribution of plots could vary widely according to the wealth of each household. Thus the size of farms varied from an average of ten to twenty *mou* in the south to seventy to one hundred *mou* in the north.[3] Farms could

THE KITCHEN GOD

Figure 11.2. The Kitchen God. Christopher H. Plopper, *Chinese Religion Seen Through the Proverb* (Shanghai: Shanghai Modern Publishing House, 1935), after p. 182.

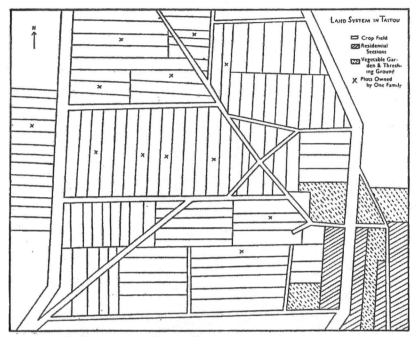

This shows the fragmentation of the crop land which belongs to families of Taitou. The fields marked with X belong to one family. The family has also a number of fields in other sections which are not shown here.

Figure 11.3.   Fragmentation of Farmland. From *A Chinese Village: Taitou, Shantung Province*, by Martin C. Yang (New York: Columbia University Press, 1945). Reprinted with permission of the publisher.

be as small as one *mou*, not enough to maintain a family's livelihood, to hundreds of *mou*.

To own land, and to increase one's land holdings, was the most important goal of every household. Only land was a secure source of livelihood, and land could never be taken away; it could only be sold. Whatever money a family might save, aside from the essential expenses of marriages and funerals, would be invested in purchases of land so its wealth might grow. Although all peasant families were essentially equal in social status, no matter how much or how little land they owned, a hierarchy of households based on land tenure nevertheless distinguished them. At the bottom was the peasant who owned no land, perhaps with no house, who worked as a hired laborer, often living with the farmer for whom he worked for wages. He might live in the house of the host family or he might live in a barn with the livestock. Next was the farmer who owned no land but rented land to cultivate from a neighboring household. Above him was the farmer who owned a small plot of land and rented additional land sufficient to maintain an independent livelihood. Next was the household that owned enough land to live comfortably with its available resources without needing to rent additional farmland, perhaps the ideal farmer. Above him in the hierarchy was the household, significantly more prosperous, that owned more land than the members of the family could work and leased some of their land to neighboring families. These last households occupied the uncertain border between the peasantry and the landlord class. But their position was apt to be tenuous and vulnerable, and they could easily fall back into lower peasant status.

For those households renting all or a portion of the land they cultivated, rent took a variety of forms, even within a single region or village. Rent might be paid as a fixed amount of money, a fixed amount of the crop in kind (e.g., wheat or rice), or a share of the harvest in kind. Each had its advantages and disadvantages depending on varying conditions. For instance, in the case of fixed rent, the advantage for the farmer when the harvest was good was that he kept everything above the rent due. But if the harvest was poor, the margin retained could vanish to almost nothing. For the peasant family, landholding was everything. It determined the family economy: the division of labor between men and women, the diversity of crops possible or available (larger amounts of land allowed greater diversity of crops among subsistence varieties and cash or market crops), and other productive activities based on the farm. Household wealth measured in terms of income distribution among families was closely correlated with land distribution. Wealthy families owned more land; poorer families owned less land. There were no famers who were wealthy but land poor.

In the north the ancient or indigenous grains of millet, wheat, sorghum, and soy beans, along with vegetables were cultivated. Wheat was the more valuable crop but was less common than millet until the means of grinding wheat flour was improved. Sorghum was a coarser grain often used to feed livestock. Besides these, cash crops included cotton (introduced in the twelfth century), hemp, sugar, and mulberry (for raising silk worms). In the south, among indigenous crops, rice predominated, along with soy beans and vegetables. Cash crops included tea, cotton, sugar, and silk. New World crops entered China from the sixteenth century and revolutionized the diet of farmers. Alien crops included maize (corn), sweet potatoes, white (Irish) potatoes, and red chili. These possessed superior nutritional value compared to indigenous crops, and were hardier and easier to grow. New cash crops included peanuts, tobacco, and opium poppies. Red chili and peanuts in particular significantly transformed Chinese cuisine in some regions, such as the provinces of Sichuan and Hunan. While rice was always considered the premier food, the elite grain, it was sometimes less available to poor farmers, for whom sweet potatoes were the staple.

THE VILLAGE

Farmers did not live on isolated homesteads in the center of their farmlands. Farm houses were clustered together, usually along a path or road passing through the area and connecting to other groups of farmhouses. Villages were such collections of households, owning or renting farmland surrounding each village. The most visible feature of the rural landscape, villages varied in appearance according to the physical environment of the region and the native materials available for construction. But villages were not corporate entities and possessed only rudimentary organizational structure. They existed in a hierarchy of rural society, a continuum from household to neighborhood[4] to village to market town. Lacking corporate identity, villages had no fixed boundaries. Farmland owned by a household within a village only in a very loose sense belonged to that village. A village typically might include from one thousand to four thousand *mou* (approximately 150 to 600 acres), distributed among cultivated land, woods, graves, and the houses of the village itself. The number of households, the basic unit of rural society, in a village might range from 100 to 400. Multiplied by a factor of five, the average size of a household, yields a village population of 500 to 2000 people.

Perhaps one or two miles separated neighboring villages with the local market town an easy walking distance of four or five miles. Villages sometimes included a small temple or school, but there were no shops or commercial establishments. Instead, goods not produced at home, such as tools, lamp oil, and medicines, had to be purchased in the market town, and agricultural cash crops produced by the household were likewise sold or traded there. Except for such infrequent contacts as these, rural society was inert, by definition sedentary. In the passive Daoist ideal of a simple society close to nature villages existed in a sort of utopian self-sufficient isolation. The inhabitants of such a country:

> Should be contented with their food, pleased with their clothing, satisfied with their homes, should take pleasure in their rustic tasks. The next place might be so near at hand that one could hear the cocks crowing in it, the dogs barking; but the people would grow old and die without ever having been there.[5]

It goes without saying that rural society was in practice far more integrated than the idyllic Daoist vision. At the very least, marriages were often contracted with families from neighboring villages, particularly because the rule of exogamy required the avoidance of marriages between same surname families or within clans. As the commercial economy developed and expanded from the late Ming, peasant life became ever more integrated into the regional and national economic fabric.

Villages varied greatly from region to region according to topography, climate, and ecology, determined by the fertility of the soil, variety of cultivations, and use of water by irrigation or rainfall. In the mountainous regions of the south, fed by abundant rainfall from monsoons, hillsides were steeply terraced to grow irrigated rice, whereas in the relatively open plains and flat areas of the north broadcast crops such as wheat depended on rainfall alone without benefit of irrigation. In the *loess* highlands of the northwest cave houses were excavated from steep embankments. In the flat plains of the northeast houses were constructed of walls of rammed earth, while houses of brick and abundant stone were typical in the lower Yangzi valley. In the lush Sichuan basin houses were constructed on bamboo frames with thatched roofs, but in the rainy south and southeast houses were built of durable brick and tile roofs. In each region the roofs, front walls, and doorways of houses were often lavishly decorated with painted scenes, designs, and figures, unique to each locale and suggesting the pride that farmers placed in their homes.

AGRARIAN POLICY

The state at both the central government and regional levels was intent on managing the agrarian economy to achieve efficient and reliable maintenance of tax revenue and effective distribution of agricultural resources. Economic development, in the sense of economic expansion as a goal of the modern state, was not a primary objective of economic thought and policy. The Kangxi emperor had, in fact, frozen the tax quotas in 1711. Before this, taxes were paid in two parts, the land tax based on land area and the labor service tax, a head tax on all adult males. These were now consolidated into one tax paid in silver. A similar reform had been implemented in the Ming by Grand Secretary Zhang Juzheng in the late sixteenth century. Formerly, a vast array of land taxes paid in grain, variable labor service taxes, and numerous surcharges kept in different accounts, which fell most heavily on the poorest segment of the peasantry, had over time become the source of numerous abuses and corruption. In 1581 all taxes were combined into a single registry (*yitiaobian*) paid as one tax in silver twice a year. Because the homophone for *yitiaobian* meant "single whip," this more colorful name stuck. The 1711 freezing of the tax quotas in the Qing became permanent in 1713. The dynasty thereby surrendered any future increment in taxation for the sake of simplified accounting in spite of significant growth in population and arable land in subsequent decades.

Payment of taxes was the responsibility of the owner of the land regardless of whether it was rented to another person. The owner was required to submit his tax payment in silver at the magistrates' *yamen* in the district city. The *yamen* dispatched tax agents to the villages to demand delinquent payments. Failure to pay could lead to physical punishment, imprisonment, and forfeiture of the property.

Nourishing and maintaining an adequate food supply, as well as a surplus to meet unpredictable emergencies, was the most important policy goal of benevolent government. One method of accomplishing this objective was to set taxes low enough so that the people could effectively plan for their own welfare: "to allow the people to nourish themselves." This was the most passive, market-oriented approach. Another, more active method in the command economy mode, with roots as far back as the Han dynasty in the second century BCE, was to purchase grain annually at the end of the harvest when abundance caused prices to fall, store it in local granaries, and subsequently sell the stored grain on the market prior to harvest or in times of dearth caused by poor harvests or during famine when scarcity led to inflated prices: "to store wealth among the people." The effect of this program, known as the "Ever Normal Granary," was price stabilization, although it was traditionally criticized as a form of profit-making by the government. The program was in continuous use during much of the Qing when Ever Normal Granaries were established in many prefectures and districts.

Besides collection of agricultural taxes, which was by far the largest share of state revenue, distribution of agricultural production in the form of various grains, and other commercial commodities such as cotton, tobacco, peanuts, tea, and silk, was an important object of economic policy. For the producer, the immediate point of distribution above the village was the market town, which was centered in an area of roughly eight to ten miles in diameter serving perhaps twenty surrounding villages. Permanent residents of the market town were not involved in agricultural work but owned the shops, teahouses, wine shops, and eating places that were the social and economic centers of peasant life. Market towns were linked with each other in larger marketing areas and connected in turn to even larger commercial centers. It is important to observe here that market towns were not administrative centers, the location of government offices. Unlike district cities, the location of the *yamen*, the headquarters of the magistrate, market towns were not surrounded by defensive walls, moats, and gates. Local agricultural produce travelled upward through the network of market towns to major commercial centers while manufactures and specialty goods circulated downward to local periodic markets for purchase by local consumers in market towns.

THE FAMILY CYCLE

Whatever the larger view of Chinese agrarian society as sedentary and quiescent, especially in the idyllic Daoist vision, the peasant household was subject to constant pressures of change both from within and from without. The vagaries of government exactions (changing taxation policies, surcharges, and fees), weather (drought, flood, and pests), political instability (civil disruptions, banditry, and war), and intrafamilial conflicts—to all of these the peasant household was extremely sensitive. Unless it had saved for times of crisis, it lived precariously on the margin of existence.

A family that grew with the birth of sons and the inclusion of daughters-in-law inevitably experienced friction between generations and between siblings. Sooner or later a married son and his wife, and any children they had, would seek to break from the family and form their own household. This breakup of an expanding family, the division of a household (*fenjia*), could have many causes, including simply personal conflicts and intrafamilial tensions. But it was inevitable. The household was not an enduring stable institution. No family ever held land longer than three or four generations, less than a hundred years. Always, the descendants of successful large landowners themselves ended as small landowners. Land was continually being bought and sold, to augment family wealth or to pay for family needs in emergencies. The advantage of *fenjia* was the additional labor that new households created; the disadvantage was the decline in aggregate wealth. But primogeniture, the inheritance of family wealth in land by the eldest son, had been abolished in China two millennia ago by the Qin, so hereditary aggregation of landed wealth was rarely possible.

Fenjia entailed the division of fields, the primary economic resources of the household, into ever-smaller plots to the male heirs either upon the death of the parents or upon voluntary breakup of the family. Such fragmentation meant that farms were composed of disconnected narrow strips, an obstacle to efficient farming practice. Each small strip necessarily allocated a portion of land to unproductive boundaries; the farmer had to walk sometimes considerable distances from plot to plot with his plow and his ox if he owned one; collective activities were difficult and technical improvements discouraged. Disputes over the boundaries between strips of land generated endless arguments and litigation among village neighbors. It was not until land reform under the Communist Revolution after 1949, when land was confiscated from landlords and small parcels were consolidated into communal farms, that the obstacles to modernization of agriculture were overcome.

The peasant family lived a cyclical existence. The shorter cycle was the annual seasonal cycle of cultivating, planting, and harvesting that rigorously governed peasant life. A longer cycle was the growth, prosperity, and inevitable decline of the family over many years. There were two routes to success. One was hard work, the persistent effort to earn enough beyond basic subsistence to buy more land. More land meant increased farm income, which was in turn used to buy more land. In most villages there was a continuous turnover in land ownership. Eventually the household's land might exceed the ability of members to work it by themselves, in which case they would lease some land to another household. Growing wealth and prosperity followed.

The other route to success was known as "plowing with the brush." If a family had a bright son and had sufficient numbers that it could spare his work in the fields, it could invest in his education, perhaps first under a tutor in the village school and later at a school in the market town. The ultimate success of the boy in the lowest level of the civil service qualifying examinations, and even rising from there, would lift the whole family through the status that would accrue to it from academic honor and the opportunities opening to new wealth. Of course, these two routes often coexisted in one family.

Usually by the third generation the seeds of decline were planted. The hard work ethic of the founder of the family's prosperity was not shared by the sons and grandsons who had not experienced the initial hardships and were raised "in the shade" of relative comfort. Their newfound extravagance drained the resources of the family, leading it eventually to end where it began, a nuclear family at the bottom of the cycle. Some might start over while some would simply expire.

The material wealth of the peasant resided completely in land. There were very few ways of saving and investing money earned from selling surplus production. Earnings went into the purchase of additional fields or into the considerable expenses of marriages and funerals. Land was usually available and could be sold again if conditions warranted, thus serving as the only viable commodity.

But there was another, spiritual quality that inhered in the land, or rather in the landscape itself that belonged to the natural order of things. The natural order and the human order—how man lived on the land and transformed the landscape and how the landscape affected those who lived on it—were joined in the conception of *fengshui*, literally "wind and water." According to the principles of *fengshui* the contours and shapes of land, hills and ridges; running water and still water; rocks and trees possessed a powerful spiritual potential that governed the fortunes of its inhabitants. Anything that was done on or to the land should abide by the spiritual forces reposing in the land, including the gods of the earth. To ignore them was to risk their malevolent influence. To conform with these forces, on the other hand, would invite the beneficent influence of the spiritual potential of the land on one's fortunes. Accordingly, buildings were situated with regard to the principles of *fengshui*; graves particularly were placed with reference to the magical properties of the landscape. To diligently observe these rules would ensure the future prosperity of the family. This was in a sense a self-fulfilling prophecy, like the saying on highway billboards, "The family that prays together stays together." Belief in the power of *fengshui* reflected a family's determination to prosper, and its determination to prosper was a good predictor of its success. The gods of the earth protected both the land and the inhabitants on the land, in a reciprocal dependent relationship.

Wang Lung rejoiced in the birth of his first son, but he experienced at the same time a pang of fear. "It did not do in this life to be too fortunate," he thought. At the candlemaker's shop

> He bought four sticks of incense, one for each person in his house, and with these four sticks he went into the small temple of the gods of the earth, and he thrust them into the cold ashes of the incense he had placed there before, he and his wife together. He watched the four sticks well lit and then went homeward, comforted. These two small protective figures sitting staidly under their small roof—what power they had![6]

In later times, *fengshui* could be an obstacle to modernization, just as *fenjia* was an obstacle to efficient farming. On a rice field on the outskirts of Taibei on Taiwan around 1976 a tall steel electric transmission tower was erected in what was formerly a peaceful, pastoral scene. The steel tower violated the benign aesthetic ambiance of the place, this offensive manifestation of modern technology. But more importantly it offended the spiritual quality that resided there. Not long after the transmission tower was built a small shrine appeared near it, no doubt to propitiate the gods of the earth who were so offended by this transgression of the good earth.

SUGGESTED READINGS

Buck, Pearl S. *The Good Earth* (New York: Pocket Books, 2005; originally published 1931). The most popular novel published on the Chinese common people, this sympathetic view strongly influenced the Western understanding of the Chinese common people.

Ch'ü T'ung-tsu. *Law and Society in Traditional China* (Paris and La Haye: Mouton, 1961). An excellent description of family, clan, marriage, social classes, law, and Confucianism in traditional China.

Eastman, Lloyd E. *Family, Fields, and Ancestors: Constancy and Change in China's Social and Economic History, 1550–1949* (New York: Oxford University Press, 1988). The evolution of Chinese society from the late Ming through the Republican period viewed from diverse perspectives.

Fei Hsiao-tung. *Peasant Life in China. A Field Study of Country Life in the Yangtze Valley* (London: Kegan Paul, 1943). A classic case study of peasant society by a famous Chinese anthropologist.

Granet, Marcel. Maurice Freedman, trans., *The Religion of the Chinese People* (Oxford: Basil Blackwell, 1975). Chinese religious belief and practice explored by an eminent French sinologist.

Johnson, David, Andrew J. Nathan, and Evelyn S. Rawski, eds. *Popular Culture in Late Imperial China* (Berkeley: University of California Press, 1985). This collection of thirteen essays presents a valuable perspective on a broad range of popular cultural themes.

Mengzi (Mencius). Trans. with an introduction by D. C. Lau, *Mencius* (Harmondsworth, England and New York: Penguin Books, 1970).

Myers, Ramon H. *The Chinese Peasant Economy: Agricultural Development in Hopei and Shantung, 1890–1949* (Cambridge: Harvard University Press, 1970). An interpretive study of the north China peasant economy from the end of the Qing through the Republican period.

Rowe, William T. *Saving the World: Chen Hongmou and Elite Consciousness in Eighteenth-Century China* (Stanford: Stanford University Press, 2001). A masterful study of the career of an influential scholar-official reformer in the eighteenth century.

Skinner, G. William. *Marketing and Social Structure in Rural China*, Association for Asian Studies, reprinted from *Journal of Asian Studies* 24.1 (November 1964), 24.2 (February 1965), 24.3 (May 1965), AAS Reprint Series. A seminal series of articles by a leading anthropologist of China on the commercial structure of rural society.

Smith, Richard J. *China's Cultural Heritage: The Ch'ing Dynasty, 1644–1912* (Boulder: Westview Press, 1983). A fascinating and informative description of the many dimensions of elite and popular culture in the Qing period.

Yang, Martin C. *A Chinese Village: Taitou, Shantung Province* (New York: Columbia University Press, 1945). A classic village study by a prominent Chinese anthropologist.

NOTES

1. Pearl S. Buck, *The Good Earth* (New York: Pocket Books, 2005; originally published 1931), 29–30.

2. The terms "farmer" and "peasant" applied to Chinese history, if not controversial, are often used interchangeably and ambiguously. A peasant is "one who

lives in the country and works the land, either as a small farmer or as a laborer." (*Oxford English Dictionary*, 1933 [Oxford University Press, 1961], vol. VII, 594). This meaning is derived from various forms of, for example, *paisaunt*, "a countryman," and is nonpejorative. "A farmer is one who cultivates a farm, whether as a tenant or owner; one who 'farms' land, or who makes agriculture his occupation." (*Oxford English Dictionary*, 1933 [Oxford University Press, 1961], vol. IV, 77). While "farmer" has many ambiguous meanings, "peasant" connotes a member of a social class.

3. *Mu* (or *mou*) was the customary unit of land area equal to roughly .15 acre (approximately 6.6 *mu* per acre), though the actual size varied somewhat from province to province.

4. Martin C. Yang refers to neighborhoods, divisions of a village having no referenced to clan, as *hutong*. Normally *hutong* refers to an alley or small street within an urban setting. Martin C. Yang, *A Chinese Village: Taitou, Shantung Province* (New York: Columbia University Press, 1945), 151.

5. Arthur Waley, *The Way and Its Power: A Study of the Tao Te Ching and Its Place in Chinese Thought* (New York: Grove Press, 1958), chapter LXXX, 241–242.

6. Pearl S. Buck, *The Good Earth*, 40.

12

Merchants and Markets

In the late thirteenth century during the reign of Khubilai Khan, the Venetian traveler Marco Polo famously commented on the astounding number of ships and the volume of trade on the Yangzi River:

> *A great number of cities and large towns are situated upon its banks, and more than two hundred, in sixteen provinces, make use of it, resulting in a traffic that would seem incredible to anyone who had not seen it. But considering its length and the number of its tributaries, it is not surprising that the cargo transported on it is incalculable. The principal commodity here is salt, which is conveyed by means of the Kiang [Yangzi], and the rivers connected to it, to the towns upon their banks, and afterwards from there to all places in the interior of the country. . . .On one occasion when Marco Polo was at the city of Sinju, he saw there no less than fifteen thousand vessels; and yet there are other towns along the river where the number is still greater.[1]*

For an inveterate merchant from the great Mediterranean commercial city-state of Venice, Marco Polo's observation is itself remarkable. It is because of such assertions that European readers of his account had trouble believing him. But what he observed suggests that the lively commercial activity of the Song, which had fallen to the Mongols in 1279, had continued apace in spite of the lack of any particular Mongol enthusiasm for trade.

Continuing down the Yangzi to the rich delta region, Marco Polo further observes:

> *Suju [Soochow] is a large and magnificent city, twenty miles in circumference. The people have vast quantities of raw silk and manufacture it, not only for their own*

consumption (all of them being clothed in silk), but also for other markets. There are among them some very rich merchants, and the number of inhabitants is astonishing.[2]

Noteworthy in these observations is his mention of salt in the former case and silk in the latter. Silk was China's most ancient commercial product—Marco traveled, after all, on the famous "Silk Road" to China—and Suzhou was then and later the center of its production. Salt had since Han times in the second century BCE been an important commodity of government monopoly.

THE SOCIAL STATUS OF MERCHANTS

The volume of local and regional trade that Marco Polo observed continued into the early Ming dynasty, although the rebellions and civil war that led to the founding of the Ming disrupted economic activity for some decades. While Marco Polo was by nature especially attuned to commercial activity (there are many notable lacunae in his account relating to cultural aspects of Chinese civilization), he clearly saw and probably was not inclined to exaggerate a vibrant world of merchants and commerce in thirteenth-century China. Yet, we must be mindful of the social and cultural context within which merchants carried on their business. In the classical Confucian view of the four classes of society— scholar (or official), farmer, artisan, and merchant—the merchant came last in this moral hierarchy. The order was based on the contribution of each class to the maintenance of the social system. Scholars at the top were the essential intelligence, the brain, without which society could not function. Farmers were the muscles, the primary producers of the wealth of the agrarian state. Artisans labored with their hands to create the tools, the material goods that supported and supplemented the farmers' production. Merchants used neither their minds nor the strength of their backs and their hands, but merely exploited the differences in supply and demand to profit themselves. It goes without saying that this depreciation of commerce did not envision commercial taxation as a vital resource of the state alongside agricultural taxes and tribute. The locus classicus of Confucian anticommercialism was Mencius, who, when summoned by King Hui of Liang, was asked by the king:

> "Sir, you have come all this distance, thinking nothing of a thousand *li*. You must surely have some way of profiting my state?" Rather contemptuously, Mencius responded, "All that matters is that there should be benevolence [*ren*] and righteousness [*yi*]. What is the point of mentioning the word 'profit'?"[3]

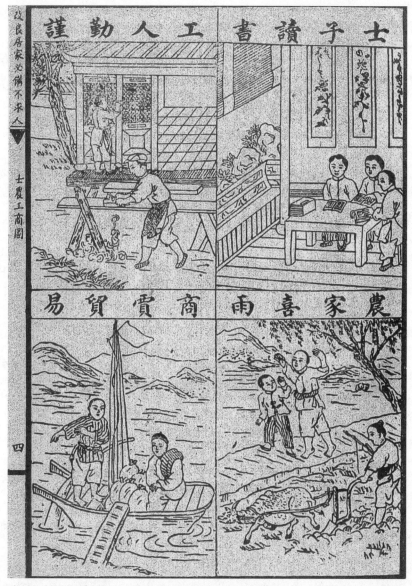

Figure 12.1. The Four Classes. *Wanshi buqiuren* (almanac) (Taibei: Wenhuan tushu gongsi, 1968).

This disdain for profit pervaded Confucian thinking for centuries. The traditional Confucian emphasis on benevolence and righteousness was so powerful that it tended to preclude any other motives, which in comparison were seen as mean and unworthy. Moreover, merchant culture of wealth and consumption was viewed by the social elite as a threat to the fundamental agrarian ideal and the established social order.

ECONOMIC EXPANSION

The long-distance interregional trade in commodities other than luxury goods that Marco Polo observed emerged in the Song, and by the late Ming had become highly developed as a "circulation economy" involving national and local markets. These commercial commodities included grain, salt, raw silk and silk fabrics, tea, cotton and cotton cloth, medicinal herbs, sugar, hemp, and vegetable oils. By the mid-Qing the central Yangzi commercial hub of Hankou swarmed with ten thousand boats and ships of all kinds, rivaling the scene that Marco Polo reported six centuries earlier.

Reforms of the taxation system in the agrarian society had a large influence on economic growth. State taxation during the Han was virtually entirely in the form of levies of taxes in kind in grain, cloth, and corvée labor. This system persisted through the long Six Dynasties period of division from the third to the sixth centuries, and was inherited by the unified empire of the Tang. By the eighth century the entire per capita taxation system had become increasingly unworkable, and the Tang was in a state of fiscal collapse. Fiscal health was restored by the "double tax" reform instituted by chief minister Yang Yan in 780. All taxes including corvée were consolidated into taxes levied twice a year on land area alone. The vital transportation of grain from the south to the capital region in the northwest was accomplished with paid labor. Progressive replacement of per capita taxes and taxes in kind continued in the Ming with the "single whip" reform of the sixteenth century. From the Tang onwards, these changes led to the growth of a money economy (including paper money and especially silver in the Ming) and a great expansion of commerce. The revival of commerce and a money economy made possible commercial taxes on commodities such as salt and tea, which became an important source of central government revenue.

By the Ming a market economy had developed on top of the traditional command economy of the state since the Han and the local customary barter economy of peasant villages and towns. We see here the intersection of coexisting economies: The customary economy at the local village and town level, largely a barter economy; the command economy driven by the state since early times, based on extraction of wealth through tribute, taxation, labor, and fees; and the market economy, a circulation economy knitting together diverse regions of China. The government's role in the latter was minimally invasive, thanks to the traditional Confucian laissez-faire attitude toward economic activity coupled with its incapacity to manage commercial activity on a local level.

The Ming began during the Hongwu reign in an economic environment that had more in common with the pre-Song patterns of classical economic activity than with the robust commercial activity of the immediately preceding Song and Yuan. One would not find such effusive observations as Marco Polo's about commerce in fourteenth century Ming. For one reason, recovery from the civil wars in the transition from Mongol to Chinese rule was several decades in the making. Perhaps a harbinger of the vigorous activity to come was the great maritime expeditions in the early fifteenth century under the Yongle emperor (1402–1424). By the mid-fifteenth century huge changes were beginning to become evident, even to people at the time. The simpler, older ways of the Hongwu era were noticeably vanishing. The most significant contribution to these changes was population growth. Although census statistics for early China are notoriously uncertain, the population of the early Ming is estimated to have been approximately 60 million. This was about what it had been more than a millennium previously during the Han. Population had fluctuated tremendously in the intervening centuries, which were marked by periods of division, rebellions, wars, and dynastic struggles. It may have reached 100 million or more in the Song before falling during the Mongol conquest. But by the seventeenth century, at the end of the Ming, the population had more than doubled to perhaps 150 million.

Expanding population pressure drove a westward migration into underutilized regions of Sichuan and Yunnan. In the early fifteenth century a series of natural calamities including flood, drought, famine, and pestilence throughout nine provinces of east, central, and northeast China caused extensive dislocation of the affected population. Shifting population was accompanied by expanding commerce that by the sixteenth century was knitting together the economy of the entire country. Itinerant merchants traveled extensively throughout the empire; this new mobility was exhibited in the popularity of short stories collected by the literary scholar Feng Menglong (1574–1646) from a variety of sources. They were written in the colloquial dialect, accessible to a wider reading public than the formal literature of the scholar elite, and reflected the growing acceptance of the itinerant merchant class.[4] The economy was becoming increasingly commercialized from the lowest levels upward as farmers became integrated in production for the markets. Surplus commodities generated by the preexisting customary economy were distributed throughout the national market economy. Widespread commercialization necessarily fostered monetization of economic transactions. This process was vastly expanded by the Spanish conquest of the Philippines in the 1570s. Huge quantities of New World silver from New Spain, carried from Acapulco in the Manila Galleon, poured into China through the growing foreign trade at Canton and Macau. Chinese luxury goods from silk to furniture were carried back across the Pacific to clothe and furnish the new wealthy colonists of Mexico and Peru, and even found their way back to Spain. Silver, the principal medium of circulation, transformed the monetary system. The "single whip" tax reform of the late sixteenth century, by which multiple head taxes and land taxes in kind were commuted to a single payment in silver, reflected the large scale economic trends since the early Ming.

This commercial revolution in the market economy, of course, was dependent on the development of long-distance transportation and communication throughout the country. Commerce and travel stimulated urbanization; the growing numbers of an emerging affluent middle class lived in cities, which attracted members of the scholar-literati social elite. Class distinctions were beginning to become less rigid. Wealth and the circulation of silver bred consumption and cultural display, of luxury goods but also of the lifestyle attributes of the scholar-elite. Printing greatly expanded from the mid-Ming, producing an abundance of books of all kinds, from scholarly classics, examination manuals and aids, travel diaries and guides, to popular entertainment literature. Books that in the early Ming were generally very expensive were now notably cheap. Printing joined the general commercialization of the economy.

THE CULTURE OF COMMERCE

The economic expansion during the Ming had transformed society. The expansion of culture followed. Cultural life in the late Ming was more varied, more complex, richer, and more pervasive than it had ever been. The Hongwu reign seemed by comparison rustic and simple—a basis, of course, for nostalgia for lost times of the past, the way perhaps America in the 1950s or the Gilded Age of the 1890s might be viewed. Fashion, style, consumption of luxury commodities, and marks of elite status such as art and artifacts assumed a new importance in society. The trends that came to a head in the late Ming were ultimately carried on in the Qing after a period of recovery from the Manchu conquest. But the Manchu tendency toward puritanical repression, both in politics and culture, dampened considerably late Ming exuberance. Still, the relaxation of the orthodox Confucian attitude toward merchants and commercial wealth had had a permanent effect. The distinctions between gentry elite and merchants were breaking down and the boundaries had become more fluid.

By the Qing, a vast hierarchical cellular structure of markets linked the levels of trade through which commodities moved. From peasant villages, surplus commodities produced by household labor and consumable goods moved upward, at first through simple exchange, to local periodic markets in towns. These markets, meeting typically two or three times in a ten-day week, were staggered so that neighboring towns' markets did not conflict. A 5-10-15-20-25-30 market by days of the month, for instance, would mesh with a 3-7-13-17-23-27 market in a nearby town. A peasant could thus avail himself of both markets during a month. At the next higher level in larger market towns, markets were open continuously. They in turn were linked with central place cities that were hubs of nationwide commerce. Goods that were not manufactured by local artisans such as iron implements, tools, and medicines, by the same token moved downward through the hierarchy to periodic markets where they could be traded or purchased by local peasants.

The social fabric of commerce likewise was becoming increasingly diversified. The long-range trade centered on commercial hub cities exhibited a functional specialization of types of merchants. Brokers acted as intermediaries between buyers and sellers, specializing in a particular commodity, such as tea. Agents operated on commissions to negotiate transactions, and between buyers and sellers. Indeed, buying and selling (*maimai*) was the very word for business in Chinese. Compradors (from the Portuguese word *compra*, to buy), who were agents of foreign merchants and their firms in their dealings with Chinese merchants, belonged to this category. Wholesalers owned goods in their own right as dealers in various commodities, selling to other merchants or to retailers. Itinerant merchants, who usually specialized in a single commodity, but sometimes expanding as opportunities presented themselves, transported goods in large quantities between places of origin and marketing centers. While they might own the boats used in transport, independent ship and boat owners represented another category of entrepreneurs hired by merchants for specific jobs. Finally, retail merchants or shopkeepers were the end point of the distribution system of large varieties of merchandise at all levels.

The number of merchants engaged in interregional and long-distance trade increased greatly with the commercial expansion in the mid-Ming. As merchants from one city frequently found themselves in a distant city as strangers among people who often spoke a different dialect, practiced different customs, and ate different cuisines, and who sometimes experienced discrimination as aliens, they began to form associations of fellow natives of their original home. These provincial guilds (*huiguan*) built guild halls where merchants could gather and reside temporarily while they conducted business in the city. They almost always had a patron deity associated with their native place, who the members celebrated with appropriate ceremonies and feasts, and usually a set of regulations governing the behavior of the members. One of the first such guilds was established in Suzhou, the major center of the silk trade, by merchants from Huizhou prefecture in Anhui province. Guilds served both economic and fraternal purposes. Thus they were also established for examination candidates traveling from distant provinces to the capital (or to provincial capitals) for the triennial imperial examinations. Although sometimes built by merchants for the benefit of fellow provincial scholars, their function was separate from the commercial *huiguan*. While the official guilds were mainly located in Beijing, as scholars converged on the capital, merchant guilds associated with their native provinces were located in many commercial cities, such as Shanghai, Hankou, Guangzhou (Canton), and Suzhou.

By the mid-Qing guilds were ubiquitous throughout China wherever trade flourished. Distinct from *huiguan*, which were like provincial clubs that controlled the movement of trade to and from home provinces, were artisan or craft guilds (known as *gongsuo*) that controlled a specific commercial craft or industry in a defined area or city, such as carpenters, millers, weavers, fishmongers, druggists, bankers, etc. All who were involved in a trade were required to join a guild and abide strictly by its rules, which included fair trade and restrictions on competition, at the risk of severe sanctions. Penalties for breach of rules included sponsoring a banquet of ten to twenty plates, theatrical performances, or monetary fines. The religious function of guilds of both kinds was vital and the guild halls incorporated temples dedicated to their patron deities. Members were expected to participate in religious festivals and were penalized for failure to do so. Indeed, the largest component of guild expenses was ritual activities. Common patron deities were Mazu or Tianhou (Mother Ancestor or Queen of Heaven), a patron of seafarers and southern coastal communities; Guan Gong (Lord Guan), variously the god of war, of scholars, and of merchants, ubiquitous throughout China; Guan Yin, the Buddhist Goddess of Mercy; and Cai Shen, the god of wealth. The first two were historical persons who had been canonized in earlier centuries.

Guild halls were the most impressive buildings in a city, with colorful façades lavishly decorated, befitting and reflecting the wealth of their members. Besides establishing regulations governing commercial activities of their members, guilds were benevolent associations. For their less affluent fellow provincials stranded in a strange city, they provided emergency aid, coffins, and burial sites. To the surrounding community they engaged in philanthropic activities to aid the poor, established firefighting brigades, and funded the construction of roads and bridges. They set up soup kitchens to provide famine relief in times of emergency, and even organized self-defense forces against civil disturbances such as banditry and rebellion.

Besides the provincial guilds (*huiguan*) serving fellow local expatriates doing business in a distant city and artisan guilds (*gongsuo*) organizing common crafts in a city were merchant guilds incorporating all the principal traders in a commercial center. Though there were few examples of such organizations, the most famous, partly because it was central to the foreign trade with China in the nineteenth century, was the Cohong at Canton. Cohong combined the word *hong*, meaning a business firm, and the prefix *gong*, meaning collective. Thus the Cohong was a joint association of thirteen *hong* merchants who were exclusively licensed to trade with Western trading firms at Canton. Evolving in the early eighteenth century, the Canton Cohong became firmly established and fixed in form by 1757. Until the Treaty of Nanjing ending the Opium War in 1842 abolished the Cohong system, it was the only avenue of Western trade with China. Its principal export was tea, for which it was virtually the only outlet. Imports included a large variety of commodities of foreign origin, especially Indian cotton and British woolens. As the tea trade grew exponentially in the nineteenth century, the lack of sufficient commodities to exchange for it created a severe balance of payments crisis that was only temporarily met by importation of large quantities of silver to pay for tea. The Cohong merchants became fabulously wealthy and were major celebrities among the community of Western traders. (The Cohong system and Western trade will be discussed at length in chapter 17.) As the operation of the Canton Cohong system suggests, economic activity and trade tended to be localized rather than generalized across the length and breadth of China (as one would expect in a modern industrial economy). The total of long distance trade that had burgeoned in the Ming was still built on the sum of regional parts.

COMMERCIAL COMMODITIES

Grain, the principal product of the economy since earliest times, had to be collected in the form of taxes in kind and moved as tribute from place to place. From the Han into the early Ming generally this was done by conscripted labor. The relocation of the capital from Nanjing to Beijing by the Yongle emperor early in the Ming required an immense effort to ship tribute grain to the north to support the new capital and the Ming northern frontier armies. Transport of grain by sea early on proved to be both so hazardous (afflicted by pirates and bad weather) and difficult to manage effectively that it was shifted in 1415 to inland shipment on the Grand Canal, which was reconstructed at immense cost for this purpose by the Yongle emperor. Transport from six southern provinces was organized by the army using soldiers as labor, employing thousands of shallow draft barges operated in convoys. The soldier-boatmen were compensated by allotments of private goods carried on the barges, making them small-scale entrepreneurs. The abuse of this system eventually led to the large movement of private goods, as well as smuggled salt, at several times the quantity of grain shipped, so that by the Qing, which inherited the system from the Ming, the Grand Canal became virtually a huge commercial enterprise managed by merchants and officials.

Marco Polo had mentioned salt and silk as principal commodities in the commerce of the late thirteenth century. Salt was a component of the traditional command economy, a state monopoly since the Han. Most salt was harvested in the lower Huai River coastal region between the Yellow and Yangzi Rivers, produced either by evaporation in large salt pans or by boiling brine. A secondary source was from salt wells in Sichuan in the west, a much more costly and difficult process. During the late Ming when grain was needed to feed the armies along the frontier, merchants received licenses to buy salt in exchange for transporting grain to the frontier. The salt was then sold to distributors. The licensed merchants soon found it cheaper and more efficient to simply hire peasants to produce the grain directly in agricultural colonies near the frontier rather than incur the expense of transport from the south. At first they received vouchers or tickets for stipulated quantities of grain transported.

In the late fifteenth century exchange of grain for salt tickets was commuted to silver payments, part of the general monetization of the economy in the mid-Ming. Henceforth the frontier merchants, mainly from Shanxi province, moved to the city of Yangzhou on the Yangzi River near the center of the salt producing region. Because the market price of salt greatly exceeded the production costs, the Yangzhou merchants became notoriously wealthy. Merchants bid on the government-issued salt licenses that, granting a monopoly to sell salt, became essentially hereditary. Taxes paid on the sale of salt became one of the largest sources of government revenue apart from the land tax. Joining the Shanxi merchants at Yangzhou were merchants from Huizhou prefecture in Anhui province, a group that was already prominent in trade nationwide. It was said that the two groups from Shanxi and Huizhou, who became the most powerful merchants in China, were both driven to settle in the Yangzhou salt trade by the poor soil and unpromising agricultural conditions of their home districts. Shanxi traders came particularly from several counties in southwest Shanxi, especially Pingyao where the founder of the group was said to have originated. While the Shanxi merchants generally were prevalent in the north, where they controlled the overland Russian tea trade, Huizhou traders, particularly those from She county, dominated in the south. The extravagant wealth of both groups was legendary. According to the late Ming scholar-official Xie Zhaozhe:

> The great merchants of Hui-chou have made fisheries and salt their occupation and have amassed fortunes amounting to one million taels [ounces] of silver. Others with a fortune of two or three hundred thousand can only rank as middle merchants. The Shansi merchants are engaged in salt, silk, reselling, or grain. Their wealth even exceeds that of the former. This is because the Hui-chou merchants are extravagant, but those of Shansi are frugal. In fact, people of Hui-chou are also extremely miserly as to food and clothing . . . but with regard to concubines, prostitutes and lawsuits, they squander gold like dust.[5]

Silk was the oldest industry in China, where it was invented in the prehistoric period. According to the legendary record the wife of the primordial emperor of China, Huangdi (The Yellow Emperor), who was purported to have lived around 2700 BCE, invented sericulture. The basic production process changed very little over centuries through the Han, when it had already become very sophisticated. China under the Han was the starting point of the famous Silk Road across central Asia to the Mediterranean where silk was in great demand among the Roman upper class. The method of silk production was maintained as a state secret, but eventually silk cocoons were smuggled out of China on caravans and the process was acquired abroad. Nevertheless, China remained the almost exclusive supplier of silk to the rest of the world, until Japan entered the trade in the late nineteenth century and displaced China in the early twentieth.

Sericulture was labor intensive, a handicraft industry based in peasant homes employing mostly female labor especially in the off-season. It began with the cultivation of mulberry trees, which could be grown on the edges of fields where they did not compete with subsistence grain crops. Mulberry leaves were fed to silkworms, the larval stage of the silk moth, held in large trays in the home. When they reached maturity the worms spun cocoons, from which the fine silk filaments were unwound and reeled into silk thread. Raw silk thread was then sold to merchants who wove it into fabric, but peasants could also do simple homespun weaving. For the labor required, the return from silk production was fairly high, making it an essential part of the household economy in many areas. From the Ming small-scale weaving workshops owned by wealthy merchants employing wage labor appeared.

The imperial court had a voracious appetite for silk, used in embroidered court ceremonial robes, the clothes of the imperial family and court ladies, decorations, and ceremonial official documents. Consequently imperial silk works were established in Beijing and at several cities south of the Yangzi River. These huge establishments, essentially artisan factories, employed corvée labor. With the growth of the money economy and the commutation of labor tax in kind to silver, the workshops switched to hired labor. After the mid-nineteenth-century Taiping Rebellion devastated the silk industry, which was centered in the region that suffered the severest impact of the rebellion, the quality of production of the official silk works deteriorated noticeably since the early Qing; compared to the fine workmanship of the early years, that of the late nineteenth century was comparatively crude. The brilliant craftsmanship seen in the many varieties of silk fabrics depended on special techniques handed down by generations in individual families, a reflection of the household nature of silk production. Households maintained their skills as secrets, and because of a reluctance to educate daughters in these techniques lest they might pass out of control of the family, they were often lost with the death of the master.

One of the curiosities of Marco Polo's account of his travels is his failure to mention tea, which by that time was a common drink in China. Perhaps it was because he circulated mainly among the Mongols, under whom he served as an official for fifteen years; the Mongols' favorite beverage was *kumiss*, fermented mare's milk, a considerably stronger drink. But tea trade with the Mongols and other peoples across the frontier was an important export commodity. Tea was introduced to China from Southeast Asia and was grown mainly in the hilly provinces of the southwest, central regions, and coastal southeast, to which it was best adapted. Tea was a state monopoly in the Tang (618–907) and became a nationwide drink in the Song (960–1279). Like silk, tea was basically an item of domestic household production, although processing and fermentation by higher-level shops was required to produce the best teas for national consumption and export. In the Northern Song, tea from Sichuan was bartered under a government program for horses for the army, supplied by nomadic peoples of the northwest frontier. Tea for domestic consumption in the Ming was not subject to government monopoly. However, the horse trade was revived as a state monopoly in tea. One-and-a-half million ounces of tea were traded for fourteen thousand horses every three years. After the tea-horse trade collapsed in the late Ming, it was revived again in the early Qing but had lapsed by the early eighteenth century.

While the salt trade was entirely a matter of domestic consumption, tea was a crucial commodity in foreign exchange as well as a significant article in local markets. It was the foreign market, where the popularity of tea grew exponentially among the British public, that transformed the tea trade. By the end of the eighteenth century the tea trade at Canton, mediated through the Cohong system, constituted virtually the entire revenue of the British East India Company and one-tenth of the revenue from taxes of the British crown. Tea comprised up to 90 percent of all exports from Canton in the early nineteenth century while China was the sole source of the world supply. By the late 1880s, however, the British had succeeded in growing tea in large plantations in the hill country of northern India and in Ceylon, cool climates to which it was perfectly adapted. The British industrial mode of production was far superior to Chinese production by independent peasant households. Individual peasant cultivators were unwilling to invest in adequate fertilization and expensive periodic replacement of over-mature tea bushes, with the result that China lost its dominance of the world market in tea by the early twentieth century.

Cotton was introduced sometime in the thirteenth century and spread rapidly in the Yangzi delta Jiangnan region as a staple crop of peasant household industry. So much cotton was planted at the expense of subsistence crops that during the famine of the 1580s there was little left to eat. Where cotton was not planted, mulberry was grown, aggravating the problem. Cotton cultivation was particularly intensive in the Shanghai area, which became the center of the industry. Cotton production became fragmented into discrete stages, including growing, ginning, carding, spinning of the yarn, weaving, calendering, and dyeing. All of these operations except the last two were possible with the proper equipment within the peasant household, which made cotton an attractive handicraft industry. Its technology changed very little until the end of the nineteenth century. Merchants were involved as intermediary agents at every stage of the process of production from ginning to weaving to dyeing. Ginned cotton was sold to spinners, the yarn sold to weavers, the finished cloth sold on the market. Thus the market economy and the customary economy were closely integrated. In the Qing cotton became the largest native industry, paired with farming itself as the basis of the customary economy. The demand for cotton in the lower Jiangnan region around Shanghai became so great that, exceeding the capacity of local production, raw cotton had to be imported from the southern provinces of Fujian and Guangdong and from the north from Shandong and Henan.

MONEY AND BANKING

The circulation economy of long-distance trade in commodities from place to place would not have been possible without an effective system of money and credit. Various forms of currency had been in use in China from antiquity, including natural vehicles of exchange like cowry shells and various forms of minted metallic money. The round copper coin with a square hole, known as *qian*, or "cash," became the standard currency in the Han for small transactions. But for larger transactions various media in standard measures were employed, such as gold and bolts of silk. Silver came into circulation by the Tang dynasty. Paper currency was introduced first in the Song period and was implemented by government mandate in the Mongol Yuan dynasty when it circulated widely. It was still in use in the early Ming, but the failure of the state to back it up caused paper currency to lose confidence and silver ingots became the standard medium for large exchanges.

Since silver was not properly coined but exchanged in units of weight of approximately one ounce (*liang* or *tael*, equal to 1.3 English ounces), in every transaction the weight and purity (fineness) had to be validated by an official assayer or shroff. Because small amounts of silver were inevitably lost in the process of assaying, an informal compensatory surcharge was collected from the payer. For instance, in paying taxes at the district *yamen*, each taxpayer would pay the surcharge in addition to the amount of tax owed. This "meltage fee" (*huohao*) became a substantial source of revenue for local and provincial governments. Being entirely extralegal and unregulated, it was the source of considerable corruption in the form of irregular payments (*lougui*, literally "customary fees," in other words, bribes) by each level of the provincial bureaucracy to the next higher level. Without these financial contributions local government administration would not have been able to meet its expenses since central government allocations to regional officials were only a small fraction of the support required. Salaries of officials, furthermore, were merely nominal stipends.

The Yongzheng emperor (1723–1735) early in his zealous fiscal reorganization banned *lougui* and mandated the legalization of meltage fees as an official source of provincial expenses, called *huohao guigong*, "returning meltage fees to the public coffers" (where in his opinion they presumably belonged). *Huohao* in various provinces ranged anywhere from 10 to 20 percent of tax payments. At the same time salaries were supplemented by additional compensation, called *yanglian* ("nourishing virtue"), paid from the legalized meltage fees, which amounted to several times the official salaries. These reforms accelerated the monetization of silver as the basis of the economy in the early Qing.

Money begat credit. Generally speaking, loans were made for purposes of consumption (seasonal purchase of seeds, expenses for weddings and funerals) not for capital accumulation. The earliest credit institutions were pawnshops, first associated with Buddhist monasteries in the fifth century. They became increasingly secularized by the Ming, and by the Qing reached the pinnacle of their popularity. Pawnshops became the most attractive alternative to investment in land, offering both security and greater profit. Pawnshops often appeared in cities as virtual strongholds, tall, sturdy brick buildings like banks designed to resist attack.

"Money shops" (*qianpu*) appeared in the Ming, dealing in small-scale exchange, usually in copper. They performed as local banks, receiving deposits, making short-term loans, and issuing notes that circulated as paper money. Money shops evolved into larger scale commercial banks dealing in silver, remitting funds, and issuing paper exchange notes, especially in Shanghai. Known as "old style" or "native" banks, they operated mainly in the south. Shanxi merchants in their extensive trade became involved in long-distance remittance of funds, at first mainly in transfer of silver bullion under guard, at the end of the eighteenth century. Operating at a higher level than the old style native banks and money shops, Shanxi banks became the most powerful traditional banks, making loans to old style banks and acting in a semiofficial capacity as fiscal agents for central and provincial governments and as repositories of government funds. They were tightly organized along family lines and regional identity, prevalent mainly in the north but operated everywhere in China. At the end of the nineteenth century modern banks (*yinhang*) made their appearance, first as branches of foreign banks such as the British Hongkong and Shanghai Banking Corporation in 1865, organized on modern open banking principles.

ECONOMIC AND SOCIAL TRENDS

During the Ming-Qing period (1368–1911) the dominant long-range development in China's economy was the transition from a command to a market economy. One consequence of this change was the increasingly passive role of the state in the economy. A second feature was the declining dependence on the land tax through the nineteenth century compared to a growing reliance on commercial taxes. While the land tax remained the primary source of revenue, commercial taxes rose in proportion to the whole. The salt tax, formerly the largest commercial tax, declined in relative importance in the nineteenth century. The foremost new nonagricultural tax was the *likin* (*lijin*, one-thousandth of a *tael* or one cash) levied on trade and goods in transit throughout the country during and after the Taiping Rebellion. *Likin* had been instituted by provincial officials to fund the regional armies that rose to fight the Taiping rebels in default of central government support. The revenues raised went entirely to provincial treasuries, completely outside the control of Beijing. Goods in transit were taxed on an ad valorem basis repeatedly at *likin* stations along all major transportation routes, both on land and water.

Third, although an integrated national commercial economy had developed by the late Ming, peasant household production at the local level of the customary economy persisted throughout this period as a base. Tea, silk, and cotton continued to be organized as handicraft industries. Also, separate merchant groups monopolized trade in separate spheres, such as the Huizhou, Shanxi, and Canton Cohong merchants, and the northern and southern ("native") banking institutions. Thus, though an extensive market economy pervaded every province of the country and united regions in a national fiscal system, the economy remained in a sense compartmentalized by specialized productive activities and fragmented by regional associations of specialized trade and marketing groups.

Fourth, the formerly sharp line between merchants and the literati-scholar class became blurred. Many merchant families increasingly adopted a strategy of social mobility to enter the official class, and literati increasingly engaged in entrepreneurial and business activities regardless of the traditional social stigma attached to business, especially as opportunities to enter officialdom declined. A conceptual transformation of the traditional Confucian view of merchants and profit had slowly evolved through the Ming-Qing period. Long-range cultural patterns were correspondingly affected. Superfluous wealth stimulated the pursuit of social and cultural rather than official and political rewards. Scholars sought the patronage of wealthy merchants, and merchants sought to accumulate intellectual and social capital by patronizing scholars and collecting vast libraries of books.

Was China in the nineteenth century on the verge of an industrial revolution which would bring it into the modern world economic order? Or was it only on the cusp of that order, looking in as a spectator but destined never to join it fully? Or was China simply pursuing its own path to a modern economy defined in its own terms? The ongoing discussion over the alleged retardation or nondevelopment of capitalism in the Western mode versus the Marxist-inspired debate over the "sprouts of capitalism" in the late traditional period has been a largely sterile exercise. It is better to understand what China was than what it was not. In some ways China's impressive late twentieth-century economic growth has stimulated such questions as the above in Chinese leaders' own minds, manifested in such rhetorical phrases as "Market-Leninism," "The Confucianization of Communism," and "Socialism with Chinese Characteristics." If some Chinese are seeking to map their own path to world economic power, they are often inhibited from discerning that path by the ambivalent and even pejorative view of their own history.

SUGGESTED READINGS

Ayao, Hoshi. Mark Elvin, trans., *The Ming Tribute Grain System* (Ann Arbor: University of Michigan, Center for Chinese Studies, 1969). Grain was transported from the Yangzi region to feed Beijing and the armies in the north since the early Ming. This competent study documents the development of the system.

Birch, Cyril, trans. *Stories from a Ming Collection: Translations of Chinese Short Stories Published in the Seventeenth Century* (New York: Grove Press, 1958). Seven stories selected from Feng Menglong's collection reflect popular life and culture from Tang times through the Ming.

Fairbank, John K. ed. *The Cambridge History of China*, vol. 10, *Late Ch'ing, 1800–1911, Part 1* (Cambridge: Cambridge University Press, 1978).

Fairbank, John K., and Kwang-Ching Liu, eds. *The Cambridge History of China*, vol. 11, *Late Ch'ing, 1800–1911, Part 2* (Cambridge: Cambridge University Press, 1980).

Gardella, Robert. *Harvesting Mountains: Fujian and the China Tea Trade, 1757–1937* (Berkeley: University of California Press, 1994). An excellent study of tea production in Fujian province and the evolution of international tea trade.

Golas, Peter J. "Early Ch'ing Guilds," in G. William Skinner, ed., *The City in Late Imperial China* (Stanford: Stanford University Press, 1977), 555–580. An informative account of Chinese merchant guilds in the Qing.

Ho Ping-ti. "The Salt Merchants of Yang-chou: A Study of Commercial Capitalism in Eighteenth-Century China," *Harvard Journal of Asiatic Studies* 17.1/2 (June 1954): 130–168. The author shows the salt merchants of Yangzhou were economically powerful and socially influential through the later Qing period.

Johnson, Linda Cooke. *Shanghai: From Market Town to Treaty Port, 1074–1858* (Stanford: Stanford University Press, 1995). Shanghai developed from a regional market center in the Song to become the queen of the treaty ports after the nineteenth-century opening of China to the West.

Li, Lillian M. *China's Silk Trade: Traditional Industry in the Modern World, 1842–1937* (Cambridge: Harvard University Press, 1981). An economic study of the silk industry and development of the silk trade from the treaty settlement with the West to the Republican period.

McElderry, Andrea Lee. *Shanghai Old-Style Banks (Ch'ien-Chuang), 1800–1935: A Traditional Institution in a Changing Society* (Ann Arbor: Center for Chinese Studies, University of Michigan, 1976). A useful short monograph on the traditional Chinese banking system.

Morse, Hosea Ballou. *The Gilds of China, with an Account of the Gild Merchant or Co-hong of Canton* (Taipei: Che'eng-wen Publishing (reprint), 1966; orig. pub. London: Longmans, Green, 1909). The classic study of Chinese merchant guilds, explaining their different types.

Peterson, Willard J., ed. *The Cambridge History of China*, vol. 9, *The Ch'ing Empire to 1800, Part 1* (Cambridge: Cambridge University Press, 2002). *The Cambridge*

History of China volumes 9, 10, and 11 (like the twin volumes on the Ming) are the standard authorities of the Qing dynasty by leading scholars of their respective fields.

Polo, Marco. Milton Rugoff, trans. with introduction, *The Travels of Marco Polo* (New York: New American Library, 1961). As a Venetian merchant Marco Polo was particularly interested in Chinese commerce. A good, accessible translation of Marco Polo's famous narration of his travels throughout the Mongol empire.

Rowe, William T. *Saving the World: Chen Hongmou and Elite Consciousness in Eighteenth-Century China* (Stanford: Stanford University Press, 2001). A masterful study of the career of an influential scholar-official reformer in the eighteenth century.

Shih Min-hsiung. E-tu Zen Sun, trans., *The Silk Industry in Ch'ing China* (Ann Arbor: University of Michigan, Center for Chinese Studies, 1976). A good description of the most ancient Chinese traditional industry.

Skinner, G. William. *Marketing and Social Structure in Rural China*, Association for Asian Studies, reprinted from *Journal of Asian Studies* 24.1 (November 1964), 24.2 (February 1965), 24.3 (May 1965), AAS Reprint Series. A seminal series of articles by a leading anthropologist of China on the commercial structure of rural society.

Wakeman, Frederic, Jr. "China and the Seventeenth Century Crisis," *Late Imperial China* 7.1 (June 1986): 1–26. This article explains China's situation in the global seventeenth-century economic crisis.

Wang Yeh-chien. *Land Taxation in Imperial China, 1750–1911* (Cambridge: Harvard University Press, 1973). An essential study of the land tax, the principal source of revenue in China, since the mid-Qing.

Watson, Andrew, trans. *Transport in Transition: The Evolution of Traditional Shipping in China* (Ann Arbor: University of Michigan, Center for Chinese Studies, 1972). Traditional shipping is discussed in its various aspects in translation of detailed articles by a number of Japanese scholars.

Whelan, T. S. *The Pawnshop in China* (Ann Arbor: University of Michigan, Center for Chinese Studies, 1979). Traces the growth of this characteristic Chinese economic institution from the mid-Qing to its relative decline in the early Republican period.

Xu Dixin and Wu Chengming, eds. *Chinese Capitalism, 1522–1840* (New York: St. Martin's Press, 2000). A very useful collection of essays on Chinese capitalism from the Marxist perspective.

Yang Lien-sheng. *Money and Credit in China: A Short History* (Cambridge: Harvard University Press, 1952). An excellent, descriptive standard work on money and credit institutions in China.

Zelin, Madeleine. "Capital Accumulation and Investment Strategies in Early Modern China: The Case of the Furong Salt Yard," *Late Imperial China* 9.1 (June 1988): 79–122. A useful article describing the production of salt by salt wells in western China.

Zelin, Madeleine. *The Magistrate's Tael: Rationalizing Fiscal Reform in Eighteenth-Century China* (Berkeley: University of California Press, 1984). An absorbing account of the complexities of fiscal reform in the eighteenth century.

NOTES

1. Marco Polo, *The Travels of Marco Polo*, edited with an introduction by Milton Rugoff (New York: New American Library, 1961), 205.
2. Marco Polo, *Travels*, 207–208.
3. Mengzi (Mencius), trans. with an introduction by D. C. Lau, *Mencius* (Harmondsworth, England and New York: Penguin Books, 1970), I, A, 1.
4. See Cyril Birch, trans., *Stories from a Ming Collection* (New York: Grove Press, 1958) for examples of colloquial short stories.
5. Quoted by Ping-ti Ho, "The Salt Merchants of Yang-chou: A Study of Commercial Capitalism in Eighteenth-Century China," *Harvard Journal of Asiatic Studies* 17.1/2 (June 1954): 143–144.

13

Official Life and
Literati Culture

Peasants plowing the yellow alluvial loess soil and digging wells in the North China plain southwest of Beijing had from time to time uncovered peculiar pieces of bone. From their fragile condition and yellow color they appeared to be very old. And some of them had strange incisions that seemed to be some sort of symbolic markings. So unlike the bones of ordinary animals, they must be the bones of dragons, auspicious beasts possessing magical powers, and therefore potentially very valuable. The peasants took these strange bones to druggists, and they eventually turned up in apothecary shops in Beijing, to be ground up for medicine. There, in the early twentieth century, antiquarians and scholars discovered them and realized that they were not "dragon bones" but the relics of a very early civilization that had occupied the Yellow River plain, and that the strange incisions were a form of primitive Chinese. Moreover, the symbols, often simple pictures, were found to be directly related to modern Chinese characters, and the inscriptions could be deciphered. Out of this discovery came the historical affirmation of the ancient Shang civilization that occupied the North China plain from roughly the eighteenth to the eleventh centuries BCE. The bones, usually scapula or flattened leg bones of large animals and the plastrons of tortoises, were instruments of divination of the will of the ancestors and thus came to be called "oracle bones." Not only did they establish the chronological validity of the Shang, heretofore believed to belong to myth, but were evidence of the antiquity of the Chinese written language.

The Chinese written language is one of the most ancient on Earth, and is the oldest in continuous use from its origins to the present time.

Chinese characters, written words, were revealed on oracle bones and bronze vessels dating from the second millennium BCE and are in essence the same, and can be read, as modern Chinese characters, allowing for evolution of stylistic forms and changes of meanings. The characters were incised on the plastrons of tortoises and flattened leg bones and scapula of oxen for use in ceremonies of divination to discover the ancestors' will, and embossed on ceremonial bronze vessels cast to commemorate important events during the Shang dynasty, circa 1700–1100 BCE. No one knows, of course, how words were pronounced in the Shang or for many centuries thereafter. Written characters are pictographic and ideographic symbols. They possess no inherent phonetic value, and are thus independent of speech. Therefore they endured, regardless of changes in speech patterns, for centuries, retaining their original meanings but acquiring layers of additional meanings and nuances through usage over time.

The word—the written word—has thus dominated Chinese culture. This is true first because the spoken language—actually several distinct spoken dialects as different from each other as many European languages—continuously evolved over time and is not directly related to the nonphonetic written language that evolved very little over the same period, and second, because of the visual calligraphic power of the written characters. The written word, as a self-contained conceptual unit, retains powerful visual impact. Thus written words defined literacy in a special way through the authority that they conveyed as autonomous visual symbols, much more than do words constructed by phonetic components in a phonetic script. Words on a sheet of paper could be arranged in an array or matrix that conveyed an additional force of meaning, as in the use of parallel lines of equal numbers of characters that reflect each other's images in a poem. Not only were written characters manipulated as visual images in ways that spoken words could not be, but patterns of characters on paper, or carved in wood or stone, as in poetry or ceremonial inscriptions or signs, acquired additional impact from their arrangement and association.

For the literati, spoken communication, if it was intended to be meaningful or important, was virtually always written down, whereupon the formal syntax and vocabulary would change. Written classical Chinese language (*wenyan*, literally "cultivated speech") had an entirely different grammatical structure from colloquial spoken language. Because of its sparse use of words, eliminating many of the connective words and particles that make speech intelligible, it was usually not intelligible if spoken. But it possessed great allusive power because of the nuances and variable meanings of written characters. Culture was only fully accessible through written words (and also illustrations, a visual form of writing). The word was everything.

BOOK CULTURE

From very early times words were recorded in continuous text as books. The Chinese invention of paper (as early as the first century BCE in the Han dynasty), and of printing (woodblock printing in the seventh-century Tang dynasty and moveable-type printing in the eleventh-century Northern Song dynasty) had an incalculable influence on the production of books. The late Ming witnessed a vast increase in publishing, based in part on technological improvements in the production of paper, especially cheap paper made from bamboo, and in woodblock printing (xylography), and also on cultural expansion and social changes from the fifteenth century. The increasing availability and low cost of books contributed to the spread of literacy. Publishers responded to a growing market for printed manuals for examination candidates and collections of successful exemplary examination essays were much in demand and widely circulated. Books of all kinds, from cheap editions of popular works of fiction to expensive reprints of classical works, including novels, poetry, anthologies, histories, philosophy and the Confucian Classics, as well as travel guides were abundantly available. The possession of books increasingly tended to define social status. Book collecting also received a powerful impetus from publishing. As books became cheaper, private libraries grew in number and size in the late Ming and early Qing. A collection of several thousand *juan* (bound chapters or volumes) was considered respectable, 10 thousand *juan* (equivalent perhaps to a thousand titles) was remarkable. Libraries of less than 30 thousand *juan* were not uncommon. One of the most famous libraries, visited by many scholars, was the *Tianyi ge* (Heaven United Pavilion), founded by the bibliophile Fan Qin (1506–1585) in Ningbo on the east coast south of Hangzhou in the mid-sixteenth century. It was preserved over several centuries as a result of extraordinary attention to security, housed in a stone building, secured by lock and key, and with a prohibition of borrowing. On Fan's death it contained 70 thousand *juan*, in several thousand titles.

THE LITERATI

Who were the literati? In spite of several decades of scholarship driven by research into Chinese social structure and social dynamics attempting to define "gentry," "scholar," and "literati," a general lack of consensus remains on the meaning of these terms in the context of traditional Chinese society. The problem is partly a matter of semantics. The basic word for literatus is *wenren*, a literate or cultivated person. The term implies someone with at least a minimal familiarity with literature, including the Confucian Classics, but excluding those with mere basic functional literacy. Parallel to *wenren* are two terms, *shi*, scholar (in origin a term for the lowest class in the feudal order of the Zhou dynasty—Confucius was a member of this class), and *shen*, often defined as gentry, or official, since the word originally denoted the embroidered sleeves of the robe of an official, an indicator of political status. Both terms imply command of the written word, more than routine literacy. Together, combined as one word *shenshi*, the term is customarily taken to designate "gentry." But this is often the crux of disagreements over terminology, since "gentry" is a term adopted from England, suggesting a social order above commoner, but is functionally unsuited to the Chinese case. English gentry typically lived in the countryside on large estates and supervised commoners living in their domain. They were fond of keeping horses and dogs and had a sentimental attachment to the land. Chinese gentry, while sometimes living in the countryside, had little sentimental connection with the land from which they drew income, and usually preferred to live in towns and cities where they could consort with their fellow literati.

Those who achieved the lowest degree in the civil service examination system, the *shengyuan* (literally "born official"), were literati by virtue of the preparation necessary to pass the examination. But this degree alone virtually never qualified its holder for official appointment. It was a transitional status between commoner and gentry, depending on the wherewithal of the individual's family. Many such "scholar-commoners" never progressed beyond this level, but enjoyed its benefits of status. *Shengyuan,* however, often filled an important function at the local level, relying on the authority of their status to act informally to mediate disputes among local residents.

Higher level degrees opened the door to official appointment. The general term for official was *shidaifu*, combining the honorific *daifu* with *shi* (scholar). Such officials certainly started out as literati, in the sense that academic achievements reflected their command of a broad range of classical literature. But they were not necessarily scholars in any meaningful sense. Many officials were more bureaucrat than literatus. They never penned a poem or essay, and their personal secretaries drafted their official documents. Thus, the notion that China was ruled by scholars, a popular European view of the seventeenth-century Enlightenment, especially fostered by the urbane and enlightened reign of the Kangxi emperor, is a distortion. Still, it is true that most officials were more than just plodding paper-pushers; they participated in a larger cultural world of classical learning, literature, art, and aesthetic appreciation. Literati here is used in this broad sense of a class of people, not all men, from very low to high social status, who were involved actively in the higher cultural world of Chinese society.

OFFICIAL AND PRIVATE SERVICE

For most literati, official service in the imperial administration was, at least initially, their primary objective. Government service provided official salaried emolument, further opportunity to acquire wealth in office to sustain an elite lifestyle, confirmed social prestige and status (including immunity from routine corporal punishment), and fulfilled a moral-political imperative to contribute to the welfare of society. Assuming a career unburdened by political or personal setbacks, an able scholar-literatus might well advance upward through the civil service examination hierarchy and through successive official appointments to reach a position of eminence and power on the national stage. This ideal course on an official career could be deflected at various stages, including repeated failures in the examination at higher levels, unsuitability for the rigors of official life and bureaucratic drudgery, and personal disinclination for a public career. Aspiring officials frequently "dropped out" of the contest for office, which imposed repeated qualifying examinations and evaluations for appointment throughout one's life. Aside from such recurrent pressures on the choice for an official career, the impact of singular events or circumstances influenced literati choices. The fall of the Ming and the Manchu conquest left many literati at sea with a sense of loss and failure. If they had served the Ming in its final years, loyalty to the fallen dynasty precluded transferring their allegiance to its successor. Though many Ming literati and officials did take official positions under the Qing, a stigma attached to such "twice-serving officials." Some literati who earned civil examination degrees under the Ming felt that they owed a debt of gratitude to the dynasty. Others felt a personal obligation to the last Ming emperor who had committed suicide upon the fall of Beijing in 1644. In their view, subjects were morally bound to follow their ruler, and some committed suicide as a mark of honor when they learned of the emperor's death. Thus, in the second half of the seventeenth century there were many loyalists (*yimin*) who refused to serve the Manchus.

In the next century, as the examination system produced an increasing number of higher degree holders while the number of official bureaucratic positions remained constant, increased competition for appointment discouraged many prospective officials. What was a man to do? A range of alternative career choices were possible for those who for one reason or another did not pursue the route to official service. Unless he had independent means the private scholar-literatus was dependent on alternative sources of income. Teaching was one. While preparing for the examinations, literati, especially those who had already earned the *shengyuan* degree, took positions with gentry families, tutoring their sons in the Classics and literature with a view to preparing them for the first examination. For more accomplished scholars, positions as lecturers in private academies were an option. Private academies burgeoned in the early- to mid-Qing, attracting advanced students preparing for higher level examinations. Many of them favored the ideological focus of their founders and patrons, such as those that Ruan Yuan founded in the late eighteenth and early nineteenth centuries, including the famous Xuehai tang (Hall of the Sea of Learning) in Canton that trained scholars in the *kaozheng* (evidential learning) movement that was Ruan Yuan's specialty.

Another alternative was employment as a secretary to a local official on his private staff (*mufu*, literally "tent government"). A member of a *mufu* was considered a *muyou*, a "friend," a coequal colleague, not an inferior employee, of the scholar-official who invited him to serve. Specializations within a typical *mufu* included particularly law and finance, the principal responsibilities of local government. Legal secretaries were the most senior, reflecting sometimes years of experience, and were responsible for much of the success of an official's administration. One of the most famous legal *muyou*, Wang Huizu (1731–1807) served as legal secretary for more than thirty years. Based on his experience he compiled two indispensable guides to local government.

Patronage of high officials and wealthy merchants offered opportunities to bright and well-trained scholars. Again, Ruan Yuan, who commanded seemingly inexhaustible financial resources, sponsored major literary projects employing numerous scholars to edit, collate, and publish compendia of classical works such as the *Huang Qing jingjie* (Qing exegesis of the Classics) as well as historical editions including the *Guangdong tongzhi* (Gazetteer of Guangdong Province). Following Ruan Yuan's own proclivities, scholars participating in these projects were particularly associated with the Han Learning (*Hanxue*) movement of the late eighteenth and early nineteenth centuries. The discovery of heretofore obscure talent by prominent figures such as Ruan Yuan was a major impetus to many literati careers. Such discoveries of talent could arise in unusual ways:

> While visiting a monastery in the mountains to avoid guests on his birthday, [Ruan Yuan] saw a poem composed by [Tan] Ying on a wall [of the monastery]. Marveling at it, he told the district magistrate: "The district has a talented person; it would be good to get him." When the magistrate asked his name, [Ruan] could not tell him, but when the magistrate found the poem and recited it to Yuan, Yuan said, "That's the one!" The next year

Yuan opened the Xuehai tang at Yuexiu to train scholars in the Classics, history, and poetry. He saw a preface, "Purification [Ceremony] of Moistened Rushes," and a lyrical poem, "Lingnan Lychee," in one hundred stanzas written by Ying that particularly moved him to admiration.[1]

Later Tan Ying was appointed director of the Xuehai tang.

The extravagantly wealthy salt merchants of Yangzhou were another source of patronage for scholars. The merchants sponsored lavish poetry contests with rich prizes, collected rare books, and supported indigent scholars, all of which redounded to the social prestige of the nouveaux-riches merchants.

Not all literati relied on the beneficence of official employers or official or merchant patronage. The expanding circulation of knowledge contingent on the boom in commercial publishing in the late Ming, and the commodification of writing, engendered a new realm of possibilities for literati employment, including writing, compiling, editing, and publishing. Literati entrepreneurs became "scholar-merchants" (*shishang*), though true to Confucian prejudices they tended to depreciate their economic activities in favor of their literary achievements.

For some literati a kind of conceit, the "urban recluse," rationalized their activities on the margin between the traditional respectable scholar-official life and the somewhat dubious mode, from an orthodox Confucian point of view, of intellectual entrepreneur. A recluse, after all, had an honorable provenance as one who chose to retreat from the stress of the political world, particularly in the late seventeenth century, as a defense against the pressures to conform to the Manchu conquest. An urban recluse could still enjoy the company of his fellow literati. A true recluse, *shanren* ("man of the mountains"), the extreme pole of withdrawal from society in a Daoist sense, an option which very few were willing to adopt because of the hardships it entailed, was generally not highly respected.

THE LADDER TO OFFICIALDOM

The aspiration of an ambitious scholar-literatus was to become an official in the imperial bureaucracy from the bottom at the poorest provincial district to the pinnacle at the metropolitan central government. Without official status and emolument, life for many literati was a constant struggle. Be that as it may, the route to becoming an official was an arduous path, beset by the risk of repeated failure and increasingly intense competition as one climbed the ladder. It began as early as age three when the prospective candidate was first introduced to the foundations of basic literacy at home, possibly by a hired tutor if the family was sufficiently well off. The first text to which the child was exposed would be the *Three-Character Classic* (*Sanzi jing*), composed of three-word phrases that successively introduced the fundamentals of Neo-Confucian doctrine. The student at first was not expected to understand the content of what he was reading but only to learn the characters and commit the text to memory. Only gradually would he begin to grasp its meaning. His education would progress to the *Thousand-Character Classic* (*Qianzi wen*), comprising one thousand characters none of which are repeated. Next would come the *Classic of Filial Piety* (*Xiao jing*) wherein the student would be introduced to a course of instruction in the fundamental Confucian *Four Books* and *Five Classics*, the basis of the orthodox school of Song Learning (*Songxue*) of Zhu Xi, upon which the civil service examinations were structured.

Moving out of private education in the home, elementary schools existed empire-wide in local districts and communities, though the coverage was often uneven. Private elementary schools were established by powerful clans, usually restricting admission to clan members. Government-mandated community schools (*shenxue*) were supplemented by charitable schools (*yixue*) which provided education for students of poor families. Above the elementary level, education became increasingly a matter of self-directed study, aided sometimes by tutors and the increasing abundance of examination preparation manuals that appeared with the vast growth of publishing in the late Ming. At the top of the educational pyramid the Imperial Academy (*Guozi jian*) was an institution less for instruction at an advanced level than for the honorary registration of successful examination candidates. In addition there were some 300 private academies (*shuyuan*) in the Qing which invited bright and promising *shengyuan* to engage in study, research, and literary compilations. Ruan Yuan's Hall of the Sea of Learning (*Xuehai tang*) was a prime example of such academies.

Beginning at the district level and at an age dependent on their intellectual capacity, students would enter the world of the examinations. For some, progress to the top could be fairly rapid; others might spend many years, perhaps their entire lives, pursuing elusive examination success. Ruan Yuan, the brilliant patron of Han Learning and high official, received the highest metropolitan degree, the *jinshi*, at the youthful age of twenty-five. Wang Huizu, the professional private secretary, earned the second provincial degree, the *juren*, at age thirty-nine after eight attempts, and the *jinshi* at age forty-six after three tries.

The first step was the district qualifying examination which was required to continue to the first level at the prefectural capital. The prefectural examination was given two out of every three years. Success here

Figure 13.1. Opening Lines of the Three-character Classic. *Mingji rili* (almanac) (Hong Kong, n.d.)

earned one the coveted *shengyuan* ("born official") degree. An estimated two million candidates nationwide sat for the district examination, of which approximately 30 thousand would be successful in receiving their *shengyuan* degree. Passing was based not on absolute criteria of mastery but on quotas set for each region and varying by region. The examiners' job was to rank all of the papers in order from top to bottom. Thus it might be that, say, of one thousand candidates sitting for the examination in one prefecture, one hundred judged to be the top papers would pass.

Examinations were held in a permanent walled examination compound. At the upper end was a hall on a raised platform for the presiding examiners, below were tiers of stalls, connected in rows, open in front, with only a simple shelf to write on and a board to sit on. The examinations lasted two to three days. Strict security governed what could be brought into the compound. The signed examination papers were numbered and copied by clerks so that the examiners read anonymous papers to avoid the possibility that they might favor a student whose name they recognized. Naturally, elaborate measures were taken by candidates, including stylistic flourishes and familiar references in the content of their essays, designed to alert the examiners to a favorite pupil.

Having passed the prefectural examination, the candidate would advance to the provincial examination offered once every three years at the provincial capital. Of the perhaps 20 to 30 thousand graduates of the prefectural examination sitting for the provincial examination nationwide, only about 1,500 could expect to win the *juren* ("recommended man") degree. The metropolitan examination was held once every three years, a few months after the provincial examination so that students would have time to travel to Beijing. For each year the metropolitan examination was given, only about 300 would receive the final *jinshi* ("presented scholar") degree. One last stage confronted the successful candidates, the palace examination before the emperor himself, by which they were finally ranked. Those awarded the first three places were celebrated as the crème de la crème of the empire, assured of the most prestigious assignments in the central government.

Both *juren* and *jinshi* were eligible for appointment, but by the mid-Qing only *jinshi* had any chance of an immediate assignment, usually as a district magistrate, the lowest level of provincial administration. Even so, because there were fewer openings than qualified candidates, a period of awaiting official appointment was to be expected.

The examination process itself did not encourage innovative or creative thought, except in adeptness in satisfying the formal expectations of the examiners. Any departure from orthodox ideology in one's examination essay would be fatal to one's chances. Examination essays were required to conform to the *bagu* (eight-leg) essay style. A question based on the classics would be posed, in which critical words or phrases had been omitted. In order to identify the omitted portions, a student would have to have committed the entire corpus of the Classics to memory. The essayist would thus be required to address the critical phrases as the core of his argument, by circumlocution, in eight prescribed sections totaling no more than 1,000 words. The prescribed essay clearly emphasized form over content, style over substance. Students spent undue amounts of time practicing and polishing their *bagu* essay style, and a good portion of the publishing industry was devoted to producing manuals that presented the latest successful *bagu* essays. Perhaps it is no wonder that many literati, faced with such an intellectually sterile exercise, simply chose not to compete. Yet for those who persisted and were successful in winning the highest degree, the rewards in prestige and access to power were enormous. The examination system created a status hierarchy based on a meritocracy (however one chooses to evaluate the merit) of knowledge, not an aristocracy of birth.

ALTERNATIVE CAREERS

The Chinese literate elite since the time of Confucius during the declining feudal age of the sixth century BCE felt a political imperative to serve the ruler in a public capacity, though moral reservations regarding the ruler's conduct could deflect this sense of obligation. Confucius himself spent his life in a quest for the ideal prince, but never found one worthy to serve. The Daoists abjured political involvement as fundamentally injurious to moral character and personal freedom. Thus a tension prevailed between Confucian and Daoist attitudes toward public service, which coexisted within many an individual: "Confucian in office; Daoist out of office." In the frenetic quotidian activity of the office, the scholar was a Confucian. In the quiet retreat of retirement, whether it was a temporary withdrawal in mid-career or at career's end, the scholar was a Daoist.

While the arduous pursuit of official appointment preoccupied a large majority of scholar-literati, there were always the leftovers, by choice or force of circumstance. For those whose antipathy for public service led them to terminate their pursuit, the *shengyuan* degree brought sufficient privileges, if at the lowest level. These joined the ranks of the nonofficial literati. Women were sometimes a significant component in this group. Since women were ineligible to take the examinations, a public literary career was difficult for them. If they were educated, their study invariably began with instruction by a family member, especially their mother if she were educated and desired the same thing for her daughter. But it was rarely if ever conceived as a route to some kind of career. If a young woman achieved a basic literacy, she could continue with self-education. In rare cases this could in turn lead to opportunities for further education and even a literary career on the margins of literati society. Yuan Mei (1716–1798), who received his *jinshi* degree at twenty-three, a famous poet, official, and libertine, educated his daughter and employed her as his secretary. He was fond of taking young women as students. In his old age he had many female students, who earned the name "moth-eyebrow academy," including at one time thirteen pupils, severely frowned upon by moralistic Confucians who believed that education was inappropriate for women. Undeterred by such condemnation, Yuan published an anthology of the poetry of twenty-three of his female pupils.

Literati women generally expressed themselves in poetry. Properly expected to avoid being seen in public, they envied the freedom enjoyed by their male friends and companions, and in a few cases resorted to disguising themselves as men. In an amusing episode recounted in his memoirs, Shen Fu (b. 1763) tells how his wife Yun, with his encouragement, dressed as a man so that they could visit a festival together. She inadvertently gave herself away when she instinctively approached a group of young women and was forced to reveal her identity. Though women were considered intellectually and morally inferior to men and confined to the home, and marriages were arranged by parents, companionate marriage became increasingly common among literati in the Qing. Li Yu (1611–1680), a prolific novelist, dramatist, publisher, and a cultural entrepreneur, could be considered a feminist for his liberal views on universal education for women and his association with literati women. Li Yu's wife was such a companion, supporting his literary endeavors. Shen Fu and his literary wife Yun, who composed poetry and participated with him in literary discussions, for more than twenty years together enjoyed a close intellectual companionship.

Nonofficial literati sought to maintain the leisure status of the educated elite. They mixed easily and frequently on a social and intellectual level with scholar-officials and between them there was no class difference. But without official salary a literatus' existence could be perilous, unless he were endowed with independent means (including family support) or some kind of consistent alternative employment or source of income. No clear boundary separated the lower literati, even those with the nominal *shengyuan* degree, from commoners and peasants. Shen Fu, for example, possessed no degree and struggled to support his family. On one convivial picnic with friends, they included in their gathering a dumpling seller they met along the way, "not an ordinary sort." Frugality, he remarked, was "knowing when to save money." His wife Yun, who invariably participated in these outings, was very accomplished at making do with very little.[2] Yet for much of their time together, though admittedly poor, they had at least one servant.

In the best of circumstances literati such as Shen Fu might enter the service of a powerful patron. But the lack of the *shengyuan* degree would be an obstacle. He could also tutor the children of scholar-gentry families. If a literatus was well-known and widely respected as a writer, such as Li Yu or Yuan Mei, he would be much in demand to sell his writings (*maiwen*), including short inscriptions, poems, prefaces to books, biographies, and epitaphs, for often handsome fees. Much more common was employment as a secretary (*muyou*) in an official's secretariat (*mufu*). Since *muyou* were treated as invited "friends," colleagues of the official, and were well paid, this was an honorable profession, as the career of Wang Huizu demonstrates. Following his father's footsteps, Shen Fu worked on and off for thirty years as a legal secretary, the most specialized and highly respected of *mufu* staff. As the social boundaries between lower literati and merchants blurred, literati became entrepreneurs, engaged in publishing and other literary activities. Li Yu's Mustard Seed Garden in Nanjing was famous as a bookstore and publishing house. On a much more modest scale, Shen Fu was forced by poverty to resort to becoming a merchant selling paintings.

LITERATI CULTURE

The lifestyles of the literati at every level were much devoted to the art of living. In this respect, rich or poor, famous or obscure, they shared a common language of culture. In both literary and visual aesthetics the goal was to exhibit discrimination and good taste. Literati taste was understood by the cognoscenti as either *ya* (elegant, refined, distinguished) or *su* (vulgar, common, unexceptional). For many the distinction was instinctive. But for the boorish *nouveaux-riches* like the Yangzhou salt merchants it had to be taught. Literati clients were very useful in instructing in such aesthetic discrimination. Since something that was elegant in one context could be vulgar in another (such as decorative objects appropriate only to the women's quarters), knowledge of this kind was not always immediately obvious. Shen Fu's memoirs, sensitive, unpretentious, charming, and often poignant, are replete with remarks and advice on taste. Yun was particularly adept at making creative and tasteful use of simple materials and objects on a limited budget. Shen Fu advises:

> When putting chrysanthemums in a vase one should select an odd number of flowers, not an even number. Each vase should contain flowers of only a

single colour. The mouths of the vases should be wide so that the flowers can spread out naturally . . . Whether the flowers should be dense or spread out, whether they should lean towards the viewer or away, *all depends on the sense of pictorial composition of someone who knows how to appreciate them.*[3]

Of course, fashion, especially from the late Ming, guided taste. The posture of refined taste could be emulated, creating kinds of fashions in behavior. One of the most enduring cultural affectations was amateurism or dilettantism in painting. Supposedly done in the studio of the literatus, literati painting was distinguished from academic or court painting, done at the dictation of a patron or the emperor. The latter was viewed as aesthetically compromised by the motive for financial gain and the absence of spontaneity, and however technically accomplished such paintings were, they were depreciated by the literati as lacking an inner spiritual quality. Yet literati painters clearly created paintings at the request of others and made good money from their sale, although the fiction was carefully preserved that they were done not for material reward.

Another kind of affectation, especially in the climate of withdrawal following the Manchu conquest, was the *shanren* (literally "man of the mountains"), someone who like a Daoist recluse withdrew from society to a rustic country retreat. The posture of *shanren* was most often adopted by the "urban recluse," one who withdrew from public service but not from the enjoyment of the society of fellow literati, a "recluse" in name only who was not a recluse in fact.

Ingredients of the literati lifestyle included the paraphernalia of things, of material culture; cuisine and food; leisure touring; and poetry. The ownership of things or objects was an obvious visual display of taste. Artisanship was an important basis for the evaluation of material objects, and particular authorship could take on an independent value, as it does in the cultures of other societies. But authorship was, and is, often easily imitated or forged. Again, Shen Fu displays an innate appreciation for objects as a source of aesthetic pleasure. In the late Ming food became a medium of expression of literati culture, for those who could afford it. Epicureanism, the enjoyment of lavish cuisines, exhibited literati taste and affluence, as it does today among Chinese in Hong Kong and on the mainland.

Leisure touring (not travel in the mundane sense) was a mark of aesthetic appreciation of scenery and place. Places that were linked to historical events and literary associations were favorite destinations of outings, occasions for feasts and banquets evoking literati fellowship. The growing popularity of leisure touring fostered its commercialization, as commercial enterprises including tea houses, wine shops, and pleasure boats sprung up around popular sites such as temples and famous natural attractions.

Of all the ingredients of literati lifestyles, poetry was ubiquitous. Poetry was the medium of communication and association among scholars regardless of other forms of intellectual and cultural activity like painting, collecting, and writing essays. Groups of literati formed poetry clubs and came together in informal social gatherings and more formal parties, devoted to poetry contests and games. More than any other intellectual endeavor, poetry was accessible to female literati. The poetry produced in these venues was collected and popularly published in large numbers of anthologies, made possible by the burgeoning printing industry that made cheap editions accessible. Anthologies were a way of displaying associations among literati and exhibiting good taste.

By the late eighteenth century the literati elite had ceased to be exclusively dependent on the state. The examinations continued to flourish as before and remained the only route to civil service appointment. Yet even this was to change in the nineteenth century when the government's increasingly urgent need for revenue to combat the crises of foreign war and domestic rebellion led to the sale of offices. But unlike earlier eras in the late Tang and Song dynasties where the examination system virtually dictated the boundaries of the ruling class, with economic and cultural expansion from the mid-Ming, the social-political elite had become far more diversified. Diminishing numbers of bureaucratic positions relative to growing numbers of qualified candidates aggravated this trend. A bureaucratic career was no longer "the only game in town" by the late eighteenth century. The Literary Inquisition of the 1770s under the Qianlong emperor, associated with the *Complete Library of the Four Treasuries* (*Siku quanshu*) project, had the effect for a time of disciplining the literati who were vigorously prosecuted and punished for sometimes innocent breaches of loyalty to the Manchus and for alleged subversion. But the Qianlong reign was the last age of abject submission to the imperial state. The expanding publishing industry since the late Ming offered vast new outlets for expression that could no longer easily be controlled by the state. Patronage opened new opportunities for intellectual and political activity. In the nineteenth century freedom of criticism challenged the dominance of the old order. Public opinion emerged as a new force.

In a counterfactual world, one could imagine that a new, vigorous dynasty succeeding the Qing might have imposed a new discipline on a cowed ruling elite, much as the founder of the Ming, Zhu Yuanzhang, did in the fourteenth century. But it was not to be. The literati had become an autonomous force.

SUGGESTED READINGS

Brook, Timothy. *The Confusions of Pleasure: Commerce and Culture in Ming China* (Berkeley: University of California Press, 1998). An innovative study of commerce and culture in the Ming, anchored to metaphorical seasons of the dynasty and biographies of salient figures in each season.

Chang, Chun-shu, and Shelley Hsueh-lun Chang. *Crises and Transformation in Seventeenth-Century China: Society, Culture, and Modernity in Li Yu's World* (Ann Arbor: University of Michigan Press, 1992). An expansive exploration of culture as reflected in the work of the idiosyncratic literatus Li Yu whose life spanned the Ming-Qing transition.

Chang Chung-li. *The Chinese Gentry: Studies on Their Role in Nineteenth-Century Chinese Society* (Seattle: University of Washington Press, 1955). The seminal study of the Chinese scholar-gentry elite, still a standard work.

Chow, Kai-wing. *Publishing, Culture, and Power in Early Modern China* (Stanford: Stanford University Press, 2004). An excellent study of the relationship between the growth of the publishing industry, culture, and political power in the late Ming.

Chow, Kai-wing. *The Rise of Confucian Ritualism in Late Imperial China: Ethics, Classics, and Lineage Discourse* (Stanford: Stanford University Press, 1994). The central role of ritual in Confucian discourse, society, and culture is examined here.

Ch'ü T'ung-tsu. *Local Government in China under the Ch'ing* (Cambridge: Harvard University Press, 1962). The best general study of the critical level of local government in the Qing period.

Clunas, Craig. *Superfluous Things: Material Culture and Social Status in Early Modern China* (Honolulu: University of Hawaii Press, 1991). A brilliant study of late Ming connoisseurship, material culture, and society.

Folsom, Kenneth E. *Friends, Guests, and Colleagues: The Mu-fu System in the Late Ch'ing Period* (Berkeley: University of California Press, 1968). Scholar-literati association in the official's private secretariat is examined here.

Hegel, Robert E., compiler and translator. *True Crimes in Eighteenth-Century China: Twenty Case Histories* (Seattle: University of Washington Press, 2009). Interesting criminal cases, usually homicide, and their investigation described here.

Ho Ping-ti. *The Ladder of Success in Imperial China: Aspects of Social Mobility 1368–1911* (New York: Columbia University Press, 1962). The path-breaking study of social mobility in the Ming-Qing period from analysis of examination records.

Ho Ping-ti. "The Salt Merchants of Yang-chou: A Study of Commercial Capitalism in Eighteenth-Century China," *Harvard Journal of Asiatic Studies* 17.1/2 (June 1954): 130–168. The author shows the salt merchants of Yangzhou were economically powerful and socially influential through the later Qing period.

Hummel, Arthur W., ed. *Eminent Chinese of the Ch'ing Period (1644–1912)*, 2 vols. (Washington, D.C.: Library of Congress, 1943–1944). In spite of its age this remains the essential comprehensive biographical reference for the Qing.

Johnson, David, Andrew J. Nathan, and Evelyn S. Rawski, eds. *Popular Culture in Late Imperial China* (Berkeley: University of California Press, 1985). This collection of thirteen essays presents a valuable perspective on a broad range of popular cultural themes.

Levenson, Joseph R. "The Amateur Ideal in Ming and Early Ch'ing Society: Evidence from Painting," in John K. Fairbank, ed., *Chinese Thought and Institutions* (Chicago: University of Chicago Press, 1957), 320–341.

Meyer-Fong, Tobie. *Building Culture in Early Qing Yangzhou* (Stanford: Stanford University Press, 2003). Following its destruction in the Manchu invasion, the reconstruction of Yangzhou cultural monuments is examined in four case studies.

Naquin, Susan, and Evelyn S. Rawski. *Chinese Society in the Eighteenth Century* (New Haven and London: Yale University Press, 1987). An examination of political, social, and economic themes in Qing China, focusing on the flourishing of related institutions in the eighteenth century.

Peterson, Willard J. *Bitter Gourd: Fang I-chih and the Impetus for Intellectual Change* (New Haven: Yale University Press, 1979). The intellectual influence of a prominent scholar-literatus during the Ming-Qing transition.

Peterson, Willard J., ed. *The Cambridge History of China*, vol. 9, *The Ch'ing Empire to 1800*, Part 1 (Cambridge: Cambridge University Press, 2002). *The Cambridge History of China* volumes 9, 10, and 11 (like the twin volumes on the Ming) are the standard authorities of the Qing dynasty by leading scholars of their respective fields.

Polachek, James B. *The Inner Opium War* (Cambridge: Harvard University Press, 1992). Early chapters discuss the role and activities of the literati in the nineteenth century.

Rawski, Evelyn Sakakida. *Education and Popular Literacy in Ch'ing China* (Ann Arbor: University of Michigan Press, 1979). The role of education in the subliterati level of society.

Rowe, William T. *Saving the World: Chen Hongmou and Elite Consciousness in Eighteenth-Century China* (Stanford: Stanford University Press, 2001). A masterful study of the career of an influential scholar-official reformer in the eighteenth century.

Shen Fu. *Six Records of a Floating Life*, translated with an introduction and notes by Leonard Pratt and Chiang Su-hui (London: Penguin, 1983). The touching and sensitive memoir of a lower level literatus-commoner. A highly recommended source for understanding literati culture.

Smith, Richard J. *China's Cultural Heritage: The Ch'ing Dynasty, 1644–1912* (Boulder: Westview Press, 1983). A fascinating and informative description of the many dimensions of elite and popular culture in the Qing period.

Twitchett, Denis, and Frederick W. Mote, eds. *The Cambridge History of China*, vol. 8. *The Ming Dynasty, 1368–1644*, Part 2 (Cambridge: Cambridge University Press, 1998). The volumes of the *Cambridge History of China* on the Ming dynasty, with chapters contributed by authorities in their respective fields, constitute the most complete and essential reference for this period.

Waley, Arthur. *Yuan Mei: Eighteenth Century Chinese Poet* (New York: Macmillan, 1956). This sympathetic biography of the idiosyncratic, popular Qing literatus describes especially his relationship with literati-women.

Watt, John R. *The District Magistrate in Late Imperial China* (New York: Columbia University Press, 1972). An important study of the district magistrate and his *yamen* where many local literati were employed as secretaries.

Whitbeck, Judith. "Kung Tzu-chen and the Redirection of Literati Commitment in Early Nineteenth Century China," *Ch'ing-shih wen-t'i* 4.10 (December 1983): 1–32. An example of literati activity in the late Qing.

NOTES

1. *Qingshi liezhuan* (Collected Biographies of the Qing), 10 vols. (Taibei: Zhonghua shuju, 1962), 36: 23 a–b.

2. Shen Fu (Leonard Pratt and Chiang Su-hui, trans.), *Six Records of a Floating Life* (London: Penguin Books, 1983), 67–68.

3. Shen Fu, 57 (emphasis added).

14

Images in the Heavens,
Patterns on the Earth

In the Chinese legendary mythology, Fu Xi was the First Man, the personification of the prehistoric Paleolithic era. As the first great culture hero, he conceived the symbolic representation of the natural world:

> When in early antiquity Pao Hsi [Fu Xi] ruled the world, he looked upward and contemplated the images in the heavens; he looked downward and contemplated the patterns on earth. He contemplated the markings of birds and beasts and the adaptations to the regions. He proceeded directly from himself and indirectly from objects. Thus he invented the eight trigrams in order to enter into connection with the virtues of the light of the gods and to regulate the conditions of all beings.[1]

The legend tells that observing the geometrical patterns on the back of a tortoise, Fu Xi invented the Eight Trigrams, the combinations and permutations of three broken and unbroken lines. At some point in the Zhou dynasty (c. 1100–246 BCE) these were incorporated as sixty-four hexagrams (combinations and permutations of six broken and unbroken lines) into the oldest Chinese Classic, the Yi Jing (The Classic of Change). The Yi Jing was an early divination manual: An elaborate process of casting the stalks of a yarrow plant derived a hexagram, which upon consultation of the manual provided an answer to a question posed by the supplicant.

The individual lines of the trigrams correspond to the fundamental cosmic principles of yin (broken line), representing dark, passive, female, and yang (unbroken), representing light, active, male. The ancient characters for yin and yang originally signified the shady side of a hill and the sunny side of a hill.

The *Yi Jing* was a compendium of constantly mutating images as the lines of the hexagrams changed from unbroken to broken and from broken to unbroken, within a closed system. Within any hexagram, the lines and their relative positions were dynamically related to each other. Flowing from the observations of Fu Xi, the hexagrams collectively were a kind of image of the pattern of the cosmic order.

Parallel with the development of the concepts of *yin* and *yang* and the sixty-four hexagrams, were the *wu xing* or Five Phases, symbolized as earth, wood, metal, fire, and water. Sometimes, perhaps under the influence of the Greek four elements of earth, air, fire, and water, the *wu xing* were conceived by Western commentators as five elements. But they are not physical elements in the same sense, but rather immaterial forces or agents. *Yin-yang* and *wu xing* eventually converged in a very early system of correlative thinking, the conceptualization of external reality (as opposed to the internal moral nature of man). Some have seen this as a proto-science, the precursor of modern scientific thinking in China. However much *yin-yang* thought was a systematic ordering of cosmology, it was not a *theory*, in that it was not subject to testing and verification. Following from the legend of Fu Xi's observations, this mode of thought was fundamentally observational and phenomenological. The Five Phases were as often correlated with directions of the compass, colors, or historical periods as with physical properties, reasoning by analogy.

PROTO-SCIENCE

Traditional Chinese naturalistic thought exhibited an intellectual proclivity for compendia of concepts or objects. The *Bencao gangmu* (literally, "Summary of roots and plants"), a systematic pharmacopoeia written in 1578 by Li Shizhen (1518–1593) contained 1,892 varieties of herbal substances and over 11,000 prescriptions, many of them highly effective in diagnosing and treating observed symptoms, superior to traditional European herbal pharmacology. But it did not lead to a modern medical science.

The premier enterprise of ancient Chinese scientific activity was astronomy in the service of calendrical science devoted to creating and maintaining the official calendar of the state. Calendrical astronomy (*lifa*, literally "the method of the calendar") was distinct from *tianwen*, astrology (literally "writing in the heavens") which only much later became the word for astronomy. An accurate calendar was a central concern of the imperial state from early times, especially with the unification of China under the Han empire in 206 BCE, for essentially two reasons. First, the agricultural economy, the foundation of the state, depended on an accurate seasonal calendar to determine the times for planting and harvest. Here, accuracy was paramount. Second, political legitimacy of the ruling house, in particular the reigning emperor, depended on the perception that the Mandate of Heaven was securely held by the monarch. Although various events might indicate the weakening of the Mandate, unpredicted astronomical phenomena were the most potent challenges to the Mandate, warnings of Heaven's displeasure. Here, predictability was paramount. Any phenomenon that could be predicted could be ruled out as an omen or portent. The cosmological order, in which the emperor stood at the center as a balance-wheel between Heaven, Earth, and Man, was influenced by Heaven and understood by divination. The emperor's ministers pointed to anomalous heavenly signs as comments on the ruler's virtue. For this reason, during the Han, computational accuracy in mathematical astronomy became increasingly refined. The function of the calendar in both its aspects became institutionalized in the Imperial Astronomical Bureau. Astronomers as scientists became bureaucrats, or vice versa.

The impetus to mathematical precision was accuracy of prediction, not theoretical understanding of the cosmos. If a lunar eclipse, which was the simplest and most common event to predict, was predicted with reasonable accuracy, all was well. Solar eclipses and comets were far more difficult. Unlike the classical Western cosmological systems of Aristotle and Ptolemy, which became the bases for understanding God's Creation, physical constructs based on geometrical models were unimportant to the Chinese. Confucianism as a state ideology was indifferent to conceptual models. For it, the issues were ethical, the nature of man's relationship to society, not his origins.

As time went on mathematical astronomy became increasingly routinized. The bases of prediction were complex periodic time cycles, which were purely computational devices, not spatial representations of reality. The basic pattern of Chinese astronomy was fixed in the Han, after which few modifications took place. Advances in the practice of mathematical astronomy reached their climax in the Song. Thereafter the practice declined and the old knowledge fell into oblivion in the early Ming.

A NEW SCIENTIFIC SPIRIT

By the late Ming the climate for science had changed. The late sixteenth century was a time of intellectual ferment and cultural vitality that fostered a reexamination of previous intellectual movements and values and an exploration of new attitudes toward the past. The Idealist School of *xin* (mind), founded by Wang Yangming in the sixteenth century as an alternative to the Rationalist Cheng-Zhu School of *li* (principle), came under increasing criticism. The Idealist School emphasized internal sources of all knowledge acquired through intuition and meditation. By the end of the seventeenth century scholars such as Fang Yizhi (1611–1671) were attacking the intellectual sterility of the abstract metaphysical discourse surrounding the Idealist School. Later in the early Qing, scholars who spanned the Ming-Qing transition, such as Gu Yanwu and Huang Zongxi, blamed the failure of the Ming on the destructive political factionalism and irresponsible self-indulgent attitudes of late Ming scholars. A new emphasis on objective sources of knowledge and empirical studies displaced the earlier intellectual fashion. Scholars exhibited a new curiosity about natural phenomena and an inquisitive attitude toward the objective world. An extraordinary number of scholar-literati took an interest in scientific and technological knowledge during this period.

The Jesuit arrival intruded into this environment in the late sixteenth century. The first of a stream of Jesuit missionaries, Matteo Ricci arrived in China in 1582 and worked his way north to Beijing, where he died in 1610. Discovering the eagerness among Chinese for superior European mathematical skills and astronomy, Ricci promoted European science as a way to gain Chinese trust. He called for more missionaries trained as scientists to follow him. Ricci pioneered the Jesuit policy of cultural accommodation first set out by Alessandro Valignano, the Jesuit father-visitor to Asia, during his field investigations in Japan. The superiority of the Jesuit science in the accurate prediction of astronomical events soon placed them in the Ming astronomical bureau. In the fluid intellectual milieu prevailing from the early seventeenth century, Western scientific knowledge stimulated among Chinese scholars interest in recovering indigenous mathematical knowledge lost since the early Ming. These efforts converged in the early Qing with the broader movement to reconstruct the genuine ancient Confucian classics, which had been corrupted and distorted by the neo-Confucian agenda of the Song. The resultant *kaozheng* (evidential research) movement became the vehicle for the revival of traditional Chinese science.

A CHINESE SCIENTIFIC REVOLUTION?

Was the early Chinese indigenous mathematics recovered through the evidential research of Chinese amateur scientists, wedded to Western mathematical astronomy introduced by the Jesuits, the beginnings of a true science in China? Some have suggested that these developments were tantamount to a scientific revolution in seventeenth century China, comparable to the scientific revolution in Europe that accompanied the discoveries of Galileo, Copernicus, Tycho Brahe, and Kepler. But the leading figures in this movement of recovery of early scientific knowledge were amateur scientists, all Confucian scholars working within a traditional context. They were ultimately committed to the traditional ideological order, not to replacing it with an entirely new paradigm. They sought not to create a rival to classical learning but to restore a part of it that had been lost. In that sense this was a scientific renaissance, not a revolution. In contemporary Europe, Galileo and Copernicus transformed the understanding of the universe and man's place in it and eventually brought down the classical cosmology.

When Galileo looked through his telescope and saw spots on the sun, heretofore viewed as a perfect unblemished body; when Copernicus convincingly showed that the earth and the other planets revolved about the sun, dethroning the earth from its place as the center of God's Creation; and when Kepler, to boot, proved the orbits of earth and the planets were not perfect circles, but ellipses, the whole classical Western cosmology of Aristotle and Ptolemy, of perfect material geometrical spheres in which man was central, was irrevocably overthrown. The Chinese traditional cosmology had no such rigorous material foundation. Secular periodic cycles in Chinese astronomy were computational conveniences only, not representations of the real world. The cosmos was not perfect; it was linked to human and earthly imperfections and flaws. Cosmological concepts such as the *Dao* (the Way), *Tian* (Heaven), and *Taiji* (the Supreme Ultimate) were not real things, they were metaphysical constructs. They were not subject to observational testing and proof. Thus changing Chinese understanding of the cosmos, whether from their own discovery or from Western revelation, did not dethrone Confucian teaching and cause a radical break in the view of the universe as it was understood. No revolution occurred.

THE POLITICS OF SCIENCE

Inevitable reactions to the new European scientific methods arose from various directions. As the Jesuit astronomers proved the predictive accuracy of their methods, they replaced the traditional Chinese and Muslim astronomers in the Qing Imperial Astronomical Bureau (*qintian jian*). The bureau was organized into a Calendar Section, an Astronomy Section, a Chronology Section, and a Muslim Section. At the very beginning of the Qing in 1644 Adam Schall von Bell, who unlike Matteo Ricci was trained as a scientist in mathematics and astronomy, was appointed director of the bureau. (He had already been aiding the Ming in calendrical reform and casting cannons, so that for the Jesuits the dynastic transition was seamless.) Under Schall's direction the Chinese in the bureau assimilated Western computational methods to create a reliable calendar.

At root, conservative scholars were opposed as much to the Jesuits' religion as their science, both of which they viewed as heterodox and alien. Chinese and Muslim astronomers whose methods had been replaced by Western ones felt an injured cultural pride caused by the implicit inferiority of native methods to imported Western knowledge. The subtitle of Schall's new official calendar, "according to the new Western methods," was particularly offensive to them. In 1657 an astronomer in the Muslim Section of the bureau, Wu Mingxuan, accused Schall of having made faulty predictions, but Schall was vindicated and Wu disgraced. As a result the Muslim Section, which no longer served any useful purpose, was abolished and incorporated into the Calendrical Section. The conservative attack was renewed in 1659 when an anti-Christian polemicist Yang Guangxian (1597–1669), aided by Wu Mingxuan, launched a campaign against the Western missionaries and criticized Schall's calendar. Yang's attack was facilitated by the ascendancy of the Oboi regency from 1661, which sought to reverse the pro-Chinese and pro-Western assimilation policies of the Shunzhi reign (1644–1661). In 1664 Yang impeached Schall for errors in astronomical calculations and accused the missionaries of plotting against the state, indoctrinating the people with false ideas, and choosing an inauspicious day for an infant prince's burial (the most serious charge). In 1665 Schall and seven Chinese astronomers were sentenced to death. But an earthquake the next day was taken as an omen of Heaven's displeasure and the sentences were dropped. However, five other Chinese were executed.

Yang, though lacking scientific expertise, was ordered to assume the directorship of the Imperial Astronomical Bureau with Wu Mingxuan's assistance, in spite of protesting his ignorance. Yang's administration was a failure. In 1668 the emperor ordered an investigation of Yang's calendar, which was found in error and Jesuit corrections substantiated. Yang, who had risen in favor with the Oboi regency, was cashiered when Oboi was condemned and his faction removed in 1669. Though Schall in the meantime had died in 1666, the Jesuits were restored to the leadership of the bureau, which henceforth remained under the control of Westerners until 1826.

Although Yang Guangxian's ineptitude in calendrical computations contributed to his undoing, the repudiation of Oboi's policies restored a climate once again receptive to the Jesuits and an appreciation of their more accurate methods. With the dismissal of the Oboi regency and the assumption of personal rule by the Kangxi emperor in 1669, the emperor, who from his youth was widely read and intellectually inquisitive, promoted Western science and patronized Chinese scientists, some of whom he assembled in the Southern Study (*nanshufang*) for instruction and discussion. In 1713 he established the *Mengyang zhai* (Studio for nurturing the young) in the imperial palace as an agency for the investigation, publication, and training in the newly recovered sciences. One of the scholars brought into the *Mengyang zhai* was the mathematician Mei Gucheng (1681–1763). During his long and distinguished career including several important posts in the central government the Kangxi emperor conferred many honors on Mei. Among his many interests was the preservation of old astronomical instruments from the previous dynasties.[2] His grandfather Mei Wending (1633–1721) was a seminal figure in the recovery movement, publishing extensively on the calendar of the Yuan and Ming, on calendrical methods, and on algebra and geometry which he believed prefigured Western works. While not himself a creative scientist, Mei Wending contributed greatly to the popularization of mathematics and astronomy and the revival of interest in earlier mathematical discoveries.

Politics and science were inextricably related. The process of calendar-making related to the auspices of the dynasty—observation, interpretation, and prognostication of celestial phenomena, omens, and portents, in an organic cosmological system that was often beyond the scope of scientific inquiry. Yet successful calendar-making in these terms required accurate predictive methods, and was improved by scientific investigation and advances in knowledge. Thus although the calendar, and the Astronomical Bureau which was charged with its computation, was devoted to an ultimately political end, it was necessarily also a scientific enterprise. A further tension existed between the demand for increased precision and conservative adherence to traditional, if outmoded and imprecise, methods and cosmological models. This tension was greatly complicated when the Jesuits became the principal exponents of methods of superior accuracy, especially since their methods were also intended to be an entrée for a different cultural order. Because the Jesuit influence displaced that of others with different vested interests, the political struggle among adherents of alternative scientific methods added another dimension to the political implications of science. Thus there were two kinds of political issues informing the practice of astronomy: First, the demand for accurate prediction as a foundation for political order, and second, the competing political influence of different scientific systems and their adherents.

The political implications of scientific activity posed a dilemma. On one hand was the desire for improved precision and accuracy committed to one political goal—imperial legitimacy through correct prediction and mastery of the natural order. On the other hand was the pressure to preserve traditional and indigenous ways committed to another political goal—legitimacy derived from adherence to traditional cultural assumptions and cultural autonomy. In other words, there were potentially competing imperatives of political legitimacy: Conformity to the objective natural order versus adherence to traditional cosmological models. How could this dilemma be resolved? At least two responses were possible. The first was exemplified by Yang Guangxian's predicament as successively the opponent of Schall's Western methods and director of the Astronomical Bureau. His response was simply to surrender the commitment to accuracy:

> Would that China have no good calendar, than that China have Westerners. Having no good calendar is no worse than the Han astronomers who, not knowing the method of apposition [between sun and moon], predicted all solar eclipses on the last day of the month. Still [the Han] enjoyed four hundred years of prosperity.[3]

The Jesuits return to favor in the Astronomical Bureau after 1669 and the Kangxi emperor's active enthusiasm for Western science did nothing to solve the dilemma. In due course, then, a second response emerged: The theory of the Chinese origin of Western science (*Xixue yuan yu Zhongguo*). The success and precision of Western science had conveyed an imputation of Chinese inferiority. But if the fundamentals of modern Western science had originated in ancient China, even though China had since lost the knowledge, European science, originally China's also, could be safely adopted without violating cultural self-esteem. Scientific accuracy and cultural integrity were reconciled. As a cultural defense, the doctrine of the Chinese origin of Western science found an influential exponent in the Kangxi emperor, and was promoted by Chinese scholars' recovery movement. However, the West and China were not symmetrical with respect to the role of scientific discovery. In the Chinese view of their own history of science, it would be as if Western scientists such as Galileo sought precedents for their discoveries in the Bible. The cultural difference in attitude was fundamental.

The trouble was that the seventeenth century was a time of great changes in Western science—a true scientific revolution was underway in the West. Scientific theories were in a state of flux, and the Catholic Church's resistance to the new science greatly complicated the situation in China. The Jesuits were constrained by Rome's injunction against heliocentrism from openly introducing the most recent European astronomy to the Chinese, although they had been availing themselves of the Copernican model in their calendrical calculations for some time. The Chinese were puzzled by apparent inconsistencies in Western cosmological models that were conveyed to them. Already Western astronomy was increasingly discredited by these unexplained discrepancies. When Copernican theory was finally introduced to China about 1760 the Chinese were thrown into confusion. Yet the Chinese had never been inhibited by a classical cosmology to which the authorities were committed. Thus the Confucian world view never exerted the benighted influence such as the Judeo-Christian mythology exerted on science in the West. Chinese mythological explanation of their origins was never a doctrine, while for the Church, Copernican cosmology was presented as a complete anathema, a form of heterodoxy.

THE PRACTICE OF SCIENCE

At the end of the eighteenth century Ruan Yuan (1764–1849), a high official and seminal figure in the Chinese scientific community of the late eighteenth and early nineteenth centuries, compiled the *Chouren zhuan* (*Biographies of mathematical scientists*). Supplemented by subsequent additions over the next century, this compendium comprised biographies and names of 675 Chinese and 205 Western scientists from antiquity to the end of the nineteenth century. Ruan Yuan, who was a leading scholar in the evidential research movement to restore the true Classics, and was an active patron of scientists if not himself a practicing scientist, envisioned the *Chouren zhuan* as a project to reconcile traditional Chinese and Western science as one. Disturbed by the imputation of China's cultural inferiority in the face of the new science from the West, Ruan subscribed to the belief that Western science had an ancient Chinese origin. The achievements of ancient Chinese science, although the knowledge of them had degenerated in China, had given birth to Western science, which the Jesuits had now brought back to China. No evidence was ever adduced to show that Western science actually originated in China and was somehow subsequently transmitted to the West—the theory was nothing more than a matter of faith engendered as a cultural defense.

What the *Chouren zhuan* does reflect, however, is that a community of scientists had taken shape in China by the nineteenth century. Scientists communicated with each other, shared their knowledge, acknowledged the priority of discoveries, and exhibited a self-image as men of science. Yet, however much scientific knowledge was perceived as an autonomous activity differentiated from humanistic knowledge promoted by the traditional examination system, it was not conceived as a distinct way to understand and master the physical universe through the discovery of abstract laws of nature. In a social sense as well, scientific activity was not yet professionalized in the modern sense, with its own institutions of recruitment and training as was beginning to happen in the West.

Chinese mathematical astronomy remained stuck in its traditional phenomenological mode through the nineteenth century, characterized by observation and categorization, without any theoretical impulse, a desire to explain the universe. No mathematization of science occurred in China, no generalization of principles. Chinese science did not develop into "modern science." Modern science was directly introduced and adopted from the West only in the twentieth century, in a secular context largely divorced from any religious agenda such as the Jesuits espoused in the sixteenth and seventeenth centuries.

What is "modern science"? It is not simply the current state of scientific knowledge and theory, a point on a constantly moving continuum—not like "modern architecture," "modern literature," or modern lifestyle, ever-changing according to the fashion of the moment. Moreover, it is not the state of scientific knowledge, say, in the late nineteenth century with J. J. Thomson's discovery of the electron in 1897, or Einstein's Special Theory of Relativity in 1915, or quantum physics circa 1925, or the Big Bang theory of the origin of the universe circa 1964, or String Theory in the 1970s. It is all of these at once yet none of these because it is not the *content* of thinking about the natural world, but the *way* of thinking about it, the methodology of understanding it, the approach to evidence and verification—what Galileo, Copernicus, Kepler, and Newton did in the early seventeenth century, that transformed the way the world is understood and truth is tested. This was a revolutionary change that did not happen in China.

The seventeenth century to the nineteenth century was a transitional period for Chinese science when Western science, mediated selectively by the Jesuits, partially melded with indigenous Chinese science, producing a kind of pseudoscience. The Jesuits had an ulterior motive that was not to convey the latest European scientific knowledge to China but Christian conversion. Science was only a means to an end. Prior to the seventeenth century traditional Chinese science was really a kind of technology— actually it was a collection of technologies in the sense that it was made up of disparate practical techniques to approach certain problems (calculating an accurate calendar, designing hydraulic irrigation and flood control works, navigating at sea, etc.) not joined in any unified or theoretical structure.

TECHNOLOGY

In the nineteenth century the mounting commercial and political assault from the West came to a point of crisis in the Opium Wars (1839–1842 and 1856–1860) and the Great Taiping Rebellion (1851–1864) that together almost brought down the Qing dynasty. One response by both high regional officials and the central government was to selectively adopt elements of perceived Western strength, mainly in the form of modern weapons and other salient aspects of Western material superiority, in defense of China's traditional order. The focus was on establishing modern arsenals and shipyards, along with supporting institutions of translation and language schools necessary to acquire and teach the skills behind the new Western technology. This activity was known as the "Self-strengthening" (*ziqiang*) movement, though it was in no sense a unified enterprise. Ultimately, as the logic of Self-strengthening expanded, it came to embrace very limited institutional reform. Its immediate impetus was to ensure the survival of the traditional imperial order in the new and threatening context of Western economic and material superiority that could no longer be simply ignored. But it was therefore essentially backward-looking. It was borrowing the West's obvious strengths but without innovating.

In the late nineteenth century a new formulation appeared, proposed by an advocate of Self-strengthening, the powerful regional official Zhang Zhidong, who borrowed the earlier rationalization for adopting Western science and mathematics: "Chinese learning for fundamental principle; Western knowledge for practical application" (*Zhongxue wei ti; Xixue wei yong*). But *yong* ("practical application") here is technology, not science; utility, not theory. In what came to be shortened as the *ti-yong* formula (an ancient Chinese heuristic dichotomy), Western *yong* included things like modern armaments, steam ships, railroads, telegraphy, and modern manufacturing based on specific Western inventions such as steam power and electricity, promoted in the West by the advantage of labor-saving but lacking the same incentive in China. The social-economic context was crucial in differentiating the two cultures. Chinese *ti* ("fundamental principle"), on the other hand, was the immutable cultural foundation of the Confucian Classics, history, literature, and philosophy.

China had technologies every bit as complex as those of the West, suited to the Chinese context as much as those of the West were to the Western context. And Chinese technologies were as ancient as those anywhere and inarguably influenced the West, such as gunpowder, paper, the compass, sericulture, and porcelain.

The cultivation of silk was invented and developed in China's Neolithic period. In the Chinese mythological record, it is attributed to the wife of Huangdi, the Yellow Emperor, third of the primordial culture heroes, of which the first was Fu Xi. There are four basic stages in the technology of silk production: The cultivation of mulberry trees on the leaves of which the silkworms feed, the raising of silkworms, the reeling of fiber from the cocoons woven by the silkworms, and weaving silk cloth from the fibers. Intensive human labor in all of these stages is essential. Left to themselves, for instance, silkworms produced a wild silk unsuitable for weaving. The technology of silk production reached an unsurpassed level in antiquity and changed very little over millennia. It remained an intensive garden-like activity perfectly adapted to the individual household economy. Silk was transported to the West on the famous Silk Road from time of the Han dynasty in the third century BCE. Sericulture was maintained as a state secret, carefully guarded, until the secret was finally breached.

Mulberry leaves are essential to produce high quality silk, the best being from white mulberry trees (*morus alba*). Trees are hardy, adaptable to a wide range of soil and climate and can be grown in areas unsuitable for other crops. Sericulture, the raising of silkworms (*Bombyx mori*), is the most sensitive of the stages, going through a cycle of hatching the eggs, feeding the worms through four molting stages during their growth, spinning the cocoons, development in the cocoon, and laying eggs by those moths allowed to emerge and mature. Silkworms are extremely susceptible to disease; the silkworm blight wiped out the industry in nineteenth-century Europe and in twentieth-century China. Reeling, from the best cocoons selected, had to be completed during a ten-day period. Coarse and fine raw silk were distinguished for different weaving methods. Mechanical reeling was introduced in the late nineteenth century, but its advantages were not as a labor-saving device but for the uniformity and reliability it produced.

Raw silk fibers were wound onto spools and made into warp and weft threads by separate processes, spinning several fibers into a single strand strong enough for weaving. Weaving was done both on small-scale household looms for smaller pieces and in large workshops employing many workers operating complex looms for larger lots. Weaving was a highly specialized profession that was maintained in particular families sometimes for centuries. The techniques that produced prized and unusual silks were preserved as family secrets, so that the techniques were often lost when the master died without an heir.

Glazed pottery in China originated as early as the Shang dynasty (c. 1700–1100 BCE). True porcelain first appeared around the third century CE. The technology of porcelain manufacture developed steadily over the next centuries, reaching a high level in the Song (960–1279) and continuing to advance in the Ming and Qing. Porcelain (called "china" in the West after its land of origin) is a highly vitrified material composed of clay and other substances, fired at very high temperatures exceeding 1200° C, at which point it becomes extremely hard and dense, and sometimes translucent. The principal ingredients in porcelain are kaolin, a very fine, almost pure white clay, and feldspar plus quartz. The word kaolin comes from the Chinese *gaoling* ("high mountain peak"), named from a mountain in Jiangxi province that was an abundant source of the clay. The nearby town of Jingdezhen became the principal manufacturing center for porcelain. Additional materials and various glazes were used to produce porcelain of a wide variety of colors and designs, such as the pale green celadon ware of the Song and the blue and white ware of the Ming. The chemistry of porcelain technology, evolved by trial and error, was extremely complex. The basic porcelain article, which was most often white, and glazes of various colors and hues including green, red, blue, and polychrome, were produced by minerals transformed at specific temperatures in the kiln, sometimes in successive firings at different temperatures.

The design of kilns constantly evolved and was central to the specialized technology of porcelain manufacturing. Small, "bun-shaped" kilns could fire at most a few hundred pieces at a time. By the Ming huge "dragon" kilns built on a 20–30° slope of a hill, up to 200 feet long and 25 feet wide, fired at the bottom with the heat rising over many steps, could fire 40 to 50 thousand small pieces at a time. The output of the imperial kiln at Jingdezhen, established in 1402, grew steadily from relatively small quantities in the sixteenth century to over 100 thousand pieces in each firing in the mid-Qing, mostly destined as gifts by the court to tributary vassal states. Large dragon kilns in Guangdong province in the south near Canton produced the famous blue-and-white "Canton ware" displaying chinoiserie themes for export to the West.

A single firing of one Jingdezhen kiln took more than twenty-four hours. In the Ming the entire process from loading the kiln, laying and feeding the fire, to cooling down and unloading the contents took five days. It is estimated that the annual output of 300 kilns at Jingdezhen alone, at forty firings per year, was about 12 million pieces. The total annual output of porcelain in the Qing may have been as high as 60 million pieces, for domestic consumption, export, and tribute.

Silk production and porcelain manufacture represented the opposite poles of indigenous Chinese technologies, both highly specialized, both exhibiting highly developed aesthetic standards, but the first was based on peasant household labor that changed very little or not at all over many centuries, while the second was based on industrial production methods that evolved considerably over the history of the technology. Both involved production of goods that were highly transportable and marketable, playing an important part in the Chinese traditional commercial economy. The technology of architecture, by contrast was quite different in the latter respects.

Architectural technology, of course, originated in the very first need for constructed shelters as Neolithic peoples emerged from the Paleolithic era of hunter-gatherer existence. The first dwellings were pit houses with a simple wooden frame supporting a thatch roof. Very early on, still in the Neolithic period, due to the abundance of fine *loess* soil in the Yellow River watershed, rammed earth walls appeared. Such walls were easily constructed by pounding damp earth into a long form, raising the form successively with each layer. The wall thus produced achieved a compact hardness that was more durable than adobe bricks, another prevalent construction method. The western-most sections of the Great Wall dating from the Han dynasty almost two thousand years ago, still visible in places in Gansu province, were built with rammed earth. This construction method persisted unchanged into the late twentieth century. Fired bricks, a later innovation, were another economical construction, especially prevalent since the Ming. Rammed earth, brick, and stone where it was available were the principal materials used in the construction of peasant houses, and were all employed in load-bearing walls. Wood, due to its high cost, was little used except for roofs in peasant houses.

For larger buildings, the houses of merchants, gentry, officials, often temples, and palaces, walls were often not load-bearing. A stout wooden framework was erected to support the heavy, often massive roof covered with baked tiles. Two styles of framework were employed: columns and beams, more common in the north, and pillars and transverse tie beams, more common in the south. With successive smaller pillars and beams erected on top of lower levels, the effect of sweeping curved roofs with over-hanging eaves was created. The larger the building, the more complex the construction. Since Neolithic times mortise-and-tenon and notched-joint construction was used, in which strength depended on the fitting of the joint alone, in interlocking pieces, not on nails and clamps. This method demanded intricate carpentry employed by expert craftsmen. The frameworks thus erected were filled by non-load-bearing curtain walls of rammed earth, adobe brick, fired brick, stone, logs or planks, or wattle and daub. Roof construction placed a premium on rapid shedding of water, for which curved tiles in alternating convex and concave rows were the superior method. Such roofs were very heavy and required strong frameworks of heavy pillars.

All Chinese buildings were measured in terms of a modular building unit, the *jian*, defined as a span between columns or walls. Thus a room, or a house, was calculated as so many *jian*. This basic design element determined the economic or social status of a building and its occupant. Sumptuary laws restricted the size of houses of commoners or people of lower classes to a certain number of *jian*, just as they restricted the kinds of apparel and the means of conveyance. Because of the variation in climate from wet to dry, warm to cold, environmental considerations exerted a large influence on architectural design and technology.

All of these technologies—sericulture, porcelain manufacturing, and architecture—and of course there were many more besides these—related primarily to specific media, not function or utility. Silk was extremely useful, both in practical and decorative senses, but its technology was governed by the exigencies of raising the insect that produced it and manipulating the material. Porcelain was likewise very durable and useful, but virtually its entire production emphasized the intricacies or forming and firing. Only architecture perhaps begins with utility and function of shelter, but thereafter the media governed the specific results.

Science is not the same as technology. Technology, though specific technologies originated in specific places, is not unique. It is easily transferrable and transportable. The technology of gunpowder and gunpowder weapons, highly developed in the Northern Song for use against the invading Jurchen in the thirteenth century, flowed easily across the border and was adopted by them against the Song, essentially equalizing the contest for supremacy. Silk and porcelain, once the techniques were learned, could be produced just as well elsewhere. Science, on the other hand, has a special cultural component that made it not so easily transportable. Eventually European science came to China. But Chinese science, so wedded to particular Chinese cosmological assumptions, faded along with the rest of the traditional Chinese world view.

SUGGESTED READINGS

Attwater, Rachel. *Adam Schall: A Jesuit at the Court of China, 1592–1666*. Adapted from the French of Joseph Duhr, SJ (London: Geoffrey Chapman, 1963). An English-language biography of the pioneering Jesuit scientist in China through the Ming-Qing transition.

Bai, Limin. "Mathematical Study and Intellectual Transition in the Early and Mid-Qing," *Late Imperial China* 16.2 (December 1995): 23–61.

Dunne, George H., SJ. *Generation of Giants: The Story of the Jesuits in China in the Last Decades of the Ming Dynasty* (Notre Dame, Indiana: University of Notre Dame Press, 1962). A popular account of the Jesuit religious and scientific enterprise in Ming China.

Eberhard, Wolfram. "The Political Function of Astronomy and Astronomers in Han China," in J. K. Fairbank, ed., *Chinese Thought and Institutions* (Chicago: University of Chicago Press, 1957), 33–70. Describes the impetus to accurate astronomical observation in the construction of the calendar in the service of the auspices of the dynasty.

Elman, Benjamin A. *A Cultural History of Modern Science in China* (Cambridge: Harvard University Press, 2006). An excellent introduction to the development of Chinese science by the Jesuits in the late Ming.

Fang Zhuofen, et al. "The Porcelain Industry of Jingdezhen," in Xu Dixin and Wang Chengming, eds., *Chinese Capitalism, 1522–1840*, part IV (New York: St.

Martin's Press, 2000), 308–326. An informative description of the technology of porcelain production.

Hummel, Arthur W., ed. *Eminent Chinese of the Ch'ing Period (1644–1912)*, 2 vols. (Washington, D.C.: Library of Congress, 1943–1944). In spite of its age this remains the essential comprehensive biographical reference for the Qing.

Jami, Catherine. "Learning Mathematical Sciences during the Early and Mid-Ch'ing," in Benjamin Elman and Alexander Woodside, eds., *Education and Society in Late Imperial China, 1600–1900* (Berkeley: University of California Press, 1994), 223–256. Discusses the development of mathematics in the early Qing.

Knapp, Ronald G. Foreword by Jonathan Spence, *Chinese Houses: The Architectural Heritage of a Nation* (North Clarendon, VT: Tuttle, 2004). A brilliantly illustrated book that also describes the technology of Chinese architecture.

Li, Lillian M. *China's Silk Trade: Traditional Industry in the Modern World 1842–1937* (Cambridge: Harvard University Press, 1981). An economic study of the silk industry and development of the silk trade from the treaty settlement with the West to the Republican period.

Mungello, D. E. *Curious Land: Jesuit Accommodation and the Origins of Sinology* (Honolulu: University of Hawaii, Press, 1985). A learned study of the Jesuit involvement in the study of China since Matteo Ricci's policy of accommodation of Chinese rites.

Nakayama, Shigeru, and Nathan Sivin, eds. *Chinese Science: Explorations of an Ancient Tradition* (Cambridge: MIT Press, 1973). A collection of nine essays on Chinese science including the contributions of Joseph Needham and pharmacological and medical science.

Needham, Joseph, et al. *Science and Civilization in China*, 7 vols. (Cambridge: Cambridge University Press, 1959–2004). The magisterial work of the great scholar of Chinese science, beginning with the philosophical foundations of Chinese scientific thinking and extending to all fields of science and technology in a large multivolume series. Needham, originally a biochemist, has been faulted for his interpretation of the achievements of China in science, but his work and that of his students who have carried it on remains the fundamental source for the study of Chinese science.

Peterson, Willard J. "Fang I-chih: Western Learning and the 'Investigation of Things,'" in William T. de Bary, ed., *The Unfolding of Neo-Confucianism* (New York: Columbia University Press, 1975), 369–411. The interaction of Western knowledge and the Confucian moral imperative in the thought of the Ming-Qing Confucian scholar.

Porter, Jonathan. "Bureaucracy and Science in Early Modern China: The Imperial Astronomical Bureau in the Ch'ing Period," in *Journal of Oriental Studies*, 18 .1/2 (1980), 61–76. A study of the bureaucratic context of mathematical astronomy in the early Qing.

Porter, Jonathan. "The Scientific Community in Early Modern China," *Isis* 73.269 (December 1982): 529–544. The development of a community of mathematical scientists as a social phenomenon in the Qing period.

Qian, Wen-yuan. *The Great Inertia: Scientific Stagnation in Traditional China* (London: Croom Helm, 1985). A brief exposition of the stagnation of the development of science in China.

Ronan, Colin A. *The Shorter Science and Civilisation in China: An Abridgement of Joseph Needham's Original Text*, Vol. 1 (Cambridge: Cambridge University Press, 1978). A very brief digest of Joseph Needham's vast history of Chinese science.

Rowbotham, Arnold H. *Missionary and Mandarin: The Jesuits at the Court of China* (Berkeley: University of California Press, 1942). Another popular but reliable account of the Jesuit missionary enterprise in China.

Schütte, Josef Franz, SJ. John J. Coyne, SJ, trans., *Valignano's Mission Principles for Japan*, vol. I, parts I & II (St. Louis: The Institute of Jesuit Sources, 1980). A scholarly study and translation of the Jesuit father-visitor Alessandro Valignano's investigation of the Christian prospects in Japan and China.

Sivin, Nathan. "Copernicus in China," in *Colloquia Copernicana* II (Warsaw: Union Internationale d'Histoire et Philosophie des Sciences, 1973), 63–122. An incisive discussion of the introduction of Copernican astronomy to China.

Sivin, Nathan. "Cosmos and Computation in Early Chinese Mathematical Astronomy," *T'oung Pao* 55 (1959): 1–73. A technical examination of computational aspects of Chinese astronomy.

Sivin, Nathan. "Why the Scientific Revolution Did Not Take Place in China—or Did It?" *Chinese Science* 5 (1982): 45–66. Addresses the ongoing controversy over the question of a Chinese scientific revolution.

Trigault, Nicolas. *China in the Sixteenth Century: The Journals of Matthew Ricci: 1583–1610*, trans. by Louis J. Gallagher (New York: Random House, 1953). The journals translated from Latin of Matteo Ricci, the pioneer of the Jesuit evangelical mission in China, containing detailed and astute observations of Chinese culture and society.

Willetts, William. *Chinese Art*, vol. 1 (New York: George Braziller, 1958). Contains a useful section on Chinese architecture.

Young, John D. "An Early Confucian Attack on Christianity: Yang Kuang-hsien and his *Pu-te-i*," in *Journal of the Chinese University of Hong Kong*, 3.1 (1975), 159–186. A very good discussion of the early Qing attack on Western science and Christianity.

NOTES

1. Richard Wilhelm, trans., *The I Ching or Book of Changes* (Princeton: Princeton University Press, 1977), 328–329.

2. Arthur W. Hummel, ed., *Eminent Chinese of the Ch'ing Period (1644–1912)*, 2 vols. (Washington, D.C.: U.S. Government Printing Office/Library of Congress, 1943–1944), 569.

3. Ruan Yuan, et al., eds., *Chouren zhuan* (Biographies of mathematical scientists), 7 vols. (Taibei: Commercial Press, 1965), IV, 451.

15

The Spiritual World

The Journey to the West (Xiyu ji), *a satirical and whimsical novel attributed to Wu Chengen in the sixteenth century, describes the miraculous birth of a monkey from a stone egg.*[1] *The protagonist of this lengthy story, Monkey, possesses magical super-simian powers, acquires immortality, and becomes a maverick, disrupting Heaven and its residents. In the course of Monkey's provocative adventures, he comes into conflict and battles a vast number of deities, gods, and spirits, none of whom are able to defeat him. These gods include, more or less in the order Monkey encounters them:*

The Jade Emperor in Heaven
The Dragon King of the Eastern Sea
The Ten Judges of the Dead
The Planet Venus
The Mighty Magic Spirit general and his armies
Vaiśravana and his third son Natha
The Queen of Heaven
Dipankara, Buddha of the Past
Lao Zi, Founder of the Dao
The Kings of the Four Quarters
The Twenty-eight Lunar Mansions
The Nine Planets
The Twelve Hours
The Bodhisattva Guan Yin and her disciple Huiyan, also known as Moksha,
the second son of Vaiśravana
The demon-king Mahābāti

The Buddha of the Western Paradise and his disciples Ananda and Kasyapa
The municipal god of the city of Chang'an

None of the names on this list are abstract concepts; they are all personified po-
tent spiritual beings who are called into service in the attempt to contain Mon-
key's mischievous antics. They represent an extraordinary array of figures from
traditional Chinese lore, Daoism, Buddhism, and popular religion, all happily
(or in the case of Monkey, unhappily) relating peacefully with each other. (But
note that Confucius and the secular sages of ancient China are conspicuously
absent. They are not gods and do not reside in Heaven.) The superior divinities
here, who appear at various critical points in the story, are The Jade Emperor in
Heaven, ostensibly the figurative Daoist lord of all the lesser deities; the bodhisat-
tva Guan Yin, the "Compassionate Sovereign;" and the Buddha of the Western
Paradise. Collectively they reflect the extreme eclecticism of Chinese religion.
Moreover, most of them exhibit in varying degrees human-like qualities. They are
all extremely powerful, but perhaps with the exception of the Buddha, they are
not omnipotent. The inhabitants of the spiritual realm of Heaven occupy a rather
human-like world, a continuum with the Earthly realm. When Monkey has at
last been contained and sealed in a mountain, the Buddha calls to his disciples to
return to the Western Heaven:

> Just as they were leaving, two messengers arrived from the Hall of Magic Mists say-
> ing, "We beseech the Tathagata. Our master is on his way." Buddha turned his head
> and a moment later saw a chariot drawn by eight phoenixes, covered by a canopy
> gleaming with jewels. There was a sound of many instruments and a chanting of innu-
> merable spirit hosts. Flower-petals fell through the air, and the smell of incense belched.
>   "I am profoundly beholden to you for dealing with that monster, said the Jade
> Emperor, when his equipage drew up, "and if you will consent to stay for a while, I
> will invite all the Immortals to join us in a feast of thanks."
>   Buddha did not like to refuse. "I could not do otherwise than to come at your Maj-
> esty's request," he said. "What small success we have had is however not my work,
> but is entirely due to the Founder of Tao and the other divinities."[2]

Chinese officials love banquets, and etiquette requires modesty. The
spiritual world of Heaven is an analog of the official bureaucratic
world on Earth, with most of the same strengths and weaknesses. Here is
no monolithic, omnipotent creator god like Yahweh, the Judeo-Christian
God. In Chinese religion, gods cannot resist a banquet, and sacrifices and
ceremonies involving gods, spirits, and ancestors are organized around
lavish provisions of food. Though popular fantasy and parody, one can
nevertheless recognize in *Monkey* the vast pantheon of Chinese religious
beliefs.

ANCESTOR WORSHIP

The bedrock of Chinese religion was the cult of the ancestor ("ancestor worship"). Its origins no doubt lay in prehistory. It became formalized in very ancient historical times in the practice of communication by the Shang kings with their ancestors by means of oracle bones, in which the large bones of oxen or the plastrons of tortoises were heated to produce cracks that were then interpreted as answers to questions posed in appropriate ceremonies to the ancestors. This was perhaps the first explicit recognition of the power of spiritual beings. Later in the succeeding Zhou period divination by consulting the hexagrams of the *Yi jing* became a more generalized vehicle to communicate with Heaven.

Deceased ancestors are believed to influence the welfare of their living descendants. Religion in this most fundamental form of belief in the continuity of the soul and its persistent influence after death pervaded every aspect of Chinese life. In concrete terms, Chinese believe that all persons possess two souls, corresponding to the fundamental *yin* and *yang* aspects of all reality. The *yin* soul is called *po*. It is the inferior, sentient soul essential to life. It stays near the body in the earth after death, but is transient. But it may become a *gui*, a malevolent spirit. The *yang* soul is called *hun*. It is the superior, ethereal, immortal soul that becomes *shen*, a good spirit. As such it is a benevolent ancestral spirit that protects its family. But people who have died without descendants to care for and respect them, or if the soul is neglected by its living descendants, that is, if it is not respected, honored, and fed, it becomes a *gui*, a hungry ghost or devil. The "less proper dead," those who were murdered, or committed suicide, or were executed, or died by drowning, the most neglected form of death, become *gui*, vengeful spirits or ghosts, malevolent forces that afflict the family and others who were the causes of their misfortune. They must be either propitiated or exorcised by elaborate rituals. They are ubiquitous and very dangerous, and because they have the capacity to inflict harm, they are feared but also respected, and must not be addressed as *gui*, which might arouse their anger, but as *haoxiongdi* ("good brethren").

Regardless of any literal belief in the persistence of ancestors' souls after death, the custom is a powerful acknowledgement of the symbolic vertical thread binding society in time, the recognition of the respect due to antecedents, the nurture of those who came before, and of obligations of those who follow. Ancestor "worship," or pious respect observed in filial piety, is the underlying sanction for social cohesion in Chinese culture. In terms of performance, the symbolic care manifested in rituals, for the comfort of the living, ensures that contented ancestors remain benevolent spirits (*shen*) that look over the continuing family tradition and protect it. Merely superstition? Maybe, but what is being exorcised

Figure 15.1. The Twenty-four Examples of Filial Piety. *Wanshi buqiuren* (almanac) (Taipei: Wenhuan tushu gongsi, 1968), 1–2.

or propitiated here? Perhaps it is the family's guilt, shame, loss, or grief for the unexpected or abnormal. The ancestral cult focuses inward to the family and lineage cohesion, rather than outward to the public realm of community and nation, binding the family as the most powerful element of Chinese society.

BELIEF AND PRACTICE

In all societies religion is an expression of culture manifested in two modes, belief (or creed, faith, etc.) and practice (performance or observation). The first takes the form of explanation. Where do we come from? Where are we going? What is our fate or destiny? What cannot be explained? What threatens us? The second takes the form of rites, rituals, or observances, the manner or form in which objects of belief or devotion are approached. Though in any religion, belief and practice are related, they are not necessarily mutually dependent on each other. Strong belief may exist in a context of weak practice. Elaborate ritual may exist in a context of weak belief. In the rationalistic spirit of the eighteenth and nineteenth centuries in Europe, religion was viewed as a set of "erroneous beliefs and illusory practices." It is always tempting to dismiss religion in this way—unless it is one's own. But one, however different, is just as valid as the other. Religion, whether in the form of belief or practice, is very real. One must always bear in mind that truth, or veracity, is never an issue in religion.

Systems of beliefs organized as coherent concepts in China emerged in the historical period at least as early as the second millennium BCE. Probably the oldest was the ancient cosmology of the correlative polar principles of *yin* (dark, female, passive), and *yang* (light, male, active), founded on observation of the perpetual cyclical seasonal change in the natural world. The original graphic meaning of *yin* was the shady or dark side of a hill, *yang* the sunny side of a hill. *Yin* and *yang* are in constant dynamic balance and fluctuation, both necessary to the process of life. The interaction of *yin* and *yang* produce the Five Agents: wood, metal, earth, fire, and water.

The symbolic representations of *yin* and *yang* constituted the divination manual, the *Yi jing* (*Classic of Change*), the most ancient of all the Classics and a constant source of reference in most later philosophical and religious thought. *Yin*, represented by a broken line, and *yang*, by an unbroken line, were combined in groups of three to form the eight trigrams, and in groups of six (combinations of two trigrams) to form the sixty-four hexagrams. The trigrams were thought to possess magical powers, and the hexagrams as constituents of the *Yi jing* were instruments of divination by means of a complex process of deriving the successive lines of a hexagram from bottom to top and consulting the manual for the interpretation of its meaning as a guide to action.

The *Dao* (path, or broadly, the Way in a metaphorical sense) was an equally ancient concept that described the primordial ontological indivisibility of nature. The earliest explicit expression of the teaching of the *Dao* was the *Dao De Jing* (*The Classic of the Way and Its Power*), attributed to Lao Zi (The Old One). As his name suggests, Lao Zi was not an identifiable historical personage, though he was supposed to be a contemporary of Confucius in the sixth century BCE. Thus, like *yin-yang* cosmology, Daoism did not originate in specific historical sources and is largely anonymous. Yet it is a highly coherent teaching. The *Dao De Jing* is a powerful impersonal religious gospel in poetic form. Its immense appeal lies in its didactic and cryptic language, inspiring endless translations and retranslations. Much more personal and more accessible in many ways is the *Zhuang Zi* (*The Master Zhuang*), by Zhuang Zhou, a definite historical figure of third century BCE, that conveys a tone of whimsical relativism and personal freedom intended to challenge the illusion of certainty of social norms.

Unlike *yin-yang* cosmology and Daoism, the lives and teachings of Confucius and his disciples and followers are well-documented in the specific historical context of the sixth to fifth century BCE late Zhou era. What emerged in the next several centuries as Confucianism, the doctrine based on Confucius' teachings, was not a belief or faith but a collection of observances and ethical principles originating in the feudal social order of Confucius' time. It was a coherent ethical system, but since it did not acknowledge spiritual or supernatural beings it cannot be considered a religion in the usual sense. The immanent moral order—how men ought to behave within society toward their family and toward their superiors—was sanctioned by Heaven. But Heaven by Confucius' time was no longer seen as an anthropomorphic deity but the moral ground of the universe. Moreover, Confucianism was not a doctrine of salvation. The immanent world of man was affirmed, not rejected. The fundamental values consistently emphasized by Confucius and his school were *ren* (human goodness, a word derived from the basic character for man) and *yi* (benevolence). Confucius believed, and his later follower Mencius in the fourth century BCE stated explicitly, that man is born good. The task was to preserve and cultivate that innate goodness.

Very different was the teaching of Buddhism. Buddhism originated in India in the sixth century BCE from the teachings of Sakyamuni, roughly a contemporary of Confucius, who upon his enlightenment following a prolonged course of meditation became the Buddha (the "Enlightened One"). Elaborated by the Buddha's disciples, Buddhism spread eastward across Central Asia to China in the second and third centuries at the end of the Han dynasty. Its doctrine of salvation from suffering was diametrically opposed to Confucianism, but held some similarities with Daoism, which facilitated the adaptation of Buddhism to the Chinese cultural environment. In Buddhism the principal and surest route to salvation was the true realization of the illusion of existence. Sincere belief, or faith, in the salvational power of the Buddha or of a bodhisattva ("enlightenment being") would ensure salvation. Another, inferior, route was practice in various forms, including devotion, meditation, and monastic asceticism. Buddhism expanded and developed in China after the third century into various sects, some derived directly from India and some indigenous to China. By the seventh century Tang dynasty it reached the peak of its power, eclipsing Confucianism and Daoism, and for a time was patronized by the imperial court as the state religion. But its influence declined thereafter, and while still a powerful cultural force in the Song period, with Confucianism resurgent, by the Ming Buddhism was relegated to its role as a popular religion and ceased to exert its former hold on elite society.

The foregoing religious traditions are all "isms," though the boundaries between them were highly permeable as each influenced the other at various times. Aside from these, other nonsystematic and "non-coherent" beliefs and practices evolved from earliest historical and prehistorical ages, constantly changing and elaborating, to become the vast arena of popular religion. Little of this popular devotion is reflected in *Monkey* because there are too many regional variations and local traditions to account for. In popular religion, performance of ritual and ceremony is generally the immediate expression of belief in divinities, gods, and spiritual beings— religious practice is a more pious aspect of devotion than belief.

THE SPIRITUAL HIERARCHY

Just as Chinese ethics is concerned above all with relationships and obligations between family members and with society at large, so is Chinese religion concerned with human relationships with supernatural beings of three kinds: ancestors, gods, and ghosts. The spiritual dimension of the world, populated by a plethora of beings, is an unseen but very real continuation of the visible secular world. The two worlds exist in a reciprocal relationship. Fundamental needs, fears, and emotions of humans, sometimes inarticulate or nebulous, in popular religion are personified as concrete personalities, residing in the spiritual dimension.

The most ancient divinity and the most pervasive presence, fundamental to agrarian society is Tu Di (The Earth God). The Chinese peasant's sense of belonging to the earth, coming from the soil and returning to the soil, the "good earth," is reflected in a saying, "The dying fox turns its head to its native hill."³ Tu Di is a manifold god, existing everywhere in one. There are Tu Di in every place where he may be worshipped or merely honored. But he is not simply a manifestation in separate images of a single deity, such as the Buddha or the Virgin Mary. He is the lowest and humblest of all the gods. He resides in simple tablets at the base of the threshold of a house, his name painted or carved in wood or stone, Menkou Tu Di (The Earth God of the Threshold), and in rustic small shrines and miniature temples on streets and beside fields. Humble though he is, Tu Di is in some way the most powerful god because he is so ubiquitous and so ancient.

Comparable to Tu Di but whose purview is within the household, Zao Jun (The Kitchen God or God of the Hearth) resides in a small altar above the stove where he can observe the daily activities of the family. He controls the family fortune (siming), when he reports to the emperor of Heaven every lunar New Year. His image on paper is burned to send him on his way on New Year's Eve, after first smearing his mouth with sugar to ensure that he will report only good things. Like Tu Di he is also a manifold god with responsibility directly for his host household.

Cai Shen (The God of Wealth) is another ubiquitous deity, but more general than Tu Di or Zao Jun. He resides in tablets higher up on the wall next to a doorway, in small shrines, or in neighborhood temples. He also appears appropriately in shrines in shops and businesses. Other minor gods include Tai Shan, the god of mount Tai, sacred mountain of the east in Shandong. Like Tu Di, he is represented in humble shrines but is not attached to individual households. And there is Lao Tai Sui (The Year God or "Father Time") who occupies larger temples where he is surrounded by subordinate deities, one for each year of the 60-year cycle. Years are numbered by the year of the cycle, so each person's birthdate falls on one of the 60 years. One offers incense and asks for good fortune from one's respective year god. Cheng Huang (The City God) is superior to Tu Di because he presides over the welfare of all of the city's inhabitants. He resides in the temple of the City God which is comparable to the yamen of a local magistrate, attended by his staff of functionaries. Naturally, he is the most bureaucratized of all of the gods.

Tu Di, Zao Jun, Cai Shen, and Cheng Huang are only the tip of an iceberg—actually the bottom tip of a spiritual hierarchy of even greater complexity and variety. Like the official political hierarchy of the secular world from subdistrict minor officials, through the district magistrate, prefect, governor and associated officials, to central government ministries, and finally to the emperor at the top, the spiritual world mirrors the official world. The Chinese emperor is the Son of Heaven; the Jade

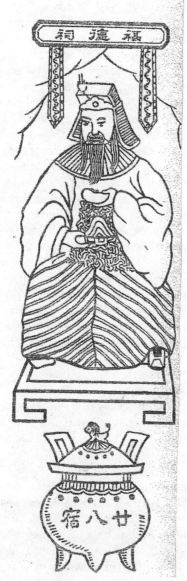

Figure 15.2. Tu Di, The Earth God. *Guang Jing Tang Tongsheng* (almanac) (Hong Kong: Hong Ming Brothers Printing Press, n.d.).

Emperor in Heaven is the emperor *of* Heaven, as Monkey learned when like an earthly Chinese rebel he sought to replace the Jade Emperor on his throne. So deeply entrenched in Chinese civilization was the idea and practice of bureaucracy that the Chinese conceived the universe, spiritual and secular, in bureaucratic terms. Many higher gods are accompanied by a retinue of attendant officials—lictors, clerks, guardians, and servants— just like earthly officials. But while no less powerful, the spiritual bureaucracy is less precisely delineated by responsibilities and powers. It is not an exact duplication of the secular bureaucracy, and for good reason. Gods and divinities of the spiritual hierarchy fill gaps in official bureaucratic competence, functions, and needs for which the average Chinese otherwise has no recourse. There are no secular officials charged with addressing issues of women's fertility or the desire for the birth of sons, the afflictions of accidents or catastrophes, medical problems, or the rectification of wrongs. The spiritual bureaucracy, however, is replete with deities who protect women in childbirth or who are called upon to ensure male children, deities who protect against fires, dog bites, smallpox, and who remedy injustices. The patronage system of the scholar-official literati world also exists in patron gods to whom the living may appeal for help in specific circumstances or occupations—Mazu, the patron of fishermen; Guan Gong the patron of scholars and merchants; and Guan Yin, "Goddess of Mercy" and protector of women. Gods are less intimidating than their counterparts in the official world. Where a commoner would be very reluctant to carry a legal complaint or supplication to a district magistrate for fear of becoming embroiled in unanticipated legal litigation, he can appeal to a god at the local temple without fear of retribution—the god needs him for his devotion expressed in incense and sacrifices as much as he needs the god for resolution of his problem.

Where did all this come from? It was not an integrated system of beliefs from early times, born at some point complete and whole. It was an ad hoc collection of spiritual responses to the exigencies of life, added to and subtracted from over many centuries.

Superior to all divinities is Heaven (*Tian*). Its basic meaning is sky, thus "the heavens." The character for heaven originally designated a great being, suggesting an anthropomorphic deity. The word became increasingly abstracted, denoting either the place where the gods dwell or the moral order of the universe and source of moral authority, as in The Mandate of Heaven (*Tianming*), or the emperor as the Son of Heaven (*Tianzi*). Heaven, represented by a circle, is paired with Earth, represented by a square. Together they are generative powers of the universe. During the Qing, the emperor conducted the annual sacrifice to Heaven at the Temple of Heaven, a large circular building, and to Earth at the Temple of Earth, a raised square platform where he performed a symbolic plowing.

Other supreme gods of the hierarchy emerged in time, including Huangtian Shangdi (The Supreme God of August Heaven), Yu Huang Dadi (The Jade Emperor in Heaven), and Xuantian Shangdi (The Supreme God of Mysterious Heaven), also known as Beidi (God of the North or the Pole Star). These three have acquired human-like characteristics and are represented in paintings and statues as awesome figures inviting veneration and supplication by the living.

Supplementing these supra-historical divinities, other divinities began as historical figures who were deified for their extraordinary virtues and deeds. They were often venerated for their specific powers to aid their worshippers, and the state repeatedly conferred exalted titles and honors upon them in an effort to co-opt their cults, as it did for Confucius. Guan Yu was a valiant warrior of the Three Kingdoms period during the aftermath of the fall of the Han in the third century. He was one of three stalwart companions of Liu Bei, the king of Shu Han state in western China and pretender to the fallen Han imperial throne. The romantic events of the struggle between the three kingdoms contending for mastery of China, and the ultimate failure of Liu Bei's cause, are fancifully captured in the great sprawling novel *Sanguo Yanyi* (*Romance of the Three Kingdoms*). Guan Yu was ultimately betrayed and killed but was deified later as an exemplar of perfect loyalty and valor as Guan Gong (Lord Guan) or Guan Sheng Dijun (Sage Emperor Lord Guan). Known first as the God of War, he is also patron of scholars and merchants, suggesting a movement to appropriate the virtues of such a powerful exemplar for other causes.

A pious young girl of the Lin family, a seafaring lineage of Meizhou, Fujian province, in tenth-century Northern Song, exhibited supernatural abilities when she was only a child. She was credited with the miraculous rescue of her father and brother from shipwreck in a storm. After she died prematurely at the age of twenty-eight she was canonized and was recognized as the patron goddess of fishermen throughout the southeastern coastal region. In subsequent centuries as her popularity grew she was accorded increasingly exalted titles as Tianfei (Heavenly Concubine) and elevated by the Qing to Tianhou (Empress of Heaven), by which name she is known in the pervasive cult centered on her throughout South China. More affectionately, she is known simply as Mazu ("Mother Ancestor" or Grandmother).

Guan Yin, "The Compassionate Sovereign," was originally the male bodhisattva Avalokitesvara in India but underwent a change in gender to become the "Goddess of Mercy" in the process of migration of the cult to China. She became the most revered of the bodhisattvas, "enlightenment beings," virtually an autonomous deity in her own right, independent of Buddhism. She is venerated in Buddhist and Daoist temples and in temples of her own everywhere. Though not strictly a deified human, her

Figure 15.3.   Guan Yin Riding a Dragon. Painting from Macau Guan Yin temple.

origins are anchored in the historical circumstances of her travel to China, which impart to her a more human touch than the more abstract supra-human deities. Mazu and Guan Yin exemplify the protection of women, a function that is rarely addressed in the secular bureaucracy. Interestingly, after the introduction of Catholicism to China in the sixteenth century, both have become easily confused with the Virgin Mary, and all three strikingly resemble each other in their iconography.

Many more lower-ranking divinities also originated as historical figures later venerated for their wisdom and valor, often with very localized followings. The origins of Tan Gong (Lord Tan) are obscure. It is claimed that he was the last emperor of the Song dynasty, then only a child, retreating with his remnant army before the advancing Mongols in the late thirteenth century to the South China coast near present Hong Kong. The story tells that there he perished, but became an immortal (*xian*) and a patron of fishermen in the coastal region. His devotion is limited to this area alone.

There is Hua Guang (God of Fires), who protects against fires. He is found mainly in urban areas where densely spaced wooden buildings are prone to catastrophic fires. Hua To was a famous physician of the former Han dynasty (second to first century BCE). He was deified as the God of Medicine and a patron of physicians. Bao Gong (Lord Bao) began as a magistrate, Bao Zheng (999–1062), also known as Longtu, in the Northern Song dynasty. His sagacity and impartial judgments led to his deification as Lord of Justice. Zhang Daoling (34–136) was an evangelical teacher of Daoism during the late Han who established a state-like community of priest-officials in western China. He is accordingly honored as the ostensible founder of institutionalized religious Daoism (as distinct from philosophical Daoism in the tradition of Lao Zi and Zhuang Zi). He was given the posthumous title *Tianshi* (Heavenly Teacher) and as the founder of the Daoist "church," is recognized as the first of a continuing line of Daoist "Popes." A scholar-official of the eighth century, Lu Dongbin, travelled throughout China, eventually becoming a recluse and a sorcerer, dedicated to overcoming evil. He is one of the Eight Immortals and the patron of druggists. The horse that carried the monk Xuan Zang to India in his quest for Buddhist scriptures during the Tang is deified as General White Horse (*Baima jiangjun*). He often appears on temple altars along with Monkey. Always paired together, Lady Jin Hua and Lady Dou Mu are protectors of women. Jin Hua is a goddess of fertility and Dou Mu is the Goddess of Smallpox.

Like female deities who as protectors of women's interests have no parallel in the official world, there is another class of gods who have no counterparts in the secular bureaucracy. These are maverick gods, unrestrained and unpredictable, and are therefore dangerous. The first

為我等祈
天后聖母

Figure 15.4. The Virgin Mary with Jesus. Painting from St. Francis Xavier Church, Coloane, Macau.

of these is Na Cha, the Third Prince. "Na Cha" is not really a name at all but an imitation of a sound, like a cry or an exclamation. However, it may correspond to Natha, the third son of Vaiśravana. Na Cha's legend tells that he was a historical figure born at the end of the second millennium BCE under supernatural circumstances. Na Cha was a monster as a child, over six feet tall. After numerous horrendous escapades, involving several potent deities, he so endangered his parents by his actions that he committed suicide at age seven. From that point he became an almost unpredictable god. Riding a fire wheel and wielding a spear, he engaged various foes guided by no clear cause or purpose. He is always depicted as a mischievous child. The second maverick god is Monkey, Great Sage Equal to Heaven, the protagonist of *Journey to the West*. Unpredictable and uncontrollable, he disrupted the established order in Heaven and on Earth. Neither Na Cha nor Monkey fit comfortably into the stable hierarchy of gods and spirits, which may explain their popularity. One who has such a proclivity for shaking up the system may seem to his followers to be a potent ally who must be appeased and whose support is worth enlisting if the other gods are unresponsive. The spiritual bureaucracy, like the secular civil order, was sometimes afflicted by pomposity and rigidity. There are always those who delight in disrupting and bringing ridicule to the establishment. Who has not wanted sometimes to stir things up? But the problem is that those maverick gods are indiscriminate in the troubles they can cause. They are no paladins of justice. In some ways the lower orders of divinities may be more real to their devotees than the relatively exalted and abstract superior gods because they are more personal. It is conceivable that one may appeal to Xuantian Shangdi (The Supreme God of Mysterious Heaven) but get further with Tu Di.

POPULAR RELIGIOUS DEVOTION

Popular or folk religion was a vibrant tradition throughout Chinese history, but because it was only peripherally connected with the literate culture it also left only tenuous traces in the written historical record. Perhaps in spite of that, or because of that, it has remained very strong into modern times. The literate elite viewed popular religion with a mixture of skepticism and antagonism, based on its potential to foster movements of social protest, and with a certain detachment. But popular religion was also exploited by the state in an effort to maintain social stability. The official patronage of deities such as Guan Gong or Tianhou with progressively more exalted titles co-opted such cults and their capacity for organized resistance to the established order. Yet at the same time, and perhaps for the same reason, during the Ming and Qing, local officials diligently performed periodic sacrifices to local gods, such as Tu Di and Cheng Huang, especially at times of urgency such as floods and droughts.

The devotion to popular religions was therefore not discontinuous across the boundaries between commoner, merchant, and literati classes. The innate eclecticism of Chinese religious belief was such that good Confucian scholars were perfectly capable of honoring popular piety just as much as they lectured their subjects on classical Confucian ethics.

Religion ceased to exert a hold on elite society and culture after the mid-Tang in the eighth century, when Buddhism languished as the state religion and Confucianism's resurgence began. Individual emperors might patronize certain religions or religious figures and themselves might be devotees. But this seldom had any effect on the vast literati-official class who effectively ruled the empire and acted as moral exemplars to the common people. So conversion of an emperor to a faith did not influence the people to conversion. In this the Jesuits in the sixteenth and seventeenth centuries were sadly deceived. They believed that if they could persuade the emperor to the Christian doctrine the whole of China would follow suit by his powerful example, and hundreds of millions of souls would be saved. But it could not and would not happen. That the emperor might be a Christian was no different than if the emperor was a Daoist or Buddhist, or was a follower of Tibetan Lamaism, which some of them were during the Ming and Qing. Confucianism is not a doctrine of salvation, while Christianity (and also Buddhism) is entirely a doctrine of salvation. The unsuccessful Jesuit attempt of accommodation with Confucianism in the early Qing foundered on this very distinction. The Chinese do not believe in salvation. In all of its rich and glorious variety, Chinese religion is an affirmation of the world. It only seeks to correct some of its deficiencies.

SUGGESTED READINGS

Buck, Pearl S. *The Good Earth* (New York: Pocket Books, 2005; originally published 1931). The most popular novel published on the Chinese common people, this sympathetic view strongly influenced the Western understanding of the Chinese common people.

Chamberlain, Jonathan. *Chinese Gods* (Hong Kong: Long Island Publishers, 1983). A useful illustrated catalog of Chinese popular deities; should be used with caution.

Ch'ü T'ung-tsu. *Law and Society in Traditional China* (Paris and La Haye: Mouton, 1961). An excellent description of family, clan, marriage, social classes, law, and Confucianism in traditional China.

Granet, Marcel. Maurice Freedman, trans., *The Religion of the Chinese People* (Oxford: Basil Blackwell, 1975). Chinese religious belief and practice explored by an eminent French sinologist.

Jordan, David K. *Gods, Ghosts, and Ancestors: Folk Religion of a Taiwanese Village* (Berkeley: University of California Press, 1972). One of the best field studies of Chinese popular religion, with an excellent treatment of religious practice and devotion.

Porter, Jonathan. *Macau: The Imaginary City: Culture and Society, 1557 to the Present* (Boulder: Westview Press, 1996). A chapter on Chinese popular religion in Macau includes the distribution and types of shrines and temples.

Smith, Richard J. *China's Cultural Heritage: The Ch'ing Dynasty, 1644–1912* (Boulder: Westview Press, 1983). A fascinating and informative description of the many dimensions of elite and popular culture in the Qing period.

Thompson, Laurence G. *Chinese Religion: An Introduction*, 3rd edition (Belmont, CA: Wadsworth Publishing, 1979). A basic short text on religion in Chinese society.

Waley, Arthur, trans., and introduction. *The Way and Its Power: A Study of the Tao Te Ching and Its Place in Chinese Thought* (New York: Grove Press, 1958). One of the best of the many translations of the Daoist classic. A word of caution: This is the most translated and interpreted religious tract in the world; many translations are unreliable and purely idiosyncratic personal interpretations.

Weller, Robert P. *Unities and Diversities in Chinese Religion* (Seattle: University of Washington Press, 1987). Another Taiwan field study, containing a good treatment of ghosts.

Wilhelm, Richard, trans. *The I Ching or Book of Changes* (Princeton: Princeton University Press, 1977). The most ancient Chinese Classic is a fountainhead of religious thought.

Wu, Ch'eng-en. Arthur Waley, trans., *Monkey* (London, New York: Penguin Books, 1961). One of China's greatest novels, written in the Ming dynasty, that is an extended narrative of religious superstition and practice as well as a social parody.

NOTES

1. Wu Ch'eng-en, *Monkey*, Arthur Waley, trans. (New York: Penguin Books, 1961).

2. *Monkey*, 86.

3. Quoted from the *Li Ji* (*Record of Rites*), in Marcel Granet, Maurice Freedman, ed. & trans., *The Religion of the Chinese People* (Oxford: Basil Blackwell, 1975), 50.

16

The Relevance of Confucius

As the disintegration of the Zhou empire gained pace after the eighth century BCE, and the social and political order began slowly to unravel, new types of men emerged from the interstices of the old feudal order. The most seriously affected belonged to the lowest stratum of the Zhou feudal hierarchy, the shi, *originally a class of warriors or knights. These new men—military tacticians, economic theorists, political strategists, a new intelligentsia—responded or reacted in diverse ways to the world that was shifting under their feet. As the transformation of the Zhou became increasingly apparent over the next few centuries, some of these new men sought to confront and perhaps to halt the decline in the feudal order. They became the teachers and philosophers of the late Zhou, a time of great intellectual ferment, as* shi *came to be redefined as scholars. They looked back to the old feudal order of the early Zhou founders, King Wu (Wu Wang) and his brother the Duke of Zhou (Zhou Gong), and before them the sages of high antiquity, as the Great Way (Da Dao).*

One critical view of the present age was expressed by a mysterious figure known as Laozi (the Old One or Elder):

> *When the Great Way was abandoned,*
> *There was humanity and morality.*
> *When cleverness and knowledge emerged,*
> *There was great hypocrisy.*
> *When the nation was in confusion and chaos,*
> *There were loyal ministers.*[1]

Such a cynical explanation condemned the great virtues of antiquity including humanity and righteousness, filial piety, compassion, and loyalty as symptoms of the declining order.

*An alternative perspective was articulated by Confucius, the great teacher of
the sixth century BCE and allegedly a contemporary of Laozi:*

> Confucius said: When the Way prevails All Under Heaven, then ritual (li), music,
> and military expeditions come from the Son of Heaven. When the Way does not
> prevail All Under Heaven, then ritual, music, and military expeditions come from
> the feudal princes. Thus it is rare that ten generations will pass before they are lost.[2]

*This second perspective contrastingly values the order-creating attributes of
antiquity, including music, ritual, and political discipline when they emanate
from the supreme ruler, not devolved on contentious feudal magnates. But what
these two expressions share is a notion of present decline from some ideal time in
the past, be it an historical age of harmony and stability or a yet more primordial
perfect era of sage kings. The idea of recurrent decline, the devolution of the social
and political order from some more ideal, if not perfect, order became a persistent
theme in Chinese political thought. The goal of sage rulers was to reverse the
process of decline and restore the ancient order.*

THE FIRST TEACHER

Confucius[3] (Kong Fuzi, Master Kong) (551–479 BCE) was only one of
many former members of the *shi* class who lived from the mid-sixth
century to the late second century BCE, embracing the period known as
the Spring and Autumn (722–481 BCE), which took its name from historical chronicles of the time, and the Warring States (403–221 BCE), also
named for a record of that violent time. Like his contemporaries, Confucius pondered the ills of his age, attempted to diagnose its problems, and
offered prescriptions for reform and change. More than any other (and
he was one of the first), Confucius looked back to the ideal world of the
early Zhou, a golden age when his heroes, particularly the Duke of Zhou,
whose descendants were enfeoffed in his own state of Lu. This age of
stability and harmony was reflected in the rituals (*li*) of that time. It was
an age that produced the great Classics that were the repository of eternal
values embedded in history.

The sources of Confucius' teachings were the Classics (of which there
were six in his time: *Yi Jing*, Classic of Change; *Shu Jing*, Classic of History; *Shi Jing*, Classic of Poetry or Odes; *Yue Jing*, Classic of Music [since
lost]; *Li Ji*, Record of Rites; and *Chun Qiu*, Spring and Autumn Annals).
It was believed in later times that Confucius edited or somehow manipulated the Classics, or even that he had written them himself, and thus in
a sense made them or claimed them as his own, especially the *Spring and*

Autumn Annals, before his death in 479 BCE. No other philosopher of those times put such stock in these ancient works. During his lifetime as he travelled about the various states seeking a patron ruler who would employ him to implement his ideas, he acquired a following of seventy-two disciples. Though Confucius himself never left a written exposition of his teachings—perhaps he didn't have to if he indeed had written the Classics—his disciples recorded his words and actions, collected after his death in the *Analects* (*Lun Yu*) (thus the repetitive format of the *Analects*).

More than a century after Confucius' death, Mencius (Mengzi, Master Meng) (372?–289 BCE) adopted and elaborated on Confucius' teachings. The book of Mencius' teachings, the *Mengzi,* expands far more extensively on the succinct statements of the *Analects.* In later times, under the influence of Neo-Confucian thinking in the Song period, a millennium after the age of the philosophers, Mencius was recognized as the greatest transmitter of the Confucian doctrine.

Mencius' essential proposition is that the fundamental nature of man is good.[4] This idea was succinctly expressed in the formulaic words of the *Three-Character Classic* (*San Zi Jing*), written in the thirteenth century, that became the basic primer for introductory indoctrination of children in schools in the Ming and Qing periods. The book is so called because each parallel sentence is composed of three characters that were recited in unison and memorized by pupils. Its opening sentences read: "In origin man's nature is fundamentally good. While his nature is mutually alike, in practice it is mutually far apart." While people's behavior may diverge toward badness under corrupting influences of their social environment, they never lose their innate goodness. In proof of this proposition Mencius offers a hypothetical example of a man, however bad, who sees a child about to fall into a well. Any such person will feel a sudden instinct of compassion, even if he does not act on it.[5] This idea, though without the assertion of man's basic goodness, was adumbrated in a typically cryptic statement by Confucius in the *Analects*: "The Master said, By nature near together; by practice far apart."[6]

The belief that human nature is essentially good but in practice often corrupted by society introduced a fundamental dichotomy in Confucianism between the optimism of the perfectible ideal of human society based on man's inherent goodness, and pessimism regarding social and moral melioration derived from man's actual behavior. This dichotomy, embedded in Confucianism, was reflected in Xunzi (The Master Xun) (c. 300–237 BCE), roughly a contemporary of Mencius, who posited that human nature is essentially bad, but by education and moral cultivation can become good. The potential, of course, was always that those social processes would fail. The implication for Xunzi's immediate followers, including especially the Legalists, was that law was the only sanction keeping man's behavior good. Thus law (*fa*) versus ritual (*li*) and goodness (*ren*) became a basic dividing line in Confucian thought. For the next millennium, until the rise of Mencius, Xunzi was the predominant thinker of the Confucian tradition.

PHILOSOPHICAL DISPUTATION

The feudal order was already moribund in Confucius' time and defunct when Mencius and Xunzi lived. The vast transformation accelerated during the last decades of the Warring States, culminating in the violent unification of the empire by one of the last surviving seven great states, the Qin. The Qin was the creation of the Legalist school, a tradition of practical statecraft going back centuries. The Confucians, constant critics of the trends which the Legalists promoted, were anathema to the Legalists. With almost totalitarian determination, the Qin would admit no dissent. Accordingly, Grand Councilor of the Qin, Li Si, instigated a ruthless destruction of the books and scholars of the philosophical schools of the late Zhou, the basis of all learning, exempting only practical books on the economy and statecraft, and Daoist works, allegedly because the First Emperor favored the school.

No regime so extreme could endure for long. Perhaps deservedly, the Qin lasted barely fifteen years. The succeeding Han dynasty (206 BCE–220 CE), moderating the extremes of the Qin, endured for almost four centuries. Confucianism, its doctrines more suitable to the administration of a centralized state, was ultimately victorious. But the Qin destruction of the learning of the Zhou created a great problem for all subsequent ages, especially for the Confucian scholars who survived. What did the sages of the Great Way of antiquity "really" say? Who, indeed, was Confucius? New texts of the Classics and the philosophical schools were produced based on "discoveries" of the lost works and on forgeries. Apocryphal books supported the cosmological inventions of Han imperial Confucianism of Dong Zhongshu (175?–105? BCE). Dong's interpretation of the cryptic *Spring and Autumn Annals* viewed Confucius as a transhistorical prophet, the "uncrowned king," whose appearance was signaled by the capture of a *lin* (female unicorn), a manifestation of the Heavenly Mandate, recorded in the concluding year of the *Annals*. In the partial vacuum in the textual record left by the Qin cataclysm, all kinds of historical constructions were possible in support of contemporary ideological agendas of the new imperial order. This movement of the Former Han came to be referred to as the New Text School.

By the last years of the Former Han, New Text learning was increasingly disputed by some scholars for its supernatural beliefs, reliance on prognostications, and incorporation of superstitious yin-yang theories. These critics asserted that early Confucian doctrine of the late Zhou had been distorted by spurious forgeries, that Confucius was not a supernatural figure but a human teacher. Though the corrected versions of the Classics promoted by these scholars may themselves have been spurious, they were known as the "old learning," in part because they were written in an old form of writing in use prior to the Qin, and thus seemingly more authentic. In the Later Han this movement became the basis for the Old Text School. The famous late Han Confucian textual scholar Zheng Xuan (127–200) produced voluminous commentaries on the Classics as well as a revised version of the oldest of the Classics, the *Classic of Change*. Replacing the New Text commentaries on the revered *Spring and Autumn Annals* was the more down-to-earth *Commentary of Zuo* (*Zuo zhuan*).

THE TRIUMPH OF NEO-CONFUCIANISM

Confucianism was already in decline in the late Han and was eclipsed during the post-Han medieval era of political fragmentation by the ascendency of Daoist mysticism and the entrance and spread of Buddhism from India into China. As a doctrine of political action based on moral rectitude increasingly wedded to the imperial state, without a centralized state in which to function, Confucianism could not flourish. The converse was also true: Buddhism and Daoism were ill-adapted to political administration. With the reunification of the empire under the Sui (589–618) and Tang (618–907) dynasties after almost four centuries of division, Confucianism was resurgent as the organizational rationale for the new imperial state. Buddhism remained the dominant religion of the old ruling class and the imperial family as long as the old aristocracy continued to dominate the social order. But with the growth of the secular scholar-gentry class supported by the civil service examination system in the Song dynasty (960–1279) the aristocracy could not survive.

Confucianism, even in its supernatural version of the Han New Text School, was a humanistic ethical philosophy that focused on the immanent social and historical context of humankind. It offered no metaphysical explanation of man's origins or existence. Understanding of human nature, such as Mencius' idea of the essential goodness of man, was the farthest Confucian thought went toward ontological theory. This metaphysical lacuna in Confucianism was filled by Buddhism and Daoism which offered systematic cosmology and moral ontology. The *Dao* (Way) of the Daoists, the primordial but unknowable progenitor, is different from both the *Dao* of Confucius, an historically anchored moral order, and from the Confucian Heaven (*Tian*), the source of moral behavior, imminent in human affairs. Buddhism embraced not only the original teachings of the historical Buddha but also a vast array of nonhistorical avatars and transcendental beings offering salvation and release from false consciousness of human existence and consequent suffering.

Song Confucians, exposed to the voluminous Buddhist sutras and the Daoist classics, and no doubt conscious of the relative inadequacy of the Confucian tradition in metaphysical thought, were deeply influenced by what they read. They were not intent on consciously distorting or revising the Classics. But into their own interpretations of the Confucian Classics, which in any case were subject to so many questions of competing understanding since the Han, they incorporated perhaps unconsciously elements from Daoism and Buddhism. Confucianism acquired a new layer of Daoist cosmology and Buddhist morality. The most influential of Confucian scholars in the Song were the brothers Cheng Hao (1031–1085) and Cheng Yi (1032–1107), and Zhu Xi (1130–1200), who synthesized the various contributions of his predecessors and was later regarded as the greatest Confucian philosopher since Mencius. Indeed, Mencius, whose philosophy possessed mystical elements not unlike Chan (Zen) Buddhism which was very influential at the time, finally came into his own.

By the Ming, the Cheng-Zhu school (so-called from the teachings of the Cheng brothers and Zhu Xi) was accepted and officially promoted as the official state-mandated orthodox Confucian tradition, the Transmission of the Way (*Dao tong*). This "new Confucianism" (Neo-Confucianism in Western parlance) was supported by the official civil service examination system, revived under the reign of the Hongwu emperor. The examination questions were all based on the interpretations of the Cheng-Zhu school. No aspiring candidate could hope to achieve success who did not thoroughly assimilate and master the official doctrine.

Zhu Xi's metaphysics was based on his concept of principle (*li*) which pervaded all things. Each thing had its own principle (*li*) which determined its material manifestation. External *Li*, the summation of all particular *li*, could be apprehended by the rational mind. Thus his school, with its quasi-scientific rationalism, was known as the School of *Li*. Accompanying his metaphysics was a moral philosophy derived from the original Confucian Classics. In order to simplify the great diversity of the original Classics into a manageable corpus, Zhu Xi reduced the essential canon to the *Four Books*, comprising the *Analects* of Confucius, the *Mengzi* of Mencius, and the *Da Xue* (*Great Learning*) and *Zhong Yong* (*Doctrine of the Mean*), two sections extracted from the *Li Ji* (*Record of Rites*). This relatively brief collection became the "Bible" of Confucianism, a sufficient doctrinal source for all ordinary Confucians. To equip him for the examinations, a fledgling Confucian would spend his early schooling committing the *Four Books* to memory, while advanced scholars would go on to study the remaining *Five Classics* and other ancient classical texts as well as the commentaries of the Han.

The Cheng-Zhu school was not without its challengers during the Ming. In the mid-Ming a divergent school arose under the illustrious official and scholar Wang Yangming (1472–1529), who derived his inspiration from Lu Xiangshan (1139–1192), a contemporary of Zhu Xi in the Song. Taking his cue from Chan (Zen) Buddhism, Wang stressed the mind (*xin*) as the source of intuitive knowledge of reality, denying the dualism between the individual mind and external reality of Zhu Xi. Reality is apprehended through spontaneous intuition; knowledge and conduct are one. The Lu-Wang school stemming from Wang Yangming, known as the School of Mind (xin) or the Idealist School as differentiated from the School of Principle (li) or the Rationalist School of Zhu Xi, enjoyed great popularity in the late Ming. Wang advocated teaching students from humble backgrounds, a populist orientation to education that included public lectures, and exerted a strong influence on his disciples and followers such as Wang Gen (1483–1541).

CONFUCIAN POLITICS

The growth of factionalism surrounding the rise of the eunuch dictator Wei Zhongxian (1568–1627) in the late Ming affected the philosophical environment of Confucianism. The Donglin party, a loosely organized association of scholar-officials resisting Wei Zhongxian's arrogation of power, adopted a puritanical Confucian program of moral rectitude, denunciation of bureaucratic power, and condemnation of the philosophical eclecticism of the Lu-Wang school. While the Donglin movement did not survive the brutal repression of the Wei Zhongxian regime, a far more coherent organization, the Fu She (Restoration Society), arose from its ashes in 1629. *Fu* means to return or renewal. The members of the Fu She aimed to purify Confucianism by returning to its roots, reviving Confucianism in its original condition before the accretions of Buddhism and Daoism in the Song. The Fu She also carried on the populist approach to education promoted by Wang Yangming and his followers. Its members included several late-Ming–early-Qing scholars, including Huang Zongxi (1610–1695) and Fang Yizhi (1611–1671), who were pioneers of the practical studies movement of the early Qing. Several of its members edited a huge compilation of essays and memorials on practical administrative and government problems during the Ming, the *Great Ming Compendium of Statecraft Writings* (*Huang Ming jingshi wenbian*). The Fu She was thus the source of the turn toward rigorous evidential studies of the Classics and scientific learning in the Qing.

The fall of the Ming amid rampant bureaucratic factionalism, incompetence of the imperial court, peasant rebellion, Manchu invasion, and general economic malaise throughout the empire had a tremendous influence on Confucians who survived the change of dynasties. In spite of that litany of fatal causes which might have been enough to convince anyone that the days of the Ming were numbered, Ming loyalists and scholar-officials were somehow unable to accept what should have appeared as inevitable. Dynasties do not last forever, and many other former Ming officials had already defected to the Manchus in spite of the stigma of being condemned as turncoats. Much like the late Zhou, literati and officials seeking to understand the collapse of the Ming turned to diagnoses of the causes of the catastrophe. Eunuch abuse of power that had become endemic during the Ming was an obvious target; less so was the weakness of late Ming emperors. Sterile bureaucratic factionalism which continued even into the Southern Ming refugee regimes was admitted as a cause of the demoralization of the official class. But beyond such institutional causes, more broadly condemned was what was seen as the metaphysical and moral abstractions of Cheng-Zhu orthodoxy that evaded pragmatic attention to the concrete troubles of the time. Dominant Cheng-Zhu Confucianism had become a heterodox learning in the critics' minds, corrupted by the philosophical detachment from worldly affairs of Buddhism and Daoism. In a related vein, the irresponsible, metaphysically self-indulgent introspective attitude of the Lu-Wang school had encouraged a penchant among its followers for "pure discussion" (*qingtan*) unsullied by practical political and social issues.

The influential Confucian thinkers who spanned the Ming-Qing transition—Huang Zongxi (1610–1695), Fang Yizhi (1611–1671), Gu Yanwu (1613–1682), and Wang Fuzhi (1619–1692)—in various ways advocated a return to practical studies and statecraft (*jingshi*) over sterile philosophical speculation. Gu Yanwu, for instance, wrote *A Record of Knowledge Diligently Accumulated* (*Rizhi lu*). Fang Yizhi turned his attention to the study of natural phenomena, physical objects, and technology, a precursor of the scientific studies of the early Qing. A common thread in these scholars' work was an emphasis on empirical scholarship, to "seek truth from facts" (*shishi qiu shi*), a counterpoise to the vacuous metaphysical speculation of the late Ming. The imperative "seek truth from facts" was a recurrent one in Chinese reformist thinking, appearing once again as a byword as late as the liberal reformist program of the "Paramount Leader" Deng Xiaoping in the 1980s which challenged the doctrinaire Maoist ideology of the previous era of the Cultural Revolution. Another theme uniting these thinkers was the importance of statecraft (*jingshi*), literally "to set the world in order," the raison d'être of the late Ming *Great Ming Compendium of Statecraft Writings* (*Huang Ming jingshi wenbian*). The basically utilitarian motivation of this movement, in contrast to the speculative orientation of Cheng-Zhu Confucianism, was manifested in the kinds of interests represented in these writings, comprising practical administrative methods, water control, calendrical studies, and geography.

QUEST FOR THE TRUE CLASSICS

All of these Confucian critics were Ming loyalists to one degree or another; all refused to serve the Manchus after 1644 in spite of earnest efforts by the Qing to woo them. Reacting to what they believed to be the corrupting influences of Buddhism and Daoism on Confucian thought, scholars of the seventeenth century transitional era searched back in time for pre-Buddhist and pre-Daoist origins of Confucianism. The problem was that the Classics themselves and related texts had been contaminated and adulterated by extraneous elements introduced by numerous commentators in the centuries following the Qin "burning of the books." To reconstruct the "true" Classics required precise, exacting research using the specialized methods of philology, etymology, epigraphy, and textual exegesis to purify the written record. Under the general rubric of "evidential research" (*kaozheng*), this quest led them back to the Later Han Old Text School for the authentic versions of the Five Classics. As Ruan Yuan (1764–1849), the great patron and seminal scholar of evidential research in the nineteenth century, explained:

> The way of the Sages is preserved in the Classics. Without explanation, the Classics are not clear. The commentaries of the Han were especially close to [the time of] the Sages compared to later discourse. . . . Our forebears observed the manner of the early generations yet still unclouded [by later commentators and interpreters]. Presumably the knowledge of those at a distance [from the originals] ultimately is not as authentic as those who were near.[7]

This enterprise of exacting scholarship led to the discovery of inauthentic elements in the Classics and even forgeries of later times, particularly in the *Classic of History* (*Shu Jing*) and the *Rites of Zhou* (*Zhou li*). The approach of *kaozheng* scholars was a profoundly historical orientation based on the *Classic of History*, the *Spring and Autumn Annals*, and the *Zuo Commentary* (*Zuo zhuan*) on the *Annals*. The search for solid evidence replaced speculative philosophy. The Classics were all considered history of the golden age of the Sages.

By the early eighteenth century the writings of the empirical research scholars produced a growing body of work that was recognized as "Han Learning" (*Hanxue*) to distinguish it from orthodox Cheng-Zhu studies or "Song Learning" (*Songxue*). The purported founder of Han Learning was Hui Dong (1697–1758), a prolific scholar and specialist on the *Classic of Change* (*Yi Jing*). Although advocates of Han Learning rejected Song Learning as not based on verifiable facts, Neo-Confucianism, that is the Cheng-Zhu tradition, remained the basis for the civil service examinations and was therefore in that sense still the official learning. But Han Learning and evidential research had taken over the scholarly world by the mid-eighteenth century. Imperial patronage for Han Learning was evident in the great literary project of the Qianlong reign in the late eighteenth century, the *Complete Library of the Four Treasuries* (*Siku quanshu*), which overwhelmingly employed Han Learning scholars at the expense of Song Learning as well as Buddhist and Daoist works. That empirical research scholarship was the intellectual mode of the mid-Qing was reflected in the work of Dai Zhen (1724–1777), a scholar influenced by Jesuit scientists, who worked on the mathematics and astronomy sections of the *Four Treasuries*.

The climax of the Han Learning movement came in the late eighteenth and early nineteenth century. Under the leadership of Ruan Yuan, the prominent high official, prolific scholar, and patron of learning, evidential research and the Old Text School dominated intellectual discourse. Ruan Yuan employed his political power and resources to advance Han Learning. While serving as governor of Zhejiang province from 1800 to 1809 he established an academy, the Lodge for Expounding the Essential Classics (*Gujing jingshe*) at Hangzhou to train students in Old Text scholarship. In 1820 as governor-general of Guangdong and Guangxi provinces in the south he founded another famous academy, the Hall of the Sea of Learning (*Xuehai tang*) at Canton, its curriculum devoted to Han Learning. Throughout his long and distinguished career, beginning in 1789 when he earned the *jinshi* degree and served in the capital in the Southern Study, through increasingly important appointments in ten provinces from Shandong south to Guangdong, Yunnan, and Guizhou and finally back to Beijing in 1835 as grand secretary with the honorary title of Grand Guardian to the Heir Apparent, Ruan Yuan was continuously engaged in the compilation and publication of collectanea of classical scholarship, including most famously the *Great Qing Explanation of the Classics* (*Huang Qing jingjie*), a compendium printed in 1829 in 366 volumes comprising 180 treatises on the Classics written during the Qing period.

Ruan Yuan had an abiding interest in Chinese science, as did previous proponents of empirical studies such as Fang Yizhi in the seventeenth century and Dai Zhen in the eighteenth. Under the impact of western science first introduced by Jesuits in the Imperial Astronomical Bureau in the late Ming and encouraged by the interest of the Kangxi emperor during the early Qing, Chinese scholars sought to rehabilitate the record of Chinese mathematics, astronomy, and calendrical science that they believed had been largely lost or neglected in previous centuries. In pursuit of this goal, Ruan Yuan compiled the *Biographies of Mathematicians and Astronomers* (*Chouren zhuan*) published in 1810 in 46 chapters (*juan*). Including subsequent supplements down to 1898 it comprised the biographies of 675 Chinese and 205 western scientists from antiquity to the end of the nineteenth century. Implicit in the goal to restore indigenous Chinese science to its proper place was the contention that Chinese and Western science were in fact one and the same and, moreover, that Western science had an ancient Chinese origin, a contention propounded earlier by the Kangxi emperor.

CONFUCIUS AS PROPHET

By the late eighteenth century Han Learning was beginning to draw its own critics. The pervasive crisis of the late Qianlong reign created by the usurpation of power and vast corruption of Heshen, the Manchu court favorite who manipulated the emperor in his old age, engendered among many scholar-officials a sense of the weakening of the moral fiber of the empire. Rebellions and growing pressure from Western trade, as well as economic and social malaise, were seen as harbingers of dynastic decline. Still working within the Han Learning enterprise, critics faulted the sterile scholasticism of evidential studies, the accumulation of arcane facts for their own sake, the emphasis on technique rather than on vision, the lack of moral compass, and the loss of political conscience and autonomy among the scholar-official class. The intellectual intimidation exerted by the *Complete Library of the Four Treasuries* project, though it had been enthusiastically embraced by most scholars, had a demoralizing influence on the class as a whole. The repeated literary inquisitions of successive reigns and the imperial condemnation of any kind of associations among officials as improper factionalism had taken their toll.

This critical mood echoed the intellectual environment of the late Ming, seeking the causes of dynastic decline in the mentality of the age. But the philosophical context had changed, from the prevailing hegemony of speculative Cheng-Zhu Neo-Confucianism and the Wang Yangming school to the tyranny of empiricism at the expense of personal moral cultivation. The quest once again for firmer moral grounding led the way farther back in time to the Former Han (206 BCE–8 CE) and a rediscovery of the New Text School represented especially by the great Confucian theologian Dong Zhongshu. This tradition was previously dismissed as wild superstition and fantasy by the pioneers of Han Learning who emphasized the Old Text learning of the Later Han as more down-to-earth and truer to what they saw as the authentic teaching of Confucius and Mencius. Central to this reorientation was the always enigmatic *Spring and Autumn Annals* which the Old Text Confucians had accepted as factual history interpreted especially by the *Zuo Commentary*. The *Annals* was the ostensible chronicle of events in Confucius' home state of Lu in eastern China from 722 to 481 BCE. Confucius was credited with editing the *Annals* which ended before his death in 479 BCE. The difficulty for all subsequent interpreters was that the *Annals* is an extremely abbreviated record. According to tradition Confucius was said to have indicated his approval or disapproval of events—the "praise and blame" theory of the *Annals*—in the esoteric phrasing of the entries. Viewed as history, the *Annals* was the record of the unfolding age of decline and disorder of the late Zhou. But the *Annals* was potentially open to numerous interpretations. The New Text scholars relied on another perspective, the *Gongyang Commentary* (*Gongyang zhuan*) on the *Annals*. Based on this commentary Dong Zhongshu wrote a history of the period, the *Luxuriant Dew of the Spring and Autumn Annals* (*Chunqiu fanlu*), that portrayed Confucius not as a learned teacher of his time, simply transmitting the wisdom of the ages, but as a prophet for all time, a charismatic visionary. At the end of the *Annals* was recorded the capture of a *lin*, a female unicorn, that was recognized as an auspicious heavenly portent that Heaven had passed the Mandate to Confucius. Confucius was thus the "uncrowned king" (*su wang*) of an abortive dynastic succession. In this view he was transformed into a transhistorical figure of mythic proportions, a Sage King speaking now across the millennia to another age of disorder.

From the end of the eighteenth century China experienced the impact of a series of pressures of mounting intensity both from Western foreign trade and cultural intrusion and from domestic disorder and rebellion, bringing down the curtain on the prosperity and confidence of the High Qing. These challenges converged in the mid-nineteenth century in the Great Taiping Rebellion and the Opium Wars, from which the Qing barely recovered. The glory days of prosperity and stability of the previous century were only a memory; the reality facing the Han and Manchu elites was dynastic decline.

By the end of the nineteenth century Confucians were confronted by the imputation that Confucianism had become irrelevant in the modern world. This realization undermined the powerful sense of exceptionalism on which the Confucian world view was based, that China was the singular center of civilization that paled off in all directions to less civilized peoples. Yet if Confucius could be conceived as not just a great humanistic philosopher of antiquity, as presented in the *Analects* of Confucius, but as a transcendent cosmological prophet with a message for all ages and all peoples, then China of Confucius would take its place among the great nations of the world, and Confucianism as one of the great religions. Thus believed the Confucian New Text scholar and thinker Kang Youwei (1858–1927). Kang was born into a prominent gentry-literati family near Canton, the epicenter of the Western intrusion. He was a bright student and, perhaps by virtue of the proximity of Western cultural influence, early on he engaged in a broad program of study of Western history and thought as well as Chinese classical learning. At one point in a period of particularly intense meditation provoked by his studies, Kang experienced a sudden vision:

> While I was sitting in contemplation, all of a sudden I perceived that Heaven, earth, and the myriad things were all of one substance with myself, and in a great release of enlightenment I beheld myself a sage and laughed for joy; then suddenly I thought of the sufferings and hardships of all living beings, and I wept in melancholy.[8]

From then on, still immersed in both Western and classical studies, Kang adopted New Text Confucianism and became an active advocate for institutional reform.

Confucius, Kang contended, was an agent of reform then, in his time, and now in the impending age of disorder. He was a model for all ages, a religious oracle comparable to the great religious prophets of the West. In *Confucius as a Reformer* (*Kongzi gaizhi kao*) Kang expounded his view of Confucius' role in history. In his radically visionary *Book of the Great Commonwealth* (*Datong shu*) Kang envisioned a future one-world utopian order into which China would lead the way. There, national boundaries, governments, racial and class distinctions, even the family would all become obsolete. New Text Confucianism had now, in the twilight of the traditional Confucian order, become detached from Confucianism itself, the abiding intelligence of the Chinese world.

The old Confucianism never recovered. It had, as its critics feared, become irrelevant in the modern world. In the early twentieth century it was ruthlessly assaulted as everything that was wrong with old decadent China. Chen Duxiu (1879–1942) belonged to the new, post-Confucian order. A revolutionary intellectual, he was a pioneer of the New Culture Movement of the second decade of the twentieth century and later a founding member of the Chinese Communist Party in 1921. In his extremely influential monthly magazine *La Jeunesse*, *New Youth* (*Xin qingnian*) in 1915 Chen challenged the new generation:

> We indeed do not know which of our traditional institutions may be fit for survival in the modern world. I would rather see the ruin of our traditional

"national quintessence" than have our race of the present and future extinguished because of its unfitness for survival. . . . The world continually progresses and will not stop. All those who cannot change themselves and keep pace with it are unfit for survival and will be eliminated by the processes of natural selection.[9]

On the eve of Kang Youwei's dream of a future utopia embracing China as a leading catalyst, Confucianism had come full circle, from the great First Teacher's reformism looking back to the early Zhou age of harmony and order to the New Text School's reformism returning to Confucius as the Eternal Sage. However he was understood, whether as First Teacher or as "uncrowned king," the great sage was regarded as the progenitor of the idea of the Chinese world as *Datong*, the great commonwealth under Heaven where the Way prevailed, a vision that if never fully realized in fact had always been the ultimate aspiration of Confucians.

Among several powerful forces promoting the continuity of Chinese civilization and history, such as geography, the agrarian economy, and the written language, the strength of tradition across millennia must be attributed to the ambivalent meaning of Confucius. Ambivalence, as opposed to simple, one-dimensional comprehension, is often a source of vitality, a dynamic tension. This was evident in the changing understanding of Confucian teaching from the sixth century BCE to the nineteenth century. Who was Confucius? For some he was and is simply a very modest and wise man of antiquity whose teaching may still offer people of later ages guidance in troubled times. For others he was the Most Holy First Teacher (*zhisheng xianshi*), a revered founding sage of a great civilization honored over centuries as the focus of a quasi-religious cult. For yet others he was the supramundane savior of the world, on a parallel with the Buddha, transcending place and time. And, in the twentieth-century era of radical revolutionary rhetoric, he was the source of all the problems that afflicted China in its struggle to survive among nations in the modern world. But however Confucius was conceived over time, Confucianism was supremely adaptable.

So powerful is the image of Confucius as a cultural icon in Chinese tradition that he is still used in the present as if he were relevant in the twenty-first century. Thus when dissident Liu Xiaobo, in prison serving a long sentence, was awarded the Nobel Peace Prize in 2010 but was not permitted by the Chinese government to travel to Norway to receive it, the Chinese came up with a "Confucius prize" as their own equivalent. And the People's Republic of China sponsors "Confucius Institutes" abroad to advance appreciation of Chinese language and traditional culture. But all of these efforts are devoid of any meaning that Confucius originally held.

SUGGESTED READINGS

Chow, Kai-wing. *Publishing, Culture, and Power in Early Modern China* (Stanford: Stanford University Press, 2004). An excellent study of the relationship between the growth of the publishing industry, culture, and political power in the late Ming.

Confucius. *The Analects of Confucius (Lun Yu)*, annotated by Arthur Waley, trans. (New York: Vintage Books, 1938). The *Analects* are brief records of Confucius' actions and words recorded by his disciples and collected after his death. They are in no way a systematic exposition of philosophy, but strong themes nevertheless clearly emerge from them.

de Bary, W. T. *The Trouble with Confucianism* (Cambridge: Harvard University Press, 1991). In six insightful essays one of the most eminent students of Confucian thought discusses the tensions and predicaments within the Confucian tradition.

de Bary, William Theodore, ed. *The Unfolding of Neo-Confucianism* (New York: Columbia University Press, 1975). An anthology of fourteen articles on the thought and practice of Neo-Confucianism.

de Bary, William, Wing-tsit Chan, and Burton Watson, compilers. *Sources of Chinese Tradition* (New York: Columbia University Press, 1960). A comprehensive anthology of translations of selections from Chinese classical works, histories, essays, and literature.

Elman, Benjamin A. "Ch'ing Dynasty 'Schools' of Scholarship," *Ch'ing-shih wen-t'i* 4.6 (December 1981): 1–41. The following articles and books by Elman present an important corpus of interpretation of Confucian scholarship and thought in the Qing era. Especially important is *From Philosophy to Philology*.

Elman, Benjamin A. *Classicism, Politics, and Kinship: The Ch'ang-chou School of New Text Confucianism in Late Imperial China* (Berkeley: University of California Press, 1990).

Elman, Benjamin A. *From Philosophy to Philology: Intellectual and Social Aspects of Change in Late Imperial China* (Cambridge: Harvard University Press, 1984).

Elman, Benjamin A. "The Hsueh-hai T'ang and the Rise of New Text Scholarship in Canton," *Ch'ing-shih wen-t'i* 4.2 (December 1979): 51–82.

Elman, Benjamin A. "Scholarship and Politics: Chuang Ts'un-yu and the Rise of the Ch'ang-chou New Text School in Late Imperial China," *Ch'ing-shih wen-t'i* 7.1 (June 1986): 63–86.

Feuerwerker, Albert. *State and Society in Eighteenth-Century China: The Ch'ing Empire in its Glory.* Ann Arbor: University of Michigan, Center for Chinese Studies, Michigan Papers in Chinese Studies No. 27, 1976. Chapter 2, "Ideology as a Unifying Element" provides a succinct evaluation of the social-political role of Confucianism.

Grimm, Tilemann. "Academies and Urban Systems in Kwangtung," in G. William Skinner, ed., *The City in Late Imperial China* (Stanford: Stanford University Press, 1977, 475–498). Scholar-literati academies were an important instrument of Confucian activity in the Ming-Qing period. See also Elman on "The Hsueh-hai T'ang."

Hummel, Arthur W., ed. *Eminent Chinese of the Ch'ing Period (1644–1912)*, 2 vols. (Washington, D.C.: Library of Congress, 1943–1944). In spite of its age this remains the essential comprehensive biographical reference for the Qing.

Jones, Susan Mann. "Scholasticism and Politics in Late Eighteenth Century China," *Ch'ing-shih wen-t'i* 3.4 (December 1975): 28–49. Another contribution to the study of Confucian scholarship and politics in the Qing.

Mengzi (Mencius). Trans. with an introduction by D. C. Lau, *Mencius* (Harmondsworth, England and New York: Penguin Books, 1970).

Naquin, Susan, and Evelyn S. Rawski. *Chinese Society in the Eighteenth Century* (New Haven and London: Yale University Press, 1987). An examination of political, social, and economic themes in Qing China, focusing on the flourishing of related institutions in the eighteenth century.

Nivison, David S. *The Life and Thought of Chang Hsueh-ch'eng (1738–1801)* (Stanford: Stanford University Press, 1966). A major intellectual biography of an influential Confucian historian of the mid-Qing.

Peterson, Willard J. *Bitter Gourd: Fang I-chih and the Impetus for Intellectual Change* (New Haven: Yale University Press, 1979). The intellectual influence of a prominent scholar-literatus during the Ming-Qing transition.

Peterson, Willard J., ed. *The Cambridge History of China*, vol. 9, *The Ch'ing Empire to 1800*, Part 1 (Cambridge: Cambridge University Press, 2002). *The Cambridge History of China* volumes 9, 10, and 11 (like the twin volumes on the Ming) are the standard authorities of the Qing dynasty by leading scholars of their respective fields.

Peterson, Willard J. "Fang I-chih: Western Learning and the 'Investigation of Things,'" in William T. de Bary, ed., *The Unfolding of Neo-Confucianism* (New York: Columbia University Press, 1975), 369–411. The interaction of Western knowledge and the Confucian moral imperative in the thought of the Ming-Qing Confucian scholar.

Polachek, James B. *The Inner Opium War* (Cambridge: Harvard University Press, 1992). Early chapters discuss the role and activities of the literati in the nineteenth century.

Waley, Arthur, trans., and introduction. *The Way and Its Power: A Study of the Tao Te Ching and Its Place in Chinese Thought* (New York: Grove Press, 1958). One the best of the many translations of the Daoist classic. A word of caution: This is the most translated and interpreted religious tract in the world; many translations are unreliable and purely idiosyncratic personal interpretations.

NOTES

1. Laozi, *Dao De Jing* (*The Classic of the Way and Its Virtue*), chap. 18.

2. Confucius, Arthur Waley, trans., *The Analects of Confucius* (*Lun Yu*) (New York: Vintage Books, originally published 1938), XVI, 2.

3. Confucius is the Latinized version given by the Jesuit missionaries in the sixteenth century, in an attempt to put Kong Fuzi on a par with the great western classical philosophers. Thus also Mengzi became Mencius.

4. Mengzi (Mencius), trans. with an introduction by D. C. Lau, *Mencius* (Harmondsworth, England and New York: Penguin Books, 1970), III, A, 1. Note that "man" is used here in the non-gendered sense of "mankind." But recognize that in fact women were not included in early Confucian thought and were regarded as possessing inferior status.

5. Mengzi (Mencius), *Mencius*, II, A, 6.

6. Confucius, *The Analects* (*Lun Yu*), XVII, 2.

7. Ruan Yuan, comp., *Gujing jingshe wenji*, 14 *juan*, in Yan Yiping, ed., *Baibu congshu jicheng*, series 44 (Taibei: Yimen yinshuguan, 1967), 3:1a.

8. Quoted in William T. deBary, et al., compilers, *Sources of Chinese Tradition* (New York: Columbia University Press, 1960), 724.

9. Quoted in Chow Tse-tsung, *The May Fourth Movement: Intellectual Revolution in Modern China* (Stanford: Stanford University Press, 1960), 46.

V

~

WHEN WORLDS COLLIDE, 1500–1870

17

The Empire and the Garden

From the sixteenth through the eighteenth century, two very different worlds, China represented by the Ming dynasty and the West represented at first by the Portuguese, came into collision. They met along overlapping boundaries in Southeast Asia and then on the South China coast in the mid-sixteenth century. What made them so different were contrasting views of the world reflected in Chinese and Portuguese cultural mentalities.

The very different mentalities of the Portuguese (and ultimately European) and Chinese worlds are reflected in contrasting cultural archetypes, expressed vividly in their most famous respective literary works of epic mythology and narrative, the Lusiads *by Luis de Camões, the poet laureate of the Portuguese nation, and* Dream of the Red Chamber *(Honglou meng) by China's most famous novelist Cao Xueqin. The two works may be understood as distillations of their respective cultures' world views. In them we find a juxtaposition of mythology, often reinterpreted, and narrative of contemporary history and culture in allegorical form. In both, the gods intrude in the process of worldly, mortal affairs, sometimes in dreams, guiding the action, interfering at critical points, and then letting events follow their courses. Yet the two portray very different perspectives of the world, one an enclosed, self-contained and introverted, garden-like totality, the other an unbounded and extroverted, but incomplete empire pursuing a destiny in the process of fulfillment.*

The Lusiads *is the epic celebration of the Portuguese race composed by Camões in the course of his travels through Portuguese Asia and back to Lisbon between 1553 and 1570. Taking the voyage of Vasco da Gama to India in 1497 as his narrative focus, Camões, inspired by classical Roman models, especially Virgil's* Aeneid, *and borrowing the pantheon of Greco-Roman mythology, exalts the Portuguese as the embodiment of a heroic legacy. The Portuguese are seen as descendants of the heroes of classical antiquity, who, while surpassing them in deed and daring as the new heroes of Christianity tested in the Crusades and the reconquest of Portugal, are recipients of a world mandate, prophesied for them by the gods. It is their destiny to establish a new world order. Jupiter, the king of the gods on Olympus, addresses his daughter Venus, along with her brother Mars, who have assumed the role of protectors of the Portuguese mariners, assuring her:*

> *Fortresses, cities, and high walls,*
> *You shall behold built by them, my child;*
> *The cruel and warlike Turks you shall see ever defeated by them;*
> *The kings of India, free and secure,*
> *You shall see by their mighty King subjected;*
> *And at last master of all, they*
> *Shall give to the Earth better laws.*[1]

The factual narrative of da Gama's voyage is interlaced with fantastic encounters with adversities and enemies which da Gama and his men must confront and overcome by bravery or cunning. These challenges are raised both by those gods who are jealous enemies of the Portuguese, and by the actual earthly enemies of the Portuguese, the Muslims and their allies. In the course of meeting these challenges, the Portuguese are constantly tested, and forced to prove their valor and the righteousness of their cause. At the threshold of the Indian Ocean on his passage around Africa, da Gama encounters the Cape of Storms (later the Cape of Good Hope) personified as the dreadful giant Adamastor:

> *Since you have come to see the hidden mysteries*
> *Of nature and the watery element,*
> *To none in all humanity permitted*
> *Whether of noble or immortal merit,*
> *Hear the punishment that I have prepared*
> *For your inordinate audacity,*
> *Over all the vast sea and on the land*
> *That you will subjugate by cruel war.*[2]

The logic of the Portuguese struggle for national unification and independence involved them in an ever-widening centrifugal movement of discovery, conquest, and subjugation. The heroic Portuguese world of the fifteenth and sixteenth centuries is portrayed as a stage in a historical continuum from classical antiquity to world empire broken by no clear boundary or resting place. It is a potentially unbounded world. The conflicts and tensions engendered by a social system in a state of flux are carried outward upon a world replete with dangers and disorder to be overcome and surmounted, an arena for adventurers and heroes. The Portuguese world, extending beyond the cramped confines of the nation, was consequently confronted by the challenge of surrounding moral disorder.

The Portuguese were the instruments of a teleological imperative of evangelical expansion and conversion to Christian law and faith, to set the world in order. Very different is the world depicted in Dream of the Red Chamber. The novel, as much a mixture of fantasy and verisimilitude in its own way as the Lusiads, is a sweeping, complex description of life within a great gentry family of late seventeenth and eighteenth century Qing China. The story centers on the younger members of the Jia family, and the ramified and often morally confused relations between them. Baoyu, the protagonist of the novel, is a boy when the story begins. His birth is as miraculous as that of Monkey in Xiyu ji. During the several years that pass as the narrative progresses, he is involved with various young female relatives, friends, and servants within the extended family, which is depicted as a virtual society within a society, administered by its own elaborate bureaucracy. The foreground of the novel is the young people's comfortable and often effete life passed within the confines of the immense garden that occupies an important part of the twin family compounds. In the background is the official world beyond the walls, in which Baoyu is expected eventually to take his place.

The events of Baoyu's story pass almost entirely within the boundaries of the Jia family compound and its refined garden. Yet the family is a world unto itself. Indeed the Chinese family, in its simple form the basic cellular unit of society, in its extended form in Dream of the Red Chamber becomes a microcosm of society as a whole. Even the hierarchical bureaucratic organization of the state, with its reliance on record keeping, is replicated within the family. Conversely, the ideal Confucian state was a family-like unit, reflecting the same moral obligations and relationships. And just as kinship ties and tensions create conflicts within the family, so can they also disrupt the larger society.

Completing the self-contained totality of the world modeled in the novel, the elaborate family garden, in turn, presents a microcosm of the natural world, just as the family is a microcosm of the human world. The Chinese scholar-literati garden was a contained world, complete and self-sufficient within its walls, where natural and artificial elements were juxtaposed in an aesthetic (and moral) balance. The architectural components of the garden exhibited a stylistic refinement and elaboration that frequently elevated superficial decorative flamboyance over substance and simplicity. By the Ming and Qing era, the process could be carried, as it was in the seventeenth century, to a point at which form was confused with substance.

He led them inside the building. Its interior turned out to be all corridors and alcoves and galleries, so that properly speaking it could hardly have been said to have any rooms at all. The partition walls which made these divisions were of wooden paneling exquisitely carved in a wide variety of motifs: bats in clouds, the 'three friends of winter'—pine, plum and bamboo, little figures in landscapes, birds and flowers, scrollwork, antique bronze shapes, and many others. The carvings, all of them the work of master craftsmen, were beautiful with inlays of gold, mother-o'-pearl and semi-precious stones. In addition to being paneled, the partitions were pierced by *numerous apertures, some round, some square, some sunflower-shaped, some shaped like a fleur-de-lis, some cusped, some fan-shaped. . . The trompe-l'oeil effect of these ingenious partitions had been further enhanced by inserting false windows and doors in them, the former covered in various pastel shades of gauze, the latter hung with richly patterned damask portieres. The main walls were pierced with window-like perforations in the shape of zithers, swords, vases and other objects of virtù.*[3]

The Chinese world was a closed, organic totality, possessing an inherent moral order governed by ritual. The traditional tribute system of relations with countries beyond the borders of the empire attempted to project the hierarchical moral order of the center over the periphery, and by ceremonial performance focus attention inward. In contrast to China's enclosed garden world, the Portuguese world of the sixteenth century was an expansive, yet incomplete and unfulfilled cultural empire. It was a world shaped by a process of continual evolution, not involution. Whereas the Portuguese world was characterized by heroic continuity, the Chinese world was characterized by hierarchical continuity.

The Chinese were content to explore the world within the confines of their own garden-world, by compressing the chaotic world within a bounded space, seemingly disordered but actually tamed and controlled in a harmoniously ordered hierarchy. If discordant elements remained they were merely part of an agreeably contained dynamic which lent excitement to the experience without requiring venturing beyond the enclosed garden-world. A writer on gardens in the seventeenth century observed, "If one can find stillness in the midst of the city toil, why should one forego such an easily accessible spot and seek a more distant one?"[4] For the Chinese the challenge was disorder within—they sought to impose an internal moral order. The Portuguese spirit was very different. While the Chinese found no impetus to venture out upon the world, the Portuguese sought to impose order on a disordered world by force beyond their borders.

Mentalities are complex things, but they were encapsulated in the careers of contemporaries from the two worlds, Henry "The Navigator" of Portugal and Admiral Zheng He of the Ming Court. Prince Henry (fl. 1415–1460), a scion of the Portuguese royal house of Burgundy, was Grand Master of the Order of Christ, which united in its crusading zeal religious and economic motives with cultural expansion. Under Henry's impetus the Portuguese thrust outward into the Atlantic, around Africa, across the India Ocean, to China and Japan. This was a potentially unbounded vision. Its origins lay in complex geographical and political motivations. The outward impulse of the Portuguese was forged in a convergence of maritime fishing experience of the Arab south and the Portuguese north, from which seafaring activities gradually expanded. The trading network embracing the Atlantic rim and the Mediterranean exploited early Italian experience, particularly from the Genoese trading empire, which contributed innovations in nautical technology to the Portuguese enterprise. This process culminated in the reconquest of Portugal from the Arabs and their Berber allies and national unification under king Afonso Henriques (1112–1185).

Zheng He (fl. 1405–1433) was Grand Commandant in the Ming Court, a Muslim as well as a eunuch. Under the orders of the Yongle emperor (1402–1424), his mission was to reestablish the tributary order over the states of Nanyang (the Southern Ocean, i.e., Southeast Asia). To this end Zheng He commanded seven expeditions of huge fleets of unprecedented size, ambitious voyages that exhibited great potential yet limited goals within finite boundaries. This was a limited, bounded vision. Its geographical and political impetus involved divided and conflicting motivations. With the collapse of the Mongol empire, the Yongle emperor sought to reassert Chinese rule over continental inner Asia, launching military campaigns to divide and rule the Mongol tribes. At the same time the emperor feared that the heir to the Ming throne whom he had usurped had survived and fled to Southeast Asia. One objective of Zheng He's expeditions was to seek him out. Thus Zheng He's efforts were directed toward the consolidation of Ming rule and the reestablishment of traditional Chinese hegemony over the surrounding regions.

There were certain similarities between the motives of Prince Henry and Zheng He. Both sought to circumnavigate lands to the south. Both sought to extend their world order: For Henry it was the supranational Christian Kingdom of God; for Zheng He it was the universal Chinese world order of *Tianxia* (All Under Heaven). Both reflected the momentum of national consolidation, following the defeat of the Mongol empire in the case of China and the reconquest of Iberia from Islam in the case of Portugal. But while Portuguese motives were harmonized in Vasco da Gama's response to the question "Why have you come?" posed by the ruler of Calicut in southern India, "We have come for Christians and spices," Chinese motives were disconnected; Nanyang was ultimately peripheral. Moreover, the Portuguese monarch, who managed the business of trade in spices from his court, was contemptuously dismissed as a "grocer king" by other European monarchs; the Chinese emperor in contrast presided over an overwhelmingly agrarian system in which commercial motives were marginal.

The Portuguese legacy was an extroverted maritime world view growing from the momentum of conquest. The world was a crusading field, uniting religious, political, and commercial objectives. Portuguese expansion led to permanent European presence in Asia, that influenced art, architecture, and literature, and transformed the Western world view. The Chinese legacy was interrupted by the abrupt end of the voyages of expansion, which were never really about conquest. China turned inward toward introversion and isolation, viewing the world as a passive moral order. This stable political, economic, and social order endured for another five hundred years, while the West experienced the tremendous transformation of the commercial, industrial, and scientific revolutions.

THE MIDDLE KINGDOM

China in the eighteenth century, and for many centuries previously, regarded itself as the center of civilization, *Zhongguo*, "The Middle Kingdom." The Chinese had a perfectly adequate understanding of the physical world, so the notion was not a literal geographic one but a conviction of cultural centrality that originated in ancient times before the first unification of China in the third century BCE. This notion had three components. The first is what may be called sinocentrism, a definition of civilized humanity based on universal norms of Confucian ethical values. There could be only one Son of Heaven, the Chinese emperor, who was the mediator between the moral order of Heaven (*Tian*) and humankind. The implication of this belief was that for the Chinese there was no concept of multiple civilizations (the modern concept of nation was not in currency). Civilization was singular; it paled off in all directions into barbarism of various degrees.

The second component is the tributary system of suzerain-vassal relations, the spirit if not the letter of which governed all contacts with other peoples however distant from the Middle Kingdom. It was a hierarchical system that bestowed the privilege of political recognition and economic intercourse by a magnanimous emperor on less fortunate peoples. The implication of this system was that for the Chinese there was no concept of international relations on the basis of equality. The world was not composed of many countries with equal claims to dignity.

The third component of the notion of the Middle Kingdom is the assurance that China's self-sufficient economy provided all of China's own needs and the superior material goods of civilization. Foreign goods, however ingenious or curious, were only exotic luxuries. The implication of this was that for the Chinese there was no concept of commerce and trade as an essential economic resource of the state.

Such a view was not a simple self-delusion on the part of the Chinese. It was shared by not a few Westerners in the nineteenth century, including S. Wells Williams, a progenitor of the field of sinology:

Comprising within its limits every variety of soil and climate, and watered by large rivers, which serve not only to irrigate and drain it, but, by means of their size and the course of their tributaries, affording unusual facilities for intercommunication, it produces within its own borders everything necessary for the comfort, support, and delight of its occupants, who have depended very slightly upon the assistance of other climes and nations for satisfying their own wants. Its civilization has been developed under its own institutions; its government has been modelled without knowledge or reference to that of any other kingdom; its literature has borrowed nothing from the genius or research of the scholars of other lands; its language is unique in its symbols, its structure, and its antiquity; its inhabitants are remarkable for their industry, peacefulness, numbers, and peculiar habits.[5]

It was not that the Chinese, once confronted with representatives of civilized nations, were quickly disabused of their confident assessment of their place in the world. The Western barbarians who arrived on the Chinese periphery from the early sixteenth century confirmed in their actions the sinocentric world view. There was no difference in their behavior from other barbarians such as Japanese pirates. Portuguese, accustomed to taking slaves throughout their maritime empire, kidnapped Chinese children as servants; the Chinese believed they captured them to eat. The eagerness of foreigners for commerce and trade in Chinese goods, and the lack of any desirable products offered in exchange, confirmed the Chinese sense of self-sufficiency. Trade would be allowed if the foreigners exhibited proper respect and observed the fixed rules of the tributary system. Thus a fundamental conflict would eventually emerge, a collision between two very different views of the world.

THE OLD CHINA TRADE

The Portuguese were the vanguard of what was to become a tide of Europeans to arrive on the South China coast, seeking trade with the Chinese empire. Shortly after the conquest of Malacca, the commercial entrepôt on the Straits of Malacca and the western terminus of Chinese commercial traffic from South China, by Afonso de Albuquerque in 1511, some Portuguese arrived in Canton aboard a hired Malay ship. During the next several decades Portuguese ships began to frequent the coastal region near Canton, which was the principal trading emporium on the south coast. The foreigners acted in such a dangerous and reckless manner that the Ming authorities at Canton were at first at a loss what to do about them. Finally, in an effort to isolate them at arm's length, they were permitted in 1557 to lease part of a small peninsula jutting out from a larger island on the west side of the Canton estuary, as a place to occupy and conduct trade. This initiative was taken entirely by local Ming officials without the endorsement of the Ming Court. Macau, the name derived from a temple to Mazu located on the peninsula, grew to become the first permanent and lasting European base on the China coast, a city of mixed Portuguese-Asian settlers with an Iberian flavor, overshadowed by the surrounding mainland. For three hundred years, enduring long after the decline of the Portuguese seaborne empire, Macau remained the sole European base in China, tolerated by the Chinese precisely because of its marginal location where its inhabitants could be easily contained and controlled.

The English arrived in Asia under the auspices of the London East India Company, founded in 1601, more than a century after the Portuguese first showed the way. They first traded at Canton in 1637 and in 1699 established a factory there. A "factory" was the site of a factor, a commercial agent, and was not then a permanent establishment. The British were required to retreat to Macau between trading seasons. By 1710 British trade had become firmly established at Canton and the British, operating under the East India Company (EIC) monopoly, which applied to all British subjects, became the principal European traders in China.

What came to be known later, after its transformation in the nineteenth century, as the "Old China Trade" developed through the eighteenth century as the characteristic system from this period. Trade was initially conducted sporadically at other ports on the China coast, but in 1757 the Qing confined all trade to Canton, the virtue of which was that it was as far as one could be from the capital at Beijing. Already in 1687 an imperial official, an officer of the Imperial Household department (*neiwu fu*) was appointed as the emperor's personal representative to oversee the foreign trade. This officer was known erroneously to the British as the "Hoppo," a corruption of Hubu (the Board of Revenue), in a fashion that became typical of the mangling of Chinese terms by the British. Strictly speaking this system was an adaptation to foreign commerce that no longer conformed to the formal exigencies of the tributary system. Western trade confined to Canton under the supervision of an imperial appointee was subject to revenue collection in customs duties that flowed directly to the Imperial Household, and to official extortion and "squeeze" by local provincial officials. In order to control and restrict the interaction of foreign traders with Chinese, in 1755 a security merchant system was implemented. A limited number of Chinese merchants permitted to deal with foreign merchants were appointed by the Hoppo. These "Hong" (from *hang*, company) merchants were licensed as a collective body known in English as the "Cohong" (*gonghang*, "collective merchants"). Fixed in form by 1760, the Cohong system became the dominant fact and institution of the Old

China Trade, the only door opening into China. Only the thirteen Hong merchants, appointed by the Hoppo, were licensed to deal with foreigners. The Cohong merchants were jointly responsible for all trade duties and fees owed by foreign merchants and for the proper order and behavior of foreigners and their debts. In 1781 the "Consoo (*gongsuo*) fund" was established, a kind of escrow account based on an ad valorem tax on trade, to redeem bad debts.

No contact between foreign merchants and Chinese officials was permitted. Only merchants, following the Confucian prejudice against commercial activity, should deal with merchants. Communication from foreign merchants had to pass through Hong merchants, and rigorous stylistic forms and avoidances were required. No foreign officials were permitted at Canton. The Hong merchants were at the mercy of local officials and the Hoppo through squeeze and extortion, so that the system was milked by the government. It was common, for instance, for the Hoppo to request from the Hong merchants large gifts for the imperial birthday or other ceremonial occasions, plus contributions to expenses of military campaigns and river conservancy. Hong merchants were appointed for three-year terms. It was said that the merchant's first year's income went to buy his appointment, the second year's income was used for "gifts" to officials, and only the third year's income was kept as profit. Even so, Hong merchants amassed great fortunes and many persisted in their appointment for many years. Yet the uncertainties of the trade were such that they could be easily bankrupted.

As foreign merchants congregated at Canton, the factories of various foreign nations and companies eventually paralleled the thirteen Hongs. During the trading season, which lasted from the spring into fall with the changing monsoons, foreign merchants resided in their factories. Each firm was assisted by a Chinese *comprador* (from the Portuguese *compra*, purchase), an agent who negotiated with the Hong merchants and conducted routine business for the firm. Women were strictly prohibited from coming up to Canton, and foreign merchants were required to depart at the end of the trading season, so that during the off season (January to May) the merchants retreated to Macau where their families resided throughout the year. Along the Pearl River waterfront, in a confined area outside the Canton city walls, two monopolies faced each other across a narrow street, physically embodied in the thirteen factories of the foreign merchants and the establishments of the Hongs. The EIC, as the doyen of the foreign commercial community, and the Cohong each exhibited similar attitudes, leaving everything to monopoly. In the late eighteenth century it was a comfortable arrangement, the only window opening to China from the West.

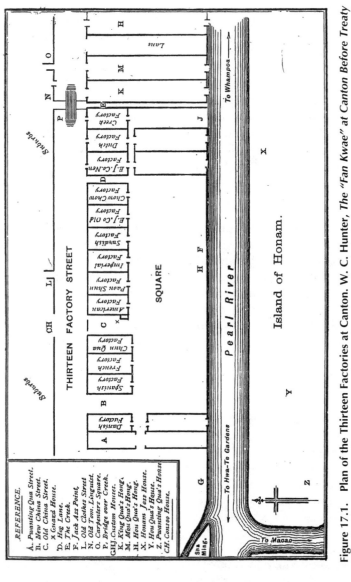

REFERENCE.

A. Pwanting Qua Street.
B. New China Street.
C. Old China Street.
x Guard House.
D. Hog Lane.
E. The Creek.
F. Jack Ass Point.
L. Old Clothes Street.
N. Old Tom. Linguist.
O. Carpenters Square.
P. Bridge over Creek.
GH] Custom Houses.
K. King Qua's Hong.
M. Man Qua's Hong.
H. Hou Qua's Hong.
X. Honam Joss House.
Y. Hou Qua's House.
Z. Pwanting Qua's House.
CH. Consoo House.

Figure 17.1. Plan of the Thirteen Factories at Canton. W. C. Hunter, *The "Fan Kwae" at Canton Before Treaty Days, 1825–1844* (London: Kegan Paul, Trench, 1882), after p. 24.

IN QUEST OF THE CHINA MARKET

Restless forces were afoot that were not content with the seemingly placid Canton order. The English bridled at the fine bureaucratic formalities that restricted communications with their opposite numbers whenever they needed to resolve disputes over trade. In 1759 they sent a company agent, James Flint, to petition directly to the Qianlong emperor. Flint was expelled and his translator was executed for their presumption to violate established rules. The second half of the eighteenth century was a critical period as English trade expanded against the increasingly stereotyped Canton system, and peaceful efforts to break out of the confinements failed.

The entire Western trade with China had become increasingly volatile as it expanded beyond the capacity of the Cohong system to accommodate it. Tea, silk, and porcelain were the principal EIC exports from Canton. From 1664, when 2 lbs. 2oz. of tea were sent to London, tea exports expanded to become the national drink of Britain, accounting for 90 percent of the trade. By 1834 three million pounds of tea were being exported every year. Imports to Canton only partially financed the export trade. British woolens, which constituted 75 percent of imports, were not especially popular with the Chinese and from 1775 were sold at a steady loss to help finance exports as well as meet the strident demands of wool growers at home. The solution was found in the "country trade" (so called because the Europeans viewed Asia as the country while the direct trade with Europe was considered the metropolitan trade) between India, progressively falling under British dominance in the eighteenth century, and Canton. British merchants licensed by the EIC carried Indian goods to China, mainly cotton, which was far more popular than woolens with Chinese consumers. Amounting to 30 percent of total British trade, the country trade helped finance the EIC export trade from Canton to London. The balance of the tea investment, ever growing, was made up by silver bullion imports, ultimately an inherently unsatisfactory balance of payments.

When the American colonies achieved independence from Great Britain, Americans, no longer British subjects, ceased to be subject to the EIC monopoly and to British taxes on tea. In 1784 the *Empress of China* sailed from Boston for China, the first American ship to enter the China trade. In the same year Parliament passed the Commutation Act, which commuted tea duties for British subjects (which, after all, had been a principal issue in the American Revolution). That, and the widespread dumping of woolens on the market, designed to capture the majority of trade for the British and ruin their rivals, were a pivot in the development of the trade. The effect was an enormous expansion of the trade against the restrictive Canton system, straining the EIC's ability to finance the trade. By 1795 the British had achieved mastery of the China trade, which the EIC, now enjoying a good, comfortable business as it adjusted to the fixed routine, was loathe to change. Moreover, preoccupation with the rising threat of Napoleon in Europe precluded any major efforts for the next two decades. But the EIC, representing the old, conservative mercantile system, was now confronted by the rising tide of laissez-faire ideology since the publication of Adam Smith's *The Wealth of Nations* in 1776. British Free Traders condemned the EIC monopoly and demanded access to the China trade denied them by the monopoly. And the Industrial Revolution, just beginning in Britain, created new pressure to seek markets as outlets for manufactured goods. No longer was the mercantile system based on the extraction of Asian goods for sale in Europe adequate to the changing reality of expanding global commerce.

Expanded trade after 1784 brought several latent problems to the fore, fostering a more urgent search for a new solution. First was the problem of financing the trade. Believing that China presented a vast, untapped market of hundreds of millions of customers for Western goods that was severely limited by the narrow Cohong system, Western merchants desired to open up a wider market in China and expand commercial relations. The myth of the China market has been the "El Dorado" of the China trade, even to the present day. In the nineteenth century it was said that if only every Chinaman would add just one inch to his gown, the looms of Manchester would keep spinning for a hundred years. Second were legal problems and conflicts. A regular treaty basis for official relations and diplomatic representation was needed to replace the strict merchant-to-merchant relations dictated by the Cohong system. Law was a basic source of friction between China and the West, arising from a fundamental difference in legal principles and practices. Legal conflicts heightened the awareness of the Western nations of the desirability for formal diplomatic relations. Chinese law was primarily penal and administrative. Commercial and civil cases were subsumed under the former, so that, for instance, a case of breach of contract was decided on the basis of criminal responsibility, and the losing party was punished under criminal law, slight compensation for the plaintiff who would recover nothing of value. Criminal law, moreover, involved the assumption of guilt, decided entirely by a magistrate. Torture was commonly employed to extract the required confession, without which punishment could not be confirmed.

Incidences of this collision of legal principles began to occur more frequently as trade relations expanded. In 1784 the British ship *Lady Hughes* fired a salute to another ship entering the Canton roads. Such salutes were a common courtesy observed among foreign ships entering and leaving the port. Chinese vendors on sampans thronged the ships selling all manner of vegetables and other goods. Unfortunately the salute from the *Lady Hughes* killed a Chinese alongside the ship. The Chinese authorities, seeking legal culpability according to law, demanded the surrender of the gunner for prosecution. When the British refused, pleading an accidental homicide, the Chinese closed the factories and surrounded the ships. The EIC capitulated and surrendered the gunner, who was executed. In 1821 an American sailor Terranova on board the ship *Emily* accidentally killed a Chinese woman in an argument while trading. When the Chinese demanded the sailor, the Americans refused to surrender him. The Chinese boarded the ship and threatened to search it. At that time opium was being traded illegally in the Canton harbor. Since the *Emily* carried contraband opium, the Americans capitulated and Terranova was executed.

Well before this incident, the British sought to launch an embassy to China to put the trade on a "firm and honorable foundation." The idea was to go directly to the emperor, as James Flint had attempted to do, confident that he would remedy the situation if he only knew the true state of affairs. It was widely believed that corrupt local officials disguised the local situation from higher authorities. The embassy was jointly sponsored by the EIC and the British crown. Lord Macartney, a former EIC official, was appointed leader, accompanied by a large contingent of experts and aids. Arriving in China in 1792, the expedition avoided Canton, and sailing up the coast, gained entry near Ningbo in central China. It was then allowed to proceed up the Grand Canal to Beijing under the banner of a tribute mission to congratulate the Qianlong emperor on his birthday. In the drawn-out negotiations on ritual and ceremony, at which the Chinese excelled, the mission came to naught. Macartney's tribute gifts, chosen to impress the Chinese with Western technological and artistic accomplishments, were considered unworthy and unremarkable. After several weeks of waiting, Macartney was granted an audience, but he had already indicated that he would refuse to perform the "kowtow" to the emperor, a ritual demanded of all subjects and foreigners alike. The kowtow (*ketou*, literally "knock the head") was known as "the three kneelings and nine prostrations." The subject kneeled before the emperor, knocked his head three times on the ground, got up, advanced, and repeated the same actions two more times. No ritual could be a more unmistakable sign of submission. Chinese officials thought nothing of it. But to Macartney, a proper British subject who bowed to no person, however exalted, other than his own sovereign, it was completely unacceptable. Manchu court officials, wishing that the affair go smoothly, were at a loss what to do. Ultimately a solution was agreed upon. A portrait of King George III was placed to one side of the throne and Macartney bowed (not kowtowed) in the direction of both the king and the emperor. For the Chinese the concession was a sign of the magnanimity of the emperor in the face of the uncouth barbarian manners of the uncivilized Europeans.

Needless to say, the embassy was a failure. Nothing the British sought was granted. In an edict of 1793 at the conclusion of the embassy the Qianlong emperor replied to George III's initial letter requesting the audience:

> We, by the Grace of Heaven, Emperor, instruct the king of England to take note of our charge.
>
> Although your country, O King, lies in the far oceans, yet inclining your heart toward civilization you have specially sent an envoy respectfully to present a state message, and sailing the seas he has come to our court to kowtow and to present congratulations for the Imperial birthday, and also to present local products, thereby showing your sincerity.
>
> We have perused the text of your state message and the wording expresses your earnestness. From it your sincere humility and obedience can clearly be seen. It is admirable and we fully approve. As regards the chief and assistant envoys who have brought the state message and tribute articles, we are mindful that they have been sent from afar across the sea, and we have extended our favor and courtesy to them, and have ordered our ministers to bring them to an Imperial audience. We have given them a banquet and have repeatedly bestowed gifts on them in order to show our kindness. . . .
>
> The Celestial Empire, ruling all within the four seas, simply concentrates on carrying out the affairs of Government properly, and does not value rare and precious things. Now you, O King, have presented various objects to the throne, and mindful of your loyalty in presenting offerings from afar, we have specially ordered the Yamen to receive them. In fact, the virtue and power of the Celestial Dynasty has penetrated far to the myriad kingdoms, which have come to render homage, so all kinds of precious things from "over the mountains and sea" have collected here, things which your chief envoy and others have seen for themselves. Nevertheless we have never valued ingenious articles, nor do we have the slightest need of your country's manufactures. Therefore, O King, as regards your request to send someone to remain at the capital, while it is not in harmony with the regulations of the Celestial Empire we also feel very much that it is of no advantage to your country. Hence we have issued these detailed instructions and have commanded your tribute envoys to return safely home. You, O King, should simply act in conformity with our wishes by strengthening your loyalty and swearing perpetual obedience so as to ensure that your country may share the blessings of peace.[6]

The opening and closing sentiments expressed in the edict were a formula repeated in all responses by Hong merchants to foreign petitions at Canton.

At the end of the eighteenth century, while the West was experiencing momentous changes, the Chinese view of the world remained static. If the Chinese were satisfied with the routine that had settled in at Canton, the British had come to the realization that China was not to be opened by normal peaceful diplomatic persuasion. The door to the China market would have to be opened by force. A thousand miles to the west a process was already underway, the significance of which was barely appreciated at the time, that was later to undermine and bring an end to the closed world of the Middle Kingdom.

SUGGESTED READINGS

Downs, Jacques M. *The Golden Ghetto: The American Commercial Community at Canton and the Shaping of American China Policy, 1784–1844* (Bethlehem & London: Lehigh University Press, 1997). A detailed account of the American merchant community at Canton and its influence on American China policy.

Greenberg, Michael. *British Trade and the Opening of China, 1800–1842* (Cambridge: Cambridge University Press, 1951). A study of the British trade at Canton leading up to the Opium War.

Hibbert, Christopher. *The Dragon Wakes: China and the West, 1793–1911* (London: Penguin Books, 1984). A comprehensive history of the Western impact on China from the Macartney Embassy to the Nationalist Revolution.

Hunter, William C. *Bits of Old China* (Taipei: Ch'eng-wen Publishing (reprint), 1976). An interesting miscellany of tales and anecdotes of the China trade by a contemporary participant.

Hunter, William C. *The "Fan Kwei" at Canton before Treaty Days, 1825–1844* (Taipei: Ch'eng-wen Publishing (reprint), 1965). The activities of Westerners in the Canton China trade through the Opium War.

Macartney, George, Earl. *An Embassy to China*, J. L. Cranmer-Bing, ed. (Hamden, CT: Archon Books, 1963). The account of Macartney's failed embassy to the Qing court in 1792–1793.

MacNair, Harley Farnsworth, ed. *Modern Chinese History, Selected Readings: A collection of extracts from various sources chosen to illustrate some of the chief phases of China's international relations during the past hundred years* (New York: Paragon Book Reprint, 1967). An excellent collection of translations of extracts of documents relating to the nineteenth century.

Morse, Hosea Ballou. *The International Relations of the Chinese Empire*, 2 vols. (London: Longmans, Green, 1910 and 1918). An early standard reference for Sino-Western relations to the end of the Qing period.

Murray, Dian H. *Pirates of the South China Coast, 1790–1810* (Stanford: Stanford University Press, 1987). Describes the revival and threat from piracy in the South China maritime world in the late eighteenth and early nineteenth centuries.

Porter, Jonathan. *Macau: The Imaginary City: Culture and Society, 1557 to the Present* (Boulder: Westview Press, 1996). A cultural and social history of the oldest continuous settlement on the China coast from the late Ming.

Porter, Jonathan. "The Troublesome Feringhi: Late Ming Chinese Perceptions of the Portuguese and Macau," *Portuguese Studies Review* 7.2 (1999): 11–35. The aggressive behavior of the Portuguese on the South China coast in the early sixteenth century presented a difficult problem for the local Chinese authorities.

Pritchard, Earl H. *The Crucial Years of Early Anglo-Chinese Relations, 1750–1800* (Pullman: Washington State College, 1936). An early but still valuable study of the formative years of Anglo-Chinese relations.

Teng Ssu-yu, John K. Fairbank, et al. *China's Response to the West: A Documentary Survey 1830–1923* (New York: Atheneum, 1970). An annotated collection of documents relating to Sino-Western relations from the Opium Wars to the early twentieth century.

Williams, S. Wells. *The Middle Kingdom: A survey of the geography, government, literature, social life, arts, and history of the Chinese empire and its inhabitants*, rev. ed., 2 vols. (New York: C. Scribner's Sons, 1883). One of the first comprehensive Western accounts of China in the nineteenth century betrays the prevalent Christian missionary attitude of the time.

NOTES

1. Luis de Camões, *Os Lusiadas*, canto II, stanza 46.

2. Ibid., canto V, stanza 42.

3. Cao Xueqin, David Hawkes, trans., *The Story of the Stone*, 5 vols. (Harmondsworth, England: Penguin Books, 1973), vol. 1, 346.

4. Quoting Ji Cheng, *Yuan Ye*, in William Willetts, *Chinese Art*, vol. 1 (New York: George Braziller, 1958), 686.

5. S. Wells Williams, *The Middle Kingdom*, revised edition, 2 vols. (New York: Charles Scribner's Sons, 1883), vol. 1, 1.

6. George Macartney, Earl, *An Embassy to China*, J. L. Cranmer-Bing, ed. (Hamden, CT: Archon Books, 1963), 336–341.

18

Opium

Across the fertile eastern Gangetic Valley of northern India in the late eighteenth century peasant cultivators, working under strict government control, harvested vast fields of poppies. Arab merchants had first introduced opium cultivation in the eighth century. The poppy plant from which opium is harvested subsequently became a staple cash crop. In the mid-seventeenth century the Dutch East India Company entered the trade, exporting opium from west Bengal to Batavia, the capital of the Dutch East Indies in Java, and from that entrepôt carried opium to other parts of the Indies and to Canton on the South China coast. The British East India Company (EIC) entered the trade in 1708 as its influence expanded in northern India, procuring, producing, and exporting opium in a rapidly growing volume to Southeast Asia and China. The EIC conquest of Bengal in the mid-eighteenth century and its expansion westward through northern India gave the British the means to monopolize the production and sale of opium from which a state-run system gradually developed, driving out the competition.

*The opium poppy (*papaver somniferum*) produces a powerful narcotic drug, used in its highly refined form in medicine as morphine. In less refined form, opium paste is heated in a small brass bowl at the end of a pipe and the vapors inhaled, "smoking" thus producing a narcotic effect. Opium is highly addictive. Moderate use may be sustained for a long time, but heavy use causes physical incapacitation, deterioration, and eventually death. Swallowed, opium is fatal. Opium was consumed throughout Southeast Asia and in China by increasing numbers of addicts, either at home by the upper classes or in opium dens by lower class townsmen and some peasants. British mothers gave laudanum, a tincture of opium, to their infants to stop their crying. Samuel Taylor Coleridge (1772–1834) was on an opium high when he composed his famous poem "Kubla*

Khan" (1816). There is no substance to the allegation born of a nineteenth-century European sense of racial superiority that the Chinese somehow had a proclivity to opium addiction.

Opium in British India was produced in a labor-intensive market-gardening regimen by skilled cultivators from specific selected castes licensed by the government. The soil was carefully fertilized, seeds sown, the young plants thinned, and the plots irrigated repeatedly. Seventy-five to 80 days after seeding the mature plants flowered. The petals were removed and 10 days later, when the capsules containing the seed pods had ripened, the cultivator slit the capsules with a knife. The sap from the capsules was repeatedly scraped off, dried, and formed into cakes. Opium agents purchased this raw opium for transport to EIC opium factories. There it was refined to an unvarying standard of purity and was packed, 80 balls to a 140 pound wooden chest, stamped with the imprimatur of the EIC guaranteeing quality. Over a million licensed peasants grew opium on more than a half-million acres in the Ganges River valley. Opium was also cultivated in Malwa in western India outside the British dominion. Malwa opium was of inferior quality and commanded only half the price of Bengal opium. The Portuguese and other merchants traded in Malwa opium through Macau, but the British conquest of western India in 1818 ended this competition and ruined the Portuguese market in Macau.

The chests of opium were shipped to the Calcutta auction, where they were sold to private merchants under license by the EIC. The market was very volatile as prices fluctuated considerably. The "country merchants," as they were known, hoped to buy low at a good price and sell high when they reached Canton, but the opposite could also be the case. In the nineteenth century the need for rapid transportation in several round trips each season fostered advances in nautical technology and the building of the famous "opium clippers," the fastest sailing ships of the age.

THE CHINA MARKET

The EIC did not itself carry opium to China. Country ships owned or leased by private English merchants licensed by the EIC carried opium purchased at Calcutta to Canton. Thus the EIC at Canton was able to deny involvement in what was essentially an illicit smuggling trade. From the beginning, the country ships, which also carried a variety of Indian products such as cotton as well as opium, off-loaded their cargoes at Whampoa about 10 miles downriver from Canton. Smaller river boats ferried cargoes, including tea to be loaded on EIC ships, to and from the port. Thus opium, while in violation of Chinese prohibitions, was being traded directly under the noses of Qing officials. Not all Western firms, it should be noted, traded in opium. But pressure to do something about the drug was rising within Chinese official circles. When Ruan Yuan was appointed governor-general of Guangdong and Guangxi, of which Canton was the capital, he drove the opium trade out of the inner Canton estuary. Seeking an alternative base for their trade, the opium merchants anchored "receiving ships" at Lintin, a small island in the middle of the outer estuary. These served as floating warehouses where the country ships from Calcutta unloaded their cargoes of opium before proceeding up to Canton. From Lintin small fast boats with large sails and rowed by more than 20 crewmen, called "fast crabs" and "scrambling dragons," smuggled the opium chests into the network of channels and branches of the river, eluding the slow Chinese coast guard junks. Chinese brokers and dealers took over the opium from there, breaking up the chests and cutting and adulterating

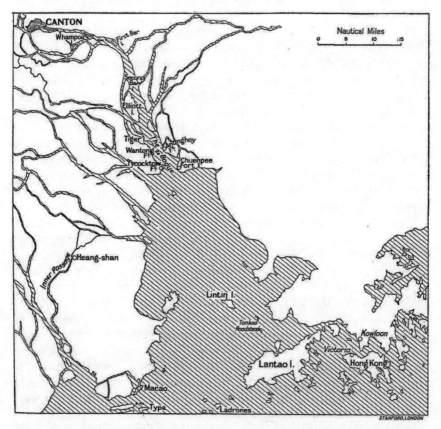

Figure 18.1. Sketch Map of the Pearl River Estuary. From *Foreign Mud* by Maurice Collis, copyright © 1946 by Maurice Collis. Reprinted by permission of New Directions Publishing Corp.

the balls for sale and distribution down the chain to individual consumers and opium dens. Immense profits were realized by the dealers and brokers along the distribution network far into the interior.

Far from dampening the trade, the expulsion of opium traders to Lintin led to a greatly expanded market. Jardine Matheson, the principal English private company, pioneered the "coast trade" of smaller coastal vessels sailing from Lintin up the China coast, putting in at various ports to seek buyers, often bribing the mandarins to look the other way. The British expanded the production and supply of opium in India in 1831, and when the EIC monopoly of the China trade expired in 1833, a large influx of new free merchants increased smuggling. Americans had the second largest share, generally dealing in Turkish opium.

An essential conflict developed between the EIC and the British government over the Macartney Embassy in 1792. The embassy had represented a compromise between two approaches to the China trade, sponsored by the Crown but led by a former EIC servant. On one side, the company was anxious not to disturb the advantageous position that it had won at Canton and the stability of the trade that had finally emerged. It represented the old mercantile age with vested interests in the status quo. On the other side, the government was under pressure from growing manufacturing interests at home and the new free traders who, influenced by laissez-faire ideology, condemned the mercantilism represented by the company. The failure of the Macartney Embassy to break out of the old Canton system and the quest for a wider marker in China confronted the fundamental problem of the "old China trade" at Canton, the lack of any commodity that the Chinese desired in sufficient quantity to balance the Western investment in the trade. Indian opium was the solution.

Through the eighteenth century, tea exports from Canton grew tremendously, to become virtually the sole article of trade for the EIC. The profits from tea were not particularly large, but from the end of the century the EIC had become much more than a commercial enterprise; it was the government of India. Duties on tea constituted one-tenth of the revenue of Great Britain. The problem was how to pay for it in the absence of a viable commodity marketable in China. Tea was purchased principally in silver, especially from New Spain via Manila, generating a major influx of silver to China. The country trade from Calcutta to Canton, made possible by the growth of British political power in India, provided funds for the tea investment at Canton, first in India cotton and then in opium. The problem for the opium merchants was how to remit profits to England without the risks of carrying large amounts of treasure. The solution was to exchange the proceeds from opium sales at the EIC office in Canton for bills of exchange on London. The EIC then used the money received to purchase tea. Thus a trilateral financial structure emerged: The profits from opium carried from Calcutta to Canton by private merchants met the tea investment there; the profits from tea carried on EIC ships from Canton to London redeemed the bills of exchange presented at the EIC offices there; and revenues of the Indian empire were thereby repatriated to London as tribute.

The odd thing about opium was that though it was in a sense the heart of the China trade it was not itself a profit source directly for either the EIC or the Qing government. Yet both sides had a powerful vested interest in maintaining the trade. For the British it was the repatriation of Indian revenues. For the Chinese emperor it was the need to preserve the source of direct revenue for domestic and military expenditures. The opium-tea trade forged a linkage between China and the global market developing in the eighteenth and nineteenth centuries. Like it or not, China was being sucked into a larger world economic system as never before.

THE CORRUPTION OF OPIUM

In 1813 Parliament terminated the EIC monopoly in India but extended its monopoly of the China trade for twenty more years. An economic boom of private traders followed that fueled the country trade. When in 1833 the EIC monopoly of the China trade ended and the company withdrew from Canton, a vacuum was created. The Select Committee of the EIC at Canton had been the responsible authority over British merchants and the doyen of the foreign community there. To fill this gap the British government in 1834 appointed Lord William John Napier British superintendent of trade as the official representative of the Crown. This action precipitated a string of counteractions that led to war between Britain and China. Napier was instructed to communicate directly with responsible Qing officials of appropriate rank, which meant the governorgeneral at Canton. This amounted to a revolutionary attempt to displace the rigidly established basis of the old system, and perpetrated a commercial and political crisis. The Chinese were aware of Napier's official status, but official contact and assumption of equality was prohibited under the rules of the Canton system, which for the Chinese had not changed. With considerable justification, Napier was regarded as a commercial agent and head merchant, which from his point of view did not comport with his aristocratic status. In fact in terms of his own instructions his status was ambiguous. The Chinese refused contact and communication at the official level, trade was stopped, and Napier was expelled from Canton. In referring to foreigners the Chinese were forced to use Chinese characters that phonetically approximated the sound of the foreign name. Because many characters are pronounced alike, the language is replete with homophones. The choice of words could be intentionally positive or negative in tone. In Chinese official dispatches and proclamations Napier was referred to by the Chinese words *Leibi* (Napier), the characters for which meant "Laboriously Vile."[1] Retreating to Macau, Napier shortly died from the emotional stress of the confrontation and the physical rigors of the tropical climate. The unresolved outcome of the Napier crisis was the realization by the British that peaceful means would not avail and that force would be necessary to break out of the constricting Canton system. Private traders were all too eager to see the government exercise it.

In the meantime an internal debate over the opium question in public and official circles grew in intensity. The problem was discussed in memorials and edicts to and from the Court and the provinces. Two fundamental objections to the opium trade emerged. The first centered on the moral and social decay caused by opium addiction. Opium was a poisonous drug that caused mental and physical degeneration among its users. Heavy addicts squandered their patrimony, violated filial piety, the family system and social cohesion were undermined, and prevalent addiction among soldiers and bannermen weakened the military forces. The second objection was economic. As the trade balance turned in the early nineteenth century as the value of opium imported to Canton exceeded the value of tea being exported, the outflow of silver to pay for opium led to a relative scarcity of silver, hoarding, and deflation of copper cash in the bimetallic currency system. The normal exchange rate was one thousand copper cash in a string to one ounce of silver, but the exchange rate rose to 1,600–2,000 cash per string. Ordinary market exchanges were in copper while taxes had to be paid in silver, and as silver rose in value prices of common goods in copper cash were inflated, placing a hardship on peasants and commoners.

Alternative solutions were aired, including the obvious ones of vigorous suppression based on prohibitions already established or legalization. Each had its partisans. Opium addiction had reached every part of the country, from towns and cities everywhere, to official *yamen*, to the palace itself, and especially throughout the demoralized Manchu banner garrisons. Public opinion was a genuine force in China, especially manifested in the collective opinion and pressure of the scholar-literati class but also increasingly among commoners. Napier misconstrued this force, believing he could play on the potential animosity of the Chinese populace toward officials and Manchus (naturally a point of extreme sensitivity for the Manchu rulers). During the crisis Napier foolishly posted a proclamation in Canton inciting the populace against the governor-general and the government. Attempts to tamper with public loyalty and stability pointed up exactly the danger the barbarians presented. The governor-general issued a counter-proclamation, violent and blunt in tone:

> A lawless foreign slave, named Laboriously Vile, has issued a notice. We do not know how such a barbarian dog can have the audacity to call himself a chief. Were he so in fact, though a savage from beyond the pale, his sense of propriety would have restrained him from such an outrage. It is a capital offense to incite the populace against their rulers and we would be justified in obtaining a mandate for his decapitation and the exposure of his head as a warning to traitors.[2]

The internal debate and discussion of the opium problem reached the point of action in late 1838 with the emperor's decision for suppression, confirming a long-standing series of prohibitions since 1729, never vigorously enforced. This time was to be different. While much of the foreign community hoped for legalization, they could hardly have been surprised by the emperor's decision. Though opium served an essential function in the trade it was nevertheless intolerable both to the Chinese and to the great majority of British public opinion and many private merchants who refused to deal in it.

GOING TO WAR

In late 1838 the Daoguang emperor (1821–1850) summoned Lin Zexu, a high official with a reputation for incorruptibility and honesty, to Beijing and in an imperial audience appointed him Imperial Commissioner with instructions to go to Canton and end the opium trade once and for all. After making a thorough study of the problem, Lin set out for Canton in early 1839 with a definite plan of action. Among the foreign merchants who were aware of Commissioner Lin's appointment there was a mood of impending crisis, mixed with cynicism that Lin, like all other officials, would be corrupted and stymied by vested interests on the spot. Shortly after arriving on March 10, Lin demanded the surrender of all opium in foreign hands and in transit to China, and a bond from each merchant undertaking not to trade in opium in the future on pain of death. The foreigners were confined to the factories, all Chinese servants and employees were withdrawn, and trade was stopped pending compliance with the demands. The Chinese believed that stopping trade alone would be a strong incentive because, though China was completely self-supporting, foreigners could not live without tea and rhubarb, which was a significant item of trade. Foreigners' physiology, it was thought, was such that their digestive systems could not function without rhubarb, a natural laxative.

On March 28 Captain Charles Elliot of the Royal Navy, who had been appointed superintendent of trade following the death of Napier, announced that he would surrender 20,293 chests of opium.

The mouth of the Pearl River where it opens into the lower Canton estuary was called in Chinese *Humen* ("Tiger's Gate") and named on foreign maps by the Latin *"Bocca Tigris."* The British slurred this name to "The Bogue." Both banks of the Bogue were guarded by Chinese forts mounting artillery, the fort at Chuanbi on the east bank being the largest. It was there that the opium was to be surrendered. Lin left Canton for the Bogue on April 10, and the next day began receiving the opium chests. On the bank of the river above Chuanbi Lin built a stockade enclosing deep, long trenches into which water from the river could be introduced and discharged. The balls of opium from the chests were broken up in the trenches by Chinese workers, mixed with water, and emptied into the river in a prolonged process taking several weeks. A reviewing stand was erected where the work could be observed by officials and foreigners, in part to dispel any notion that the opium was not being destroyed. (Contrary to popular legend, Lin did not burn the opium in great bonfires.) Lin prayed at the temple of Mazu, the Queen of Heaven, whose origin was Lin's home province of Fujian, to ask forgiveness for his pollution of the river. There is a kind of ironic symmetry here between Chinese popular religious piety and Western Christian pious self-confidence in laissez-faire Christianity.

Captain Elliot had promised the British merchants that the government would indemnify them for the loss of the opium, valued at 6 million dollars, a significant inducement to them to comply with the surrender. In the meantime the British, who had no intention of accepting a fait accompli and were ready to go to war, were assembling a naval squadron in India for dispatch to China. Britain had emerged from the defeat of Napoleon in 1815 as the master of the seas and the greatest world power. The British government was willing to fight a war with China to preserve opium as the essential means of transferring wealth from the Indian empire to London.

One of Britain's demands was for a base on the China coast comparable to the Portuguese settlement at Macau. When the large British Royal Navy squadron arrived, comprising several powerful frigates and armed steamships, it anchored in the harbor between Hong Kong island and the mainland at Kowloon. The first battle of the Opium War was fought at Kowloon Point on September 4, 1839, when the British squadron opened fire on Chinese naval junks protecting Kowloon from a British landing. As in all subsequent engagements during the next three years, British firepower was devastating, inflicting complete destruction and defeat on Chinese forces. Invariably, however, Chinese and Manchu commanders

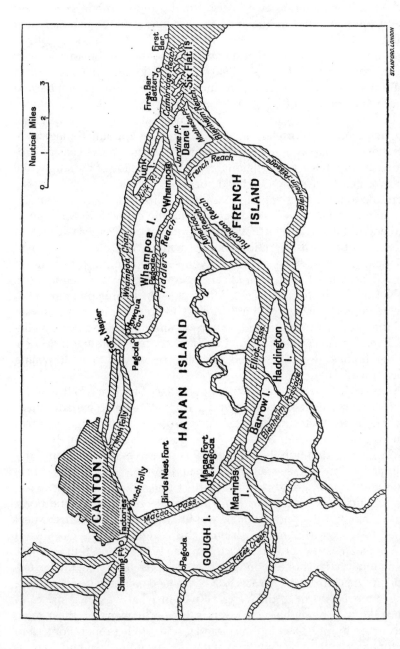

Figure 18.2. Sketch Map of the Vicinity of Canton. From *Foreign Mud* by Maurice Collis, copyright © 1946 by Maurice Collis. Reprinted by permission of New Directions Publishing Corp.

reported to the throne victorious defeats of the English. On November 3, in the Battle of Chuanbi, two British frigates repulsed a large Chinese fleet which was attempting to admit past the Bogue an English merchant ship that had signed the guarantee. However, the British soon realized that nothing would avail in limiting hostilities to the Canton area, so they sailed up the coast, and in July 1840 the considerably enlarged British Expeditionary Force, reinforced by Indian native infantry, bombarded and occupied the city of Dinghai on Zhoushan Island on the southern side of Hangzhou Bay. Karl Friedrich August Gutzlaff, a "Prussian buccaneer missionary interpreter" for the British, was appointed magistrate of Dinghai.[3] Gutzlaff was known for taking passage on the coastal clippers, dispensing Bibles and religious tracts over one side of the ship while opium was being off-loaded on the other side.

Intending to force their way up to Canton, in 1841 the English returned to the south. On January 7, in a large assault, the Bogue forts were bombarded and occupied, and virtually the entire Chinese fleet was destroyed upriver. One of the most significant engagements of the war, this impelled the Manchu prince Qishan, who had been sent to Canton to investigate Commissioner Lin's failure to eradicate opium, to enter into negotiations with the British. The result was the Convention of Chuanbi on January 18, ceding Hong Kong Island to the British. While playing for time, Qishan lacked the authority to cede Chinese territory and in fact had been explicitly ordered by the emperor to hold fast and concede nothing. In March, when his duplicity was discovered, he was arrested and taken to Beijing in chains for trial.

In August 1841 the new British plenipotentiary Sir Henry Pottinger arrived in Hong Kong accompanied by a greatly augmented expeditionary force. "The Early Victorian Vikings" now proceeded north again, "sacking one coastal town after another."[4] The British forces ultimately numbered 25 ships of the line, 14 steamers, 9 support vessels, and ten thousand infantry. One of the steamships, a heavily armed EIC paddle-wheel steamer, the *Nemesis*, greatly impressed the Chinese with its ability to run circles around the Chinese war junks regardless of weather conditions. Amoy, a major trading port in Fujian, was attacked and occupied, the fleet returned to reoccupy Zhoushan Island, and Ningbo, a large city inland from Zhoushan, was captured in October. The British paused there while the Qing mounted a counteroffensive that was planned as the final extermination of the barbarians in March 1842. It failed completely. From there Pottinger moved north to the Yangzi River in what was the final campaign of the war. Shanghai was taken in June, Zhenjiang on the Yangzi was occupied in July, blocking the Grand Canal, while preparations were made for an assault on Nanjing in August. At that point the Qing government, facing the inevitable, capitulated and on August 29, 1842, signed the Treaty of Nanjing on Pottinger's flagship HMS *Cornwallis*.

The two negotiators, Pottinger, the English aristocrat, and Qiying, a Manchu imperial clansman trusted by the emperor, the successor to the disgraced Qishan, confronted each other across an immense cultural divide. Qiying, urbane and ingratiating, particularly was caught in a difficult predicament. On one hand he had to mollify the powerful English, on the other hand he had to assure the emperor that he was being tough with his adversaries. In a situation all too familiar in the annals of diplomacy, the two parties exuded a genial manner of personal respect and friendship during the lengthy negotiations. Qiying and Pottinger exchanged portraits of each other's wives, and Qiying offered to adopt Pottinger's son. But playing on the emperor's sympathy, in private dispatches Qiying protested how difficult it was to endure the offensive manners of the barbarians.

The terms of the Treaty of Nanjing included an indemnity of $21 million which included the cost of the opium destroyed plus the expense of the war; opening five ports to trade, including Canton, Amoy (Xiamen), Fuzhou, Ningbo, and Shanghai; equal access to officials of corresponding rank; British consuls appointed to each port; abolition of the Cohong; a moderate uniform tariff on imports and exports; and cession of Hong Kong. The treaty made no mention of opium. The treaty finally accomplished the opening of China so long sought by the British and the other Western powers. Or so it seemed.

Pottinger and Qiying met again in 1843 to negotiate the Supplementary Treaty of the Bogue which set conventional tariff levies and established the Most-Favored Nation Clause. The latter provided that any provision secured by one country subsequently would automatically accord to all other parties to treaties, ensuring that all would be treated equally. This provision fit well with the traditional Chinese predilection for playing barbarians off against each other. The American Treaty of Wangxia was signed between the United States negotiator Caleb Cushing and Qiying at Macau in 1844. It provided for explicit extraterritoriality, according to which foreign nationals charged with crimes in China would be tried by consular courts of their own country; a clause allowing the purchase of books and hiring of teachers in the five ports; and for revision of the treaties after twelve years. The Treaty of Whampoa with France in 1844 further established the toleration of Roman Catholic missions in the treaty ports. In order to equalize this provision among all powers it was extended to Protestant missions as well. Collectively these treaties came to be known as the "Unequal Treaties" because they denied or impinged on Chinese sovereignty in ways that European nations would not have negotiated between themselves. Extraterritoriality violated the principal that a sovereign nation has legal authority over foreign nationals within its borders; the Most-Favored Nation clause denied China the ability to negotiate differentially with other nations; and the tariff convention likewise prevented China from raising or lowering tariffs selectively with other nations. The treaties were all imposed under duress and remained a potent symbol of China's impotence and subordination to Western imperialism. Extraterritoriality, the most resented of the unequal provisions endured through the Qing and long into the post-revolutionary Nationalist period, and was not finally abolished until 1943, as a concession to the Nationalist regime in a gesture to raise morale under the Japanese invasion during the Second World War. (Japan, also afflicted by unequal treaties in the nineteenth century, managed to negotiate an end to extraterritoriality by 1900.) On October 1, 1949, when Mao Zedong, announcing the founding of the People's Republic of China in Tiananmen Square, proclaimed that China had at last "stood up," he was mindful of China's liberation from Western imperial domination.

INCOMPLETE SETTLEMENT AND THE RENEWAL OF WAR

In spite of the treaties, the spirit and practice of the tributary system did not immediately topple. If the British and the other powers saw the treaty provisions as defining a new set of opportunities for wider trade and diplomatic relations, the Chinese viewed them, in a lawyerly fashion, as maximally allowable terms of interaction. To any requests for official contact, the Chinese referred Western officials to the Canton authorities, thus maintaining the effect of the Canton system to relegate barbarians to a place as remote from Beijing as possible. Foreign affairs were still under Canton jurisdiction. The British were frustrated by Chinese resistance and intransigence at every turn. Increasingly the Western powers sought greater regularization of trade, expanded opportunities for access to the China market, and regular and official diplomatic contact. For the powers, the settlement was incomplete. But as the date for revision of the treaties after twelve years approached, originally included in the American treaty of 1844, China resisted every effort at negotiation.

Once having gone to war and pried open the Chinese door part way, Britain was all the more ready to apply force again. An arrogance of power had come to infect the British imperial mentality, born in part by contempt engendered by the ease with which Chinese resistance was swept away. The vaunted Manchu empire under the reign of the glorious Qianlong emperor of a century earlier, logging victory after victory in the far reaches of Central Asia and Tibet, once regarded with awe by

European observers, was now moribund. The Victorian sense of moral superiority and self-confidence of a ruling elite was bred in the Afghan War of 1839–1842, the annexation of the Sind in 1843, the war against the Sikhs in 1845–1848, the defeat of a vast Mogul assault by a few British soldiers led by Robert Clive at Arcot in central India in 1751, and even the defeat of Catherine the Great of Russia in the Crimean War of 1854. A sense of racial superiority pervaded the British view of China.

All that was needed in China was a causus belli. Conveniently this was presented by the Lorcha *Arrow* incident in 1856. A lorcha is a hybrid ship with a Western hull and Chinese rigging and sails. The *Arrow* was a hybrid in even more ways, Chinese owned, commanded by an English captain, with a Chinese crew, sailing under Hong Kong registration that had expired, and flying the British flag. The Chinese navy boarded the ship searching for opium, still contraband, and removed several Chinese crewmen. The British, claiming dubious jurisdiction, demanded the return of the crewmen. The Chinese at first refused, then complied. But the British complained that the concession was unsatisfactory and that their flag had been insulted. The French found their own cause when a French Catholic missionary, the Abbé Chapdelaine, who had illegally entered the interior, was arrested by a local magistrate and executed. French efforts to exact reparations were unavailing. Thus, relying on such dubious pretexts, began the Second Anglo-Chinese War.

The British opened hostilities at Canton in 1856 and occupied the city in 1857. They set up their own puppet administration, searched the files in the governor-general's *yamen*, and carried off to Calcutta the current hard-line governor-general, Ye Mingchen. Then, a combined British and French expeditionary force sailed north to Tientsin (Tianjin), the port closest to Beijing, in 1858, skipping the existing treaty ports along the way. Russian and American ships followed along, hoping to pick up benefits from the others' actions. The British and French bombarded the Dagu forts guarding Tientsin. Their approach so near to the capital had the desired effect, and the Chinese agreed to negotiate. Qiying, who had successfully concluded the 1842 negotiations for the Treaty of Nanjing, was brought out of retirement. However, having examined the Canton *yamen* records, the British discovered Qiying's duplicity and his disparagement of Pottinger in his dispatches to the throne and refused to negotiate with him. Thus fatally embarrassed, he was withdrawn by the Court and ordered to commit suicide. Four new Treaties of Tientsin (British, French, American, and Russian) were signed, including provisions for ten new ports, some on the Yangzi; diplomatic legations in Beijing; a 5 percent ad valorum tariff duty on a list of export and import commodities including opium (thus legalizing the drug); and opening all China to missionaries. The most significant provision was the last, since it effectively extended extraterritoriality inland. But the prospect of diplomatic legations in Beijing where the foreigners would be able to spy on the inner workings of the Middle Kingdom was anathema to conservative high officials and Manchu clansmen.

A split soon opened between the peace party of negotiators and regional officials who possessed more realistic appreciation of barbarian affairs on one hand and a xenophobic war party at the capital that reacted to the concessions granted by the treaties. The war party and the Court led by the Xianfeng emperor were adamantly opposed to permanent residence of diplomatic representatives in Beijing and the assumption of equality of relations. This had been the most crucial point in the Qianlong emperor's rejection of the Macartney Embassy's request in 1793. Nothing had changed in this respect a half-century later. On one hand the British were equally intransigent, but at the same time they were aware that pushing the Qing too hard might fatally undermine the dynasty. What had now been gained with such effort would then all be lost. On the other hand, the issue was potentially driving a wedge between Chinese and Manchu. For Manchus the survival of the dynasty was at stake; for Han Chinese, who had seen dynasties come and go, the survival of traditional society and culture was foremost. Thus the Manchu political elite was above all politically opportunistic and made the decision for peace possible.

A year later the British and French returned to Tientsin to exchange ratifications of the treaties. In the interim the Qing Court under the influence of the conservative faction had second thoughts, and had rebuilt the Dagu forts and mounted Western artillery. Attempting to land at low tide, the allied infantry were subjected to devastating fire at the Battle of Muddy Flats and forced to withdraw ignominiously. Separately the Americans expediently bypassed the forts and got to Beijing. Refusing to kowtow, they failed to exchange ratifications. But the Chinese, now realizing the dire consequences of their actions, followed the American delegation and exchanged ratifications on board ship. The Russians also managed to accomplish the exchange separately. Predictably angered and humiliated by their unexpected defeat, the allies returned once again in 1860. Avoiding frontal assault on the forts, they fought inland to Beijing. On their approach and fearing their wrath, the Court abandoned the capital and fled across the Great Wall to the summer palace at Rehe. In retaliation for the mistreatment of a party of emissaries under a white flag, the expeditionary forces looted and destroyed the Manchu summer palace west of Beijing. In one of the greatest acts of cultural vandalism in war, irreplaceable treasures and architectural monuments built and collected in the Kangxi and Qianlong reigns were lost, including one of the only surviving manuscript copies of the great encyclopedia of the Ming Yongle reign, the *Yongle dadian* (1424).

Having reestablished its dominance at Court, the peace party sent Prince Gong, brother of the Xianfeng emperor, down to Beijing to sign a revised set of treaties that reflected additional terms, including the cession of Kowloon, the territory on the mainland opposite from Hong Kong island, and indemnities of 8 million *taels* each to be paid to Britain and to France. The Western powers had now extracted everything that they had first sought from the now prostrate Qing.

THE TREATY SYSTEM

Beginning in 1860 a new order of Sino-Western relations replaced the old Canton system with profound implications for the survival of Imperial China. It would be fair to say that the final countdown to the end, while it was a protracted process, began at this time. Shanghai, one of the first five ports opened, formerly a regional market center near the mouth of the Yangzi River, by virtue of its location at the intersection of the coastal and inland axes of commerce, soon became the queen of the treaty ports and a great Westernized city. More than any other port, Shanghai became the entry point for Western commercial and cultural influences, quickly displacing Canton. The walled International Settlement and the adjacent French Settlement along the Wusong River leading into the Yangzi were established as exclusive enclaves and symbols of foreign power. A sign, perhaps an apocryphal relic of the early twentieth century revolutionary movement, on the gate of the public park in the International Settlement, read "No dogs or Chinese allowed." With the opening of the interior to foreigners, Christian missionary imperialism, a corollary of economic imperialism, penetrated remote towns and villages under the protection of the treaties, eroding social and cultural cohesion of rural society. When the Taiping rebels approached Shanghai and occupied the Chinese city in 1854, causing a breakdown of Chinese customs collection, the task of collecting the revenue was assumed by a new agency, the Chinese Imperial Maritime Customs, under foreign leadership and jointly staffed by foreigners and Chinese. Under the direction of Sir Robert Hart until the end of the nineteenth century, the agency expanded its reach to embrace construction of navigation aids, a postal service, and steamship construction.

The treaty system brought to China a new and unfamiliar order with a transformative power that could not be opposed or deflected. In the past, barbarian conquerors (such as the Mongols and Manchus) invaded in such large numbers, ruling large segments of the Chinese population that they were ineluctably sinified and assimilated. Such was the case with the Khitan Liao dynasty from the tenth century, the Jurchen Jin dynasty from the twelfth, and even the Mongol Yuan conquest of the Song in 1279, though the Mongols tried more than their predecessors to retain their separate identity. The Manchus settled a substantial portion of their population below the Great Wall and while they also took measures to guard against loss of ethnic identity and frontier martial virtues, emperors from Kangxi to Qianlong despaired over the seduction of Manchu clansmen by Han culture. Even military superiority ultimately counted for little. But the new European barbarians were only the remote appendages of political, military, and cultural power still anchored in their own capitals thousands of miles away. Protected in their walled enclaves, they were immune from assimilation. As Qiying learned in negotiating the Treaty of Nanjing in 1842, the Westerners could not be handled with the old methods of barbarian management. From the late nineteenth into the twentieth century the treaty ports became the principal catalyst in the transformation of China, areas beyond Chinese control where a new Chinese middle class, evolved from the compradors of the Canton system and disconnected from the classical Confucian tradition, emerged. Iconoclasm and nationalism fed by the Western stimulus attacked the old traditions as inadequate and, much worse, irrelevant in the new world order where Chinese and Western claims to universality now competed.

As the Western expeditionary force approached Beijing in 1860, the Xianfeng emperor abandoned the city with his entire Court and fled to the Manchu summer palace at Rehe across the Great Wall, leaving behind his brother Prince Gong to negotiate with the foreigners. In the summer of 1861 the emperor, both physically and mentally weak, died. A group of conservative Manchu imperial clansmen attempted to assert themselves as regents for the new child emperor, though they lacked the formal authority to do so. Later in that year the relatively moderate Prince Gong, representing the appeasement party of high officials advocating accommodation with the foreigners, along with the two young Empress Dowagers Cian (widowed empress of the Xianfeng emperor) and Cixi (his principal concubine and mother of the new emperor), staged a coup d'état, arresting the would-be conservative regents. The two dowager empresses now sat as legitimate regents for the newly enthroned Tongzhi ("Shared Governance") emperor (1862–1875), ruling "from behind the screen," powerful but unseen behind the throne. Thus began the Tongzhi Restoration, an era that brought a promise of reform of aging institutions.

SUGGESTED READINGS

Bridgeman, Elijah Coleman, and S. Wells Williams, eds. *The Chinese Repository* (A periodical published by the American Board of Commissioners for Foreign

Missions), 20 vols. (Canton: 1832–1851, reprint). This periodical published for twenty years at Canton is a rich source for a great variety of primary materials covering the years before and after the Opium War. Especially useful for the growth of the opium trade and the controversy surrounding it from both the Western and Chinese perspectives.

Chang Hsin-pao. *Commissioner Lin and the Opium War* (Cambridge: Harvard University Press, 1964). A good account of Lin Zexu's efforts to suppress the opium trade.

Collis, Maurice. *Foreign Mud: The Opium Imbroglio at Canton in the 1830s and the Anglo-Chinese War* (New York: W.W. Norton, 1946). A popular but balanced history of the opium crisis at Canton and the Opium War.

Downs, Jacques M. *The Golden Ghetto: The American Commercial Community at Canton and the Shaping of American China Policy, 1784–1844* (Bethlehem & London: Lehigh University Press, 1997). A detailed account of the American merchant community at Canton and its influence on American China policy.

Fairbank, John K., ed. *The Cambridge History of China*, vol. 10, *Late Ch'ing, 1800–1911, Part 1* (Cambridge: Cambridge University Press, 1978). This standard reference for late Qing history contains an incisive chapter on the Opium War.

Fairbank, John King. *Trade and Diplomacy on the China Coast: The Opening of the Treaty Ports 1842–1854* (Stanford: Stanford University Press, 1969). An authoritative study of the negotiation of the treaty ports between the settlement of the first Opium War and the renewal of war in the 1850s.

Greenberg, Michael. *British Trade and the Opening of China, 1800–1842* (Cambridge: Cambridge University Press, 1951). A study of the British trade at Canton leading up the the Opium War.

Gulick, Edward V. *Peter Parker and the Opening of China* (Cambridge: Harvard University Press, 1973). A biography of a medical missionary who played a significant role in diplomatic activities in China through the mid-nineteenth century.

Hibbert, Christopher. *The Dragon Wakes: China and the West, 1793–1911* (London: Penguin Books, 1984). A comprehensive history of the Western impact on China from the Macartney Embassy to the Nationalist Revolution.

Hunter, William C. *The "Fan Kwei" at Canton before Treaty Days, 1825–1844* (Taipei: Ch'eng-wen Publishing (reprint), 1965). The activities of Westerners in the Canton China trade through the Opium War.

MacNair, Harley Farnsworth, ed. *Modern Chinese History, Selected Readings: A collection of extracts from various sources chosen to illustrate some of the chief phases of China's international relations during the past hundred years* (New York: Paragon Book Reprint, 1967). An excellent collection of translations of extracts of documents relating to the nineteenth century.

Morse, Hosea Ballou. *The International Relations of the Chinese Empire*, 2 vols. (London: Longmans, Green, 1910 and 1918). An early standard reference for Sino-Western relations to the end of the Qing period.

Polachek, James B. *The Inner Opium War* (Cambridge: Harvard University Press, 1992). Early chapters discuss the role and activities of the literati in the nineteenth century.

Pritchard, Earl H. *The Crucial Years of Early Anglo-Chinese Relations, 1750–1800* (Pullman: Washington State College, 1936). An early but still valuable study of the formative years of Anglo-Chinese relations.

Spence, Jonathan D. "Opium Smoking in Ch'ing China," in Frederic Wakeman, Jr., and Carolyn Grant, eds., *Conflict and Control in Late Imperil China* (Berkeley: University of California Press, 1975), 143–173. An interesting study of opium consumption and addiction in China.

Teng Ssu-yu, John K. Fairbank, et al. *China's Response to the West: A Documentary Survey 1830–1923* (New York: Atheneum, 1970). An annotated collection of documents relating to Sino-Western relations from the Opium War to the early twentieth century.

Van Dyke, Paul A. *Merchants of Canton and Macao: Politics and Strategies in Eighteenth-Century Chinese Trade* (Hong Kong: Hong Kong University Press, 2011). An encyclopedic study of the activities of Chinese merchants in Western trade, with reproductions of original documents and including individual biographical chapters on nine merchants.

Wakeman, Frederic, Jr. *The Fall of Imperial China* (New York: The Free Press, 1975). A standard textbook on the late imperial period from the end of the Ming to the end of the Qing.

Wakeman, Frederic, Jr. *Strangers at the Gate: Social Disorder in South China, 1839–1861* (Berkeley: University of California Press, 1966). A study of the impact of the Opium War on social stability in the South China Canton hinterland.

Williams, S. Wells. *The Middle Kingdom: A survey of the geography, government, literature, social life, arts, and history of the Chinese empire and its inhabitants*, rev. ed., 2 vols. (New York: C. Scribner's Sons, 1883). One of the first comprehensive Western accounts of China in the nineteenth century betrays the prevalent Christian missionary attitude of the time.

NOTES

1. H. B. Morse, *The International Relations of the Chinese Empire, v. 1, 1834–1860* (1910), 126. In a note Morse explains the use of the Chinese words *lao*, or *lei*, and *bi*, meaning "Laboriously Vile," for Napier preceded by the word *lu* for "Lord."

2. Quoted in Maurice Collis, *Foreign Mud: The Opium Imbroglio at Canton in the 1830s and the Anglo-Chinese War* (New York: W. W. Norton, 1946), 144.

3. Arthur Waley, *The Opium War Through Chinese Eyes* (London: George Allen & Unwin Ltd., 1958), 222.

4. Waley, *The Opium War*, 157.

19

The Heavenly Kingdom

One of the greatest wars in modern history of the last century and a half ravaged China in the mid-nineteenth century. It was an age of war, the first wars fought on a modern scale of organization and military technology, from the American Civil War, to colonial wars and internecine conflicts around the globe. But the war in China dwarfed them all in terms of size of the forces engaged, the technology of the weapons employed, and the number of lives lost and destruction wrought. A member of the party of Lord Elgin, the British plenipotentiary who negotiated the treaty ending the Second Opium War in 1858, described the scene at Zhenjiang on the Yangzi River downstream from Nanjing:

> Landed on the right bank, and walked to Chinkiang [Zhenjiang] over about two miles of plain, intersected by the remains of rough earthworks. This strip of level ground, which intervenes between a range of hills and the river, was until recently the abode of a thriving and industrious population. Scarce a year has elapsed since it was the scene of violence and bloodshed, the theatre of an action between the Rebel and Imperialist forces. The devastation is now widespread and complete. A few of the peasantry have crawled back to the desolate spots which they recognize as the sites of their former homes, and, selecting the heaps of rubbish which still belong to them, have commenced to construct out of them wretched abodes—roughly thatching in a gable-end that has escaped the general destruction, or replacing the stones which once composed the walls with strips of mattings. Miserable patches of garden were being brought into existence between the crumbling, weed-covered walls; but the destitute appearance of the scanty population served rather to increase than diminish the effect which this abomination of desolation was calculated to produce.
>
> We entered the city by the north gate, and might have imagined ourselves in Pompeii. We walked along deserted streets, between roofless houses, and walls overgrown with rank, tangled weeds; heaps of rubbish blocked up the thoroughfares, but they

obstructed nobody. There was something oppressive in the universal stillness; and
we almost felt refreshed by a foul odor which greeted our nostrils, and warned us that
we had approached an inhabited street.

At a spot where a few chow-chow shops, and two partially inhabited streets
crossed each other, was the most lively place in town. We obtained a small share of
interest here from a mob of hungry, ragged boys; but the people generally seemed
too much depressed even to stare at a barbarian, and we strolled unmolested in any
direction our fancy led us.

On our way to a fort which crowned a bluff overhanging the river, we passed
under some handsome stone arches, which were still standing conspicuous amid
the destruction, by which they were surrounded. From our elevated position we
commanded an extensive view over the area enclosed by the walls of the city, which
was thickly strewn with its ruins. . . . The population of Chinkiang was formerly
estimated at about 500,000, it does not now probably contain above 500 souls.[1]

With the alteration of only a few words this scene could as well be taken for a
description of Hiroshima in 1945.

By the nineteenth century the bonds that held China together, however tenuously at times, were beginning to loosen and unravel. It was not simply a matter of political decline caused by bureaucratic corruption and factionalism, as in the late Ming. It was not simply a matter of economic stress occasioned by natural and human disasters, such as floods, drought, and famine. It was not merely religiously inspired popular upheaval, as during the White Lotus Rebellion at the turn of the eighteenth century. It was not the challenge of barbarian invaders, which the Manchus presented in the seventeenth century. Nor was it the erosion of moral coherence and cultural confidence such as afflicted the late Ming and early Qing. It was all of these, and more.

Population growth is generally acknowledged to have played a leading role. Under the influence of peace and prosperity of the High Qing, population increased from approximately 150 million in the late seventeenth century to perhaps 450 million by the early nineteenth century. While increasing agricultural production based on an expansion of arable land at first kept pace with the demands of a growing population, demographic changes had manifold consequences. The number of local officials did not increase to keep pace with the increased population, so that the ratio of officials to population declined and the ability of officials to administer local issues suffered. By mid-century floods and attendant famine increased pressure on regions of central and south China. The lower course of the Yellow River began to shift to the north of the Shandong peninsula in 1851, devastating vast areas of populated farmland. Such natural disasters set local populations in motion seeking relief in new regions where they disrupted settled communities and provoked social tension. Progressive decline in bureaucratic morale and competence, and prevalent corruption became endemic since the vast scandal of Heshen's abuse of power at the end of the Qianlong reign.

From early in the century both the legitimate tea trade and illicit opium smuggling had become entrenched in commercial networks extending throughout south and central China. Confiscation of opium and disruption of trade during the Opium War caused extensive economic hardship among the sizeable population that had come to profit from the trade. Whether legal, or later legalized, opium had become a huge problem in the social milieu of south China. Successive defeats of Qing forces by the British in the Opium War, however much the court sought to minimize its failures, created a popular perception of weakness and loss of legitimacy of the Manchus. In spite of the dynasty's success in claiming the Mandate in the early years, the Qing as an alien conquest dynasty was now coming back to haunt it in its declining years. More serious was the existential challenge of Protestant Christianity that was more than simply an alien religion but projected a vision of Western wealth and power that asserted a new superiority. The sinocentric claim to the priority of Confucian civilization was no longer persuasive.

These influences were pervasive throughout the country but were concentrated in the south. The Canton region and its hinterland were earliest and longest affected by the fluid conditions of the maritime world and foreign influences. As the British established their permanent base in Hong Kong, pirate bands, driven inland by the campaign against coastal piracy, fed endemic banditry, and ethnic hostility between indigenous local populations and ethnic immigrants fostered a climate of social conflict. In the interior districts of Guangdong and the hinterland province of Guangxi to the west a toxic mix of local ingredients was creating the conditions for the incubation of a dissident movement.

VISIONS OF A NEW ORDER

Hong Xiuquan (1814–1864) was peculiarly affected by the social instability of the Canton region. He belonged to a family of modestly well-off peasants from Hua county north of Canton, members of the Hakka community ubiquitous in the region. The Hakkas were settlers who had migrated into Guangdong and Guangxi from Fujian and other regions to the north over the previous several centuries. The name Hakka means "guest people" (*kejia*) in local dialect, as distinct from the indigenous Punti, "original population" (*bendi*). Though both groups were ethnic

Han Chinese, the Hakka had distinct customs and dialect; the women did not practice footbinding and wore distinctive dress. Thus while there was little to otherwise distinguish them as immigrants, they continued to suffer discrimination from the original settlers.

In spite of his later fame, Hong's early life is obscure. He was evidently a bright child who showed an interest in books, and read classics and history. Impressed by his intellectual ability and hoping as all families did that a successful son could raise the family's fortunes, his parents sent him off at age fourteen to Canton, thirty miles to the south of Hua, to sit for the civil service examinations in 1827. There was nothing remarkable in this about Hong. His ambition to enter the scholar-literati class was typical for aspiring scholars such as himself. He passed the qualifying examination in 1827, but failed the first, prefectural level examination for the *shengyuan* degree. Here again, most candidates failed this examination upon their first attempt since the quota was very restrictive. Returning home, Hong persisted in his studies. On one hand, from the evidence of his later writings, he clearly had assimilated Confucian ideology and classical history that were the prerequisites for success in the examinations. On the other hand, in light of his later experiences, Hong perhaps lacked the kind of single-minded focus that was such a stultifying feature of the civil service system. Failures were routine for all but the most brilliant scholar-literati. Most survived repeated disappointments.

Hong returned to Canton in 1836 for his second attempt. Again he failed. While in the city he heard a Chinese Christian convert preaching to the crowd and distributing Christian literature. It was then that he received a book, a collection of tracts, entitled "Good Words to Exhort the Age" by Liang Afa, an early Protestant convert and first Chinese Christian minister. During this time Hong was employed as a teacher in his home district, tutoring young pupils who were themselves in the early stages of examination preparation. The next year he returned to Canton and failed for the third time. This failure and his family's disappointment had a devastating effect on Hong's mental state. Returning home, so weak that he had to be carried in a sedan-chair, he suffered a severe nervous breakdown, which kept him bedridden for forty days. During his illness he experienced graphic trance-like dreams, which he related to his family and friends following his gradual recovery. In his dream he recalled that he ascended to Heaven where he was greeted by a woman who informed him that she was his mother. All of his internal organs were removed and replaced by pure ones. He was then presented to his father, the Heavenly Father, a tall man in black robes and wearing a long golden beard, and the Heavenly Father's first son, Hong's older brother. The Heavenly Father lamented that the demons had overcome the world with depravity and vice, and he commissioned Hong as Heavenly King to return to earth to exterminate the demons. Unfortunately for the Manchus, they were identified as the demons.

Following his emergence from his dream, Hong was transformed, now referring to himself as a sovereign ruler. Yet his visions remained inexplicable. But he gradually calmed down and resumed his study for the examinations, which he attempted one more time in 1843. He failed for the fourth time, but this time he was angry at the government and the Manchus whom he blamed for his failures. He continued to teach in local schools. It was not until a little while later that a friend, visiting him, noticed the book "Good Words to Exhort the Age," which Hong had never read after receiving it in Canton seven years earlier. His friend borrowed it, and returned excited to urge Hong to read it. For Hong the book was a revelation of the meaning of his dream. Now he knew that the Heavenly Father was the Christian God, his older brother was Jesus, and his mission on earth was to carry out the command of God, to destroy the demons corrupting the world.

Hong was already deeply imbued with Confucian teachings and ethics through his own extensive study for the examinations and his teaching in village schools. The new doctrines of Protestantism did not so much replace Confucianism in his mind as become assimilated with it. Confucian utopianism of the *Datong*, the Great Unity, fit well with his newfound Christian eschatology. Hong now gave up once and for all his pursuit of the examinations and began preaching in Guangdong and among Hakka communities in Guangxi, first converting his own family members. He must have been a very persuasive, perhaps charismatic, figure. One of his first converts was his cousin Feng Yunshan and another was his younger cousin Hong Rengan. They baptized each other in their new faith as the pamphlets had taught them. Feng Yunshan in particular was the mastermind of a new organization that took shape amid the tense social milieu of ethnic conflict and militarization of local communities defending against bandit groups in Hakka communities in Guangxi. Feng organized the Society for the Worship of God (the "God Worshippers") that incorporated the growing numbers of converts to their cause. At first the God Worshippers were merely one of the many such local self-defense militias.

Hong Xiuquan and Hong Rengan in the meantime returned to Canton where they met the American Southern Baptist missionary, Issachar J. Roberts. The two received instruction from Roberts during part of 1847. When the missionary had reservations regarding the sincerity of Hong Xiuquan's Christianity and did not baptize him, Hong returned to Guangxi. There he found the God Worshippers had greatly expanded under Feng Yunshan's influence, attracting a diverse following of peasants, rural workers such as charcoal burners, and unemployed miners. Talented new leaders had also joined, including Yang Xiuqing, an illiterate charcoal burner, and Xiao

Chaogui, both Hakkas. The fervent iconoclasm of Hong and Feng—they smashed the idols in local schools and Confucian temples—had already evoked the anger of the social elite. The growing militancy of the movement led to the first direct clash with local authorities in late 1850. Feng Yunshan had already created a rudimentary military organization. In the first engagement with regular government troops in January 1851 at Jintian, Guangxi, the God Worshippers were victorious and were now regarded by the authorities as rebels. In a ceremonial gathering shortly afterward, Hong declared the Heavenly Kingdom of Great Peace (Taiping Tianguo) with himself as Heavenly King (Tian Wang).

At this point the fledgling movement was still groping, unclear as to its ultimate destination while its organizational structure was constantly evolving. As Jintian was untenable, the army moved north to Yongan, the first walled city they occupied, in late 1851. There, under pressure of a gathering siege by government forces, their organization took definitive shape. All those who joined the movement were required to surrender their property and wealth to the communal Sacred Treasury, from which all would be supported. Segregation of the sexes was decreed, prohibition against cohabitation strictly enforced. Women were enrolled in separate military units. Only when the Earthly Paradise had finally been achieved would the prohibitions be lifted. No doubt one factor in Taiping mobility was that Hakka women did not practice footbinding, allowing them to follow the army on the march. The army acquired precise organizational structure based on classic military models from the ancient *Rites of Zhou* (*Zhou Li*). Soldiers were indoctrinated in Taiping Christian doctrine and all followers were required to attend daily religious assemblies, with prayers and sermons. Strict moral discipline was enforced. At Yongan, Yang Xiuqing was appointed supreme commander and named Eastern King, while Xiao Chaogui was named Western King, thus creating a collective leadership.

However radical the ideology and organization of the initial Taiping insurrection, it was still at heart a religious movement. It was not a highly articulated enterprise with a well-conceived theoretical rationale, like the Bolshevik movement grounded in "scientific Marxism." It was ad hoc and evolutionary, subject to the changing views of its leaders. Moreover, unlike the rigorous discipline of Communism, the constant need to recruit new soldiers, or even to coerce new followers who lacked the commitment of the original Guangdong-Guangxi warriors, led to a change in the complexion of the Taiping as it gathered force.

Under pressure of the siege of Yongan, the Taiping broke out and resumed their march. They still did not know their destination, but merely responded to conditions that presented themselves. The army marched north down the watershed of the Xiang River through Hunan, followed by the ineffectual Qing armies at their heels. They besieged the Hunan capital Changsha but failed to take it, and moved on. This brought them to the mighty Yangzi River and a fateful choice. By now, with an army numbering tens of thousands, they had captured thousands of boats. They could have crossed the river while their momentum would have carried them north, unstoppable, across the North China plain to Beijing, where no doubt the dynasty would have fallen within months. A story, likely apocryphal, tells that the leaders asked the advice of an aged Yangzi boatman, who told them that the north was an inhospitable dry and barren place, but that down river were huge cities stockpiled with grain and treasure, all within their grasp. So they sailed down river, attacking city after city, until they reached the greatest of them all, the former Ming southern capital at Nanjing. This was the promised Heavenly Capital they had been seeking, which they stormed and captured in March 1853.

The Taiping now gradually changed, from movement to stasis. Their institutions adapted to holding cities and administering territory. But while they had laid plans on paper to distribute agricultural land, collect land taxes, and establish civil service examinations, they lacked stable territorial control to put them into effect. They relied on expropriation of wealth and confiscation for revenue. Rarely daring to stand up to the Taiping in a decisive frontal battle, the imperial armies that had dogged their heels all the way from Jintian now assembled their forces around Nanjing. Over the next two years they slowly tightened the noose. At the same time, changes were underway among the leadership. Hong as Heavenly King was increasingly isolated in his lavish palace in the manner of traditional Chinese emperors, with a huge harem and bedecked in costly robes. Already he had become progressively marginalized by the Western King Xiao Chaogui who, before his early death in 1852, claimed to be the oracle speaking for Jesus, Hong's elder brother, and by the Eastern King Yang Xiuqing who claimed to be the oracle speaking for the Heavenly Father himself, Hong's father. Yang adopted ever more grandiloquent titles with corresponding authority. In his quest for ever more power, Yang established himself as the highest ideological leader, a spiritual figure responsible for all success. Hong's cousin Feng Yunshan, the genius behind the initial God Worshippers organization, had been killed during the march through Hunan, a loss of a vital moderating influence. The collective leadership of the early movement was lost in the struggle for absolute power. Hong's authority itself was increasingly threatened. It was likely that Yang was plotting to usurp the Heavenly Throne.

In a bold foray from Nanjing in 1856, the Taiping hurled back and dispersed the besieging imperial forces under the command of Imperial Commissioner Xiang Rong. The sudden release of pressure of the lengthy siege unloosed the smoldering tensions within the Heavenly Capital.

Hong had become convinced that he must act before Yang's schemes had matured. He secretly recalled to the city generals who resented Yang's arrogance. In September the conspirators attacked and assassinated Yang and his faction. A bloodbath ensued that lasted for many days, with tens of thousands killed.

The removal of Yang Xiuqing's faction and his influence left the Taiping with no able leaders with the vision to carry on the movement. The Heavenly Court was now dominated by Hong's incompetent, self-serving relatives, and cohesion and purpose of the movement evaporated. The most able military leaders, Shi Dakai, one of the original adherents from the Guangxi days, and Li Xiucheng were involved in far-flung military campaigns away from the capital. Saving the day, Hong Rengan arrived at Nanjing in 1859. An early convert and younger cousin of Hong Xiuquan, he had followed a divergent path initially, having extensive contacts with Westerners in Hong Kong and Shanghai. When he arrived in Nanjing he was a breath of fresh air, greeted enthusiastically by Hong Xiuquan as one who could deliver the Taiping from its crisis, and was raised immediately to high rank and made virtual prime minister of the Taiping. In a sense if Hong Xiuquan was the prophet, then Hong Rengan was the teacher, with broad experience and understanding of the modern world. For a time he revitalized the movement with moderate reforms and an emphasis on more orthodox Christianity. But it was too late to turn the Taiping around, and his efforts were vitiated by now endemic factionalism and fragmentation of the movement. The dynasty was reassembling its forces to besiege Nanjing once more. At the same time, Li Xiucheng's threatening approach toward Shanghai in 1860 prompted several foreign missions of British, French, and Americans to the Heavenly Capital, to warn the Taiping against interference with Western commerce. Foreign neutrality was beginning to fray as Western intelligence of the Taiping revealed both its unorthodox religious ideology and its lack of understanding of the Western world. As Taiping leadership disintegrated, a vast number of new "kings" (*wang*) were created to reward loyal followers, diluting their authority and prestige. And as the coherence and organization of the Taiping armies weakened, they degenerated into disconnected plundering operations beyond the control of Nanjing.

ZENG GUOFAN

From the beginning Qing efforts to suppress the rebellion were beset by incompetence and fragmented leadership. Qing commanders, whether Manchu or Han, were reluctant to commit their forces for fear of the consequences of defeat to their own careers; engaged in dilatory tactics; and were inhibited by entrenched bureaucratic habits. Soldiers were generally poorly trained, poorly paid (if paid at all), and poorly equipped. Qing generals were constantly replaced and reappointed. Nanjing was twice invested in 1856 and 1860 and the besieging armies twice defeated by the Taiping. At almost any point a serious, determined, and organized resistance could have stopped the Taiping.

Although it did not as yet fully appreciate the true magnitude of the Taiping threat, the Court in 1852 ordered the appointment of respected local retired officials and gentry leaders to raise militia in their home provinces to pacify the areas the Taiping armies had traversed. Government-sanctioned militias (*tuanlian*, literally "drilling and grouping") were a traditional measure of local pacification used as recently as the late eighteenth century to counter the White Lotus rebellion. It was a measure often born out of desperation that the Court was very loathe to endorse for fear of empowering local Han leaders in ways that could later come to threaten central authority.

In 1853 Zeng Guofan, a high central government official, had returned home on leave to his native province of Hunan to mourn the death of his father, when he was appointed militia commissioner of Hunan. Only a year before, the Taiping armies had passed north through the province on their way to the Yangzi, leaving in their wake disorder from banditry and Taiping remnants. This breach of mourning ritual, taken so seriously by pious Confucians, was justified by the urgency of the national crisis. Zeng saw himself as a facilitator, not a military commander, and called on respected fellow provincial colleagues to raise local militia forces. The Court expected no more, but Zeng soon realized that the traditional militia model was inadequate to the task facing him, and he created a new model of a regional army which soon was known as the Xiang Army, borrowing the traditional name for Hunan. It was organized on entirely different principles from officially sanctioned government armies such as the Green Standard Army, a provincial constabulary under central government control whose officers were routinely appointed by Beijing. Instead, Zeng selected as his subordinate commanders trusted colleagues, who in turn selected their subordinates from among their friends, and so on down the line, so that at the bottom, each soldier enjoyed a personal relationship with his immediate superior officer. The units were well trained and regularly paid at a much higher rate than government troops. Recruits were drawn from solid peasant stock, not the unreliable urban riffraff, and discipline was strict. The worst punishment for infraction of discipline was for an officer to report the offense to the offender's parents. The army was indoctrinated in Confucian ethics, countering Taiping military indoctrination in Christian morality, and morale was high.

To support such an army Zeng had to rely on local sources of revenue since direct government appropriations were inadequate. He was forced to appeal constantly to provincial officials for grants-in-aid. Eventually a new form of revenue was devised, the *likin* (*lijin*, one-thousandth of a *tael*), assessed ad valorum on all goods in transit at repeated stations along major routes. The Xiang Army was hugely successful in pacifying Hunan. Its success and the urgent need to deal with the Taiping dictated that the Court approve its move out of Hunan, and Zeng began a laborious campaign of descending the Yangzi, attacking city after city held by the Taiping. To enable him to fight on the water, he created an auxiliary naval force, but the task was not easy and the Xiang Army suffered numerous setbacks. Branches of the army were formed to campaign under Zeng's protégés and his brothers. The expansion of his efforts made financial support ever more difficult, but the Court was reluctant to remove the fetters on Zeng's authority.

With the dispersal and failure of government armies besieging Nanjing in 1856 and again in 1860, plus the demonstrated effectiveness of Zeng's Xiang Army, the Court finally had no choice but to concede to Zeng overall command and authority over the anti-Taiping campaign. Once he was appointed imperial commissioner and governor-general of the central provinces of Jiangsu, Jiangxi, and Anhui in 1860, Zeng now directly commanded regional financial and military resources of the provinces. The fear remained that given such unprecedented powers Zeng would aspire to replace the dynasty himself. The concern was not unfounded, and rumors alleged that such a course was urged on him by some close associates.

Zeng's appointment in 1860 was the turning point in the Taiping war. Zeng was a virtual generalissimo directing a supra-provincial campaign by armies raised and led by his various lieutenants and protégés, supported by the extraordinary mobilization of revenues including the *likin* tax and customs revenues. His strategy was to move from the west down the Yangzi taking successive cities, while Li Hongzhang, his principal lieutenant, advanced from the east through Jiangsu toward Nanjing. Small private mercenary forces under the command of a succession of foreigners—the Americans Frederick Townsend Ward and Henry A. Burgevine, and the Englishman Charles George Gordon—leading the Ever Victorious Army, were hired by Chinese merchants to protect Shanghai. Employing modern training and discipline, these forces were modestly involved in the last stages of the offensive. Nanjing was invested by Zeng Guofan's younger brother Zeng Guoquan. The Heavenly Capital fell in July 1864. Hong Xiuquan was already dead, on June 1, 1864. The fall of the city was followed by a great massacre. Remnant Taiping forces fled south, including Hong's son the Junior King and Hong Rengan, to continue the movement, but both were soon captured and executed. The last Taiping forces were destroyed in Guangdong in early 1866, having come geographically almost full circle in the course of fifteen years.

REBELLION, REVOLUTION, OR CIVIL WAR?

The Heavenly Kingdom's challenge failed. It failed as much for defects in leadership as for losing the contest for allegiance of the scholar-literati elite, military incompetence, or lack of religious vision. Indeed, almost to the end the Taiping showed extraordinary resilience in military command, and religious conviction remained steadfast. Initial motivations of the Taiping movement sprang from a complex intersection of endogenous and exogenous influences on Hong Xiuquan and his immediate followers. On one hand were repeated failures to pass the civil service examination at the very first level, thwarting the traditional route to social and political advancement. In itself this was not remarkable since most candidates initially failed and some never succeeded. Hong Rengan was another notable example. The intensity of examination competition was an inherent aspect of traditional culture. Severe stress occasionally led to dissidence and antisocial behavior, but was usually channeled by the family system and the social order into nondestructive outcomes. A case in point is Kang Youwei (1858–1927), whose intense preparation for the examinations caused him also to experience visions of a utopian order. But Kang was a member of a distinguished gentry family and not an ethnic minority. Wang Tao (1828–1897) was another. He passed the prefectural examination with distinction in 1845 but failed the second-level provincial examination in 1846. His failure led him to attack the system including the eight-legged examination style. For several years he experienced constant dreams which ceased only in 1849 and which he recorded in a dream diary. In 1854 he was exposed to Christianity and was baptized.

On the other hand was exposure to Christian doctrine at Canton in the midst of the traumatic conflict of the Opium War and incipient challenge to Manchu legitimacy. If examination failure was a relatively routine experience for most aspiring candidates for civil service appointment, exposure to Christian evangelization coupled with foreign invasion by Westerners was a radicalizing experience. These influences as well as the ethnic tensions between Hakka and Punti, growing local lawlessness and banditry, and militarization of the social order converged in Hong Xiuquan's visions and his explanations for them.

In attempting to understand the Taiping Heavenly Kingdom an inevitable question arises: What sort of phenomenon was this? Was this the genesis of classic rebellion in the context of severe social, economic, and political dislocation? Was it a righteous millennial religious movement inspired by one man's oracular vision? Was it civil war between competing forces contending for political dominance? Or was it a true modern revolution that failed? To varying degrees all of these definitions have been advanced to explain the Taiping. The principal difficulty here is distinguishing between rebellion and revolution. Revolutions either succeed or they are labelled rebellions. Rebellions that succeed usually become revolutions.

Clearly for Imperial China the world had changed in the nineteenth century. As with the tea trade, the opium trade, and the treaty system, China was now acting within a global context as never before. The incubation of the Taiping movement was crucially conditioned by the international context. By contrast the Manchu revolution of the seventeenth century unfolded within the Inner Asian sino-barbarian dynamic that was centuries old and thoroughly indigenous. (At the very most the exogenous influence of the Jesuits provided artillery technology equally to both sides of the conflict.) Yet the Taiping leaders consistently failed to appreciate the extent to which they were acting within an international context. They had virtually no understanding of the Western world, including the ambivalent views of the Qing held by Western powers; the critical importance of opium in the structure of trade; the vital importance of commercial access to the Chinese market by the West; and the issue of Christian orthodoxy versus heterodoxy in Western minds. The Taiping, after all, whether they realized it or not, were playing a Western game in which they were insensitive to Western precedence in Christian history and doctrine. Again, unlike Marxism-Leninism, the archetype of modern political revolutionary ideology, which displayed a masterful understanding of history and the contemporary world order, and possessed a powerful and coherent theoretical and practical program for action and acted on it accordingly, the Taiping had no such systematic foundation aside from utopian visionary faith. Taiping truth was highly personal and naïve.

LEGACIES

The final destruction of the Taiping was a vindication of the support the Qing received from the scholar-official class who were overwhelmingly Han. For them, in this conflict, Manchu alien ethnicity was not an issue. But for many others the Taiping apocalypse was a manifestation of Heaven's wrath, the instrument of retribution for the moral failings of individual Chinese as well as the dynasty. The end of the cataclysm saw little self-righteous moralizing. Too many lives had been lost, too much material and intellectual culture had been destroyed, too much economic wealth had been wiped out.

The drama of Taiping dynastic politics was played out within the larger drama of the Qing's rise and fall, and followed much the same course. After settling down at Nanjing, the Taiping resembled more and more a traditional dynastic movement. Aside from bizarre elements of colorful Taiping costumes and extravagant titles, and the veneer of Biblical Christian doctrine infused with their leaders' personal claims to religious authority, the Taiping was not so different from other historical challenges to Chinese dynastic rule. In that sense the Taiping challenge to the Qing and the Manchus was increasingly blunted and became merely an ethnic attack on barbarian rulers.

The story of the Taiping is as much about its ultimate suppression and its physical impact as about its genesis and development as a popular movement. Aside from its memory in later revolutionary consciousness— Sun Yatsen, the "Father of the Chinese Revolution," grew up aspiring to be another Hong Xiuquan—it had little influence on Qing or post-Qing ideology and religious culture. Its impact was on institutional and social changes into the twentieth century and the material destruction wrought by the war. The turning point in the war, and more broadly for the late Qing as well, was the appointment in 1860 of Zeng Guofan as governor-general and imperial commissioner. Zeng straddled a critical juncture between traditional and modern China, both the best example of the old Confucian order then in decline and an unconscious harbinger of the new transformation then emerging. One may draw an instructive parallel between Zeng Guofan and Wu Sangui, the Ming general guarding the Great Wall against the Manchus when Beijing fell to the rebels of Li Zicheng in 1644. Wu and Zeng both threw in with the Manchus against domestic Han rebels for the sake of Confucian culture. But this was the last time this choice could be made. In 1860 Confucianism was still crucial and vital enough to make the Taiping challenge premature, but the choice even then was confusingly muddled by the new forces of the West outside the traditional frame of reference. Fifty years later the choice would no longer be for the Manchus.

Although Zeng never exploited his power to displace the Manchu Court and exalt his position (as the dynasty feared he would), the Court never could recover the power and authority it ceded. Zeng Guofan's protégés, and their protégés in turn, monopolized regional power through the last years of the Qing and into the post-revolutionary era, where they became the warlords of the early twentieth century. Within a half-century of 1860, the Manchus had become irrelevant.

SUGGESTED READINGS

Cohen, Paul A. *Between Tradition and Modernity: Wang T'ao and Reform in Late Ch'ing China* (Cambridge: Harvard University Press, 1974). An intellectual biography of a Chinese reformer who was a journalist and a Christian convert.

Fairbank, John K., ed. *The Cambridge History of China*, vol. 10, *Late Ch'ing, 1800–1911, Part 1* (Cambridge: Cambridge University Press, 1978). This standard reference for late Qing history contains an incisive chapter on the Opium War.

Gernet, Jacques. Janet Lloyd, trans., *China and the Christian Impact: A Conflict of Cultures* (Cambridge: Cambridge University Press, 1985). The study of Christianity in China since the Ming by a leading authority.

Hibbert, Christopher. *The Dragon Wakes: China and the West, 1793–1911* (London: Penguin Books, 1984). A comprehensive history of the Western impact on China from the Macartney Embassy to the Nationalist Revolution.

Jen Yu-wen. *The Taiping Revolutionary Movement* (New Haven: Yale University Press, 1973). A thorough, sympathetic history of the Taiping by a leading student of the movement.

MacNair, Harley Farnsworth, ed. *Modern Chinese History, Selected Readings: A collection of extracts from various sources chosen to illustrate some of the chief phases of China's international relations during the past hundred years* (New York: Paragon Book Reprint, 1967). An excellent collection of translations of extracts of documents relating to the nineteenth century.

Meyer-Fong, Tobie. *What Remains: Coming to Terms with Civil War in Nineteenth-Century China* (Stanford: Stanford University Press, 2013). This study focuses on the human and material ravages of the Taiping war and the attempts to come to terms with the destruction and losses in subsequent decades.

Porter, Jonathan. *Tseng Kuo-fan's Private Bureaucracy* (Berkeley: University of California, Center for Chinese Studies, China Research Monographs no. 9, 1972). A study of the *mufu* system as greatly expanded by Zeng Guofan in the service of defeating the Taiping Rebellion.

Spector, Stanley. *Li Hung-chang and the Huai Army: A Study in Nineteenth-Century Chinese Regionalism* (Seattle: University of Washington Press, 1964). Leader of an offshoot of Zeng Guofan's Xiang army, Li Hongzhang became the most powerful Chinese official of the post-Taiping era.

Spence, Jonathan D. *God's Chinese Son: The Taiping Heavenly Kingdom of Hong Xiuquan* (New York: W. W. Norton, 1996). A brilliant sympathetic biography of the leader of the Taiping Rebellion; perhaps the best account of the movement.

Teng Ssu-yu, John K. Fairbank, et al. *China's Response to the West: A Documentary Survey 1830–1923* (New York: Atheneum, 1970). An annotated collection of documents relating to Sino-Western relations from the Opium War to the early twentieth century.

Wakeman, Frederic, Jr. *The Fall of Imperial China* (New York: The Free Press, 1975). A standard textbook on the late imperial period from the end of the Ming to the end of the Qing.

Wakeman, Frederic, Jr. "The Secret Societies of Kwangtung, 1800–1856," in Jean Chesneaux, ed., *Popular Movements and Secret Societies in China, 1840–1950* (Stanford: Stanford University Press, 1972), 29–47. The growth of secret societies in South China in the early nineteenth century contributed to the general social unrest through this period.

Wakeman, Frederic, Jr. *Strangers at the Gate: Social Disorder in South China, 1839–1861* (Berkeley: University of California Press, 1966). A study of the impact of the Opium War on social stability in the South China Canton hinterland.

NOTE

1. MacNair, Harley Farnsworth, ed., *Modern Chinese History, Selected Readings* (New York: Paragon Reprint, 1967), 373–374.

VI

CONTINUITY IN CHANGE, 1870–1900

20

Self-Strengthening and
Its Fate

History is change. Perception of change comes from a sense of the flow of time. The Chinese knew this as well as anyone. Their consciousness of change was expressed by a work of great antiquity, generally acknowledged to be the first of the revered Classics, the Yi Jing *(The Classic of Change). The Classic envisions a process of contingent change, continuous mutation of components,* yin *and* yang, *within a closed harmonious cosmic order. Time in this conception is not a teleological process, progressing from an original state to a conclusion. The universe is uncreated and unending. Yet the Chinese were aware of great singular changes in their history that were irreversible. According to the* Dao De Jing, *the premier Daoist canon, in early antiquity following the age of the legendary sage kings (second millennium BCE), the Great Way, the perfect moral order, was abandoned and artificial social distinctions arose. In the third century BCE the rise and conquest of China by the authoritarian Qin state forever extinguished the feudal order during which the virtuous sage philosophers, including Confucius and Mencius, had established the foundations of humanity and righteousness. And in the 1850s Zeng Guofan, in his proclamation calling his fellow scholar-officials to arms against the Taiping Heavenly Kingdom, warned of the greatest threat to the traditional moral learning in the two millennia since those hallowed times.*

Though few Chinese statesmen and scholars appreciated it at the time, the Opium War presented the Middle Kingdom with an inescapable ultimatum: Adapt to the new challenge from the West and survive, or succumb and die. The challenge was soon greatly magnified by the internal threat of the Taiping Rebellion. To adapt, it gradually became clear, meant to change. But how to change? As they had done so often in the past, Confucian scholars seeking rationale for change had recourse to the Yi Jing. *The first hexagram of the* Yi Jing *is* Qian, *comprising six unbroken* yang *lines. It represents Heaven (*Tian*). The corresponding Image (*xiang*) of* Qian *reads: "Because Heaven's actions are vigorous and persevering, the superior man (*junzi*) engages ceaselessly to strengthen himself (*ziqiang*)."*[1]

THE SELF-STRENGTHENING MOVEMENT

The inspiration for the Self-Strengthening Movement from the 1840s arose from this notion that China's defense in the face of war and rebellion must come from within, as the superior man strengthens himself under the imperative of Heaven's robust action. The costs of war and rebellion dictated that the Qing dynasty undertake vigorous measures to ensure its survival. Moreover, the very survival of China itself was now at stake. But the problem was that neither the authority of the *Yi Jing* nor the teachings of history sanctioned the sort of radical change that now was called for.

Self-strengthening efforts evolved in a succession of stages over a period of almost half a century. In 1840 Imperial Commissioner Lin Zexu, impressed by the power of British warships in the initial battles of the Opium War, advocated adoption of Western naval technology. The paddle-wheel steamer *Nemesis* had run circles around cumbersome Chinese war junks. Some Chinese at first believed the paddle-wheels were powered by men inside the ship, but soon came to appreciate the power of steam. Commissioner Lin was the first self-strengthener. But the appreciation of Western military technology was limited to a very few officials on the scene who were isolated in the vast conservative bureaucracy. Lin's proposals fell on deaf ears. The Court simply did not believe that an emergency existed that could not be handled in the traditional way of reemphasizing the moral values of humanity (*ren*) and righteousness (*yi*).

Two decades passed before serious self-strengthening efforts were inaugurated. In 1860, after the Chinese made a futile last-ditch stand against the Western powers, Britain and France occupied the imperial capital to enforce the acceptance of the second round of treaties ending the Second Opium War. The emperor fled with the Court to the Manchu summer palace across the Great Wall. The Taiping were just then at the zenith of their power as their military campaigns struck out east to Shanghai and north toward Beijing. Senior Court officials and regional leaders now acknowledged that a turning point had been reached, that China confronted grave and unprecedented threats.

Self-strengthening enterprises, including arsenals, shipyards, and technical schools, were now established in the principal treaty ports where access to Western technology was most direct. Funds to support these projects were diverted from the *likin* tax on goods in transit and from customs revenue. Even the imperialist powers, fearful that their hard-won commercial privileges would be jeopardized if the dynasty collapsed, offered their support. Still, few scholar-officials were persuaded of the necessity of the adoption of Western technology; commitment to traditional learning as a priority remained as strong as ever.

In spite of persistent opposition, the next decade was the heyday of the Self-Strengthening Movement. Arsenals employing Western advisers and technicians were opened at Shanghai, Tianjin, and Nanjing: shipyards were established at Fuzhou and Shanghai; training schools teaching Western language, technology, and science were opened at Beijing, Shanghai, and Fuzhou; and educational missions of Chinese students were sent to the United States and France. These projects reached maturity in the 1870s and demonstrated commendable successes. But thereafter they experienced significant decline. The flux of change described by the *Yi Jing* would have predicted as much. By 1895, two decades later, self-strengthening reform was a failure and China was once again prostrate before the power of Western weapons.

THE SEDUCTIVENESS OF TECHNOLOGY

The first lesson drawn from the initial confrontation with the British at Canton was that the source of their superior strength was their military technology. Institutional strength, the training of their soldiers, the command of their armies was never considered. This was true as well with the Mongol invaders and their predecessors in the thirteenth century. The Chinese were never ready to accept that the other's culture could be a basis of their superiority. There was a comforting seductiveness in this conclusion. If only the Chinese could acquire the same guns as the West had, they would possess the same power to defend themselves. It was like the role of the Colt revolver in the old American West. It was the great equalizer; the gun made he who held it the equal of anyone. Thus guns and ships were the immediate priority. Military technology was sufficient to defend China against foreign invasion and to defeat domestic rebellion. The issue was not perceived as a more fundamental one of culture and institutions.

The first self-strengthening efforts were small, ad hoc affairs established by Zeng Guofan and his protégés in the early campaigns against the Taiping: The Hunan Gun Bureau set up in 1853, three small arsenals and a shipyard in Jiangxi in 1855–1856, and the Powder Bureau established in Wuchang by Hu Linyi. When Zeng recaptured the city of Anqing, upriver from Nanjing, he founded the first substantial production facility, the Anqing Arsenal in 1861. Anqing attracted some prominent mathematical scientists, including Li Shanlan. Now with Zeng Guofan's acquisition of plenipotentiary powers over the financial and military resources of the lower Yangzi provinces of Jiangnan, self-strengthening expanded and began to flourish. The Jiangnan Arsenal established by Li Hongzhang at Shanghai in 1865 absorbed the work of the Anqing Arsenal, producing ships as well as guns. Li had then taken over from Zeng Guofan the campaign to suppress the Nian Rebellion in north China. Requiring a source of munitions to supply his army closer to its theater of operations in northern Anhui, he moved a smaller arsenal from Suzhou and established the Nanjing Arsenal in 1867. Before the Nanjing Arsenal was fully operational, the Zongli yamen, the ad hoc committee of high officials under the leadership of Prince Gong, which was responsible for foreign affairs of Western nations and foreign-related projects, ordered Li to send machinery and personnel from Jiangnan to establish an arsenal at Tianjin, near Beijing. The Tianjin Arsenal began production in 1868 to supply armaments to the northern armies.

About the same time Zuo Zongtang, governor-general of the eastern coastal provinces of Zhejiang and Fujian and a fellow Hunanese protégé of Zeng Guofan, promoted a project to establish a shipyard and arsenal at Fuzhou, the capital of Fujian province. The Fuzhou Shipyard opened in 1866 and began to build a variety of steam-powered ships, including both paddle-wheel and screw-driven ships, on a variety of hybrid wooden and ironclad hulls. In all of these enterprises foreign engineers and directors played a crucial role. An important issue from the beginning for all of these projects was the choice between importing armaments from the West versus manufacturing them in China by trained Chinese. In the image of self-strengthening from the *Yi Jing*, Zeng Guofan, Li Hongzhang, and Zuo Zongtang all strongly believed that China must learn the "secrets" of Western technological superiority for itself. Western technicians and engineers were essential to train Chinese in the engineering sciences and methods to manufacture armaments, but would eventually be released when Chinese had mastered the knowledge. Thus the educational function of the arsenals and shipyards was seen to be as important as their industrial output.

In 1862 the Tongwen guan (Interpreters College) was founded in Beijing by the Zongli yamen. In the beginning, manuals in English, French, and German necessary to operate industrial machinery had to be understood, so instruction began in languages. Li Hongzhang in 1863 established the

Guang fangyan guan (Foreign Language Institute) at Shanghai. One thing led to another. Mathematics and astronomy taught by foreign instructors were added to the curriculum of the Tongwen guan, and by the mid-1860s the curriculum had expanded to resemble a small liberal arts college with political economy and international law added. At the Fuzhou Shipyard, Zuo Zongtang, its benefactor, and its director Shen Baozhen regarded steamship production as a byproduct of its principal mission to teach Chinese the skills to build, organize, and operate a modern fleet.

The logical extension of such domestic programs was to send Chinese students abroad to study Western learning at its source. Rong Hong, a Westernized Chinese educated in Macau and Hong Kong, went on to the United States to become the first Chinese to graduate from a Western college (Yale) in 1853. Upon his return to China, Rong offered his services to Zeng Guofan. In 1864 Zeng commissioned Rong to buy machinery in the United States for use in the Jiangnan Arsenal—"Machines that make machines" as Rong put it. After his return, Rong proposed to Zeng an educational mission to the United States and in 1872 led the first group of twenty students, who enrolled in various schools in New England. A traditional Chinese scholar was appointed as co-director to continue the students' classical education in order to guard against their assimilation to Western culture. Over the next several years successive cohorts of students were sent to America, totaling more than a hundred. About the same time a second mission of students was sent to France from the Fuzhou Shipyard, whose foreign director was a Frenchman, Prosper Giquel.

YANGWU

All of the *ziqiang* (self-strengthening) projects in a broad sense belonged to the *Yangwu* (foreign affairs or Western matters) movement. *Yangwu* was a less pejorative term than *yiwu* (barbarian affairs), previously applied to matters relating to foreigners, to which Westerners objected. A well-defined but small cadre of *yangwu* experts had emerged since the 1840s. One of the most influential and prescient *yangwu* experts was Feng Guifen (1809–1874), who is often credited as the first to use the term *ziqiang*. Feng was a traditional scholar who earned his *jinshi* (presented scholar) degree in 1840 and subsequently served for many years in the central government and as an adviser to Zeng Guofan and Li Hongzhang. His interest ranged widely over modern scientific and technical subjects, which took shape in a series of influential essays that circulated among self-strengthening-minded officials. Wei Yuan (1794–1856) was a traditional scholar (*jinshi* 1844) who turned his attention to Western affairs while working for Lin Zexu. His most famous work was *Haiguo tuzhi* (Illustrated treatise on the maritime nations) published in 1844. A later adviser on the staffs of both Zeng Guofan and Li Hongzhang, where he gained experience in Western affairs, was Xue Fucheng (1838–1894), who served for several years in the 1890s in China's diplomatic service in London and Paris. These and other *yangwu* experts, such as Zhao Liewen, who served in Zeng Guofan's private secretariat (*mufu*), generally learned their specialty from experience on the job.[2] There was no systematic body of knowledge that provided a foundation for dealing with the West, nor any coordinated effort to train such experts.

Institutional adjustments accompanied the new appreciation by the Court of China's desperate situation following the catastrophic defeat of its forces and the occupation of the capital by the British and French, and the rise of the Taiping threat to the dynasty following their second breakout from Nanjing and expansion toward Shanghai and the north in 1860. Prince Gong and other high officials proposed the creation of an ad hoc organization, the *Zongli geguo shiwu yamen* (Office in general charge of the affairs of the various nations), "Zongli yamen" for short, in 1861. The charge of the Zongli yamen was essentially the management of the entire range of matters involving Western nations, including diplomatic relations, treaties, self-strengthening , and *yangwu* generally. The Zongli yamen acted as a subcommittee of the Grand Council and included most of its members. Prince Gong, brother of the Xianfeng emperor who died in 1861, and uncle and regent of the succeeding Tongzhi emperor, directed the Zongli yamen until his dismissal in 1884.

The second innovation was the creation of two imperial commissioners for trade for the northern and southern treaty ports, respectively. These high officials, including Zeng Guofan and Li Hongzhang at various times, directly oversaw most of the self-strengthening projects as well as the collection of the customs revenues from Western trade, under the direction of the Zongli yamen. A third innovation evolved from the collapse of customs collection at Shanghai during the 1853 uprising of the Small Sword Society. Because Chinese officials were prevented from collecting customs from foreign merchants during the crisis, Western diplomatic personnel stepped in to collect them on behalf of the Chinese government. From this arrangement evolved a permanent institution, the Imperial Maritime Customs under foreign direction, with Chinese and European staff. A Briton, Sir Robert Hart, served as its inspector general through most of its existence to 1911. The Imperial Maritime Customs administration directed revenues to self-strengthening enterprises, and proposed and sponsored new projects such as coastal navigation aids and postal service. These institutional innovations were not reforms in the true sense. Rather, they were ad hoc adjustments prompted by the new context of the Western presence on the China coast and the demands of the treaties. In the case of the Zongli yamen, it was explicitly stated in the memorial proposing its establishment that it would be abolished as soon as the problems that occasioned it ceased to exist, and management would revert to the old system.

OBSTACLES TO REFORM

The output of the self-strengthening enterprises was at first of poor quality. Ships were slow and extremely inefficient to operate. Artillery was poorly made and sometimes dangerously defective. But manufacturing competence and skills of Chinese workers improved steadily. Europeans later reported positively on the quality of ships built by the Fuzhou Shipyard and the high standard of workmanship. Yet as European military technology rapidly advanced in the nineteenth century, outpacing the fledgling Chinese efforts, the arsenals were in a constant race against obsolescence. The rate of rifle production at the Jiangnan Arsenal in 1875 was only twelve per day, made with iron barrels and not of uniform construction, so that parts were not interchangeable, below the common standard of the industrial revolution. The arsenal did not manufacture Remington-type repeating rifles until 1871, but these were inferior to the original purchased models. The problems went much deeper. However praiseworthy some of the modernization efforts were, they were isolated within the vast conservative traditional culture, which not only did not appreciate their importance, but also feared their corrupting impact on traditional cultural values. Powerful conservative officials at the Court, who had no direct contact with the Western threat or with the Taiping Rebellion and knew of these things only through reading reports in memorials to the throne, actively blocked modernization proposals. Woren (d. 1871), a learned and respected Mongol grand secretary, attacked the expanded curriculum of the Tongwen guan (Interpreters College), asserting in a memorial to the Tongzhi emperor:

> Astronomy and mathematics are of very little use. If these subjects are going to be taught by Westerners as regular studies, the damage will be great. . . Your slave has learned that the way to establish a nation is to lay emphasis on propriety and righteousness, not on power and plotting. The fundamental effort lies in the minds of the people, not in techniques.[3]

Even though Western armaments had demonstrated their clear advantage over rebel forces, both the Taiping and the Nian, the majority of Chinese still resisted their adoption for moral reasons.

Structural issues embedded in the social and cultural context of self-strengthening efforts undermined their effect. The China Merchants' Steam Navigation Company, founded by Li Hongzhang at Shanghai in 1873 to transport tribute grain from the Yangzi River region to Tianjin, was organized according to the *guandu shangban* ("official supervision and merchant management") formula. *Guandu* meant "official supervision" performed by regional officials. *Shangban* referred to "merchant management." Official supervision was afflicted by the persistence of traditional official *yamen* practices and attitudes, the tendency of officials to look on their role as a source of personal enrichment and career advancement, and "squeeze" at the expense of rational business practice. Merchant management was based on the comprador background of the managers who were hampered by inadequate sources of treaty port capital, familial loyalties, foreign competition, and adversity to risk-taking. The system suffered from the liabilities of both components.

In a more passive way, against the bureaucratic inertia of the vast traditional institutional structure of Imperial China, the voices of the *yangwu* experts and self-strengtheners were lost in the wilderness. As opponents were only too glad to point out, there was no place in the existing institutional order for the employment of the products of the new technical schools and foreign educational missions. As long as the centuries-old examination system continued to flourish as the route to a respected career, Western learning was a dead end. In the absence of radical political and cultural reform, traditional cultural and social values continued to exert a powerful attraction.

MODERNIZATION AND WESTERNIZATION

The entire complex of problems associated with the self-strengthening reform movement raises a perennial issue surrounding the debate regarding modernization and Westernization. Are the two identical? Could China have modernized without becoming Westernized, an anathema to so many scholar-officials? Or is one the precondition for the other? Modernization, after all, began with the Industrial Revolution in England in the eighteenth century and spread around the world from there. All other nations were always following the model of their predecessors. To become modern usually meant to become more like the first to experience the Industrial Revolution. Moreover, modernity meant fundamental social and cultural change in the modernizing society, changes in social structure, intellectual outlook, economic organization, and political values that originated in the West—in other words, Westernization. In nineteenth-century China even the most enthusiastic self-strengtheners rejected Westernization even while they supported Western learning. The concept of modernization in its general sense would have been alien to them.

Advocates of self-strengthening often spoke of discovering the secrets or mysteries of Western learning, particularly those aspects in which the West was clearly superior such as technology and science, as if they could be detached from the root of Western learning generally. They viewed Western technical knowledge as a set of arcane practices that had to be unlocked, perhaps something the foreigners were protecting for themselves. Once China unlocked these secrets and mastered their use it would be on a par with the West. This notion evoked an ancient dichotomy in Chinese traditional thought, *ti* (essence or fundamental structure) versus *yong* (practical application or technique). It was formulated in a popular slogan stated by Zhang Zhidong later in the century, *Zhongxue wei ti, Xi xue wei yong* (Chinese learning for fundamental values, Western learning for practical application). Western military technology as *yong* could be adopted as a shield to protect Chinese culture as *ti*. The strength of the West lay in its practical techniques, not in its cultural foundations, to which Chinese civilization was clearly superior. Advocates of self-strengthening believed that Western technology could (and must) be applied only within the context of Confucian tradition, particular Western ingenuity within a universal Confucian ethic. The problem with the *ti-yong* formulation was that Western *yong* was itself a product of Western civilization, and was thus organically linked to Western *ti*. The two could not so easily be pried apart. The Chinese failed to see the implications of their limited approach that the adoption of Western *yong* would inexorably undermine and erode Chinese *ti* because Western *ti* was inevitably admitted with it.

In the genesis of the Self-Strengthening Movement, China was challenged by surprisingly superior Western military power (and subsequently by the Taiping as well), and responded with efforts to rectify its weakness, just as Lin Zexu observed the devastating effects of British steamships and advocated a program to learn their secrets. Herein lies a logically persuasive thesis, the challenge-response model, to explain China's experience in the last century of the Qing to deal with the unprecedented arrival in force of the modern West. The challenge-response formula became a widely accepted paradigm among students of modern Chinese history over the last half-century to understand the anguish and trauma (as well as successes) of China's confrontation with the modern world. It has helped to illuminate the inherent weakness and shallowness of China's actions in the nineteenth century. If, for instance, one examines another time of traumatic confrontation, the Mongol invasion of the thirteenth century, we find there no calls for, and no need to adopt, Mongol military technology and culture. China had previously endured such challenges and this one too would pass. But the same could not now be said for the challenge of the modern West.

The trouble with the challenge-response model is that it is a Eurocentric view of history, born of the European mastery of the world in the nineteenth century. It is, first, unidirectional: It was not Europe being challenged by China and forced to respond, but the other way around. Second, China in this view is seen as an essentially passive, inert, and reactive entity only. In the Eurocentric view, China was retarded, Europe advanced. This nineteenth century view was succinctly described by William Gascoyne-Cecil in 1911:

> For centuries China has been the land that never moved. It had a political history full of wars and bloodshed, of intrigue and murder; periods of darkness and desolation; but the country remained essentially the same country. There might be some small alterations in its custom, but China was distinctly unprogressive.[4]

In human psychology, challenges are positive, fostering growth; responses to challenges are judged in the light of their effective outcome. But China, after all, was driven by its own internal logic, which until the arrival of the modern West had produced one of the most creative civilizations in human history.

THE CHANGING CONTEXT

The consequences of China's confrontation with foreign and domestic challengers since the first half of the nineteenth century involved pervasive unintended changes in institutional, political, economic, social, and geographical forms that did not arise from a considered response to challenges. First was the growth of regional power at the expense of central authority of the dynasty. While the Court was constantly mistrustful of its provincial officials, ever vigilant for any actions, by commission or omission, that might undermine dynastic legitimacy, it was perforce dependent on men on the spot. A fixed principle of central unified government was division of authority between competing officials and frequent punishment and replacement for lack of success. But as incompetent generals were successively defeated by foreign troops and Taiping armies, the Court was forced to accept the increasing role of quasi-private provincial armies. In 1860 the Court bowed to the inevitable and granted Zeng Guofan plenipotentiary powers over the Taiping suppression campaign. Again in 1864 in appointing Zeng to supreme power to suppress the Nian Rebellion in the north, the Court acknowledged its dependence on Han

Chinese to save the dynasty in 1868. In the following decades Zuo Zong-tang's campaigns against the Muslim rebels in Shaanxi-Gansu (1862–1873) and in Xinjiang (Chinese Turkestan) (1876–1877) preserved the Manchu Central Asian empire. The devolution of regional power to Zeng, Zuo, and Li Hongzhang, and their institutional heirs was irreversible.

Second was a concomitant shift of the political center of gravity to the provinces at the expense of central control. Revenues from commercial taxes such as *likin* and foreign customs funded programs that strength-ened provincial influence. Regional officials increasingly dictated official appointments, developing coteries of close associates and supporters. Third, the locus of political power shifted from Manchus to Han Chinese. Manchus had predominated in higher provincial posts since the begin-ning of the dynasty. The Qing had sought to balance the much larger numbers of Chinese officials against the minority of Manchus by favoring Manchu appointments disproportionately in the central government and higher provincial administration. By the nineteenth century the situation had reversed and Manchu influence waned. Governors-general, who were almost exclusively Manchu early in the dynasty, were greatly out-numbered by Han in the later years of the Qing.

Fourth was the progressive militarization of the social order. This was evident at first in the appearance of local village armed militia in the inland regions of south China in response to the disintegration of social order in the Opium War years, as villages sought to protect themselves against marauding bandits and pirates driven inland by the British. The Taiping transition from a local religious sect to an armed movement was fostered in this environment. Larger provincial militias organized to com-bat the Taiping continued the trend, and the supra-provincial regional armies of Zeng Guofan and his protégés were the climax of the process, the harbinger of the warlord era of the twentieth century.

Fifth, with the rise of the comprador-merchant class in the treaty ports and expansion of professional military careers associated with the new armies, career patterns were expanding and barriers between the scholar-literati and the rest of society were loosening. The erosion of the tradi-tional social-political elite by the late nineteenth century made pigeonhol-ing of social classes into scholars (*shi*) and merchants (*shang*) no longer possible. Although the civil service examinations retained their hold, new intellectual groups such as journalists and reformers were appearing. The social structure was becoming much more fluid.

Finally, sixth, a broad geographical divergence between two Chinas opened up, coastal China of the treaty ports, characterized by urban de-velopment, Western cultural influence, and commercial activity oriented outwards, and inland China of the interior provinces, characterized by traditional rural economy and culture, and persistence of old social norms. Traveling from a modern treaty port to its rural hinterland only a few miles inland involved crossing a distinct cultural divide. The dichotomy between littoral and hinterland has endured even to the present, affecting the implementation of modernizing programs.

These changes marked the irreversible decline not just of the Qing dynasty but of the entire imperial order itself. The system that was built by the Hongwu emperor of the Ming, inherited from the Ming by the Qing, and reconstructed by Hong Taiji, Dorgon, and the Kangxi and Qianlong emperors was now coming permanently unraveled, not to be revived again.

THE FAILURE OF SELF-STRENGTHENING

In late 1874 the Zongli yamen called for an extensive national policy debate among high officials regarding the priority to be given to maritime versus frontier defense. The call for debate was prompted on one hand by the poor record of the Jiangnan Arsenal's production of steamships over the previous decade, and on the other hand by the impending campaign led by Zuo Zongtang to restore Qing control over the inner Asian frontier. The domestic construction of steam-powered warships had proven extraordinarily costly compared to foreign purchase, with indifferent results. The Central Asia campaign over the next several years was expected to be even more expensive. During the course of the military campaign and reconstruction in its aftermath from 1876 to 1881, 51 million *taels* (a measure of one ounce of silver) were expended, a cost the government could barely sustain. In 1875 the Court decided in favor of frontier defense, thus reaffirming the great eighteenth-century conquests of the Qianlong emperor in Xinjiang. Perhaps almost predictably the dynasty thus chose to reassert China's traditional inner Asian orientation, as the Yongle emperor had done in the early Ming, at the expense of maritime defense of the east China coast whence the real threat was soon to come. Ironically, the decision doomed the Self-Strengthening Movement. And in fact, as soon as the fateful decision was made, a series of assaults on China's integrity came from the sea, not the land.

The pathetic tale of the demise of the Self-Strengthening Movement over the next two decades reveals the predicament that Imperial China now found itself in. The movement was not just the idiosyncratic obsession of a few visionary statesmen and scholars—Lin Zexu, Zeng Guofan, Li Hongzhang, Zuo Zongtang, Wang Tao, Feng Guifan, Xue Fucheng, Ding Richang, Shen Baozhen, Wei Yuan, and Guo Songdao. It could have been the salvation of China as an autonomous nation, if not of Imperial China specifically. Harbingers of the fate of self-strengthening came in a succession of military defeats, the very thing the movement had been intended to forestall. In 1871 some fishermen from the Ryukyu (Liuqiu) Islands were killed on Taiwan (Formosa) by aborigines there. The ambiguous status of the islands as tributary of both China and Japan led to a dispute between the two nations over competing claims to sovereignty. In 1874 Japan sent a naval expedition to Taiwan to exact reparations over what it considered an offense to its sovereign claim to the Ryukyus. Governor-general Shen Baozhen dispatched a naval squadron from the Fuzhou naval base to Taiwan. But the ships were incapable of opposing even Japan's relatively inferior force, and China failed to engage the Japanese on land. By default China conceded sovereignty of the Ryukyus to Japan and paid an indemnity in compensation for the victims.

Since the 1860s the French had been expanding their control over the territory that was to become French Indo-China, embracing Cochin-China (South Vietnam), Annam (North Vietnam), Cambodia, and Laos. Annam was historically a close tributary state of China, and French expansion was resisted by Chinese irregular forces known as the Black Flag. War between France and China eventually broke out in 1884 after inconclusive negotiations. The French navy attacked Fuzhou and destroyed most of the fledgling Chinese navy as well as the Fuzhou Shipyard that the French themselves had helped to build. In the Treaty of Paris in 1885 ending the war, the Chinese acknowledged de facto French possession of Annam. The Qing had incurred enormous expenses and debts in prosecuting the war.

Effective response to the French naval threat had been weakened by disjointed Chinese military organization. Division of command between commissioners for the southern and northern ports meant that no unified military command existed; the north could ignore the predicament of the south. To correct this weakness the Court created a Navy yamen, a kind of Chinese Admiralty, staffed by Manchu princes and Court officials based in Beijing, comparable to the Zongli yamen, intended to unify the navy command.

In a series of escalating moves Japan now began to challenge both China's hold on its tributary vassal Korea and Russia's expanding influence in the northeastern provinces of Manchuria. Imitating United States Commodore Matthew Perry's opening of Japan by threat of naval force in 1853, Japan opened Korea in the same manner in 1875. A treaty negotiated between the two nations recognized Korean independence. Not a party to the treaty, China, however, still regarded Korea as a tributary state, leaving its status unresolved. Increasing Japanese influence in Korea prompted a reactionary anti-foreign faction to attack the Japanese legation in Seoul in 1882. China and Japan both intervened in the Korean troubles in 1884 by sending military forces backing opposing factions,

Japan responding to the attack on its interests, China invoking the responsibility of its suzerain status over Korea in the tributary system. Impending war between the two states was forestalled by a negotiated settlement in 1885 between their respective principal statesmen, Li Hongzhang and Ito Hirobumi, which provided for the withdrawal of the forces of both sides, Korean freedom to organize itself independently, and a stipulation that advance notice be given by either side of intention to intervene in the future.

Domestic unrest continued to mount, breaking out in 1894 in a rebellion, the Tong Hak (Eastern Wisdom), against the Korean throne. Invoking its tributary right, Korea called for Chinese protection, and Chinese forces intervened without advance notification. When Japan then also intervened, negotiations for mutual withdrawal broke down and open war commenced. In naval engagements off Yalu in northern Korea and Shandong in the Yellow Sea, and land battles in Korea, Manchuria, and Taiwan, Chinese forces were crushingly defeated. In spite of all its efforts at self-strengthening over the previous decades, Chinese armaments proved to be no match for Japanese modern weapons, while the command structure of the Chinese army and navy was riddled with corruption and the persistence of traditional cultural and social values inconsistent with modern military discipline. The Treaty of Shimonoseki ending the war was negotiated under the good offices of the United States in 1895. China recognized the independence of Korea; ceded Taiwan, the Pescadore Islands, and the Liaodong peninsula in Manchuria to Japan; granted new trade privileges to Japan; and paid a crushing indemnity to Japan.

The Sino-Japanese War marked the total failure of self-strengthening. The outcome not only stunned the Chinese, who had continued to regard Japan as an inferior client state whose culture was derived from China's, but shocked Europeans as well, who had not appreciated the weakness of China's modernization nor fully grasped the success of Japan's. It was one thing for China to be defeated by Europeans bearing Western arms but quite another to be defeated by another Asian country that had only recently adopted them. The Western view of both nations was forever changed. The breakup of China into colonial fragments ruled by Western powers and Japan was now only a matter of time.

The deficiencies of the Chinese navy revealed in the Sino-French War were supposed to have been remedied by the creation of the Navy Board at Beijing. In 1860 the British and French expeditionary forces, as a punitive retaliation against the Court, had destroyed the old summer palace built by the Kangxi and Qianlong emperors. More than a humiliating military defeat, this act stood out as an intolerably shameful loss of dynastic prestige. The monarchy was determined to restore its self-esteem by building a new summer palace. In the greatest irony, the Empress

Dowager Cixi used the Navy Board to divert huge sums to the extravagant construction of the new summer palace to the west of the capital. At a time of drastically diminishing revenues and increasing expenditures, the project absorbed hundreds of millions of *taels*. In the shallow lake of the palace garden a marble pavilion in the form of an ornate barge was built, seemingly tethered to the shore, where Cixi could enjoy the summer breezes. On each side of the barge are large marble representations of paddle wheels, immobile symbols of modern technology standing in mute reproach to the misdirection of vital funds from the real navy crushed by the Japanese.

JAPAN AND CHINA: A COMPARISON

How was it that China's attempts to modernize were such a complete failure while Japan's were so brilliantly successful? A comparison of the experience of Japan since the Meiji Revolution overthrew the Tokugawa feudal regime in 1868 with the Tongzhi Restoration that followed China's defeat in the Second Opium War in 1862 tells the tale. The feudal system of Japan was by nature fluid, not static. Since the mid-eighteenth century the tight, centralized control maintained by the Tokugawa shogunate over the feudal order was breaking down. Many of the roughly 250 feudal fiefs (*han*), particularly in western Japan where Western influence was strongest, were becoming more autonomous and growing in strength. Economic development engendered new commercial classes as *han* towns became vibrant centers of economic activity. New cultural forms blossomed in the towns, responding to the new wealth of the townsmen. With the end of internecine feudal warfare following consolidation of Tokugawa rule in 1600, the ruling feudal warrior class, the *samurai*, gravitated to the affluent life of the towns and their rich pleasure quarters. The Tokugawa capital at Edo (later Tokyo) became a huge urban center where the *daimyo*, the feudal rulers of the *han*, resided half of each year in extravagant mansions with their many retainers, as the Tokugawa attempted to control their movements. Yoshiwara, the pleasure district of Edo, became a playground for the *samurai*. But urban living and its cultural attractions were expensive. *Samurai* stipends issued in rice were fixed since the beginning of the Tokugawa. Inevitably the *samurai*, living beyond their shrinking means became indebted to brokers (*chonin*) and merchants (*shonin*) who exchanged their rice stipends for cash. The status of the *samurai*, still observing feudal military discipline and privileged to wear two swords, was eroding.

In contrast, China's scholar-official class maintained its hold on traditional culture and status conferred by the examination system since the

Song. No great changes had affected their role as the ruling social and political elite by the nineteenth century. Conservative to the core, the scholar-gentry, with a vested interest in supporting the traditional social order, holding fast to traditional cultural values, resisted any and all fundamental political or social reforms. The ruling scholar-gentry elite of the Qing had everything to lose and nothing to gain from radical revolutionary change, be it arriving from the West or from Taiping rebels. The halfway efforts of the post–Tongzhi Restoration never amounted to truly significant institutional change.

The *samurai* elite of Japan, however, had nothing to lose and everything to gain in leading fundamental institutional and political reform under the Tokugawa. In 1868 young *samurai* leaders from the western *han* overthrew the regime, embraced radical institutional reform, and established a modern nation state under the new Meiji emperor. Subsequently the group of young *samurai* oligarchs in the space of a decade abolished feudal stipends, the privilege of carrying swords, and feudal social distinctions; rapidly assimilated Western knowledge, both technical and institutional; and embarked on the building of a modern and effective army and navy. Certainly the deeply imbedded role of military values and organization in the Japanese feudal system enhanced the ability of the Japanese to build, support, and command military forces in the new context of political institutions derived from the West.

The results of these contrasting historical backgrounds were all too clear in the outcome of the Sino-Japanese War of 1894–1895. Japanese ships and soldiers were commanded by the new officer class, heirs of the *samurai*, who had adopted the technological and social systems of the West but were imbued with the military values necessary to make them work. Chinese ships and soldiers, otherwise equal to the Japanese in technical advancement and human qualities, were commanded by scholar-officials whose focus was as much on traditional attractions of social and cultural status and deep-rooted habits of evasion of responsibility as on commitment and devotion to the commonweal. Meiji leaders adopted a concerted policy to build a modern, centralized state and military to equal those of the West, while the Manchu and Chinese officials of the Qing Court failed to adopt a determined policy of investment in industry and defense. The consequences of this difference were to persist into the mid-twentieth century.

Perhaps the problem goes back to the Chinese notion of change derived from the *Yi Jing*, from which the watchword *ziqiang* comes. In the *Yi Jing*, *ziqiang* arises from within the subject in an internal dialectic with *Tian* (Heaven). But nineteenth-century *ziqiang* came not from Chinese *Tian* but from the Western *Gestalt* with which a true creative dialectic had yet to be established.

SUGGESTED READINGS

Cohen, Paul A. *Between Tradition and Modernity: Wang T'ao and Reform in Late Ch'ing China* (Cambridge: Harvard University Press, 1974).

Fairbank, John K., ed. *The Cambridge History of China*, vol. 10, *Late Ch'ing, 1800– 1911, Part 1* (Cambridge: Cambridge University Press, 1978). This standard reference for late Qing history contains an incisive chapter on the Opium War.

Fairbank, John K., and Kwang-ching Liu, eds. *The Cambridge History of China*, vol. 11. *Late Ch'ing, 1800–1911, Part 2* (Cambridge: Cambridge University Press, 1980).

Feuerwerker, Albert. *China's Early Industrialization: Sheng Hsuan-huai (1844–1916) and Mandarin Enterprise* (New York: Atheneum, 1970). A biography of a principal nineteenth-century industrialist and self-strengthening official.

Feuerwerker, Albert, Rhoads Murphey, and Marcy C. Wright, eds. *Approaches to Modern Chinese History* (Berkeley: University of California Press, 1967). A collection of twelve essays mostly by students of modernization and self-strengthening enterprises in the nineteenth and twentieth centuries.

Folsom, Kenneth E. *Friends, Guests, and Colleagues: The Mu-fu System in the Late Ch'ing Period* (Berkeley: University of California Press, 1968). The *mufu* (official's private secretariat) was an important agency involved in reform in the nineteenth century.

Hao, Yen-p'ing. *The Comprador in Nineteenth Century China: Bridge between East and West* (Cambridge: Harvard University Press, 1970). Compradors bridged the institutional and cultural gap between Chinese treaty port merchants and Western trade, becoming themselves a new urban class. This is one of the first studies of compradors as a group.

Hibbert, Christopher. *The Dragon Wakes: China and the West, 1793–1911* (London: Penguin Books, 1984). A comprehensive history of the Western impact on China from the Macartney Embassy to the Nationalist Revolution.

Kennedy, Thomas L. *The Arms of Kiangnan: Modernization in the Chinese Ordinance Industry, 1860–1895* (Boulder: Westview Press, 1978). A critical study of the Jiangnan arsenal, one of the earliest efforts at modernization.

Leibo, Stephen A. *Transferring Technology to China: Prosper Giquel and the Self-strengthening Movement* (Berkeley: University of California, Center for Chinese Studies, China Research Monograph no. 28, 1985). The French adviser to the Fuzhou shipyard was a strong advocate of technical education of Chinese under the auspices of Chinese modernizing officials.

Porter, Jonathan. "Foreign Affairs (*Yang-wu*) Expertise in the Late Ch'ing: The Career of Chao Lieh-wen," *Modern Asian Studies* 13.3 (1979): 459–483. Discusses the career of a foreign affairs adviser in Zeng Guofan's *mufu*.

Porter, Jonathan. *Tseng Kuo-fan's Private Bureaucracy* (Berkeley: University of California, Center for Chinese Studies, China Research Monograph no. 9, 1972). A study of the *mufu* system as greatly expanded by Zeng Guofan in the service of defeating the Taiping Rebellion.

Rawlinson, John L. *China's Struggle for Naval Development, 1839–1895* (Cambridge: Harvard University Press, 1967). A thorough study of China's efforts to create a modern navy from stimulus of the Opium War to the disastrous outcome of the Sino-Japanese War of 1895.

Rudolph, Jennifer M. *Negotiated Power in Late Imperial China: The Zongli Yamen and the Politics of Reform* (Ithaca: Cornell University, East Asia Program, 2008). As a kind of ad hoc foreign office created as a result of the second Opium War, the Zongli Yamen became the principal agency of self-strengthening enterprises through the late nineteenth century.

Teng Ssu-yu, John K. Fairbank, et al. *China's Response to the West: A Documentary Survey 1830–1923* (New York: Atheneum, 1970).

Wakeman, Frederic, Jr. *The Fall of Imperial China* (New York: The Free Press, 1975).

Wright, Mary C. *The Last Stand of Chinese Conservatism: The T'ung-Chih Restoration, 1862–1874* (Stanford: Stanford University Press, 1957). A classic and important investigation of the Tongzhi Restoration and the predicament of Confucian reform.

Yung Wing [Rong Hong]. *My Life in China and America* (New York: Henry Holt, 1909). The autobiography of the first Chinese student to graduate from an American university who went on to lead the educational mission to the United States in the 1870.

NOTES

1. Cheng Yi, *Shenyi tang Yi Jing* (The *Yi Jing* from the Studio of Cautious Transmission), 4 vols. (Beijing, 1885), vol. 1, 5a.

2. On Zhao Liewen, see Jonathan Porter, "Foreign Affairs (*Yang-wu*) Expertise in the Late Ch'ing: The Career of Chao Lieh-wen," *Modern Asian Studies* 13.3 (1979), 459–483.

3. Teng Ssu-yu, John K. Fairbank, et al., eds., *China's Response to the West: A Documentary Survey 1830–1923* (New York: Antheneum, 1970), 76.

4. Lord William Gascoyne-Cecil, *Changing China* (London: James Nisbet, 1911), 3.

Epilogue
The Twilight of Imperial China

The traditional explanation of dynastic change as an inevitable cyclical process is succinctly expressed at the beginning of the Romance of the Three Kingdoms (Sanguo Yanyi), *the epic narrative of the fall of the Han dynasty at the end of the second century:*

> *They say the momentum of history is ever thus: the empire, long divided, must unite; long united, must divide.*[1]

Chinese history is not reducible to such simple cyclic change, but the dynastic cycle still possessed a compelling logic. It was first expressed in the declarations of Wu Wang ("The Martial King") and the Duke of Shao at the beginning of the Zhou dynasty in the twelfth century BCE. As a description of the pattern of Chinese history it is enshrined in the long tradition of official historiography, beginning with Sima Qian's Shi Ji (Historical Records) *published in 100 BCE, the model on which Ban Gu's* Qian Han Shu (History of the Former Han) *(ca. 100 CE) was based, and followed by 25 official dynastic histories, each written by the succeeding dynasty. Even the Qing has its own official history, written, and revised once to correct an anti-Manchu bias, by the Republic of China.*

The fall of the Ming and the rise of the Qing took place within traditional parameters of dynastic change, including peasant rebellion, bureaucratic-social struggle, barbarian invasion, and military insurrection. By the end of the Qing, those parameters had not only evolved, they had changed fundamentally. From the 1890s new conditions spelled the end not just of the Qing but of Imperial China. These included aggressive Western imperialism; intrusive Christian proselytism sanctioned by the Unequal Treaties; an increasing willingness among the literate class to consider radical reform; the evolution of Confucianism from the ethical foundation of civilization to one ideology among many world ideologies; the transformation of the gentry-literati class into an increasingly autonomous intelligentsia; the emergence of nationalism; and the growth of a revolutionary movement oriented to the West.

1895 AS A WATERSHED

The Sino-Japanese War and the Treaty of Shimonoseki in 1895 sounded the death knell of Imperial China. The formal end of the Qing did not come until the abdication of the Manchus in January 1912, but Imperial China was already defunct, persisting only on the momentum of its massive moribund institutions. The events following the war—the 1898 Reform Movement and the "Hundred Days of Reform," the Empress Dowager Cixi's coup d'état imprisoning the Guangxu emperor in 1898, the Boxer Uprising of 1899–1900 and its defeat, and the conservative reform program in the first decade of the twentieth century—were aimless efforts, too little, too late to resurrect or salvage the old order from irrelevance. The civil service examination system, the hallowed underpinning of the entire traditional structure, was abolished in 1905. Post-1895 Imperial China was no longer a viable entity.

China's defeat by Japan had a stunning effect on both Chinese and Westerners. It was, first, a huge blow to China's self-esteem that completely changed the terms of debate regarding China's efforts to modernize. It revealed the bankruptcy of self-strengthening and the pervasive extent of bureaucratic corruption. It gave impetus to the revolutionary movement as well as to radical institutional reform. And it prompted the obvious negative comparisons with Japan's brilliantly successful military modernization. For the Great Powers, it was a stunning revelation of China's moribund condition that changed the Western assessment of its future as a nation. China lost much of the vestigial respect for a great empire that had persisted for so long in Western minds. Admiration for an ancient civilization, however flawed, in the modern world, changed to contempt for a decrepit state post-1895. Japan, the spunky little country growing powerful by diligent emulation of Western models, fit the Western affection for an admired underdog, not decrepit China. The Western nations now anticipated China's impending breakup, predicated on the belief that the Chinese were not a cohesive people. They lacked a national spirit of determination and common public identity. Sun Yatsen (1866–1925), leader of the fledgling revolutionary movement in the 1890s, later characterized the Chinese people as a "sheet of loose sand" upon which the Western powers could act at will. For Sun, nationalism, the cement that would weld them together as a strong force, was as yet only embryonic:

> What is the standing of our nation in the world? In comparison with other nations, we have the greatest population and the oldest culture, of four thousand years duration. We ought to be advancing in line with the nations of Europe and America. But the Chinese people have only family and clan groups; there is no national spirit. Consequently, in spite of the four hundred million people gathered together in one China, we are in fact but a sheet of loose sand. We are the poorest and weakest state in the world, occupying the lowest position in international affairs; the rest of mankind is the carving knife and the serving dish, while we are the fish and the meat.[2]

Sadly, it was once family that was the great strength and core of Confucian culture. Nationalism was a modern phenomenon.

CARVING THE CHINESE MELON

Acting on the pretext of the killing of two German Catholic missionaries in 1897 in western Shandong, where anti-Christian xenophobia had grown virulent, Germany demanded a leasehold on Jiaozhou Bay in southern Shandong peninsula. The regional city of Qingdao would become the center of German economic and cultural penetration of the province. This triggered a scramble for territorial concessions by the major powers. Russia quickly followed suit, obtaining a twenty-five-year lease of Port Arthur at the tip of the Liaodong peninsula in Manchuria and neighboring Dalian Bay. Ironically, this was the very area that Japan had been forced by the Tripartite Intervention of Russia, France, and Germany in 1895 to retrocede to China, after obtaining the region in the Treaty of Shimonoseki. Each concession by China justified the next, while China was helpless to oppose the process. France demanded a lease on Guangzhou Bay in Guangdong province, adjacent to its colony in Indochina, in 1898. As the greatest power opposed to exclusive division of territory, Britain at first avoided joining the scramble for concessions. But it was persuaded in the same year by China to occupy Weihaiwei in northern Shandong as a counterweight to Russian and German influence. Japan, having acquired Taiwan in 1895, demanded the nonalienation by China of Fujian on the mainland opposite Taiwan, tantamount to staking an exclusive claim on the province. The United States, like Britain opposed to alienation of exclusive spheres of influence, advocated equal opportunity for exploitation of China for all nations' economic interests and opposed transportation and tariff barriers erected by nations in their respective spheres. This policy was proposed by secretary of state John Hay to the various nations separately and, upon receiving positive, if ambivalent replies, Hay declared agreement with the Open Door Policy in 1900. But the United States in the meantime had acquired the Philippines as spoils from the Spanish-American War in 1898, and thus had its own colony in close proximity to China.

In the scramble for concessions the imperialist powers had effectively drawn figurative dotted lines across the map of China, along which future colonial divisions would dismember the country. The Open Door Policy contributed to halting this potential process. Also influential was the emergence of Chinese nationalism in response to China's predicament. But the "Carving of the Chinese Melon" remained a vision in Western minds, as evident in Lord Charles Beresford's *The Break-up of China* (1899), an economic assessment of future Western prospects in China.

THE REFORM MOVEMENT OF 1898

The threatened "Carving of the Chinese Melon" energized the Reform Movement led by the scholar Kang Youwei (1858–1927) since the mid-1880s. Kang's career, like Sun Yatsen's on a parallel track, spanned the critical years from the Taiping Rebellion and the Second Opium War to the National Revolution of the 1920s. The fear that China would soon succumb to imperialist conquest made serious institutional reforms all the more urgent. Through gentry-literati study societies formed by Kang and his followers, a growing number of liberal reform newspapers, and a blizzard of memorials to the Zongli yamen and the throne, Kang proposed a battery of institutional reforms that went beyond the technological modernization program of the Self-Strengthening Movement. Aside from structural reforms such as new ministries of translation, commerce, and industry, Kang proposed to fortify Confucianism as a national religion through a government ministry of religion, to establish Confucian churches, and to count the calendar from Confucius' birth. These proposals contributed as much to the weakening of Confucianism, as they relegated it to a mere "faith" or ideology among many.

The Guangxu emperor (r. 1875–1908), upon reaching his majority in 1889, assumed actual power, while the Empress Dowager relinquished formal power in retirement. The young emperor was influenced in favor of new liberal ideas by his palace tutors, who introduced him to such liberal thinkers as Feng Guifen, and by his own reading in Western learning and study of foreign languages. By 1898 Kang Youwei's thinking had become more radical. In January 1898 he had an interview, arranged by the emperor, with the Zongli yamen. His memorials were now studied by the emperor, and in June Kang had his first imperial audience. In an edict, the emperor announced a national policy of reform. What followed was the "Hundred Days" of reform, during which the emperor promulgated more than a hundred decrees following Kang's advice. Among the most significant measures were reform of the examination system to end the eight-legged examination essay style and to include essays on current affairs and policy, and to open official discussion of institutional reform.

Inevitably the reforms evoked a powerful conservative reaction. The parallel with the Major Reform program of Wang Anshi (1021–1086) that was undone by a hostile bureaucracy is notable. In both cases, the rapid pace of the reform decrees and the restructuring of central government processes antagonized the great majority of the bureaucracy and Court officials, who had a vested interest in the unchanging stability of the old order. The Empress Dowager, who saw her influence under attack, finally staged a coup d'état in late September, imprisoning the emperor on an island in a lake in the palace, rescinding the reform edicts, and arresting and executing many of the reformers. Cixi now resumed direct power until 1908, when she died within hours of the Guangxu emperor, whom she allegedly poisoned so that he would not have the satisfaction of outliving her to see the end of her reactionary regime.

THE HEARTS AND MINDS OF THE PEOPLE

The Empress Dowager and her allied Manchu princes now turned to the most reactionary conservative force to defend against Western imperialist aggression and the threat to China's geographical integrity. Christian imperialism was emboldened by dynastic weakness in the face of Western imperialist aggression after 1895 and the expansion of protections afforded by the Unequal Treaties' provision of extraterritoriality. Chinese provincial and local officials were reduced to cringing submission to the slightest foreign demands in response to missionaries' and their converts' complaints of harassment and intimidation, and the threat of further military coercion. Western Shandong, the focus of German Catholic missionary proselytism, partly owing to the weakness of gentry influence there, had a long history of banditry and militancy, dating back to the Northern Song reign of Emperor Huizong in the early twelfth century. Popular xenophobia and the anti-Christian movement were directly linked to provocation of aggressive imperialism of the 1890s. Reflecting the culmination of years of inarticulate pent-up frustration and humiliation at the hands of foreigners, and polarization of local society between Chinese Christian converts protected by missionary exploitation of extraterritorial rights under the umbrella of the Unequal Treaties, and non-Christian Chinese villages, resentment and anger erupted in late 1899 in the explosive uprising of Boxers United in Righteousness (*Yihe quan*) in western Shandong. The Boxers gathered on local village fields or boxing grounds to practice simple martial arts exercises (thus the name boxers or fists) and magical possession by gods and heroes from popular fiction, such as Monkey and Guan Gong, which they believed imparted invulnerability to swords and guns. Carrying flags bearing the slogan "Revive the Qing, Destroy the Foreigners" (*Xing Qing, mie yang*) they rose up out of villages and towns in Shandong and the metropolitan province of Zhili, and spread across the north China plain, attacking and killing foreigners, missionaries, and their Christian converts in the spring of 1900. Emphasizing their loyalty to the throne, they had changed their name to Militia United in Righteousness (*Yihe tuan*). By the summer they converged on Beijing, the seat of the hated foreign presence and the diplomatic missions that had been the last reluctant concession to the Western powers in 1860.

Reactionary bureaucrats and Manchu princes saw the Boxers as an instrument of national salvation and defense of the dynasty, a cathartic whirlwind to expunge the Western presence where everything else had failed. A popular mass movement of such energy, they realized, could not be safely thwarted or opposed without incurring final, fatal alienation and attack on the dynasty itself. The Boxers possessed the appeal of rare unity of popular sentiment embracing the whole spectrum of social classes: powerful nobles intent on driving out the foreigners, scholar-gentry defending Confucian tradition against Christianity, xenophobic peasantry, bandits, and unemployed mobs.

In a debate on what policy the Court should adopt toward the Boxers, at a mass audience of ministers and Princes in mid-June, the Empress Dowager interrupted the discussion:

> Perhaps their magic is not to be relied upon, but can we not rely on the hearts and minds of the people? Today China is extremely weak. We have only the people's hearts and minds to depend upon. If we cast them aside and lose the people's hearts, what can we use to sustain the country?[3]

The Court therefore took the decision to support the Boxers, which was tantamount to a declaration of war against all the foreign powers. The Boxers besieged the foreign legations quarter for 55 days from mid-June to mid-August 1900. An International Relief Expedition comprising contingents of Japanese, German, Russian, British, French, Austrian, Italian, and United States troops marched from Tianjin, defeating the Boxer resistance, and relieved the legations on August 14.

Revenge was severe. Terms of the Boxer Protocol of 1901 specified punishment of guilty princes and officials, a massive indemnity of 450 million *taels*, establishment of a permanent legation guard, destruction of the Dagu forts near Tianjin, prohibition of importation of arms for two years, stationing of foreign troops along the Tianjin-Beijing corridor, and suppression of civil service examinations for five years in cities where the Boxers had been active and had enjoyed the support of the scholar-gentry. The enormous indemnity, equivalent to one *tael* for every subject, was equal to more than four times the annual revenue of the nation. The most crippling punishment the allies might well have demanded was the removal of the Empress Dowager, who after all was ultimately responsible for failing to stop the uprising. But the powers knew that the dynasty might thereby fall, and its continued existence was the one thing that guaranteed their continued economic domination of China. This consideration mitigated the severity of their demands.

If the Boxers failed as an instrument of dynastic salvation in the face of implacable Western imperialism determined to dominate China, the uprising nevertheless engendered an emerging Chinese nationalism that began to bring cohesion to Sun Yatsen's "sheet of loose sand," and thus discouraged further moves by the powers to dismember China.

JUDGMENT

That the dynasty's days were numbered was evident to those attuned to the signs of change in the last decade of the Qing, as it was at the end of the Ming, when rebels gathered in strength, barbarians pressed upon the Great Wall, and bureaucratic factionalism ate away at institutional cohesion. But whereas obvious contenders for succession to the Mandate existed at the end of the Ming—though the issue was then still in doubt— none had clearly emerged at the end of the nineteenth century, not the Boxers, not the Japanese, not the reformers. It was not even clear whether the "momentum of history" would repeat itself again, though there were forces in motion that were pulling China in new directions. Another half-century would pass before the struggle between the array of contenders was resolved. By then the old order was only a memory, not a compelling logic. Or was it?

The Communists condemned China's imperial past as a dark era of oppressive feudalism and imperialism, mitigated only by occasional bright flashes of righteous peasant resistance and rebellion. The glorious future of Liberation proclaimed in 1949 had put all that behind them. The Nationalists, somewhat more forgiving, considering that the Guomindang (Nationalist Party) elite enjoyed a continuity with the old gentry social elite, nevertheless rejected the oppressive rule of the alien Manchu conquerors. But one may be forgiven for taking the rhetoric of post-revolutionary condemnation of the traditional imperial past with a considerable dose of skepticism. Is the Leninist dictatorship of the People's Republic of China any different than the authoritarian autocracy of the Qianlong emperor or the Wanli emperor? Is the murderous slaughter of Chinese "Rightists" during the Great Proletarian Cultural Revolution more forgivable than the Hongwu emperor's beating and execution of thousands of suspected traitorous officials? Is the contemporary implacable persecution of political dissidents more acceptable than any autocratic emperor's pursuit of heterodox beliefs?

Hexagram forty-eight of the Yi Jing comprises the trigrams for Wood below and for Water above. It signifies The Well (Jing). The Judgment (or Decision) associated with the hexagram says:

> *The Well. Although the city may change, the well does not change. Neither does it diminish nor does it gain. Those who come and go to the well, draw from it. When the well-rope does not quite reach the water, or the jug breaks, there is misfortune.*[4]

Jing has two levels of meaning. First, most simply, it denotes the common well of a village or walled town. Although a town's location may move, the well cannot. Second, it connotes the "well-field" (jingtian) system, a utopian agrarian order that allegedly existed in remote antiquity (third millennium BCE), but was first mentioned in the Classic Zhou Li (Rites of Zhou) from the third century BCE. The unit of the well-field was nine square fields of equal size arranged in the pattern of the character jing (井). The central field, the "common field," belonged to the ruler and contained the well, used by the surrounding eight families cultivating their respective fields. The fields were divided by ditches, and mulberry trees for sericulture grew on the boundaries. Larger ditches separated each nine-square unit, or well-field, from the others around it, and so on across the flat plain. In both meanings, the well, or well-field system, was the anchor of a primordial social order. The well was taken both as literal fact and as metaphor, a physical feature of ancient land tenure and an image of harmonious social organization. Thus the well is an analog of government, the central benefit to the people and the source of life. But danger lies in its interruption or loss.

The Yi Jing is all about continuity in change, and The Well suggests this in its image of continuity underlying change: the town may change or move but the well as a life-giving source endures. Hexagram forty-nine, following Jing, The Well, is Ge, Revolution. The original meaning of ge is to molt, to change one's skin. Revolution in this sense is an ordered process of change, however abrupt. The antithesis of order is luan (disorder, confusion, turmoil, anarchy). The Well represents the foundational order, insurance against luan, the greatest anathema to Confucians.

Jingtian may never have existed. But the jingtian ideal was a recurrent model from its first appearance in classical writings in the late Zhou or Han (second millennium BCE to first century BCE). It reappeared repeatedly as an ideal-typical institution in the thinking and proposals of reformers from Wang Mang (33 BCE–23 CE) in the Han and Wang Anshi (1021–1086) in the Song to Huang Zongxi and Gu Yanwu in the late Ming–early Qing. Why? Because jingtian possessed the powerful appeal of allegedly concrete evidence for an institution that represented the very ground of historical continuity, that lay at the very beginning of history, as early as the Yi Jing itself. Even at the end of the Qing and into the Republican and Communist periods in the twentieth century, the question of jingtian's actual existence as well as its metaphorical significance was still being debated by scholars and revolutionaries. Was jingtian an ancient precedent for modern socialism? Was it a prescription for the present and the future? Or was it only a myth, existing in the imagination, like so many other mythological creations of the Chinese legendary record? Yet the perennial attraction of order in change was never in question.

SUGGESTED READINGS

Esherick, Joseph W. *The Origins of the Boxer Uprising* (Berkeley: University of California Press, 1987). An excellent, critical study of the rise and development of the Boxer movement from the 1890s to its climax in 1900.

Fairbank, John K., and Kwang-ching Liu, eds. *The Cambridge History of China,* vol. 11, *Late Ch'ing, 1800–1911, Part 2* (Cambridge: Cambridge University Press, 1980).

Sun Yat-sen. Frank W. Price, trans., *San Min Chu I: The Three Principles of the People* (Taipei: China Cultural Service, n.d.). An official translation of the principal work of Sun Yat-sen, expounding his political philosophy.

Wilhelm, Richard, trans. *The I Ching or Book of Changes* (Princeton: Princeton University Press, 1977). The most ancient Chinese Classic is a fountainhead of religious thought.

NOTES

1. Moss Roberts, trans. and ed., *Three Kingdoms: China's Epic Drama by Lo Kuan-chung* (New York: Pantheon Books, 1976), 3.

2. Sun Yat-sen, *San Min Chu I: The Three Principles of the People,* Frank W. Price, trans. (Taipei: China Cultural Service, n.d.), 5.

3. Quoted in Joseph W. Esherick, *The Origins of the Boxer Uprising* (Berkeley: University of California Press, 1987), 289.

4. Cheng Yi, *Sheng tang Yi Jing* (The *Yi Jing* from the Studio of Cautious Transmission), 4 vols. (Beijing: 1885), vol. 4, 35b.

Selected Bibliography

Amitai-Preiss, Reuven, and David O. Morgan, eds. *The Mongol Empire and Its Legacy*. Leiden: Brill, 2000.

Attwater, Rachel. *Adam Schall: A Jesuit at the Court of China, 1592–1666*. Adapted from the French of Joseph Duhr, SJ. London: Geoffrey Chapman, 1963.

Atwell, William S. "From Education to Politics: The Fu She." In William T. de Bary, ed., *The Unfolding of Neo-Confucianism*. New York: Columbia University Press, 1975, 333–367.

Ayao, Hoshi. Mark Elvin, trans. *The Ming Tribute Grain System*. Ann Arbor: University of Michigan, Center for Chinese Studies, 1969.

Backhouse, E., and J. O. P. Bland. *Annals and Memoirs of the Court of Peking*. Taipei: Ch'eng Wen Publishing (reprint), 1970; originally published 1914.

Bai, Limin. "Mathematical Study and Intellectual Transition in the Early and Mid-Qing." *Late Imperial China* 16.2 (December 1995): 23–61.

Balasz, Etienne. H. M. Wright, trans. *Chinese Civilization and Bureaucracy: Variations on a Theme*. New Haven: Yale University Press, 1964.

Bartlett, Beatrice S. *Monarchs and Ministers: The Grand Council in Mid-Ch'ing China, 1723–1820*. Berkeley: University of California Press, 1991.

Birch, Cyril, trans. *Stories from a Ming Collection: Translations of Chinese Short Stories Published in the Seventeenth Century*. New York: Grove Press, 1958.

Bodde, Derk. *China's First Unifier: A Study of the Ch'in Dynasty as Seen in the Life of Li Ssu (280?–208 B.C.)*. Leiden: E. J. Brill, 1938.

Bol, Peter K. "Government, Society, and State: On the Political Visions of Ssu-ma Kuang and Wang An-shih." In Peter P. Hymes and Conrad Schirokauer, eds., *Ordering the World: Approaches to State and Society in Sung Dynasty China*. Berkeley: University of California Press, 1993, 128–192.

Bridgman, Elijah Coleman, and S. Wells Williams, eds. *The Chinese Repository* (A periodical published by the American Board of Commissioners for Foreign Missions). 20 vols. Canton: 1832–1851, reprint.

Brook, Timothy. *The Confusions of Pleasure: Commerce and Culture in Ming China.* Berkeley: University of California Press, 1998.

Brown, Claudia. *The Great Qing: Painting in China, 1644–1911.* Seattle: University of Washington Press, 2014.

Buck, Pearl S. *The Good Earth.* New York: Pocket Books, 2005; originally published 1931.

Camões, Luis de. *Os Lusíadas.* Reis Brasil, ed. Lisboa: Editorial Minerva, 1964.

Cao Xueqin. David Hawkes, trans. *The Story of the Stone.* 5 vols. Harmondsworth, England: Penguin Books, 1973.

Chamberlain, Jonathan. *Chinese Gods.* Hong Kong: Long Island Publishers, 1983.

Chan, Hok-lam. "The Rise of Ming T'ai-tsu (1368–1398): Facts and Fictions in Early Ming Official Historiography." *Journal of the American Oriental Society* 95.4 (1975): 679–715.

Chang, Chun-shu, and Shelley Hsueh-lun Chang. *Crises and Transformation in Seventeenth-Century China: Society, Culture, and Modernity in Li Yu's World.* Ann Arbor: University of Michigan Press, 1992.

Chang Chung-li. *The Chinese Gentry: Studies on Their Role in Nineteenth-Century Chinese Society.* Seattle: University of Washington Press, 1955.

Chang Hsin-pao. *Commissioner Lin and the Opium War.* Cambridge: Harvard University Press, 1964.

Chang, Michael G. *A Court on Horseback: Imperial Touring and the Construction of Qing Rule, 1680–1785.* Cambridge: Harvard University Press, 2007.

Cheng Yi. *Sheng tang Yi Jing* (The *Yi Jing* from the Studio of Cautious Transmission). 4 vols. Beijing: 1885.

Chesneaux, Jean, ed. *Popular Movements and Secret Societies in China 1840–1950.* Stanford: Stanford University Press, 1972.

Chow, Kai-wing. *Publishing, Culture, and Power in Early Modern China.* Stanford: Stanford University Press, 2004.

———. *The Rise of Confucian Ritualism in Late Imperial China: Ethics, Classics, and Lineage Discourse.* Stanford: Stanford University Press, 1994.

Ch'ü T'ung-tsu. *Law and Society in Traditional China.* Paris and La Haye: Mouton, 1961.

———. *Local Government in China under the Ch'ing.* Cambridge: Harvard University Press, 1962.

Cleaves, Francis Woodman, trans. and ed. *The Secret History of the Mongols (Yuan chao bishi).* 2 vols. Cambridge: Harvard University Press, 1952.

Clunas, Craig. *Superfluous Things: Material Culture and Social Status in Early Modern China.* Honolulu: University of Hawaii Press, 1991.

Cohen, Paul A. *Between Tradition and Modernity: Wang T'ao and Reform in Late Ch'ing China.* Cambridge: Harvard University Press, 1974.

Collis, Maurice. *Foreign Mud: The Opium Imbroglio at Canton in the 1830s and the Anglo-Chinese War.* New York: W. W. Norton, 1946.

Confucius. *The Analects of Confucius (Lun Yu).* Annotated by Arthur Waley, trans. New York: Vintage Books, 1938.

Crawford, Robert B. "Eunuch Power in the Ming Dynasty." *T'oung Pao*, second series, 49.3 (1961): 115–148.

Crossley, Pamela Kyle. *A Translucent Mirror: History and Identity in Qing Imperial Ideology*. Berkeley: University of California Press, 1999.

———. *The Manchus*. Oxford: Blackwell Publishers, 2002.

———. *Orphan Warriors: Three Manchu Generations at the End of the Qing World*. Princeton: Princeton University Press, 1990.

Dardess, John W. *Conquerors and Confucians: Aspects of Political Change in Late Yuan China*. New York: Columbia University Press, 1973.

———. *Ming China, 1368–1644. A Concise History of a Resilient Empire*. Lanham, Maryland: Rowman & Littlefield, 2012.

de Bary, William Theodore. "Chinese Despotism and the Confucian Ideal: A Seventeenth-Century View." In John K. Fairbank, ed., *Chinese Thought and Institutions*. Chicago: University of Chicago Press, 1957, 163–203.

———. *The Trouble with Confucianism*. Cambridge: Harvard University Press, 1991.

———, ed. *The Unfolding of Neo-Confucianism*. New York: Columbia University Press, 1975.

de Bary, William Theodore, Wing-tsit Chan, and Burton Watson, compilers. *Sources of Chinese Tradition*. New York: Columbia University Press, 1960.

Downs, Jacques M. *The Golden Ghetto: The American Commercial Community at Canton and the Shaping of American China Policy, 1784–1844*. Bethlehem & London: Lehigh University Press, 1997.

Dunne, George H., SJ. *Generation of Giants: The Story of the Jesuits in China in the Last Decades of the Ming Dynasty*. Notre Dame, IN: University of Notre Dame Press, 1962.

Dreyer, Edward L. *Early Ming China: A Political History, 1355–1435*. Stanford: Stanford University Press, 1982.

Eastman, Lloyd E. *Family, Fields, and Ancestors: Constancy and Change in China's Social and Economic History, 1550–1949*. New York: Oxford University Press, 1988.

Eberhard, Wolfram. "The Political Function of Astronomy and Astronomers in Han China." In J. K. Fairbank, ed., *Chinese Thought and Institutions*. Chicago: University of Chicago Press, 1957, 33–70.

Elliott, Mark C. *Emperor Qianlong: Son of Heaven, Man of the World*. Longman Library of World Biography, Peter Stearns, ed. New York: Longman, 2009.

———. *The Manchu Way: The Eight Banners and Ethnic Identity in Late Imperial China*. Stanford: Stanford University Press, 2001.

Elman, Benjamin A. *A Cultural History of Modern Science in China*. Cambridge: Harvard University Press, 2006.

———. "Ch'ing Dynasty 'Schools' of Scholarship." *Ch'ing-shih wen-t'i* 4.6 (December 1981): 1–41.

———. *Classicism, Politics, and Kinship: The Ch'ang-chou School of New Text Confucianism in Late Imperial China*. Berkeley: University of California Press, 1990.

———. *From Philosophy to Philology. Intellectual and Social Aspects of Change in Late Imperial China*. Cambridge: Harvard University Press, 1984.

———. "The Hsueh-hai T'ang and the Rise of New Text Scholarship in Canton." *Ch'ing-shih wen-t'i* 4.2 (December 1979): 51–82.

————. "Scholarship and Politics: Chuang Ts'un-yu and the Rise of the Ch'ang-chou New Text School in Late Imperial China." *Ch'ing-shih wen-t'i* 7.1 (June 1986): 63–86.

Elvin, Mark. *The Pattern of the Chinese Past*. Stanford: Stanford University Press, 1973.

Esherick, Joseph W. *The Origins of the Boxer Uprising*. Berkeley: University of California Press, 1987.

Fairbank, John K., ed. *The Cambridge History of China*, vol. 10. *Late Ch'ing, 1800–1911, Part 1*. Cambridge: Cambridge University Press, 1978.

————, ed. *Chinese Thought and Institutions*. Chicago: University of Chicago Press, 1957.

————. *Trade and Diplomacy on the China Coast: The Opening of the Treaty Ports 1842–1854*. Stanford: Stanford University Press, 1969.

Fairbank, John K., and Kwang-Ching Liu, eds. *The Cambridge History of China*, vol. 11. *Late Ch'ing, 1800–1911, Part 2*. Cambridge: Cambridge University Press, 1980.

Fang, Zhuofen, Tiewen Hu, Rui Jian, and Xing Fang. "The Porcelain Industry of Jingdezhen." In Xu Dixin and Wu Chengming, eds., *Chinese Capitalism, 1522–1840*, part IV. New York: St. Martin's Press, 2000, 308–326.

Fei Hsiao-tung. *Peasant Life in China: A Field Study of Country Life in the Yangtze Valley*. London: Kegan Paul, 1943.

Feuerwerker, Albert. *China's Early Industrialization: Sheng Hsuan-huai (1844–1916) and Mandarin Enterprise*. New York: Atheneum, 1970.

————. *State and Society in Eighteenth-Century China: The Ch'ing Empire in Its Glory*. Ann Arbor: University of Michigan, Center for Chinese Studies, Michigan Papers in Chinese Studies no. 27, 1976.

Feuerwerker, Albert, Rhoads Murphey, and Mary C. Wright, eds. *Approaches to Modern Chinese History*. Berkeley: University of California Press, 1967.

Folsom, Kenneth E. *Friends, Guests, and Colleagues. The Mu-fu System in the Late Ch'ing Period*. Berkeley: University of California Press, 1968.

Gardella, Robert. *Harvesting Mountains: Fujian and the China Tea Trade, 1757–1937*. Berkeley: University of California Press, 1994.

Gernet, Jacques. Janet Lloyd, trans. *China and the Christian Impact: A Conflict of Cultures*. Cambridge: Cambridge University Press, 1985.

Giles, Herbert A. *A Chinese Biographical Dictionary*, 2 vols. Shanghai: Kelly & Walsh, 1898.

Golas, Peter J. "Early Ch'ing Guilds." In G. William Skinner, ed., *The City in Late Imperial China*. Stanford: Stanford University Press, 1977, 555–580.

Goodrich, L. Carrington, and Chaoying Fang, eds. *Dictionary of Ming Biography, 1368–1644*, 2 vols. New York: Columbia University Press, 1976.

Granet, Marcel. Maurice Freedman, trans. *The Religion of the Chinese People*. Oxford: Basil Blackwell, 1975.

Greenberg, Michael. *British Trade and the Opening of China, 1800–1842*. Cambridge: Cambridge University Press, 1951.

Grimm, Tilemann. "Academies and Urban Systems in Kwangtung." In G. William Skinner, ed., *The City in Late Imperial China*. Stanford: Stanford University Press, 1977, 475–498.

Gulick, Edward V. *Peter Parker and the Opening of China*. Cambridge: Harvard University Press, 1973.

Guy, R. Kent. *The Emperor's Four Treasuries: Scholars and the State in the Late Ch'ien-lung Era*. Cambridge: Harvard University Press, 1987.

——. *Qing Governors and Their Provinces: The Evolution of Territorial Administration in China, 1644–1796*. Seattle: University of Washington Press, 2010.

Hao Yen-p'ing. *The Comprador in Nineteenth Century China: Bridge between East and West*. Cambridge: Harvard University Press, 1970.

Hartwell, Robert. "Demographic, Political, and Social Transformations of China, 750–1550." *Harvard Journal of Asiatic Studies* 42.2 (December 1982): 355–442.

Hegel, Robert E., compiler and translator. *True Crimes in Eighteenth-Century China: Twenty Case Histories*. Seattle: University of Washington Press, 2009.

Henderson, John B. "Early Ch'ing Critique of Traditional Chinese Cosmography," unpublished paper, 1978.

Hibbert, Christopher. *The Dragon Wakes: China and the West, 1793–1911*. London: Penguin Books, 1984.

Ho Ping-ti. *The Ladder of Success in Imperial China: Aspects of Social Mobility, 1368–1911*. New York: Columbia University Press, 1962.

——. "The Salt Merchants of Yang-chou: A Study of Commercial Capitalism in Eighteenth-Century China." *Harvard Journal of Asiatic Studies* 17.1/2 (June 1954): 130–168.

——. "The Significance of the Ch'ing Period in Chinese History." *Journal of Asian Studies* 26.2 (February 1967): 189–195.

Huang, Pei. *Autocracy at Work: A Study of the Yung-cheng Period, 1723–1735*. Bloomington: University of Indiana University Press, 1975.

Huang, Ray. *1587: A Year of No Significance: The Ming Dynasty in Decline*. New Haven: Yale University Press, 1981.

Huang, Zongxi. *Mingyi daifang lu (A Record of Perseverance in Adversity in a Time of Darkness)*. In Yan Yiping, compiler, *Baibu congshu jicheng*. Taibei: Yiwen yinshuguan (reprint), Daoguang 19 (1840).

Hucker, Charles O. *China's Imperial Past: An Introduction to Chinese History and Culture*. Stanford: Stanford University Press, 1975.

——, ed. *Chinese Government in Ming Times: Seven Studies*. New York: Columbia University Press, 1969.

Hummel, Arthur W., ed. *Eminent Chinese of the Ch'ing Period (1644–1912)*. 2 vols. Washington, D.C.: U.S. Government Printing Office/Library of Congress, 1943–1944.

Hunter, William C. *Bits of Old China*. Taipei: Ch'eng-wen Publishing (reprint), 1976.

——. *The "Fan Kwei" at Canton before Treaty Days, 1825–1844*. Taipei: Ch'eng-wen Publishing (reprint), 1965.

Hymes, Robert P., and Conrad Schirokauer, eds. *Ordering the World: Approaches to State and Society in Sung Dynasty China*. Berkeley: University of California Press, 1993.

Jami, Catherine. "Learning Mathematical Sciences during the Early and Mid-Ch'ing." In Benjamin Elman and Alexander Woodside, eds., *Education and Society in Late Imperial China, 1600–1900* (Berkeley: University of California Press, 1994), 223–256.

———. "Western Mathematics in China, Seventeenth Century and Nineteenth Century." In Patrick Petitjean, Catherine Jami, and Anne Marie Moulin, eds., *Science and Empires: Historical Studies about Scientific Development and European Expansion*. Dordrecht, Netherlands: Kluwer Academic Publishers, 1992, 79–88.

Jen Yu-wen. *The Taiping Revolutionary Movement*. New Haven: Yale University Press, 1973.

Jenner, W. J. F. *The Tyranny of History: The Roots of China's Crisis*. London: Penguin Books, 1992.

Johnson, David, Andrew J. Nathan, and Evelyn S. Rawski, eds. *Popular Culture in Late Imperial China*. Berkeley: University of California Press, 1985.

Johnson, Linda Cooke. *Shanghai: From Market Town to Treaty Port, 1074–1858*. Stanford: Stanford University Press, 1995.

Jones, Susan Mann. "Scholasticism and Politics in Late Eighteenth-Century China." *Ch'ing- shih wen-t'i* 3.4 (December 1975): 28–49.

Jordan, David K. *Gods, Ghosts, and Ancestors: Folk Religion of a Taiwanese Village*. Berkeley: University of California Press, 1972.

Kahn, Harold L. *Monarchy in the Emperor's Eyes: Image and Reality in the Ch'ien-lung Reign*. Cambridge: Harvard University Press, 1971.

Kennedy, Thomas L. *The Arms of Kiangnan: Modernization in the Chinese Ordinance Industry, 1860–1895*. Boulder: Westview Press, 1978.

Kessler, Lawrence D. *K'ang-hsi and the Consolidation of Ch'ing Rule 1661–1684*. Chicago: University of Chicago Press, 1976.

Knapp, Ronald G. Foreword by Jonathan Spence. *Chinese Houses: The Architectural Heritage of a Nation*. North Clarendon, VT: Tuttle, 2004.

Kuhn, Dieter. *The Age of Confucian Rule: The Song Transformation of China*. Cambridge: Harvard University Press, 2009.

Kuhn, Philip A. *Rebellion and Its Enemies in Late Imperial China: Militarization and Social Structure, 1796–1864*. Cambridge: Harvard University Press, 1970.

———. *Soulstealers: The Chinese Sorcery Scare of 1768*. Cambridge: Harvard University Press, 1990.

Legge, James, trans. *The Chinese Classics*, 5 vols. Hong Kong: Hong Kong University Press, 1970 (1960).

Legge, James, trans. *The Four Books*. Shanghai: Chinese Book Company, 1930.

Leibo, Steven A. *Transferring Technology to China: Prosper Giquel and the Self-Strengthening Movement*. Berkeley: University of California, Center for Chinese Studies, China Research Monograph no. 28, 1985.

Leung, Man-kam. "Juan Yuan (1764–1849): The Life, Works, and Career of a Chinese Scholar-Bureaucrat." Unpublished dissertation, University of Hawaii, 1977.

Levathes, Louise. *When China Ruled the Seas: The Treasure Fleet of the Dragon Throne, 1405–1433*. New York: Oxford University Press, 1994.

Levenson, Joseph R. "Ill Wind in the Well-field: The Erosion of the Confucian Ground of Controversy." In Arthur F. Wright, ed., *The Confucian Persuasion*. Stanford: Stanford University Press, 1960, 268–287.

Li Chu-tsing, and James C. Y. Watt, eds. *The Chinese Scholar's Studio: Artistic Life in the Late Ming Period: An Exhibition from the Shanghai Museum*. New York: Thames and Hudson, published in association with Asia Society Galleries, 1987.

Li, Lillian M. *China's Silk Trade: Traditional Industry in the Modern World, 1842–1937.* Cambridge: Harvard University Press, 1981.

Lin, Yutang. *The Gay Genius: The Life and Times of Su Tungpo.* New York: J. Day Co., 1947.

Liu, James T. C. *China Turning Inward: Intellectual-Political Changes in the Early Twelfth Century.* Cambridge: Council on East Asian Studies, Harvard University Press, 1988.

———. "The Neo-Traditional Period (ca. 800–1900) in Chinese History: A Note in Memory of the Late Professor Lei Hai-tsung." *Journal of Asian Studies* 24.1 (November 1964): 105–107.

———. *Ou-yang Hsiu: An Eleventh-Century Neo-Confucianist.* Stanford: Stanford University Press, 1967.

Lufrano, Richard John. *Honorable Merchants: Commerce and Self-Cultivation in Late Imperial China.* Honolulu: University of Hawaii Press, 1997.

Ma Huan. J. V. G. Mills, trans. and ed., *Ying-yai Sheng-lan: "The Overall Survey of the Ocean's Shores."* Cambridge: Cambridge University Press, 1970.

Macartney, George, Earl. *An Embassy to China.* J. L. Cranmer-Bing, ed. Hamden, CT: Archon Books, 1963.

MacNair, Harley Farnsworth, ed. *Modern Chinese History, Selected Readings: A collection of extracts from various sources chosen to illustrate some of the chief phases of China's international relations during the past hundred years.* New York: Paragon Book Reprint, 1967.

Mann, Susan. *Local Merchants and the Chinese Bureaucracy, 1750–1950.* Stanford: Stanford University Press, 1987.

Martzloff, Jean-Claude. "Space and Time in Chinese Texts of Astronomy and of Mathematical Astronomy in the Seventeenth and Eighteenth Centuries." *Chinese Science* 11 (1993–1994): 66–92.

McElderry, Andrea Lee. *Shanghai Old-Style Banks (Ch'ien-Chuang), 1800–1935: A Traditional Institution in a Changing Society.* Ann Arbor: Center for Chinese Studies, University of Michigan, 1976.

Mengzi (Mencius). Trans. with an introduction by D. C. Lau. *Mencius.* Harmondsworth, England and New York: Penguin Books, 1970.

Menzies, Gavin. *1421: The Year China Discovered America.* New York: William Morrow, 2003.

Metzger, Thomas A. *The Internal Organization of Ch'ing Bureaucracy: Legal, Normative, and Communication Aspects.* Cambridge: Harvard University Press, 1973.

Meyer-Fong, Tobie. *Building Culture in Early Qing Yangzhou.* Stanford: Stanford University Press, 2003.

———. *What Remains. Coming to Terms with Civil War in Nineteenth-century China.* Stanford: Stanford University Press, 2013.

Michael, Franz. *The Origin of Manchu Rule in China: Frontier and Bureaucracy as Interacting Forces in the Chinese Empire.* New York: Octagon Books reprint, 1965.

Morse, Hosea Ballou. *The Gilds of China, with an Account of the Gild Merchant or Cohong of Canton.* Taipei: Che'eng-wen Publishing Company (reprint), 1966. Orig. pub. London: Longmans, Green, 1909.

———. *The International Relations of the Chinese Empire.* 3 vols. London: Longmans, Green, 1910 and 1918.

Mote, F. W. *Imperial China, 900–1800*. Cambridge: Harvard University Press, 1999.

Mote, Frederick W., and Denis Twitchett, eds. *The Cambridge History of China*, vol. 7. *The Ming Dynasty, 1368–1644, Part 1*. Cambridge: Cambridge University Press, 1988.

Mungello, D. E. *Curious Land: Jesuit Accommodation and the Origins of Sinology*. Honolulu: University of Hawaii, Press, 1985.

Murray, Dian H. *Pirates of the South China Coast, 1790–1810*. Stanford: Stanford University Press, 1987.

Myers, Ramon H. *The Chinese Peasant Economy: Agricultural Development in Hopei and Shantung, 1890–1949*. Cambridge: Harvard University Press, 1970.

Nakayama, Shigeru, and Nathan Sivin, eds. *Chinese Science: Explorations of an Ancient Tradition*. Cambridge: MIT Press, 1973.

Naquin, Susan, and Evelyn S. Rawski. *Chinese Society in the Eighteenth Century*. New Haven and London: Yale University Press, 1987.

Needham, Joseph, et al. *Science and Civilization in China*. 7 vols. Cambridge: Cambridge University Press, 1959–2004.

Nivison, David S. "Ho-shen and His Accusers: Ideology and Political Behavior in the Eighteenth Century." In David S. Nivison and Arthur F. Wright, eds., *Confucianism in Action*. Stanford: Stanford University Press, 1959, 207–243.

———. *The Life and Thought of Chang Hsueh-ch'eng (1738–1801)*. Stanford: Stanford University Press, 1966.

Oxnam, Robert B. *Ruling from Horseback: Manchu Politics in the Oboi Regency, 1661–1669*. Chicago: University of Chicago Press, 1970.

Parsons, James Bunyan. *Peasant Rebellions of the Late Ming Dynasty*. Tucson: University of Arizona Press, 1970.

Peterson, Willard J. *Bitter Gourd: Fang I-chih and the Impetus for Intellectual Change*. New Haven: Yale University Press, 1979.

———, ed. *The Cambridge History of China*, vol. 9. *The Ch'ing Empire to 1800, Part 1*. Cambridge: Cambridge University Press, 2002.

———. "Fang I-chih: Western Learning and the 'Investigation of Things.'" In William T. de Bary, ed., *The Unfolding of Neo-Confucianism*. New York: Columbia University Press, 1975, 369–411.

Plopper, Clifford H. *Chinese Religion Seen Through the Proverb*. Shanghai: Shanghai Modern Publishing House, 1935.

Polachek, James B. *The Inner Opium War*. Cambridge: Harvard University Press, 1992.

Polo, Marco. Milton Rugoff, edited with introduction. *The Travels of Marco Polo*. New York: New American Library, 1961.

Porter, Jonathan. "Bureaucracy and Science in Early Modern China: The Imperial Astronomical Bureau in the Ch'ing Period." *Journal of Oriental Studies* 18.1/2 (1980): 61–76.

———. "Foreign Affairs (*Yang-wu*) Expertise in the Late Ch'ing: The Career of Chao Lieh-wen." *Modern Asian Studies* 13.3 (1979): 459–483.

———. *Macau: The Imaginary City: Culture and Society, 1557 to the Present*. Boulder: Westview Press, 1996.

———. "The Scientific Community in Early Modern China." *Isis* 73.269 (December 1982): 529–544.

———. "The Troublesome Feringhi: Late Ming Chinese Perceptions of the Portuguese and Macau." *Portuguese Studies Review* 7.2 (1999): 11–35.

———. *Tseng Kuo-fan's Private Bureaucracy.* Berkeley: University of California, Center for Chinese Studies, China Research Monograph no. 9, 1972.

Pritchard, Earl H. *The Crucial Years of Early Anglo-Chinese Relations, 1750–1800.* Pullman: Washington State College, 1936.

Qian, Wen-yuan. *The Great Inertia: Scientific Stagnation in Traditional China.* London: Croom Helm, 1985.

Qingshi liezhuan (Collected Biographies of the Qing), 10 vols. Taibei: Zhonghua shuju, 1962.

Rawlinson, John L. *China's Struggle for Naval Development, 1839–1895.* Cambridge: Harvard University Press, 1967.

Rawski, Evelyn S. "Economic and Social Foundations of Late Imperial Culture." In David Johnson, et al., eds., *Popular Culture in Late Imperial China.* Berkeley: University of California Press, 1985, 3–33.

———. *Education and Popular Literacy in Ch'ing China.* Ann Arbor: University of Michigan Press, 1979.

———. *The Last Emperors: A Social History of Qing Imperial Institutions.* Berkeley: University of California Press, 1998.

Reischauer, Edwin O., and John K. Fairbank. *East Asia: The Great Tradition.* Boston: Houghton Mifflin, 1958.

Richards, J. F. "The Indian Empire and Peasant Production of Opium in the Nineteenth Century." *Modern Asian Studies* 15.1 (1981): 59–82.

Roberts, Moss, trans. and ed. *Three Kingdoms: China's Epic Drama by Lo Kuan-chung.* New York: Pantheon Books, 1976.

Ronan, Colin A. *The Shorter Science and Civilisation in China: An Abridgement of Joseph Needham's Original Text.* Vol. 1. Cambridge: Cambridge University Press, 1978.

Rossabi, Morris. *Khubilai Khan: His Life and Times.* Berkeley: University of California Press, 1988.

Rowbotham, Arnold H. *Missionary and Mandarin: The Jesuits at the Court of China.* Berkeley: University of California Press, 1942.

Rowe, William T. *China's Last Empire: The Great Qing.* Cambridge: Harvard University Press, 2009.

———. *Hankow: Commerce and Society in a Chinese City, 1796–1889.* Stanford: Stanford University Press, 1984.

———. *Saving the World: Chen Hongmou and Elite Consciousness in Eighteenth-Century China.* Stanford: Stanford University Press, 2001.

Ruan Yuan, comp. *Gujing jingshe wenji, 14 juan.* In Yan Yiping, ed., *Baibu congshu jicheng,* series 44. Taibei: Yimen yinshuguan, 1967.

Ruan Yuan, et al., eds. *Chouren zhuan* (Biographies of mathematical scientists), 7 vols. Taibei: Commercial Press, 1965.

Rudolph, Jennifer M. *Negotiated Power in Late Imperial China: The Zongli Yamen and the Politics of Reform.* Ithaca: Cornell University, East Asia Program, 2008.

Schütte, Josef Franz, SJ. John J. Coyne, SJ, trans. *Valignano's Mission Principles for Japan*, vol. I, parts I & II. St. Louis: The Institute of Jesuit Sources, 1980.

Schwartz, Benjamin. *The World of Thought in Ancient China*. Cambridge: Harvard University Press, 1985.

Shen Fu. *Six Records of a Floating Life*. Translated with an introduction and notes by Leonard Pratt and Chiang Su-hui. London: Penguin, 1983.

Shih Min-hsiung. E-tu Zen Sun, trans., *The Silk Industry in Ch'ing China*. Ann Arbor: University of Michigan, Center for Chinese Studies, 1976.

Sivin, Nathan. "Copernicus in China." In *Colloquia Copernicana* II. Warsaw: Union Internationale d'Histoire et Philosophie des Sciences, 1973, 63–122.

———. "Cosmos and Computation in Early Chinese Mathematical Astronomy." *T'oung Pao* 55 (1959): 1–73.

———. "On 'China's Opposition to Western Science during Late Ming and Early Ch'ing.'" *Isis* 56 (1965): 201–205.

———. "Why the Scientific Revolution Did Not Take Place in China—or Did It?" *Chinese Science* 5 (1982): 45–66.

Skinner, G. William. *Marketing and Social Structure in Rural China*. Association for Asian Studies, reprinted from *Journal of Asian Studies* 24.1 (November 1965), 24.2 (February 1965), 24.3 (May 1965), AAS Reprint Series.

Smith, Paul J. *Taxing Heaven's Storehouse: Horses, Bureaucrats, and the Destruction of the Sichuan Tea Industry, 1074–1224*. Cambridge: Harvard University Press, 1991.

Smith, Richard J. *China's Cultural Heritage: The Ch'ing Dynasty, 1644–1912*. Boulder: Westview Press, 1983.

So, Kwan-wai. *Japanese Piracy in Ming China during the 16th Century*. East Lansing: Michigan State University Press, 1975.

Spector, Stanley. *Li Hung-chang and the Huai Army: A Study in Nineteenth Century Chinese Regionalism*. Seattle: University of Washington Press, 1964.

Spence, Jonathan D. *The Death of Woman Wang*. New York: Penguin Books, 1979.

———. *Emperor of China: Self-portrait of K'ang-hsi*. New York: Alfred A. Knopf, 1974.

———. *God's Chinese Son: The Taiping Heavenly Kingdom of Hong Xiuquan*. New York: W. W. Norton, 1996.

———. *The Memory Palace of Matteo Ricci*. New York: Viking, 1984.

———. "Opium Smoking in Ch'ing China." In Frederic Wakeman, Jr., and Carolyn Grant, eds., *Conflict and Control in Late Imperil China*. Berkeley: University of California Press, 1975, 143–173.

———. *Treason by the Book*. New York: Viking, 2001.

———. *Ts'ao Yin and the K'ang-hsi Emperor: Bondservant and Master*. New Haven: Yale University Press, 1966.

Spence, Jonathan D., and John E. Wills, Jr., eds. *From Ming to Ch'ing: Conquest, Region, and Continuity in Seventeenth-Century China*. New Haven: Yale University Press, 1979.

Stover, Leon E. *The Cultural Ecology of Chinese Civilization: Peasants and Elites in the Last of the Agrarian States*. New York: New American Library, 1974.

Struve, Lynn A. "Huang Zongxi in Context: A Reappraisal of his Major Writings." *Journal of Asian Studies* 47.1 (August 1988): 474–502.

———. *The Southern Ming, 1644–1662*. New Haven: Yale University Press, 1984.

———, ed. and trans. *Voices from the Ming-Qing Cataclysm: China in Tigers' Jaws.* New Haven: Yale University Press, 1993.

Sun E-tu Zen. "Mining Labor in the Ch'ing Period." In Albert Feuerwerker, et al., eds., *Approaches to Modern Chinese History.* Berkeley: University of California Press, 1967, 45–67.

Sun Yat-sen. Frank W. Price, trans., *San Min Chu I: The Three Principles of the People.* Taipei: China Cultural Service, n.d.

Taylor, Romeyn. "Yuan Origins of the Wei-so System." In Charles O. Hucker, ed., *Chinese Government in Ming Times.* New York: Columbia University Press, 1969, 23–40.

Teng Ssu-yu, John K. Fairbank, et al. *China's Response to the West: A Documentary Survey 1839–1923.* New York: Atheneum, 1970.

Thompson, Laurence G. *Chinese Religion: An Introduction.* 3rd edition. Belmont, CA: Wadsworth Publishing, 1979.

Trigault, Nicola. *China in the Sixteenth Century: The Journals of Matthew Ricci: 1583–1610.* Trans. by Louis J. Gallagher. New York: Random House, 1953.

Tsai, Shih-shan Henry. *Perpetual Happiness: The Ming Emperor Yongle.* Seattle: University of Washington Press, 2001.

Twitchett, Denis, and Frederick W. Mote, eds. *The Cambridge History of China,* vol. 8. *The Ming Dynasty, 1368–1644, Part 2.* Cambridge: Cambridge University Press, 1998.

Urgunge Onon, trans. *The Secret History of the Mongols: The Life and Times of Chinggis Khan. Yuan ch'ao pi shih.* Richmond, Surrey: Curzon, 2001.

Van Dyke, Paul A. *Merchants of Canton and Macao: Politics and Strategies in Eighteenth-Century Chinese Trade.* Hong Kong: Hong Kong University Press, 2011.

Wakeman, Frederic, Jr. "China and the Seventeenth-Century Crisis." *Late Imperial China* 7.1 (June 1986): 1–26.

———. *The Fall of Imperial China.* New York: The Free Press, 1975.

———. *The Great Enterprise: The Manchu Reconstruction of Imperial Order in Seventeenth-Century China.* 2 vols. Berkeley: University of California Press, 1985.

———. "High Ch'ing: 1683–1839." In James B. Crowley, ed., *Modern East Asia: Essays in Interpretation.* New York: Harcourt, Brace, World, 1970, 1–28.

———. "The Secret Societies of Kwangtung, 1800–1856." In Jean Chesneaux, ed., *Popular Movements and Secret Societies in China, 1840–1950.* Stanford: Stanford University Press, 1972, 29–47.

———. *Strangers at the Gate: Social Disorder in South China, 1839–1861.* Berkeley: University of California Press, 1966.

Wakeman, Frederic, Jr., and Carolyn Grant, eds. *Conflict and Control in Late Imperial China.* Berkeley: University of California Press, 1975.

Waley, Arthur. *The Opium War Through Chinese Eyes.* London: George Allen & Unwin, Ltd., 1958.

———. *Yuan Mei: Eighteenth Century Chinese Poet.* New York: Macmillan, 1956.

———, trans., and introduction. *The Way and Its Power: A Study of the Tao Te Ching and Its Place in Chinese Thought.* New York: Grove Press, 1958.

Walker, Kathy Le Mons. *Chinese Modernity and the Peasant Path: Semicolonialism in the Northern Yangzi Delta.* Stanford: Stanford University Press, 1999.

Wang Yeh-chien. *Land Taxation in Imperial China, 1750–1911.* Cambridge: Harvard University Press, 1973.

Watson, Andrew, trans. *Transport in Transition: The Evolution of Traditional Shipping in China.* Ann Arbor: University of Michigan, Center for Chinese Studies, 1972.

Watt, John R. *The District Magistrate in Late Imperial China.* New York: Columbia University Press, 1972.

Wei, Peh T'i. "Internal Security and Coastal Control: Juan Yuan and Pirate Suppression in Chekiang 1799–1809." *Ch'ing-shih wen-t'i* 4:2 (December 1979): 83–112.

Weller, Robert P. *Unities and Diversities in Chinese Religion.* Seattle: University of Washington Press, 1987.

Whelan, T. S. *The Pawnshop in China.* Ann Arbor: University of Michigan, Center for Chinese Studies, 1979.

Whitbeck, Judith. "Kung Tzu-chen and the Redirection of Literati Commitment in Early Nineteenth Century China." *Ch'ing-shih wen-t'i* 4.10 (December 1983): 1–32.

Wilhelm, Richard, trans. *The I Ching or Book of Changes.* Princeton: Princeton University Press, 1977.

Wilkinson, Endymion. *Chinese History: A New Manual.* Cambridge: Harvard-Yenching Institute, 2013.

Will, Pierre-Etienne. Elborg Forster, trans. *Bureaucracy and Famine in Eighteenth-Century China.* Stanford: Stanford University Press, 1990.

Willetts, William. *Chinese Art.* vol. 1. New York: George Braziller, 1958.

Williams, S. Wells. *The Middle Kingdom: A survey of the geography, government, literature, social life, arts, and history of the Chinese empire and its inhabitants,* rev. ed., 2 vols. New York: C. Scribner's Sons, 1883.

Wong, George H. C. "China's Opposition to Western Science during Late Ming and Early Ch'ing." *Isis* 54 (1963): 29–49.

Wright, Mary C. *The Last Stand of Chinese Conservatism: The T'ung-Chih Restoration, 1862–1874.* Stanford: Stanford University Press, 1957.

Wu Ch'eng-en. Arthur Waley, trans., *Monkey.* London, New York: Penguin Books, 1961.

Wu, Silas H. L. *Communication and Imperial Control in China: Evolution of the Palace Memorial System, 1693–1735.* Cambridge: Harvard University Press, 1970.

——. *Passage to Power: K'ang-hsi and His Heir Apparent, 1661–1722.* Cambridge: Harvard University Press, 1979.

——. "Transmission of Ming Memorials and the Evolution of the Transmission Network, 1368–1627." *T'oung Pao,* second series, 54.4/5 (1968): 275–287.

Xu Dixin and Wu Chengming, eds. *Chinese Capitalism, 1522–1840.* New York: St. Martin's Press, 2000.

Yang Lien-sheng. *Money and Credit in China: A Short History.* Cambridge: Harvard University Press, 1952.

Yang, Martin C. *A Chinese Village: Taitou, Shantung Province.* New York: Columbia University Press, 1945.

Young, John D. "An Early Confucian Attack on Christianity: Yang Kuang-hsien and his *Pu-te-i.*" *Journal of the Chinese University of Hong Kong* 3.1 (1975): 159–186.

——. "Science and Religion: The K'ang-hsi Emperor and Christianity." Paper presented to the International Symposium on Ch'ing Archival Collections, Taipei, Taiwan, July 1978.

Yung Wing [Rong Hong]. *My Life in China and America*. New York: Henry Holt, 1909.

Zelin, Madeleine. "Capital Accumulation and Investment Strategies in Early Modern China: The Case of the Furong Salt Yard." *Late Imperial China* 9.1 (June 1988): 79–122.

——. *The Magistrate's Tael: Rationalizing Fiscal Reform in Eighteenth-Century China*. Berkeley: University of California Press, 1984.

Index

About the Author

Jonathan Porter is professor emeritus in history at the University of New Mexico. He received his PhD in Chinese history from the University of California at Berkeley in 1971, and taught Chinese, Japanese, and Asian history, and historical methods at the University of New Mexico from 1969 to 2011. His research interests include imperial China, the social history of Chinese science, and Macau. He is the author of three books, including *Macau, The Imaginary City: Culture and Society, 1557 to the Present*, and seventeen articles on the history of China and Macau.